MW00700196

NON-GOVERNMENTAL ORGANIZATIONS, MANAGEMENT AND DEVELOPMENT

Non-Governmental Development Organizations have seen turbulent times over the decades; however, recent years have seen them grow to occupy high-profile positions in the fight against poverty. They are now seen as an important element of 'civil society', a concept that has been given increasing importance by global policy makers. This book has evolved during the course of that period to be a prime resource for those working (or wishing to work) with and for NGOs.

The third edition of *Non-Governmental Organizations, Management and Development* is fully updated and thoroughly reorganized, covering key issues including, but not limited to, debates on the changing global context of international development and the changing concepts and practices used by NGOs. The interdisciplinary approach employed by David Lewis results in an impressive text that draws upon current research in non-profit management, development management, public management and management theory, exploring the activities, relationships and internal structure of the NGO.

This book remains the first and only comprehensive and academically grounded guide to the issues facing international development NGOs as they operate in increasingly complex and challenging conditions around the world. It is the perfect resource for students undertaking studies of NGOs and the non-profit sector, in addition to being an excellent resource for development studies students more generally.

David Lewis is Professor of Social Policy and Development at the London School of Economics and Political Science. A social anthropologist by training, he holds degrees from the Universities of Cambridge and Bath. His main interests are th theory and practice of international development, non-governmental organi (NGOs) and civil society, and rural development.

Professor Lewis has given us an indispensable text on the evolution of management ideas in international development. It is a domain full of tension between the forces of professional management and social activism. Lewis brings an anthropologist's sensibility to this inquiry, showing that the messy realities of development require NGOs to craft new pluralistic models of management.

Alnoor Ebrahim, *Associate Professor, Social Enterprise Initiative,*
Harvard Business School, USA

This third edition comprehensively addresses the conceptualization, theory, and practice of NGO management. With the current global trend to delegate public-sector tasks to NGOs and allocate vast resources to them, it is more important than ever to understand their roles and how they are managed. This book provides such in-depth and critical understanding in accessible language and is illustrated with insightful examples. I strongly recommend this book to students and development practitioners alike.

Dr. Sylvia I. Bergh, *Senior Lecturer in Development Management and Governance,*
International Institute of Social Studies,
Erasmus University Rotterdam, The Netherlands

In this thoroughly revised and updated 3rd edition of *Non-Governmental Organizations, Management, and Development*, David Lewis brings an anthropologist's sensitivities to understanding the operation and challenges faced by development NGOs. These important organizations play central, fast-growing, and often controversial roles in fostering equitable development and poverty alleviation throughout the world. Dr. Lewis draws on his detailed knowledge of organization theory and development studies, as well as his considerable practical fieldwork experience, to produce a book that breaks through the conventional categories to offer a highly original and nuanced understanding of this complex and rapidly evolving field. More than merely a textbook, *Non-Governmental Organizations, Management, and Development* is essential reading for scholars and practitioners alike.

Richard P. Appelbaum, *Ph.D., MacArthur Chair in Sociology and*
Global & International Studies, Co-PI, Center for Nanotechnology and
Society, University of California at Santa Barbara, USA

'Management is management'. Maybe, but in the NGO world, where political, social and financial uncertainties are the default position, it isn't that straightforward. This important and wide-ranging book by a thoughtful veteran of the sector should be essential reading for those who think they understand the management challenges faced by NGOs, including NGO managers themselves.

Ian Smillie, *writer, researcher and consultant on NGOs and*
international development

David has done it again! This is a superb, well-researched, comprehensive and objective portrayal of NGOs, their philosophy, practices and challenges. Yet another significant contribution from him on the discourse and the art and science of development.

A. Mushtaque R. Chowdhury, *Ph.D., Vice Chair and*
Interim Executive Director BRAC, Bangladesh

NON-GOVERNMENTAL ORGANIZATIONS, MANAGEMENT AND DEVELOPMENT

Third Edition

David Lewis

Routledge
Taylor & Francis Group

LONDON AND NEW YORK

First published 2001, second edition published 2006
as *The Management of Non-Governmental Development Organizations*

by Routledge
2 Park Square, Milton Park, Abingdon, Oxon OX14 4RN

and by Routledge
711 Third Avenue, New York, NY 10017

Third edition published 2014

Routledge is an imprint of the Taylor & Francis Group, an informa business

British Library Cataloguing in Publication Data
A catalogue record for this book is available from the British Library

Library of Congress Cataloging-in-Publication Data
Lewis, David, 1960–
Non-governmental organizations, management and development / David
Lewis. – Third edition.
pages cm
Includes bibliographical references and index.
ISBN 978-0-415-81649-6 (hardback)–ISBN 978-0-415-81650-2
(pbk.)–ISBN 978-0-203-59118-5 (ebook) 1. Non-governmental
organizations. I. Title.
JZ4841.L49 2014
338.9–dc23
2013035571

ISBN: 978-0-415-81649-6 (hbk)
ISBN: 978-0-415-81650-2 (pbk)
ISBN: 978-0-203-59118-5 (ebk)

Typeset in Bembo and ITC StoneSans
by Cenveo Publisher Services

CONTENTS

LIST OF ILLUSTRATIONS

Figures

Tables

Boxes

ACKNOWLEDGEMENTS

There are a great many people who have helped me during the long, slow period of this book's emergence. At the London School of Economics, I would like to thank David Billis and Margaret Harris, former colleagues at the erstwhile Centre for Voluntary Organization (CVO) who first set me the challenge of writing about the management of NGOs; and Howard Glennerster, who encouraged me to write a book based on my NGO lectures. I would also like to thank Helmut Anheier, who in 1999 steered the CVO into a new phase at LSE as the Centre for Civil Society (CCS), and more recently Jude Howell, director of CCS since 2003, for her valuable advice and support. I owe a very large debt of gratitude to all the students who have taken the LSE Management of NGOs Masters course since 1995. I have learned a great deal from the perspectives of a diverse and experienced group from Asia, Africa, Latin America, North America, Europe and the Caribbean. I also learned a lot from co-teaching the course at various times with Arti Sinha, Nina Bowen, Hakan Seckinelgin, Jo de Berry and Nuno Themudo. Many of the comments of these NGO practitioners and researchers are, I hope, reflected or addressed in these pages, although the gaps, shortcomings and limitations are of course entirely my own.

Many visiting speakers and researchers at LSE, and in particular Bruce Britton, Harry Blair, John Clark, Mike Edwards, John Farrington, Marie-Claude Foster, John Hailey, David Hulme, Jacqui MacDonald, Allister McGregor, Roger Riddell, Salil Shetty, Graham Thom, Tina Wallace and Geof Wood, have over the years discussed many of these themes with me. I have also benefitted from a lively group of Ph.D. students over the years at LSE, including Mônica Mazzer Barroso, Preecha Dechalert, Nandita Dogra, Paola Grenier, Marit Haug, Hammad Hundal, Sarah Lister, Nisrine Mansour, Tasneem Mowjee, Alejandro Martinez Natal, Ebenezer Obadare, Salma Shawa and Nuno Themudo. I would also like to thank many people in the NGO world who have given me the opportunity to observe or to work with NGOs in the field: F.H. Abed, Q.F. Ahmed, Shaheen Anam, Keiko Asato, A.M.R. Chowdhury, Aine Fay, Rick James, Mahbubul Karim, Aurea G. Miclat-Teves, 'Nibi Oloniyo and Md Shahabuddin are just a few. Finally, I would like to thank Nazneen Kanji for her encouragement and support throughout the writing process, and Kamil Kanji for his help with the bibliography.

David Lewis
Department of Social Policy
London School of Economics

A note on the second edition

When this book was first published in 2001, I had no idea that five years later I would have the opportunity to revise and expand it in order to meet increasing interest in the field of NGO management.

Aside from a selective updating of the text, then, the main addition to this second edition has been to draw upon the knowledge of a range of colleagues (some of them former students) working in the NGO sector around the world who have kindly provided me with material for additional and up-to-date information for text box examples of NGO management issues. Here I am particularly grateful to Markus Ketola, Alisha Myers, Mónica Tapia, Yaaminey Mubayi, Agnes Kithikii, Stephan Judge, and Armine Ishkanian. I have also benefitted greatly from useful feedback on the first edition of the book provided by colleagues who have used the book. These include Daniel D'Esposito, Alnoor Ebrahim, Jo Beall, Nidhi Srivinas, Diana Mitlin, Simon Batterbury, Paul Opoku-Mensah, and Tony Bebbington. I particularly thank Ann Marie Thomson for her detailed feedback, and an anonymous referee. I'm also grateful for comments from students of Ann Marie's NGO course at University of Indiana, including Megan Hershey, Bobae Park and Rana DeBey and other anonymous contributors to my informal survey. I wish to thank Francesca Heslop and Emma Joyes at Routledge for their commitment to and encouragement with this second edition. Finally, I could not have written this book without the love, patience and support of my partner, Nazneen Kanji.

June 2006

A note on the third edition

More than a decade after first writing this book, NGO management remains an important yet understudied field. When the publishers asked me to consider updating this book for a new edition, it was a difficult request to resist. I have given it what I hope is a thorough overhaul.

In revising this volume for a second time, I decided to try to improve the book in three main ways. First, I have updated the content in the light of the wider changes that have taken place in the world of international aid and development, and the contexts in which NGOs work. To reflect this, I have also dropped the Northern/Southern (NNGO/SNGO) terminology because I think it a binary distinction that oversimplifies an increasingly complex development NGO landscape. Second, I have substantially restructured the book, in the hope that the main arguments can be made more clearly. I have moved away somewhat from the text book layout style of the second edition, because I felt it had become cluttered and difficult to read, and moved material such as the discussion questions (for those using the book as a course text) to the website. Third, I have changed the title to reflect a more discursive, analytical approach that will I hope draw more readers from both the management and the development fields.

In preparing the revised edition, I spoke to a range of people who helped update me with their insights on an NGO scene that is changing fast in many ways, even while it seems to me that many of the key NGO management issues remain very much the same. I also occasionally drew upon a set of life history interviews with NGO leaders and activists conducted in the UK, Bangladesh and the Philippines during 2006-7, collected as part of an earlier Economic and Social Research Council (ESRC) project on sector boundary crossing (Grant reference RES-155-25-0064).

In particular, I would to thank Martin Kyndt, Brian Pratt, Mónica Tapia, Tom Dichter, John Hailey and Jane Cotton each of whom kindly shared their views, recent experiences and ideas with me. I am also extremely grateful to Shaheen Anam, Sylvia I. Bergh, Stephen Biggs, Sarah Binion, Frederik Claeyé, Willem Elbers, Renuka Fernando, Ashima Goyal Siraj, Richard Holloway, Armine Ishkanian, Markus Ketola, Carolyn Miller, Pooja Rangaprasad, David Satterthwaite, Sinead Walsh and Emma Wilson for very useful input and ideas. I wish to thank Clare Weaver for doing an excellent job with copy-editing the book and especially for being willing to accommodate last minute changes.

Finally, I would not have been able to complete this book without the patience and loving support of my family, and in particular, my wife Nazneen.

August 2013

ABBREVIATIONS

ASSEFA	Association of Sarva Seva Farms (India)
BRAC	Bangladesh Rural Advancement Committee
BRLC	Baptist Rural Life Centre (Philippines)
CBO	Community-based organization
CSO	Civil society organization
DFID	Department for International Development
GAN	Global action network
GONGO	Government-organized NGO
GSO	Grassroots support organization
ICVA	International Council for Voluntary Agencies
ID	Institutional development
IDR	Institute of Development Research
IIED	International Institute for Environment and Development
IMF	International Monetary Fund
INGO	International NGO
INTRAC	International NGO Research and Training Centre
LFA	Logical framework analysis
MBO	Management by objectives
MJ	Manusher Jonno ('for the people')(Bangladesh)
NGDO	Non-governmental development organization
NGO	Non-governmental organization
NK	Nijera Kori (Bangladesh)
NNGO	Northern NGO
OD	Organizational development
OECD	Organization for Economic Cooperation and Development
PLA	Participatory learning and action
PPA	Programme partnership agreement

PO	People's organization
PRA	Participatory rural appraisal
PRSP	Poverty reduction strategy paper
PSC	Public service contractor
PVO	Private voluntary organization
SEWA	Self-Employed Women's Association (India)
SIDA	Swedish Agency for International Development Cooperation
SNGO	Southern NGO
TSO	Third sector organization
UNDP	United Nations Development Programme
USAID	United States Agency for International Development
VO	Voluntary organization

PART I

The conceptualization of NGO management

1

INTRODUCTION

In the old days, rich countries had NGOs which focused on helping poor countries. The world's not so simple anymore.

Cooper (2012)

This book is about non-governmental organizations, better known as 'NGOs' or sometimes more specifically as 'non-governmental development organizations'. NGOs go back a long way. Britain's Save the Children Fund (SCF) was founded by Eglantyne Jebb in 1919 after the trauma and destruction of the First World War. Oxfam, originally known as the Oxford Committee Against the Famine, dates back to 1942, when it was established in order to provide famine relief to victims of the Greek Civil War. The US agency CARE (Cooperative for Assistance and Relief Everywhere) had its origins in sending US food packages to Europe in 1946.

NGOs are usually understood to be 'third sector', not-for-profit organizations concerned with addressing problems of global poverty and social justice and working primarily in the developing world. An NGO has an identity that is 'legitimised by the existence of poverty' (Fowler 1997). Some people link NGOs to concepts of charity, while others understand them in more political terms as 'civil society organizations', meaning that they are groups of organized citizens, independent from the government or business sectors. NGOs tend to go about their work either directly through the provision of services to people in need, or indirectly through partnerships, campaigning work and policy advocacy to bring about wider structural change that will improve the position of people living in poverty. While there is general agreement that development NGOs have been growing in numbers and increasing their profile in recent years, no one knows how many NGOs there are in the world. In 1946, there were 41 international NGOs registered at the United Nations (UN), while today there are more than 2,800. There are believed to be over one million NGOs in India, and 200,000 in the Philippines (OECD 2009).

International NGOs are estimated to raise around US$20–25 billion each year, as compared to official development assistance flows of US$104 billion (OECD 2009). In 2009, around 13 per cent of the total development aid provided by OECD countries was channelled to or through NGOs, a total of around US $15.5 billion (OECD 2011).

There has been an explosion of academic and practical literature on NGOs over the past few decades, but more attention has generally been given to 'what NGOs do' rather than 'how NGOs work' as organizations. The large scale of resources commanded by NGOs means that there is growing interest in how these resources are utilized. In a rapidly changing and complex world, people working in NGOs also require more and more in the way of relevant knowledge and skills. NGO management is therefore an important – though still relatively underappreciated – topic. Many people argue that this third sector contains a distinctive type of organization that is different in important ways from the more familiar forms of private sector business or public sector agency. NGO management can be seen as a specialized field that warrants its own study because it requires new creative thinking that goes beyond both existing conventional business management approaches and public sector management science. NGOs face complex, multifaceted challenges in their work and, at the same time, they have distinctive organizational characteristics. In general, NGOs have arguably failed to communicate a clear 'story' about just how complex and difficult NGO management is. Under pressure from donors and publics, they often seek instead to present simplicity and effectiveness rather than the true complexity and messiness of their work.

While we may identify NGOs as a specific category of third sector organization, we must also recognize that there are many different types. Some NGOs are small self-help groups or informal associations working at the community level with a membership that barely reaches double digit figures and no paid staff, drawing instead on volunteers and supporters who may be motivated by politics, religion or some form of altruism. Others are large, highly bureaucratized service-providing organizations with corporate identities and thousands of staff, many of whom may increasingly see their work in terms of a professional career. Some organizations see themselves as part of the world of development agencies and institutions working to eliminate poverty and injustice, while others are recreational societies or religious organizations with specialized purposes. Some take a mainstream growth-centred 'modernization' approach to development, while others are more interested in alternatives to the mainstream and view development in terms of popular mobilization and empowerment. Some NGOs depend on outside funding, while others mobilize resources locally through their own fund-raising initiatives or through membership fees and subscriptions. Some are private member-benefit in orientation, while others are public benefit.

This book is primarily concerned with NGO management from the perspective of organizations working in the field of development – as opposed to those that work primarily in humanitarian or emergency relief – in Africa, Asia, Latin America and the Caribbean, as well as those in the 'post-socialist' areas of the former Soviet bloc. Readers who wish to pursue further and in more depth issues of development in relation to NGOs – as distinct from the broad management perspectives presented in this volume – are referred to *Non-Governmental Organizations and Development* by David Lewis and Nazneen Kanji (2009), which forms a companion piece to this book. Effort has been made in the text wherever possible to present material and examples from across the globe. However, readers will notice that there is more material drawn from the context of South Asia than from elsewhere, reflecting the author's own experience.

The structure of the book

The chapter map provided (Figure 1.1) offers a guide to the overall structure of the book. Part I is concerned with the *conceptualization* of NGO management, and its wider backdrop. Chapter 1 introduces the book's main structure, themes and basic argument. NGO categories and terms are introduced (Figure 1.2), and shifting public attitudes to NGOs and their work are briefly discussed. Different attitudes to NGO management are broadly characterized as the generic, distinctive and adaptive views, the final of which is the approach taken in the book. The key concepts introduced in the chapter include *NGO diversity* and the *NGO management debate*.

Chapter 2 sets the scene by framing the field of NGO management in general terms. First, NGOs are distinguished from other types of third sector organizations, and development NGOs are then distinguished from other types of NGO. The strengths and weakness of existing academic and other literature on NGOs is briefly reviewed. Different views, both positive and negative, of the work of NGOs are then explored. NGO management is then introduced as a complex but under-researched subject, requiring a focus on both organizations and their environment. The

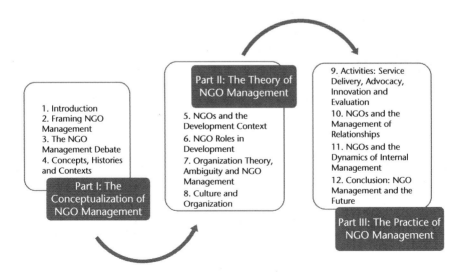

FIGURE 1.1 Chapter map.

challenges of NGO management are set out as lying broadly in three distinct but related domains: (i) internal structures and processes, (ii) the activities NGOs seek to undertake, and (iii) relationships with other institutional actors. All are set against a fourth domain of the organizational environment (Figure 2.1). In each domain, we also find three main roles: (i) the delivery of services, (ii) efforts to catalyze political change and innovation, and (iii) the attempt to build synergies through development partnerships. As a result, a synthesis of ideas from a range of sources will be needed in order to build a composite model of NGO management (Table 12.1). This will be the main task of the book. The key concepts introduced in this chapter include *civil society, third sector* and *hybridity*.

Chapter 3 begins with an exploration of the broad idea of management, and the ways this can be related to development NGOs. Reasons for the longstanding ambiguous attitude to the idea of management among many NGOs are discussed. There has been a recurring 'NGO management debate' that has been taking place since the 1980s, a theme that will be returned to throughout the book. It then considers some distinctive challenges faced when relating different kinds of management ideas to the field of development NGOs. Taking forward the idea of developing a composite model of NGO management, four main sources of ideas are discussed: mainstream business management, public sector management, development management and non-profit management are each shown to have useful relevance. This makes it possible to establish a conceptual framework for thinking about NGO management based on a 'composite' model that draws on different management traditions (Lewis 2003). The key concepts discussed in the chapter include *management, managerialism, new public management* and the *composite model of NGO management*.

Leaving behind questions of organization and management, Chapter 4 discusses context and broad categories, definitions, and labels (Table 4.1). Development NGOs are found all over the world, and work within very different environments. First, it briefly reviews the history and contexts around the world that have given distinctive shapes to the emergence and evolution of development NGOs. While all NGOs share some common characteristics, their different histories across various geographical locations mean that there are also distinctive variations within and between contexts. The chapter concludes with an overview of the relatively recent rise of NGOs within the international development field. The key concepts discussed in the chapter include *neoliberalism, third sector* and *civil society*.

In Part II, we explore the *theory* of NGO management in the context of development work. It seeks to explain how NGOs have come to be seen as important actors in development, and the various approaches that can be used to understand the management challenges that they face. Continuing with this exploration of the context in which NGOs operate, Chapter 5 focuses on the various ideas of development that have emerged, and both mainstream and alternative versions are identified. Different approaches to development have viewed NGOs in various ways (Figure 5.1). The chapter then moves on to trace changing relationships between NGOs and this 'development industry' that emerged after the Second World War that includes the United Nations, multilateral and bilateral donors, and growing numbers of private funding sources. Many NGOs receive resources from the aid system, but face a set of challenges in their relationship with it, including dealing with unequal power relations within development partnerships, and keeping up with the rapidly changing frameworks of international aid. Furthermore, while NGOs are traditionally understood as organizations that work in 'developing' countries, the global balance of power is now changing such that simple distinctions between developing and developed appear increasingly outmoded. The key concepts discussed in the chapter include *development, alternative development, 'big D'/'little d' development, humanitarian relief, international aid* and *the aid effectiveness agenda.*

Chapter 6 returns to the level of the organization and sets out in more detail the main roles played by development NGOs. These roles were previously identified at three levels as those of implementation, catalysis and partnership. The challenges of each one are introduced and then briefly discussed using some examples. The implementation role is increasingly central to mainstream development approaches and is concerned with the delivery of services to those in need, which raises issues of cost, contracting, quality and targeting as well as broader contextual ones of accountability and citizenship. A crucial question is identified as whether service delivery by NGOs is viewed in the longer term as a means or simply as an end. The catalyst role is often contrasted with that of implementation, and takes in advocacy, community empowerment and innovation and is generally associated with radical or alternative development. Finally, partnership is discussed as an increasingly central policy concept that seeks to build synergies between different kinds of organization in the public, private and third sectors. For NGOs, the key challenge is identified as building active rather than dependent partnerships. The chapter then moves on to consider what makes an NGO an effective organization, and reviews some of the evidence that has been produced in relation to NGO performance. The key concepts discussed in the chapter include *implementation, partnership, advocacy, innovation, contracting* and *effectiveness.*

Chapter 7 discusses the ways that NGO management is characterized by a high level of ambiguity, given its composite, multi-stranded nature. The chapter begins with an exploration of the ways different traditions within organization theory (including modernist, symbolic-interpretative and postmodern) are relevant to our understanding of NGO management. Following from this discussion, aspects of resource dependence, neo-institutionalism and evolutionary theory are discussed in relation to development NGOs. This leads us to consider leadership and learning within NGOs as key management issues. In the second part of the chapter, continuities between organization theory and anthropological work on organizations are explored. The argument is made that given the nature of NGOs and their work, an anthropological approach provides a particular useful disciplinary lens through which to analyze power relations, and the local cross-cultural encounters that characterize development work. Finally, both organization theory and anthropology are shown to highlight the concept of ambiguity as helping to explore key aspects of NGO management, such as the increasingly blurred boundaries between associational and bureaucratic worlds, and between the public, private and third sectors in many societies. Key new concepts discussed in this chapter include *organization theory, resource dependence, neo-institutionalism, organizational life cycles, organizational worlds theory* and *ambiguity*.

Moving away from issues of structure, Chapter 8 is concerned with the complexity of cultural issues in NGO management. It begins by looking at the organizational culture that NGOs seek to promote in their working styles, leadership and interactions with communities. The chapter explores work that discusses different types of organizational culture that have been identified within organizations, and considers relationships between gender and organization culture. Turning to wider societal culture, the chapter considers work that tries to identify wider cultural factors influencing organizational life, including Hofstede's influential work. Finally, approaches that move away from over-generalized culturalist assumptions are introduced in order to engage more fully with issues of complexity, power and hybridity that increasingly characterize the world of NGO management. Key concepts discussed include *internationalization, culture, organizational culture* and *hybrid organizational systems*.

Part III is concerned with the practice of NGO management. It contains four chapters, three of which each focus on a key area of NGO activity. These are broken down into the three interlocking circles of organization, activities and relationships that are outlined in the conceptual framework in Figure 2.1.

Chapter 9 returns to the main activities undertaken by development NGOs. It expands upon the earlier discussion in Chapter 6 in the light of the issues raised in preceding chapters, and discusses in more depth the challenges of service delivery, advocacy and innovation. Following from this is a discussion of NGO experiences with evaluation, which remain unsatisfactory, and the resultant need for NGOs and donors to think in new ways about approaches to evaluation. The chapter concludes with a brief discussion of the question of scale, and asks whether scaling up NGO work is a necessary precondition for success. Key new concepts discussed include *innovation, evaluation* and *scaling up*.

In Chapter 10, NGO relationships with communities, state, business and other development agencies are discussed. Introducing a strategic management framework that distinguishes between control, influence and appreciation (Figure 10.1), the chapter first argues that NGO managers cannot afford to focus only on the organizational dimensions of their work. The second part of the chapter is concerned with the complex task of managing multiple accountabilities, which lies at the heart of the management of each of these relationships. Different approaches to accountability are then discussed, including external regulation and internal accountability systems within NGOs. The chapter then goes on to review NGO relationships with government, business and local communities in the light of the preceding discussion, and draws out the key challenges for NGO managers. Finally, we return to the increasingly common but often problematic idea of partnership (Figure 10.2). Key new concepts discussed in this chapter include *strategic management, accountability, contracting, gap filling, social capital, corporate social responsibility* and *partnership*.

Chapter 11 brings us to explore aspects of the dynamics of internal management within development NGOs. It focuses on an increasingly complex set of organizational issues, and draws on emerging issues from the field of third sector management to explore their relevance to NGOs. The nature of third sector leadership, the governance of third sector organizations, and the management of volunteers are each explored using third sector literature. The chapter then moves on to discuss the small but growing literature on the internal organization of NGOs, and reflects on capacity building and organizational learning. The management of information is identified as a key area of NGO management that is gaining in importance as technology advances. Finally, we look at various approaches to organizational change, and the need to engage with high levels of complexity that these entail. Key concepts discussed in this chapter include *third sector management, voluntarism, governance, bureaucratization, capacity building, information management, organizational change* and *complexity*.

Chapter 12 concludes by drawing the themes of the book together and considering the overall theme of 'NGO management', its changing forms and its future. The composite model that draws on four different areas of management (business, public, development and third sector) is set out, along with the ideas of synthesis and improvisation that remain central to the practice of NGO management (Tables 12.1 and 12.2). Finally, three central issues are highlighted for the future – hybridity, ambiguity and uncertainty. Key new concepts discussed in this chapter include *improvisation, turbulence* and *diversity*.

The approach to NGO management

Since NGOs became viewed as central actors in development during the late 1980s, a debate about NGO management has taken place that has broadly been polarized around two positions: those who see NGOs as well-meaning but disorganized and therefore in need of sounder management tools and techniques, and others who argue instead that NGOs should fear those seeking to apply more mainstream management because it may threaten their distinctive values or damage their creativity. Instead, this line of argument goes, NGOs need to develop their own alternative appropriate approaches that embody the principles, ideals and values that they seek to deploy in their work.

While there is some merit to both positions, we will see that there are more complex issues involved. Indeed, there can be no single approach to understanding or performing the management of NGOs. We identify three main schools of thought in this book. The first is the *generic* management view that assumes that 'management is management' and that development NGOs should simply strengthen and improve their management by drawing strongly on mainstream business thinking. The second is the *adaptive* view of NGO management, where it is argued that while generic management may be useful and relevant to development NGOs, it cannot be applied in a straightforward way. It therefore needs adapting in the light of NGOs' distinctive values, structure, culture and type of work. The third pushes this point further and argues for a fully *distinctive* view of NGO management. This view suggests that managers of NGOs face a unique combination of challenges that are different to those encountered by other types of organization. The development of appropriate organizational responses will require further experimentation and research that engages with the real organizational worlds in which these organizations operate, and in ways that can generate new concepts, models and tools where necessary.

All three perspectives can therefore make potentially important contributions. In taking this approach forward, the book makes the argument for a 'composite' model of NGO management that acknowledges two basic truths: (i) the continuing relative lack of available knowledge that exists of this subject field compared to other forms of management, and (ii) the need to view NGO management as a constantly shifting synthesis of management perspectives that is dependent on a range of complex factors linked to context and task. Within an improvisational process of building appropriate practice, NGO managers generally need to draw on ideas from four areas: business management, public management, third sector management and development management. The precise strategic management mix required will necessarily depend on a particular organization's mission, culture and values, and on the forces operating in its wider environment, such as the demands of donors, or the requirements of government.

Each organization needs to find its own unique optimal management composition. None will ever get this totally right, but some NGOs are more effective than others in pursuing this goal. A combination of external and internal pressures means that no organization ever stands still in terms of its scale, activities and identity. For example, an NGO's position within the third sector may shift and take on hybrid characteristics, and these may have implications for the way that it is organized. For example, an NGO that seeks to generate resources from the market to reduce its dependence on funders may increasingly draw on business management ideas, but an NGO moving more fully into government service contracting may need to engage further with public management traditions.

Features of the book

The references in the book bring together relevant classic and contemporary academic research on NGO management, alongside many 'grey' literature references to agency reports, NGO evaluations and other official documents.[1] The subject and author index gives the reader a systematic way to access further information about each of the topics covered, and the means to follow up in more detail on the authors whose work has been drawn upon in the writing of this book.

This third edition includes many new references from the literature that reflect the changing landscape of NGO management in the period since 2007. However, I have also avoided gratuitously scattering contemporary references throughout the text when an older source or example continues to illustrate a particular point or an idea. In my view, many policy debates on development policy and management are imprisoned within an historical 'perpetual present', where there is an unhelpful emphasis on the promise of delivering 'the next big thing' often at the expense of learning from even the recent past (Lewis 2009). My approach is to try to build on experience by maintaining a historical perspective on NGOs and development.

There is also a website associated with the book (http://www.routledge.com/books/details/9780415816502). This contains additional materials useful for teachers and students who are using this book for teaching, including chapter learning objectives, discussion questions and links to relevant web sites and video clips.

Terminology

The study of NGOs is a field in which there are an unusually large number of complex and confusing terms, abbreviations and acronyms. NGOs work not just in the development field but also in human rights or environment, as well as in other diverse spheres such as arts, sport and recreation. Most researchers and policy makers tend to stick to 'NGO' in common usage whether they are referring to development NGOs, human rights NGOs or any other type. The use of 'NGDO' is used by a few authors in their texts (e.g. Fowler 1997) but is not widely used, and is to my mind, a rather clumsy abbreviation. In the first edition of this book, the attempt was therefore made to try to keep things simple by using the generic term 'NGO' throughout, rather than deploying the additional 'D'. As with the second edition, for clarity I begin by explaining the different sub-categories of NGO (Figure 1.2). A glossary is also provided at the end of the book to help guide the reader through this complexity.

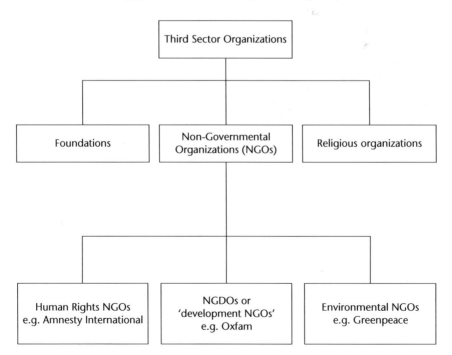

FIGURE 1.2 Situating development NGOs within the third sector.

Around the start of the twenty-first century, the label 'NGO' began to lose a little of its earlier shine and it has in some quarters fallen out of favour (Box 1.1). Some organizations that once described themselves as NGOs came to prefer other terms – such as 'civil society organizations' (CSOs), 'not-for-profit' agencies or 'social enterprises'. There are multiple, sometimes contradictory, reasons that have contributed to this change: criticisms that many NGOs have come to be seen as inefficient or over-professionalized, that they are unaccountable to those they claim to serve, or an association in certain contexts with opportunism and corruption. There are also critics of the dominance of neoliberal development policies that have come to see NGOs as part of the problem rather than the solution, and who now associate NGOs with the maintenance of the status quo rather than with attempts to change it.

However, I continue to use the abbreviation 'NGO' for three main reasons. The first is that I think it better to keep to the terms most people still use 'on the ground' and in the UN. The second is that the majority of texts on development NGOs on which I draw use the term 'NGO', and it would probably confuse matters even further to have different terms used side by side in the text. Finally, I think

---

Box 1.1 THE 'BUSINESS OF HELPING'?: NGO MANAGEMENT IN THE HEADLINES

'Sins of the secular missionaries' (Economist, 29 January 2000)

In particularly florid journalistic style, this article argues that NGOs, 'once little more than ragged charities', increasingly act as large-scale private contractors for Western governments. It also suggests that in many developing countries NGOs have become vehicles for unscrupulous individuals to connect opportunistically with aid resources. The article then goes on to chart the increasing scale of NGO operations, and argues that 'non-governmental' is often a misnomer because many NGOs increasingly depend on public funds. Overall, the article is critical of this new 'business of helping' and while it acknowledges that many NGOs 'do achieve great things' it hints darkly that NGOs 'can also get into bad ways because they are not accountable to anyone'.

'Hearts and minds at any cost' (The Guardian, 13 July 2004)

This article argues that humanitarian efforts have been increasingly co-opted into the 'war on terror'. It illustrates the ways that boundaries between public and private agencies in Iraq and Afghanistan have been eroded, making it difficult for NGOs to exist in an independent and critical 'civic space' away from both US government policy and the terrorists. The article to some extent blames many of the NGOs themselves for having outgrown their 'charitable' origins and become largely funded by governments.

'The $1.6 trillion non-profit sector behaves (or misbehaves) more and more like big business' (*Newsweek*, 5 September 2005)

This story covers the growth and scale of the NGO sector and argues that greater regulation is needed. It begins by describing Oxfam GB's Director Barbara Stocking, referring to her 'no-nonsense manner' and 'power broker's schedule'. It suggests many NGOs 'are dropping their image as anti-capitalist do-gooders and adopting the look of the Fortune 500 companies that they have been known to criticise'. But the article also comments on the search by many NGOs for more independent non-governmental sources of income from private giving and fair trade activities, citing the Iraq conflict as a wakeup call to some NGOs. While Oxfam GB with more than half a million individual donor supporters was able to take a clear position against the war, the article points out, CARE USA, which receives approximately half its income from the US government, had to 'tread softly'. In Iraq, the US government compelled US NGOs to display American logos on aid deliveries and has required that discussions with the press be officially cleared first.

The Truth About NGOs: Haiti (*BBC Radio*, 5 January 2012)

This was one of three hard-hitting programmes that asked difficult questions about NGO work in the contrasting settings of Haiti, India and Malawi. Despite the tabloid style title, these programmes were good examples of balanced and investigative public service broadcasting. Yet each took a far more critical tone than would arguably have been the case a decade ago. This episode begins: *'NGOs are facing what some describe as a mid-life crisis. Hard questions are being asked. Should international NGOs be a conduit for aid? And are they ignorant of local realities, wasteful and undermining of democracy? As we approach the second anniversary of Haitian earthquake we take a look at the Caribbean country sometimes referred to as "the republic of NGOs" ...'*

---

other terms are not used consistently and it therefore makes sense to keep things simple.[2]

I use the term NGO in its broad form in this book. It includes both national and international organizations, those from both 'industrialized' and 'developing' country contexts, organizations that are funded from the development industry and those that are not, and finally both membership and non-membership organizations. I do not follow the convention in some texts that the use of the term NGO implies an organization that receives foreign aid (though many NGOs of course do so) or that an NGO is necessarily formally registered as such.

Finally, this is not a book about 'how to manage an NGO'. Other people would be far more qualified than I am to write such a book, although I have my doubts, given the diversity of organizations, approaches and contexts, whether it would be very useful to do so. The tone of this volume is therefore intended to be discursive rather than prescriptive. It is hoped that by reviewing the relevant literature, a preliminary understanding of our subject can be achieved, and that through further action, debate and research, this understanding can be taken forward. The intended main audience for this book will be researchers and students of development management, social policy and non-profit management, at either graduate or undergraduate level. I hope also that those interested in managing development organizations and people working 'on the ground' in NGOs might also find the book useful.

2

FRAMING NGO MANAGEMENT

> While bookshops may brim with the latest and greatest tomes on running a
> more successful corporation and there are endless courses and seminars to
> attend, there is little to help leaders of INGOs with the relatively more com-
> plex task of managing an INGO.
>
> *Ronalds (2010: xiv)*

Introduction

This chapter introduces the complicated subject of development NGOs, and discusses the main sources of information that we have about them. Our knowledge
base, particularly about the *management* of NGOs, is limited in some important ways.
It also considers some of the criticisms that have been made about development
NGOs. Putting both of these observations together, this chapter makes the argument that we need to understand more about NGO management because we need
to address knowledge gap, and that doing so will help with the normative challenges
of improving NGO performance. The chapter ends with a basic conceptual framework with which to frame our exploration of the subject of NGO management.
This is based on the main roles and   activities of NGOs, the diversity of organizations and contexts, and on the idea that in order to understand NGO management
we will need to draw upon a range of other management fields.

Surveying the landscape: the ubiquity of NGOs

Some two decades ago the US academic Lester M. Salamon (1994) wrote of a
'global associational revolution' that was taking place. He suggested that third sector
organizations, so called because they form an important arena of social, cultural,
economic and political activity alongside the state and the market, were growing in

numbers and playing increasing roles in public policy. Whether providing services to citizens, promoting particular kinds of values, forming the basis for community self-help initiatives or campaigning on public issues, third sector organizations have gained an increasingly high profile right across the world. They are active across a vast spectrum of activities from welfare services to sports and leisure, and from political activism to arts and culture (Salamon and Anheier 1999). Since the end of the Cold War and the rise of neoliberal policy agendas in particular, they have become a feature of most societies.

Non-governmental organization (NGO), a designation normally associated with organizations working in the field of development, environment or human rights, are a subgroup of the third sector organizational family. The acronym NGO originated after the Second World War in the context of the newly formed UN. Although the UN was primarily an organization of governments, provision was made for certain international citizen organizations that were independent from UN member governments, to observe and participate in UN affairs. These organizations were concerned with issues that included development, human rights, peace and environment. Many of these were not new organizations. For example, the Red Cross had existed since the nineteenth century. But recognition by the UN provided these organizations with an important new international status and elevated their profile. While NGOs are a subgroup of organizations within this wider third sector, NGOs themselves also form a highly diverse organizational category (Figure 1.2).[3] The primary focus of this book is on non-governmental *development* organizations, as opposed to other forms of NGO whose focus may lie more squarely within the fields of environment, conservation, human rights, peace building, the arts or a range of other less related specialized activities.[4]

NGOs are 'third sector' organizations that are engaged in development, poverty reduction and social justice work at local, national and global levels. Some NGOs set out simply to deliver services to people who need them, while others are activist groups campaigning for a better world. Many NGOs try to combine both aims. The profile of NGOs has increased steadily among development policy makers, activists and researchers in both the rich industrialized countries of the 'North' and among the low-income, aid recipient countries of the 'South'.[5]

For Mitlin *et al.* (2005: 4), what is crucially important about NGOs is not so much their capacity to undertake specific tasks as the roles that they may play in generating new ideas and in demonstrating 'alternatives' to the status quo:

> NGOs exist as alternatives. In being 'not governmental' they constitute vehicles for people to participate in development and social change in ways that would not be possible through government programmes. In being 'not governmental' they constitute a 'space' in which it is possible to think about development and social change in ways that would not be likely through government programmes … they constitute instruments for turning these alternative ideas into, and alternative forms of participation, into alternative practices and hard outcomes.

BOX 2.1 NGOs AND 'CIVIL SOCIETY'

By the 1990s, NGOs were being connected in the minds of policy makers with a newly rediscovered idea: 'civil society', or the uncoerced space for citizen action that was believed to lie between state and market. It was argued that a strong civil society was good for development because it provided an arena for citizen voice and curbed the excesses of government and private sector. Development agencies also favoured the idea that if synergies and common purposes could be fostered between government, business, and civil society, this would strengthen economic, political and social development.

The idea of supporting civil society became a key development objective for donors, and was conceptualized at three levels. The first was the *organizational level* (individual NGOs) where there was a need seen to clarify organizational values, identities and strategies (linking longer-term vision and project activities, learning from experience), to build organizational capacities for governance, decision making and conflict management, and to develop human resources (mobilizing skilled staff without undermining social commitment) and organizational learning (building systems to avoid losing experience in the day-to-day demands on time). A second was the *sector level* (viewing civil society as a sector) where NGOs and other civil society actors such as associations or grassroots movements were seen as needing to create opportunities for building shared perspectives and joint action, such as through coordinated networks and campaigns. They could also promote mechanisms to represent key sectorial issues, such as alliances to ensure that land reform or minority rights remained on the policy agenda. Finally, the third was the *societal level* where NGOs were viewed as able to create institutions to establish and safeguard the independence of the civil society sector itself, such as legislation that gives proper voice to NGOs in policy dialogue, and consultations with civil society over the reform of policy.

Source: Brown and Tandon (1994); Howell and Pearce (2001)

NGOs have also come to be seen by many as part of an emerging 'civil society' in many countries that may serve to balance or challenge the excesses of the state and the market (Hadenius and Uggla 1996; Glasius *et al*. 2004) (Box 2.1).

The importance of NGOs goes well beyond the worlds of narrowly defined international development and humanitarianism. In the field of international relations and politics, there has been a growth of interest in non-governmental networks of environmental, gender and human rights campaigning organizations (Keck and Sikkink 1998; DeMars 2005). Within public policy, NGOs in many countries are involved as contractors and lobbyists nationally as well as internationally. They are also part of the world of social policy. Deacon *et al*. (1997) draw attention to the ways in which international non-state actors are increasingly contributing to transnational social policy under processes of economic, technological and cultural change which have together become loosely referred to as 'globalization', and the potential role of NGOs in working to link poor people with the benefits of globalization is discussed by Tembo (2004).

Related to this is the emerging concept of 'global civil society'. Social scientists and activists have increasingly deployed this concept in relation to a wide range of public action undertaken by different non-state actors, including protests about genetically modified (GM) food, policy activism on climate change and opposition to international trade rules (Anheier *et al.* 2001). For example, the G8 Gleneagles, Scotland summit held in the summer of 2005 generated discussion, demonstrations and policy advocacy initiatives among a wide range of non-governmental actors that included NGOs, trade unions, religious groups and social movements (Glasius *et al.* 2006). More recently, the Occupy Movement that emerged in the wake of the 2008 financial crisis is another example that has combined nonviolent occupations of urban spaces, media activism and non-hierarchical forms of decision making (Maskovsky 2013). At the time of writing, NGOs are also lobbying hard within the Big If campaign – continuing in the tradition of 2005's Make Poverty History Coalition – to persuade the governments attending the June 2013 G8 meeting in Fermanagh, Northern Ireland to tackle the causes of global hunger.

Many NGOs are also active in long-term humanitarian work in contexts that are sometimes termed 'complex political emergencies', such as Sudan or Somalia (Bennett 1995). From post-conflict reconstruction roles in the wars in Iraq and Afghanistan to natural disasters such as the 2004 Asian tsunami, the 2005 floods in New Orleans, or the 2010 Haiti earthquake, the global profile of humanitarian NGO work has never been higher. Relief work is often distinct from development, but it cannot be completely separated from it, for two main reasons. The first is that development NGOs tend originally to emerge to meet immediate needs in the wake of war or natural disaster. The Red Cross was born of the Crimean War, Oxfam the Greek Civil War, and BRAC the Bangladesh Liberation War and the devastating hurricane and flooding that followed it. Indeed, as we will explore in Chapter 3, David Korten's (1990) 'NGO generations' typology provided a model of organizational change that show how organizations – along with their management systems – evolve over time from an initial focus on individual and societal responses to meeting immediate people's needs during disaster and conflict, towards a longer-term focus on development that seeks to address the root causes of poverty and vulnerability in more sustainable ways.

The second is that distinguishing between relief and development is not always straightforward. In some contexts both sorts of activities may be needed side by side. The capacity to deal with disaster by minimizing its consequences is an outcome of a society's progress in wider development, as is the capacity to reduce the likelihood of manmade disasters happening. The boundaries between meeting immediate needs and pursuing longer-term development are by no means clear-cut, and may require a complex set of organizational responses and strategies that address both causes and effects. Many development NGOs therefore have departments concerned with both types of work, and they may also have units that carry out advocacy that cuts across relief and development. These complexities also have important implications for how an NGO is managed.

Finally, it is important to recognize that the development NGO sector must be seen in ideological context. The rise of NGOs and other non-state actors is part of the wider neoliberal economic and social re-ordering of modern societies, as well as to the ways that citizens may seek to shape or oppose this trend. For example, some social scientists seek to understand the way NGOs increasingly mediate relationships between global processes, states and local lives (Fisher 1997 and 2010; Hilhorst 2003). As Wiebe Nauta (2006: 149) has suggested, understanding NGOs needs to be undertaken in ways that 'embed' an account within the wider dynamic historical, political and socioeconomic processes to which any organization is linked.

Research and policy literature on NGOs

What *do* we know about development NGOs and their management from existing research? During the 1990s, a growth of writing about development NGOs took place from within development studies. Much of this work was celebratory in tone, because NGOs seemed to offer a way out of the deadlock of minimal progress in reducing global poverty during what was sometimes described as the lost decade of the 1980s. While such work presented a mainly positive picture, it tended to be funded by development agencies, and/or written by people directly involved with or sympathetic to NGO work (e.g. Drabek 1987). However, while this material drew useful attention to the importance of what NGOs were doing, in retrospect it is possible to see that it also had some key limitations. It was a literature that sometimes tended towards the descriptive rather than the analytical, tended to focus on individual organizational cases rather than the broader picture, and it frequently carried a prescriptive or normative tone (Clarke 1998; Najam 1999; Lewis 2005; Tvedt 2006; Lewis and Opoku-Mensah 2006). Some of the further reasons for this weak knowledge base are discussed in Box 2.2.

Furthermore, very little of this literature has concerned itself with management issues (Billis 1993). Instead, the focus was mainly on NGO roles in development processes and on the potential of NGOs to challenge existing policy and practice (Lewis 1999a). One therefore has to look quite closely to uncover the small but evolving history of initiatives and studies that have engaged with NGO management issues. During the mid-1980s, an NGO Management newsletter began appearing, published by the International Council for Voluntary Agencies (ICVA) in Geneva. It laid some useful groundwork for discussing the concept of NGO management, and carried some lively debates, but had ceased publication by the early 1990s, as discussed in the next chapter.

In the wider literature, it was not until early in the new millennium that development studies fully acknowledged the field of NGO management. This took place with publication of a 'reader' volume that drew together a diverse collection of academic and practitioner writings on the topic, later updated as a 'companion' to NGO management (Fowler and Edwards 2002; Fowler and Malunga 2010). Yet

BOX 2.2 NGOs AND RESEARCH: ISSUES AND CHALLENGES

Despite the attention that NGOs have received, it is arguable that the research base of knowledge about how they work as organizations and the activities that they undertake remains relatively under-developed and overly normative. There are several sets of reasons for this weak literature. First, knowledge about NGOs is often constructed by applied contract researchers or consultants who are funded by development agencies more interested in positive findings and evaluation results than reflection and critical lessons. Second, NGOs are themselves sometimes resistant to giving access to outside researchers, for reasons to do with their prioritization on their work (and an impatience with purely 'academic' research aims), and their vulnerability as organizations to unfavourable publicity. NGOs are reluctant to open themselves up to scrutiny when their own positions may be fragile in relation to funding and reputation. The result is that 'Typical NGO literature is largely produced by insiders, has an activist flavour, presents simple solutions for complicated development dilemmas, depends heavily on jargon, and perpetuates many myths about NGOs' (Nauta 2006: 149). Many NGOs themselves carry out research in the course of their work, for example on issues that help them to assess impact, or to assist with advocacy and campaigning. Some NGOs have also formed productive research partnerships with universities and other research institutions.

Some NGOs have helped to innovate, with local communities, new ways of thinking about and doing research. For example, Action Aid Bangladesh has undertaken community-level work with local partner organizations that seeks to build on local knowledge and history. The principle and practice of *gono gobeshona* (which means 'people's research' in Bengali) has encouraged and facilitated local community members to conduct their own enquiries into local signs of climate change, reflect on these and to take appropriate adaptive action (Action Aid 2009). During a field visit in 2010, a group of village women talked us through their reconstruction of the recent environmental trends in this drought-prone area, using picture maps and timelines that they had developed at community level, showing how drought is increasing and season lengths are changing. As a result, a range of local adaptation responses are being developed and implemented, including experimenting with new crop varieties such as wheat, new water-efficient cultivation methods, reduced-water latrines and adapted communally-located tube-well pumps. At the same time, this approach seeks to raise awareness for embarking on local and international campaigning on mitigation as well as local-level adaptation.

Source: Action Aid Bangladesh (2009); author field notes

there remains a continuing lack of attention given to NGO management compared to other forms of management, and to other forms of research on NGOs. A further problem has been that where research *has* been carried out into the internal management and organizational development of NGOs, it has tended to be narrowly technical and prescriptive, and has paid insufficient attention to wider context and politics (Stewart 1997). All this has created an important knowledge gap in which NGOs' management is left largely unexplored. This needs to be addressed, since as Udoh James (1998: 229) has pointed out, 'management capacity is the lifeblood of all organizations, irrespective of whether they are private entities, public agencies, not-for-profit concerns or non-governmental varieties'.

All this stands in stark contrast to the considerable attention that is given to management in the fields of for-profit business and government. Management has become a diverse field of academic study, practical writing and popular literature. It encompasses approaches to management that are laden with high theory as well as, at the other end of the spectrum, those taking a more 'hands-on' training approach. The field is characterized by a rapidly changing succession of popular management fads and management 'gurus' all seeking to deliver the latest ideas and techniques to managers, a phenomenon that has itself become a lucrative business (Bate 1997). At the same time, in the public sector, what used to be called 'public administration' has metamorphosed into 'public management', reflecting the elevation of the idea of private sector management into a dominant force across all levels and corners of society.

Alongside this has been the rise of academic research on the wider third sector particularly within industrialized country contexts. Some of this third sector literature engages with questions of organization and management, sometimes termed 'non-profit management'. Perhaps ironically, given the lack of work on NGO management, this remains a largely unexplored area for researchers familiar only with the world of international development (Lewis 1999a). In this book I make the case for the greater linking of insights from both of these literatures, while also recognizing the need to be attentive to the limits of sharing such ideas across contexts, given the fact that such work rarely moves beyond the United States or Britain in its geographical focus (Hailey 2006).[6]

Approaching the field of NGO management will therefore require us to engage in an act of improvisation in which we gather, magpie like, ideas from across different disciplinary research areas and diverse contexts. In this book, we suggest that there *is* a distinctive emerging field of NGO management, but that it is best viewed in 'composite' terms as a hybrid or synthetic field drawn from the domains of business management, development management and non-profit management. In order to take this forward, we need to first understand the key management challenges that are faced by development NGOs, focusing on both *internal* and *contextual* issues. In the field of development, these NGO management challenges follow from the types of work undertaken by NGOs and can be summarized as: (i) *delivery* of new or improved services to sections of communities that are in need; (ii) efforts to *catalyze* social, economic and political change processes at the level of society, groups or individuals; (iii) attempts to create synergies among different agencies and initiatives through the building of *partnerships*.

The book aims to build a conceptual framework through which the distinctive challenges of the management of NGOs can be understood and analyzed. In a modest way, it is hoped that this approach can cast some new light on the subject of NGOs, and perhaps offer some new perspectives on management itself.

NGOs, advocates and critics

During the 1990s, despite having been around for decades, NGOs were discovered anew and for a while they became 'flavour of the month' in mainstream development circles. Discouraged by the lack of progress that had been achieved within traditional government-to-government development assistance that was the norm during the 1960s and 1970s, NGOs came to be regarded as a 'magic bullet' that could solve longstanding development problems. NGOs were initially viewed as capable of working more directly with people living in poverty (instead of having development aid captured by elites connected to government), of having the flexibility to respond quickly and appropriately to local problems (thereby challenging the traditional 'top-down' approaches common to the prevailing government-led development projects), and as capable of helping to build a new alternative set of development ideas and practices that challenged the dominant view of development as economic growth and technological change (by bringing in ideas about sustainability, empowerment, participation, gender, human development and multidimensional perspectives on poverty).

For many years, the dominant view of NGOs has been a benign one of essentially heroic organizations seeking to 'do good' for others in difficult circumstances. However, today NGOs face many critics. The title of Michael Edwards and David Hulme's (1992) influential book on development NGOs (based on an influential Manchester conference that attracted considerable international attention) was *Making a Difference: NGOs and Development in a Changing World*. A 2007 book from a later Manchester conference held on NGOs in 2005 edited by Bebbington *et al.* was less confidently titled *Can NGOs Make a Difference?*, reflecting a decline in confidence that NGOs were all that their advocates claimed them to be. Even more ominous was Hans Holmén's (2010) book on NGOs that carried the title *Snakes in Paradise: NGOs and the Aid Industry in Africa*.

Of course, there have always been criticisms of international charity, philanthropy and general 'do gooding' that date back at least to the Victorian era. But more recently the view of development NGOs as organizations that unproblematically carry out good work has evolved into something more objective and questioning, and rightly so. Criticism is not only confined to organizations carrying out well-meaning service delivery to those in need. For example, Mallaby (2004) suggested that some campaigning NGOs have simply become self-interested 'professional agitators' and have also grown out of touch with many of the ordinary people that they claim to represent. In 2013, a *New York Times* article by Peter Buffett raised concern about the 'charitable-industrial complex' that allows the wealthy to feel good while others are denied the possibility of structural change:

> The rich sleep better at night, while others get just enough to keep the pot from boiling over. Nearly every time someone feels better by doing good, on the other side of the world (or street), someone else is further locked into a system that will not allow the true flourishing of his or her nature or the opportunity to live a joyful and fulfilled life.[7]

Nor should all NGOs necessarily be seen as 'progressive' organizations.[8] While a great many NGOs work towards social transformation, others may equally be seeking simply to preserve the status quo. Morris–Suzuki (2000: 68) points out, 'NGOs may pursue change, but they can equally work to maintain existing social and political systems'. For example, Ronalds (2010: 56) describes the ways some religious international NGOs have lobbied conservative governments in majority Catholic and Muslim countries on issues that limit women's rights, and have contributed to the US's refusal to ratify the UN International Convention on the Rights of the Child.

Criticisms of NGOs have therefore been made from multiple standpoints. On the left, some criticize the use of NGOs as part of wider privatization agendas that are informed by neoliberal ideology. There has been a general shift by development donors away from support to governments towards privatized and potentially less accountable forms of development intervention that rely on NGOs as private actors (Hanlon 1993; Tvedt 1998). Critics see NGOs as facilitating neoliberal policies and capitalist transformation, serving merely as 'safety nets' for those harmed by withdrawal of state services and a new reliance on markets. Some critics also see NGOs as formal organizations that sap away the potential of radical grassroots action by activists and social movements by processes of institutionalization and professionalization (e.g. Kaldor 2003). Yash Tandon (1996) has argued that development NGOs play roles in sustaining and extending neo-colonial relations. More recently, Choudry and Kapoor (2013) offer a critique of what they and others term 'NGOization', a term that has come to be used by critics to refer to the depoliticization of activism through professionalization, and to the limiting of political space by insisting that social change can only be pursued 'as opportunities permit *within* existing structures'. They acknowledge that 'some NGOs do act in opposition, mobilize, and are committed to supporting and building broad social and political movements, but these constitute the minority and are often marginalized' (p.13).

On the political right (broadly defined), there are often two sets of criticisms. One is that NGOs are poorly organized, over-idealistic and wasteful, and need to be reformed based on the logic of a more professionalized market-based private sector approach. These critics place a strong emphasis on the need for better regulation and control of NGOs. The other is that NGOs are the enemies of the free market and that their role in promoting global governance challenges the established interests of governments and business. For example, US neoconservatives came to view NGOs as potentially harmful to US foreign policy and business interests. The American

---

BOX 2.3 THE LACK OF AGREEMENT AND EVIDENCE ABOUT THE EFFECTIVENESS OF NGOs

There are many perceived strengths of NGOs, but little hard data to support the claims that are often made. It is claimed that in comparison with government the main advantages of NGOs are social (a greater gender and poverty focus); economic (greater performance and efficiency, the ability to innovate and adapt); political (an emphasis on participation and human rights and an independence from government agendas); and cultural (a sensitivity to need and a focus on appropriateness of interventions) (Cernea 1988; Anheier 1990). However, many of these claims remain unsubstantiated. Vivian and Maseko (1994) also show that evidence for NGO performance is somewhat scanty. Judith Tendler's (1982) oft-quoted study provides an important critique of NGOs drawn from a wide USAID survey: NGOs were often top down in their decision making, villagers were in practice only rarely involved in project designs, local elites may well influence or control NGO programmes, and most NGOs tended to use well-known techniques and only rarely innovated. Other critiques stress the role of NGOs as resource brokers rather than change agents (McGregor 1989; Hashemi 1989); as palliatives to real structural change (Arellano-Lopez and Petras 1994); the vested interests which exist between donors, NGOs and states (Sanyal 1991; Hanlon 1991); NGO limitations in relief work (de Waal and Omaar 1993); and NGO problems with sustainability and impact. More recently, there have been attempts to evaluate using experimental methods such as RCTs, generating new evidence for example that requires us to be more realistic about the gains that microfinance can offer (Banerjee and Duflo 2011). A recent review by Banks and Hulme (2012) suggested a continuing mixed picture in which NGO work has been undermined by funding increases and rapid growth, and by concerns about legitimacy as NGOs had moved further from the realities of local people, and away from their roots.

Source: UNDP (1993)

Enterprise Institute (AEI), a think-tank that was close to the Republican administration of George W. Bush, set up an NGO 'watchdog' website (www.ngowatch. org). It lists a set of grievances in relation to NGOs that includes their support of 'global governance' agendas, their efforts to restrict US room for manoeuvre in foreign policy and their attempts to influence the power of corporations and, by extension, the 'free market'. In Russia, the government of Vladimir Putin has seen frequent raids on the offices of both local and international NGOs in a crackdown on civil society that is seen as challenging an increasingly authoritarian state.[9]

There are also organizational criticisms of NGOs. In Bangladesh, for example, a report by Transparency International (2006) on NGO governance is typical in identifying a long list of organizational shortcomings around the ways the country's extensive NGO sector operates. These range from allegations of predominantly top-down decision making and lack of financial transparency, to inadequate levels of accountability to stakeholders and exaggerated performance evaluations. Humanitarian NGOs have also come in for considerable criticism for their alleged lack of coordination and inefficiency, from Somalia during the early 1990s to Haiti in 2010 (de Waal and Omaar 1993; Schuller 2012). NGO roles in post-conflict reconstruction and state building in Afghanistan have also faced widespread criticism (Ghani and Lockheart, 2010).

The Economist's article in 2000 entitled 'The sins of the secular missionaries' perhaps marked the moment when the NGO bubble was punctured, and a backlash began to set in. Questions were asked about issues of accountability, probity and effectiveness. These days NGOs are fair game in some areas of the media, variously criticized as ineffectual do-gooders, over-professionalized large humanitarian business corporations or self-serving interest groups (see Box 1.1 for some examples).

Western donors in general have also become a little less enamoured with NGOs than they once were. By the end of the 1990s, official aid no longer saw NGOs as a 'magic bullet', and shifted back towards a renewed emphasis on government-to-government aid delivery mechanisms (such as budget support) in order to influence developing country governments more directly (Craig and Porter 2003). It became more common to hear donors and governments speak in terms of CSOs, 'citizen organizations', 'community associations' or 'faith-based groups' rather than NGOs. There was a sense in which NGOs are thought to have disappointed in some way, or that they were overrated in the past. Large-scale evaluations of support to NGOs such as that commissioned by the DAC in 1997 tended to show mixed results (Box 2.4). These changes of language and emphasis nevertheless continue to reflect the fact that non-state actors play increasingly important roles.

In spite of the criticisms, the amount of international assistance going to NGOs in development, humanitarian and post-conflict reconstruction contexts remains high. Although the statistics are notoriously unreliable, the flow of foreign aid to NGOs is believed to have increased from around US$7.3 billion in 2001 to US$15–27 billion by the end of the decade (Ronalds 2010). These significant figures, along with the fact that NGOs receive a less easy ride these days than perhaps they did in the 1990s, speak to the continuing importance of understanding their management strategies and challenges more clearly and systematically.

The fact that NGOs have become the focus of criticism from both right and left of course reflects their growing importance and their diversity. The validity of many of these criticisms also indicates the need for a stronger focus on NGO management in order to protect the integrity of the sector. Long gone are the days when NGOs could simply rely on the 'moral high ground' to justify their work and provide legitimacy. Long-term generally pro-NGO writers such as Michael Edwards *et al.* (2000: 40) have for some time been emphasizing the need for development NGOs to raise their organizational game, suggesting that few NGOs have structures that can genuinely respond to grassroots demands, that decision making within 'partnerships'

BOX 2.4 THE 1997 DAC DONOR EVALUATION OF NGO IMPACT

A key study of donor and NGO evaluations of projects and programmes concluded it was difficult to assess the impact of NGOs because few organizations
kept benchmark data or maintained effective monitoring systems. Most evaluations were weakened by a preoccupation with 'impact' rather than learning,
and the report argued that this led to a reduction of risk-taking and innovation
because funding had come to depend only on impact. The results of the DAC
evaluation showed that while NGOs may be more effective than government
in reaching the poor, they tend not to reach the very poorest section of the
population; that more than 85 per cent of projects met their objectives (which
is much higher than government); that the rate of innovation was less than is
often assumed or claimed; that assessments of cost-effectiveness were inadequate because fixed costs were usually ignored in the calculations; that sustainability was difficult to assess because few NGOs collected data after a project
had ended, but that the poorer the people involved, the less likely was sustainable impact to be achieved; that NGOs were more generally gender focused;
and finally that replicability was rarely considered in evaluations.

Source: Riddell (1999)

---

remains highly unequal, and that the legitimacy of NGOs (particularly those rooted
in the North) is open to question:

> NGOs must be leaders in cultivating a global moral order that finds poverty
> and violence unacceptable. They must be exemplars of the societies they want
> to create, and work much harder to mainstream civic values into the arenas of
> economic, social and political power…

The lively debate about NGOs and their work, along with a set of criticisms that
need to be taken extremely seriously, suggest a pressing need to focus in more depth
on organizational issues.

The diverse NGO organizational universe

The sheer diversity of organizations that fall into the general category of 'NGO' is
daunting. NGOs can be large or small, formal or informal, externally funded or
driven by volunteers, charitable and paternalistic, or radical and empowerment
based. One NGO might combine several of these different elements at any one
time. Some NGOs are relatively prosperous, while others live a 'hand-to-mouth'
existence, ever more concerned with the need to secure their own organizational
survival in the face of donor or public apathy, or struggling to exist in the context
of political oppression or suspicion. NGOs are constantly dealing with change,

locked into an unpredictable context in which it alternates between periods of affluence (in which they are favoured by donors who provide extensive funding and leave them with problems of rapid growth and formalization) and periods in which resources can suddenly dry up.

Some brief organizational examples can be used to illustrate this diversity. The Bangladeshi NGO BRAC is a formal, bureaucratically structured NGO that works closely with government in the delivery of a wide range of services in urban and rural areas, and it is now one of the largest NGOs in the world (Lovell 1992; Smillie 2009).[10] It employs more than 97,000 people and works in 78 per cent of Bangladesh's villages (BRAC 2004). In its organizational structure and behaviour, BRAC to some degree mirrors aspects of government with its formal hierarchy, and aspects of the private sector with its multiple non-for-profit business activities that help it to generate income. But BRAC also challenges prevailing public and business orthodoxy: with pro-poor social business initiatives, and participative working styles. It also tackles head on two other NGO norms: first, it has identified strategies to generate most of its income itself, freeing it from dependence on development donors[11]; and second, it has expanded and begun operating internationally in Asia and Africa, challenging the idea that only Western NGOs are able to do international work of this kind.

At the other end of the scale are very small organizations such as Vetwork UK. Activists interested in improving animal health in low-income farming communities in poor countries set up this NGO in 1996. It began as an information network on the internet, run by a small but dedicated group of professionals volunteering their time and specialized skills.[12] It was a value-driven, 'virtual organization' (in Handy's 1995 phrase) at the cutting edge of thinking about the third sector, relying on information technology and international solidarity to challenge the conventional distinction between a 'Northern' NGO which works in a developing country through country offices, or with a 'Southern' NGO partner organization from that country. This example illustrates a new (or perhaps reviving) trend across Europe and North America: the rise of the private micro-INGOs (sometimes known as the 'my NGO phenomenon') that are established by volunteers who wish to engage more directly in face-to-face contact with people in need, and who often choose to work outside what they see as the limitations of the formal aid bureaucracy (Pratt 2009; Kingsbergen and Schulpen 2011).

Building a conceptual framework for NGO management

What types of management problems have come to be identified in relation to development NGOs? The subject of NGO management defies simple generalization, but there are general themes and issues that can be explored. For example, Sahley (1995) highlighted six recurring areas of organizational weaknesses for NGOs: (i) a focus on short-term details rather than on longer-term horizons and strategy; (ii) the wish to respond immediately, with little time for learning or reflection; (iii) a tendency for 'over-committed and emotional' rather than achieval

NGO responses; (iv) an inability to decentralize decision making or build true collaboration or partnership with other agencies; (v) imposition of individual agendas on the overall NGO organizational remit; and (vi) a tendency for NGOs to maintain a 'grant mentality' rather than seeking to mobilize resources more widely, due to the persistence of an insecure funding climate which inhibits planning. Each of these remains true today for many organizations.

The first task is to build a simple conceptual framework that will allow us to take forward the project of understanding NGO management in a systematic way. This task combines knowledge of the various literatures described earlier with my own practical experiences from the NGO and development field from the past two decades, including sustained teaching of reflective practitioners at Masters level in the UK.[13]

Figure 2.1 sets out three interrelated areas of NGO activity and provides a basic conceptual framework for thinking about NGO management. Despite their diversity, all NGOs need to manage in three main areas: the organizational domain of their *internal structures* and processes; the *activities* that they undertake in line with their aims and vision, which may be in the form of projects or programmes, campaigns or services; and finally their management of *relationships* with other institutional actors – the state, the private sector, other NGOs and organized components of the communities in which NGOs operate. These can be portrayed as overlapping circles since, while each is a distinctive sphere of activity, all three are clearly interrelated. A further three-fold distinction is needed in order to disaggregate the different

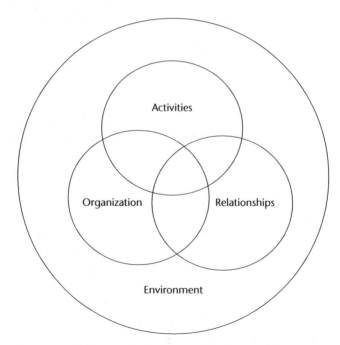

FIGURE 2.1 A conceptual framework: four inter-related areas of the NGO management challenge.

roles engaged in by development NGOs: the three distinct but sometimes overlapping roles of *implementer, catalyst* and *partner* (this will be explored in more detail in Chapter 5). Within each area of NGO management set out in Figure 2.1, each of these three roles is possible – within the organization's own systems, in the performance of its activities, and in the relationships it seeks to build.

All three domains are necessarily located within the broader *environment* in which NGOs work. This needs to be seen as a crucial variable, against which the analysis of any particular NGO must be placed. This has political, historical, geographical and cultural dimensions. As Thomas Carroll (1992: 38) once observed, 'all NGOs operate within a contextual matrix derived from specific locational and historic circumstances that change over time'. For example, when a change of government takes place in a particular country such change may open up new space for NGO activity, or conversely it may bring in new restrictions on what NGOs can do. This makes it difficult to draw NGO management lessons from a specific country context and apply them to another in any straightforward way.

For example, Bangladesh is a country that has become known internationally for its well-documented large-scale NGO sector. When people try to learn lessons from high profile NGOs in Bangladesh it is important to recognize that these have been shaped by a highly distinctive set of political and historical processes, including the war of liberation that led to separation from Pakistan in 1971, the setting up of a new state from scratch, and large-scale humanitarian disaster that led immediately to massive inflows of foreign assistance (Lewis 2011). As a result, not all observations about the sector in one context can be fruitfully applied to NGOs in others.

The question of contextual factors – with the exception perhaps of the context of funding – has on the whole not been given sufficient attention in the NGO literature. Too much focus on the organizational dimension may obscure the landscape within which people organize, and through which their activities are given meaning. We need to go beyond the level of the organization. For example, Hans Holmén (2010: xv) writes about the context of African NGOs, suggesting that 'NGOs are not always formed for the reasons or with the objectives that Western supporters assume'. Such reasons and objectives are usually multifaceted – social, economic, political – and complex. They may include making use of available opportunities, the use of organizing as a form of resistance to the status quo, or as a way of adapting to unwelcome pressures of change.

Furthermore, as Fowler and Malunga (2010) have argued, the environment in which many NGOs operate is an increasingly difficult one. One set of challenges is to improve professionalism while resisting the dangers of 'managerialism', defined as the unwarranted and often ideological reliance on purely *technical* problem solving. As Power (1997: 142) has shown in his analysis of the 'audit society', there has been a steady momentum in UK and other Western societies towards the reshaping of public life around 'evaluation, assessment, checking, and account giving' that raises some critical questions about 'programmatic ideals of "performance" and "quality" and the technologies through which they are made operational' (p.142). This pressure is increasingly felt not only within the domestic contexts of Western societies but also in the international aid industry that extends from these societies (Wallace *et al.* 2013).

Another key contextual challenge is to continue to mobilize and access the resources an organization needs on as close as possible to an organization's own terms. Here the changing environment offers new opportunities – in the form of new donor entrants in the world of international aid, and new forms of more socially aware capitalism – but also a set of constraints. One important constraint has been the global financial crisis that has been making the availability of resources less certain since the late 2000s. Yet the response of seeking more funds from private sector sources raises potentially difficult questions about NGOs' ability to maintain core values and identities, and there is growing pressure from governments and donors for the measurement of performance and results. For example, at the time of writing the UK media reported criticisms from the Charity Commission that the salaries of the chief executives of NGOs in the Development Emergencies Committee (DEC) might be becoming too high, suggesting that it might be perceived by the public as being out of step with the values of these organizations.[14]

As we will see in Chapter 3, managing the link between the organization and its environment is crucial. Some research suggests that negotiating the boundary between the organization and its environment may be one of the main keys to working effectively. Organization theory for example emphasizes the importance of the 'boundary spanner' role as being a particularly powerful one for managers, because it allows for innovative connections to be made between internal systems and external information and other resources. A key finding from Crutchfield and Grant's (2007: 35) study of twelve high performing non-governmental organizations was that NGOs that were adept at working across boundaries were more effective than those that placed their main focus on building strong internal systems.

Conclusion

In this chapter, we have framed the idea of NGO management in the context of the imperfect knowledge base that we have in relation to the subject, and emphasized the need to address increasingly difficult questions about how NGO work and how well they do. We began exploring the diversity of the organizational universe of development NGOs. Having set the scene for exploring the issue of NGO management and established a basic conceptual framework for this purpose, we turn in the following chapter to investigate in more detail an 'NGO management debate' that lies at the heart of the field. We explore the four areas – business management, development management, public management and third sector management – from which we can draw relevant concepts and ideas to help us with this task.

3

THE NGO MANAGEMENT DEBATE

Criticised by governments for their lack of professionalism, NGOs are then accused of bureaucratisation when they do professionalise.

Ian Smillie (1995: 147)

Introduction

This chapter explores different understandings of management, problems of 'managerialism', and tendencies for some NGO to shun the world of management. Indeed, there has been a longstanding tension between those who argue that development NGOs should apply a basic 'nuts and bolts' generic approach to management like any other organizations, and others who argue instead that the specific nature of NGO work and values requires them to rethink the idea of management from the ground up and throw away the rule book. Both sides of this debate make valuable points, and a composite approach is therefore required, in which NGO management is seen as requiring improvisation and synthesis to draw from different sources of ideas and practices. The chapter explores some of the main approaches to management in different theoretical traditions and institutional settings, in order to consider ways these might be applied to development NGOs.

The concept of management

Management has become a vast research field with a range of different approaches and paradigms. What is actually meant by 'management'? There is a wide range of definitions that are available – from the practical to the philosophical, and from the normative to the analytical. These include functional definitions such as 'getting the work done by the best means available' to more diffuse yet equally relevant ideas about the aim of managing as 'the reduction of anxiety'.

Some views of management place a strong emphasis on issues of 'control and authority', while others are more concerned with managing through 'enablement and participation'. Indeed, the analysis of management has generally tended to distinguish two main groups of approaches. The first is 'blueprint' or 'scientific' management that stresses control, hierarchy and instrumentality, and such approaches are often stigmatized as being 'top down' by development people who argue that they pay insufficient attention to the needs of those people who are on the receiving end of development work. The second is 'people-centred' or 'enabling' management, which by contrast emphasizes process, flexibility and participation, and which has found favour in approaches to development work that place people and communities at their centre. Development in this approach is understood as being co-produced by development workers and local people. Managers in development NGOs have often been keen to distance themselves from the 'command and control' side of management in favour of more participatory approaches, since the organizational culture of NGOs is one in which managers often choose to see themselves as 'facilitators', 'organizers' or 'coordinators'.

Such distinctions have long generated controversy within the NGO sector. For example, in a rarely early survey of the directors of US NGOs undertaken by Stark Biddle (1984), there was a clear reluctance evident among most the managers consulted to accept that their organizations could be run like other organizations. This was because of a strong perceived sense of 'difference' within these organizations, which managers saw as stemming from a distinctive set of staff values that prioritized community participation, the need for the NGO to be as close as possible to poor people, and the aim of trying to maintain high levels of organizational flexibility. Managers worried that if they acted like traditional managers (whom they understood as behaving in a top–down way), they would somehow become 'contaminated' by the 'mainstream' values of hierarchy and authority. Perhaps ironically, the data generated by this study nevertheless pointed to a set of basic management weaknesses that existed among these organizations. Some basic management tasks were apparently not being fully performed within this 'alternative' approach to management.

A second important aspect of thinking about management that is need to recognize a distinction made between values and action – between what is sometimes termed the 'instrumental' and 'expressive' dimensions of management processes. For example, in the context of the British voluntary sector, Paton (1991) has argued that the *functions* of management (such as controlling, planning, motivating, directing or monitoring) can be distinguished from the *style* of this management (such as consultative, participatory, cooperative or top–down). In other words, the fact that something 'gets done' is only one aspect of management, because it may also be important to consider the *way* in which it gets done. This dichotomy is particularly important for thinking about third sector organizations such as development NGOs because they normally tend to assert the primacy of 'values' in the way they present themselves and their work.[15]

Some NGOs have even sometimes suggested that the fact that they are trying to do something about a problem may be more important than worrying about whether what they are doing is effective or adequate (Riddell and Robinson 1995). Indeed, studies of organizations have often raised interesting questions about the nature of organizational 'success'. For example, in addition to addressing specific stated social problems, other forms of 'success' may include the idea of being seen to be trying to do something about a problem, or placating a political constituency, or serving an ideological purpose (Seibel 1999).

We also need to distinguish the concept of *managerialism* from that of management. Christopher Pollitt (1993) defines managerialism as an apparently self-evident, though in practice seldom tested, truth that 'if things are better organised they will improve'. This is an ideological assumption that brings controversial and even contradictory implications. It tends to create a type of thinking that decrees that when new challenges or problems arise solutions can always be found from within the status quo, a perspective which can easily become oppressive and even exploitative to staff. It can also suggest, with more idealistic overtones, that answers to problems can be found 'to hand' and solutions can be built with the help of creative thinking and leadership.

At the core of managerialism is the idea that progress requires increases in economically defined productivity, along with the application of increasingly sophisticated technologies. In this model, it is managers – as distinct from other elements within an organization – who hold the key to positive change. In the international development sector, as Elbers (2012) has argued, this translates into the idea that 'development can be planned and controlled as long as the right management tools are applied' (p.175) and leads to the danger that 'doing things right' may become more important than 'doing the right things'. Furthermore, in the managerialist worldview it is the private sector that is seen as the main source of creativity for all organizations, from which all other sectors must learn. Advocates of managerialism tend to identify opposition to itself among its 'enemies' the public sector and civil society (usually in the form of bureaucrats and trade unions). Managerialist approaches may address certain types of problems, but may also limit broader discussions of management. One obvious danger for NGOs is that other kinds of organizational values such as friendship, voluntary cooperation or politics become undervalued. Wallace *et al.* (2006: 165) found that NGOs in Uganda and South Africa feel pressure to use whatever training resources they have available to ensure that their managers can complete donor documentation 'to a satisfactory level' instead of using it to train their frontline staff on other equally relevant issues such as recognizing gender inequality, building communication and listening skills, or facilitating the inclusion of marginalized people.

Yet a rejection of managerialism is not to be confused with a rejection of management itself. Stark Biddle (1984) and Dichter (1989a) both argue that a more rational application of management means to ends would help many organizations. However, within an organization driven primarily by development values, one of the key management challenges is the need to maintain the expressive aspect of the organization's values and work while maintaining or increasing the effectiveness of its work.

So what are the alternatives to the ubiquitous rise of managerialist ideology? Nilima Gulrajani (2010: 142) makes an argument for reviving the Romantic philosophical tradition within development management. Romanticism, she argues, provides an alternative to managerialism because it places people at its centre, avoids excessive linear means–ends thinking, and is capable of dealing with uncertainty. It usefully suggests that 'modernity is a contested goal whose achievement derives from intricate, inter-connected and nonlinear processes lacking universally applicable answers to the practical and ethical problems of life'.

Managerialism is not only an ideology, it is also a set of practices. For many NGO managers, the growth of managerialism is symbolized by the rise of the logical framework approach (often known as the 'log frame') as a tool for project planning. Created in 1979 by the US consulting firm Practical Concepts Incorporated as a 'scientific approach to design and evaluation', the log frame is believed to have drawn on ideas and tools that had originally been developed to manage military projects and the space programme (Hall, 2012). It has come to be used across the large parts of the international development industry (Box 3.1).

While some NGOs have voluntarily adopted the log frame as a planning tool, others have found that is imposed as a requirement of funding agencies when the application for a grant is made. The log frame takes the form of a 'four by four' matrix designed to imposed clarity and logic on the planned project. Along the vertical axis are the categories of inputs, outputs, purpose and goal, and on the horizontal axis each column is described using four further categories: narrative summary, objectively verifiable indicators, means of verification, and the listing of key assumptions. Managers are required to complete the framework in consultation with stakeholders (meaning the project's intended beneficiaries, other community members, funders and government), and the document forms the template for the basic plan that helps to steer a project from inception to completion. It also provides a means for monitoring progress towards a project's objectives.

Some NGO managers acknowledge that the log frame helps to systematize planning, while others dislike it because they find that its linear logic of means–ends thinking may oversimplify reality and depoliticize thinking. Doubts are also regularly raised about the level and quality of consultation that takes place around the design of the log frame, particularly in relation to the least powerful stakeholders. At a more conceptual model, logic models of this kind also come under criticism because they assume a closed system model of organization and intervention, even though in the real world performance will be 'contingent'. Projects, for example, are better viewed as open systems where there is a need to be willing to take risks, appreciate uncertainty, innovate and make adjustments during the course of a project, and engage with the possibility of failure (Ebrahim and Rangan 2010).

Managerialism is a constantly changing set of ideas and practices, and the log frame is just one example. Other tools are in use, with many claiming to offer ways around some of these problems. One that is currently gaining traction along development NGOs is the theory of change approach (Box 3.2), which aims to make clearer the theory and evidence that underpins a proposed intervention (INTRAC, 2012).

BOX 3.1 NGOs AND THE LOGICAL FRAMEWORK

The logical framework was developed in the 1970s as a tool for international development project planning and monitoring by Practical Concepts Incorporated, a private consultancy firm in the United States (Hall 2012). Used widely by development donors, the 'log frame' – as it is often known – has been a controversial management tool for development NGOs. While it can lend structure and coherence to a project idea, some NGO managers have resented what is seen as a lack of flexibility and a reliance on simple, technocratic 'means-ends' thinking. Others have resented its imposition by donors and its use as a condition of funding.

During recent work in Sri Lanka, Renuka Fernando studied the experiences of one NGO. Sarvodaya, the oldest and largest NGO in Sri Lanka, has been using log frames since the late 1990s. It was first introduced by a Dutch foundation, *Novartis*-Oxfam. After a decade of exposure, the log frame is now commonplace – required by numerous donors and recognizable to most NGO staff. Drawing on interviews and observations with staff, she built up a 'balance sheet' of log frame pros and cons that can be summarized as follows. On the positive side, it provides a 'framework' for understanding a project, programme or development ambition; it helps staff to think with the 'logic' of causation, noting that their particular activity is connected to a larger goal; it is useful in all stages of the project, from planning, monitoring, evaluation and mapping the next project; it forms a portable document that can be taken into both the field and to donor meetings; it can be used with other tools, such as budgets, project cycles and activity plans to synchronize different areas of work; it provides a visual layout for a project that is memorable; its listing of assumptions can be used as a starting point for thinking about 'risks' and risk mitigation techniques.

Less positively, staff report that they must regularly 'relearn' log frame analysis depending on the changing format required by donors; the terminology and overall concept of the log frame does not always translate well into local languages and works best in English; the choice and meaning of terms such as 'inputs', 'outputs', 'outcomes' and 'impact' varies per project; the 'quality' of indicators rests on the ability to harass appropriate baseline data and existing systems to track progress; in projects that work in distant sites and with numerous levels of staff, it can be difficult to periodically collect data that resonates with the log frame; its contents, and especially its phrasing, are usually subject to political scrutiny and oversight from host and donor governments; it can be difficult and costly to train staff due to the variations in formats and terminology. The 'pros' largely speak to the endless 'potential' of the log frame, and supporters point to exemplar cases of user applications. Like many tools, it can be used well or badly. On the other hand, the 'cons' point to continuing underlying difficulties around unequal stakeholder relationships, problems of 'measurement', and struggles over limited resources within NGOs.

Source: Renuka Fernando, personal communication

Some recent versions of theory of change explicitly recognize the need to pay closer attention to the importance of context, pointing out that 'a theory of change cannot stand alone', and that 'a desired change in one context may have a different effect in another' (USAID 2013).

Ambiguous NGO attitudes to management

Development NGOs have on the whole been reluctant to engage fully with the idea of 'management'. Partly as a result, there is only a relatively small field of distinctive research that has emerged around this theme. There are perhaps six main reasons why this has been the case.

The first is what might be termed the 'priorities elsewhere' problem. Many NGOs are characterized by a 'culture of action'. NGO leaders and staff may not wish to devote time to thinking about organizational questions if it interferes with the primary task of 'getting out there and doing something'. This may, as Korten (1987: 155) suggests, be particularly true of NGOs in their early stages of evolution. The origins of many NGOs lie in the efforts of key individuals to mobilize people based on altruism where there may simply be an appeal to 'high moral purpose' over and above professional or technical qualifications and experience. As a result, people in NGOs have often not taken management very seriously. While committed to doing good, being activists, or promoting solidarity, they have often been reluctant managers.

A second is the widespread view, particularly among the public and donors, that 'management costs money'. People feel, understandably, that NGOs should use almost all their funds for working with people who are living in poverty or who are marginalized. In this view, NGOs should not spend money on administrative overheads or waste too much time on administrative questions. As Smillie (1995: 151) suggests, there is a 'powerful public myth that development should be cheap', which has led in some quarters to a tendency to take low NGO administrative overheads as one of the main criteria for judging the success of their work.

A third reason is the fact that development NGOs may be established by left of field people who are consciously searching for 'alternatives' to conventional or mainstream thinking. For such people, management, with its strong associations with the business and the public sectors, may be viewed as tainted ground. Management may been seen as positioned far too close to what Robert Chambers (1994) has called 'normal professionalism', which runs against the grain of NGO values and priorities. Normal professionalism, in Chambers' view, is an ideology that prioritizes the wrong things: it gives preference to rich over poor, 'blueprints' over adaptation, things over people, quantity over quality, and the powerful over the weak. This led David Korten (1990: 156) to point out that some NGOs 'actively espouse an ideological disdain for management of any kind, identifying with it the values and practices of normal professionalism, and placing it in a class with exploitation, oppression and racism'. Feminist theorists too have raised similar concerns around power and the social validation of knowledge so that the challenge for

BOX 3.2 USING 'THEORIES OF CHANGE' TO DESIGN AND PLAN INTERVENTIONS

Although the log frame has remained a dominant tool, new approaches that claim a less mechanistic approach to design and planning of interventions have emerged. One that has recently been attracting attention is the Theories of Change (ToC) approach that aims to address the need for NGOs to conceptualize more fully how envisaged changes will take place, and to consider the evidence that makes such change plausible.

Rather than merely focusing on what is being *done* (outputs), proponents of ToC argue that the approach encourages a stronger focus on what is to be *changed* (outcomes). It can also be used to check monitor progress during the intervention, maintain transparency, test causal links within the change pathways of the project, document lessons learned, and report to donors and boards. There are different understandings and uses of ToC among different agencies that have emerged. For some, it is simply a better, more detailed logical framework. For others, it may be opening up new ways of thinking more politically about change processes, and making better connections with wider research evidence in relation to their area of work. For this reason, it is probably better thought of as a cluster of different approaches rather than a single tool. One organization that has been experimenting with different ways of using ToC is The Asia Foundation (TAF).

TAF has worked for example with partners in Nepal on introducing local-level community mediation as a service delivery project to promote improved access to justice for excluded groups. The NGO provided training in this approach to small local dispute resolution that had the advantage of solving disputes without one party losing face, and took some pressure off an over-burdened formal justice system. As experience with community mediation grew, staff learned that there were other benefits, such as empowerment, building respect, and in the post-conflict and potentially unstable setting of Nepal, elements of peace building and strengthened community relationships and social harmony. The ToC approach made it possible for the Asia Foundation to monitor progress and understand some of these new insights, and discuss with different stakeholders. It undertook action research to better understand these emerging ideas and hypotheses around different types of project impacts, and to make course corrections to the project, such as updating their training materials.

While the ToC approach originally emerged during the 1990s within the field of US community development as a form of logic planning model in which an organization makes explicit the sequence of changes it is attempting to bring about in order to reach its goal, it has evolved further in the development field. Used carefully, it may lead organizations to consult more fully with

> stakeholders and engage in more depth with the available evidence in order
> to make clearer and strengthen the assumptions that underpin an intervention
> that claims to bring about a desired change.
>
> *Source*: INTRAC (2012), author field notes, August 2012

NGOs is 'to achieve a kind of professionalism shaped according to their own
models and principles, rather than those uncritically adopted from business, for-
profit organizations' (Smyth 2002: 114).

A fourth reason is the 'unplanned growth' problem, common across the third
sector as a whole. With time, an NGO may experience rapid growth and change,
leaving it always one step behind in its thinking about organizational responses to
growth and change. NGOs that have started out as small, informal structures in
which management issues could be dealt with on an *ad hoc*, informal basis, may
rapidly grow in size if they find favour with funders or become more successful. In
this case they may find themselves developing more complex, multidimensional
structures, projects and programmes but may not immediately realize that they need
new ideas, systems and procedures to cope. Arguably, it was the neoliberal expansion
of the development NGO role that generated what interest there was in NGO
management in the first place, and much of it was concerned with growth and
expansion.[16]

A fifth reason for reluctance relates to the power of external forces. As NGOs
have grown closer to funders, they may be required to develop new systems of
accountability, and their efficiency and effectiveness may be questioned and challenged. These outside pressures may create strong and unwanted 'professionalizing'
pressures on NGOs (Smillie 1995). This may generate resentment that much of the
impetus for thinking about management – as in the case of the log frame discussed
above – comes from outside the organization, and is therefore viewed suspiciously
as imposed rather than something that emerges organically from an NGO's own
agenda. A good example is the efforts of international NGOs to undertake capacity
development of their partner organizations. This was sometimes seen as something
that international NGOs 'did' to developing country NGOs rather than as a two-
way, exploratory learning process (Lewis 1998c; Simbi and Thom 2000).[17]

A sixth reason is simply the diversity of NGO forms and structures, which makes
it difficult to offer generalized insights. When the category of development NGO
includes small informal groups as well as large hierarchical agencies, there may be
little common ground to be found in thinking about how they are managed.

There is a sense in which NGOs can therefore be characterized as reluctant
managers. However, a small but evolving history of initiatives dealing with NGO
management issues has been in place since the 1980s. Interest in management and
organizational issues in the North, as we have seen, started to appear in 1986 when
the Geneva-based International Council for Voluntary Agencies (ICVA) first published its *NGO Management Newsletter*. This laid the early groundwork for discussing

the concept of NGO management, and carried some lively debates. It had ceased publication by the early 1990s.[18] In the UK, the International NGO Research and Training Centre (INTRAC) was established in the UK in 1991 and has grown steadily since that time.[19]

In the US, the Institute of Development Research (IDR) in Boston provided new work on organizational issues for NGOs for many years, while in India the Society of Participatory Research in India (PRIA) continues to pursue NGO organizational training and research agendas. The subject of NGO management grew further with renewed interest in the idea of 'civil society', which led to the rise of global citizen organizations such as Civicus. Despite these complexities, and the overall lack of research attention that NGO management receives, 'a school of NGO management science' (Stewart 1997) did emerge in a modest way in the 1990s and continues to exist within a few specialist niches. For example, the Feinstein International Centre at Tufts University in the US currently provides a wealth of new research on NGO management in the humanitarian action field.

The foundations were laid early on for the NGO management debate, which has taken the form of a discussion between two broad positions among writers on NGOs and development. One group was excited by the new emphasis on 'alternative' management practices, such as empowerment, participation and other bottom–up approaches, while the other was frustrated by the ways in which the idealism of NGOs, along with the growing expectations of funders and policy makers, often seemed to outstrip NGOs' own understanding and practice of basic management skills.

From this first perspective, David Korten (1987) identified a set of 'alternative management approaches' as a paradigm emerging among some development NGOs. Influenced by the work of Robert Chambers and others, these were tried to address problems that had become apparent within the existing top–down approach. Korten (1987: 156) spoke of 'a new development professionalism', in which

> Rather than supporting central control, [these NGOs] … support self-assess-ment and self-correction driven by a strong orientation to client service and a well-defined sense of mission. Highly developed management systems pro-vide rich flows of information to facilitate these self-management processes.

An example of this provided by Korten was the evolution within NGOs of an exist-ing 'hand me down' concept of 'strategic planning', in which a specialized planning unit developed a static blueprint that was then often resisted by staff at other levels of the organization, into the newer idea of 'strategic management', which, if under-taken properly, could become a more inclusive, consultative process that brings staff at all levels of the organization into the identification and implementation of organ-izational choices.

Other writer-practitioners focused less on idealism and more on management basics. Thomas Dichter (1989a: 387) argued that development NGOs needed to be able 'to walk before they can run'. He described an organization he had encoun-tered in which leaders and staff were given courses in 'participatory' leadership training by a well-intentioned development organization when in his view what they really needed to learn was far more basic practical management skills such as 'how to set up and keep administrative, accounting, book-keeping, and record-keeping systems for the co-op'. In another example, Dichter related how an international NGO, planning to establish a presence in West Africa, had provided a preliminary state-of-the-art 'development management' training to its expatriate executive director, who then made two basic mistakes when he set up the local country office. First, the director did not pay attention to the need to make sure that the right person was carefully recruited for the job, and without any feel for local culture or job markets appointed a person too quickly who had then turned out to be unsuitable. Second, he neglected to make sure that basic information systems were established, selected an office in an inappropriate area of town, and ignored the practical need to put in place a proper vehicle maintenance programme.

Dichter's central message was that NGO management needed to start 'plain' rather than 'fancy'. A preoccupation with experimental, participatory development management styles should not be prioritized at the expense of more basic management tasks. NGOs needed to understand budgeting and personnel issues; they needed to analyze the markets, legal framework and policy environment within which they operated; and they required a proper knowledge of how to maintain relationships, information systems and assets. Dichter's position was close to what we might term the 'management is management' idea – the argument that no matter what kind of organization we are talking about, generic management rules always apply. Rejecting simple North/South, business/voluntary or top-down/bottom-up dualisms, Dichter (1989a: 385) suggested that basic management principles

> are not that different for North and South, or for business and the not-for-profit sector. ... Indeed, if 'good' management in a generic sense exists, it encompasses task, people, process and organization. What makes for salient differences are context and the ends of management. These cannot be ignored, any more than we can forget that different theories of management are themselves contextual.

It is understandable that both Western and non-Western NGOs have been strongly drawn to people-centred participatory management ideas, because these may fit well with many NGOs' overall ideologies and objectives. But such ideas have usually originated in stable, strongly defined organizations in the context of strong supporting structures and institutions. These conditions, Dichter argued, were unlikely to exist in many of the poorer regions in which NGOs tend to be active. Dichter's assumptions were perhaps oversimplified in assuming that the global South is 'under-organized' compared to the rich world. Such dualist thinking can be misleading. But his argument was a useful comment on the tendency for well-meaning outsiders (and sometimes insiders) who set up NGOs to overlook the basics in favour of putting their idealism into practice. As we have seen, there is a tendency within the wider third sector for organizations to rush headlong towards management approaches that may not always be appropriate.

This was a vivid description of how these somewhat prosaic management short-comings quickly undermined NGO efforts to carry out their work, no matter how well intentioned they were. It is a recurring theme. For example, Michael Edwards (1999a) found in a study of NGO work in South Asia that lack of attention to 'the basics' of management was an important contributory factor in the failure of NGO initiatives, such as selecting appropriate staff and local partners, maintaining a clear sense of purpose and goals, and maintaining good communications with clients and constituents (Box 3.3). Among idealistic organizations in the women's movement in the United States, those seeking to reject formal organizational forms in favour of experimental collectivism had led in some cases to 'the tyranny of structurelessness', failure in organizational capacity so that charismatic leadership and individualism dominated, with the unwelcome subordination of organizational aims to personal agendas (Freeman 1973).

BOX 3.3 CONTRASTING ORGANIZATIONAL CHARACTERISTICS OF TWO NGOs IN SOUTH ASIA

Edwards (1999a) contrasts the organizational characteristics of two NGOs in South Asia. The first organization, which was the more successful, had 'inspirational but not overbearing' leadership, which was respected both by staff within the organization and by members of the disadvantaged communities within which the NGO was active. However, a shared organizational culture had been built up through long-term education and dialogue about the causes of poverty and the appropriate response to it, which created a high level of commitment, selflessness and 'a determination to hand over power at every opportunity' during the course of the NGO's development work. This had the result that local community groups, rather than the NGO itself, were gradually strengthened through the NGO's work. By contrast, another NGO which was judged less successful in the study, was characterized by a strong director whose personal influence shaped the work undertaken to the detriment of middle-level and junior staff further down the hierarchy, who found themselves with very little opportunity to influence decisions or events. For example, a new credit scheme was introduced from the top without consultation, despite the fact that local staff had learned from their own informal efforts that such a design could not work properly. Consultation at the country office level took place not with country staff, but with the headquarters in London, which led not only to missed opportunities for learning, but also to extremely high overheads. Important preconditions for success such as risk-taking, communication and initiative were all discouraged by this excessive centralization and bureaucracy.

Source: Edwards (1999a)

Today there are continuing efforts among many development NGOs to strive to improve management practices, along with more interest among management researchers to identify the distinctive features of how NGOs organize. For example, Crutchfield and Grant (2007: 35) aimed to understand how twelve successful organizations managed their work. The findings challenged the conventional assumption that improving internal systems is the key to improving effectiveness:

> The secret to their success lies in how high-impact nonprofits mobilize every sector of society – government, business, nonprofits, and the public – to be a force for good. In other words, greatness has more to do with how nonprofits work *outside* the boundaries of their organizations than with how they manage their own *internal* operations. The high-impact nonprofits we studied are satisfied with building a 'good enough' organization and then focusing their energy externally to catalyze large scale change.

More than two decades later, the NGO management debate is still running. The idea of 'good enough management' as a pragmatic, flexible, improvised approach once again takes issue with those who continue to argue that third sector organizations do not pay close enough attention to the 'nuts and bolts' of mainstream management.

The increased attention paid to the management of NGOs has had both a positive and a less benign side. For example, as we have seen, the issue of capacity development (see also Box 11.3) indicated a concern that NGOs in developing countries could, with the right kind of organizational support, strengthen their roles as development actors in providing services, build more democratic political processes and advocate for policy change and development rights. Yet this trend also brought the risk of increased managerialism through a proliferation of training initiatives and one-way support. Subsequent debates over power and autonomy led many to question international assumptions about local organizations, and to a suspicion of the widely used concept of 'partnership' that was (and still is) so readily deployed within development and NGO discourses from the 1990s onwards (Lewis 1998c; Lister 2000; Bebbington 2005; Hoksbergen 2005).

What has emerged from all this is an ambiguous, sometimes contradictory view of management in relation to development NGOs. The NGO management debate that follows from the work of Stark Biddle (1984) and Dichter (1989a) – about whether NGOs should follow the mainstream management rules, or develop their own alternative approaches – remains important. It continues among many of today's NGOs, where one senior executive in a leading UK development NGO has spoken of their time at the organization since the mid-2000s as being mainly about the overhaul of basic management systems to create a more professional environment in which managers are free to manage and make decisions (rather than everyone being involved), and remedying a situation where the organization had in the past paid insufficient attention to such basic matters as lines of decision making and work role descriptions.

In essence, this tension has continued to produce two contradictory trends. Some organizations continue to see management as being 'in the way' of their work, at best a remnant of a previously undesirable mainstream, and continue to play down its value and importance. Other organizations sense the need to make a closer connection with what they see as proper, professional management ideas and tools and rush headlong towards the solutions promised by the management experts, often from the private sector. If we are to build further on the small foundation that exists around NGO management knowledge, we will clearly be required to venture further afield into the different but related fields of business management, development management and third sector management. While development NGOs are a distinctive category of organization in many respects, they also face a set of management problems that they share, at least in part, with all other kinds of organizations. It therefore follows that NGO management can in part be understood by exploring relevant ideas from within the wider world of management.

Business management

The study of management is a diverse and elusive field. It has been characterized as 'a mysterious thing in so far as the more research that is undertaken the less we seem to be able to understand' (Grint 1995: 3). There is academic research, as well as a bewildering range of popular 'self-help' books.[20] In common with development, there are also tensions between theorists and practitioners. There are also two strong elements of bias to be found in the wider management literature. The first is that management studies has usually been concerned with the management of commercial businesses. The second is that mainstream management has focused strongly on Western ideas and models, while NGOs tend to work predominantly within non-Western cultures and contexts. There will therefore be considerable areas of NGO management where such ideas may not apply.

Modernist management writers such as F.W. Taylor (1856–1915), who talked of 'scientific management', and Henri Fayol (1841–1925), who developed a theory of 'administrative management', both laid the early foundations of the field. They based their analyses on an understanding of organizations as logical 'machines' that required systemic maintenance and fine-tuning. Management was seen as a rational science in which improvements in efficiency could be produced by the 'right' changes to structure and process. This remained a strongly Western rationalist approach to managing organizations, and despite the emergence of less top-down and more participatory strains of modernism, continues to inform much of the neoliberal 'technical' discourse of management. The classical management theorists drew to some extent on principles that came from military and engineering thinking, and saw management chiefly in terms of 'planning, organization, command, coordination and control' (Morgan 1997: 18). The use of scenario planning (Box 3.4) is an example of a business management approach now transferred to development NGO work that embodies both the strengths and weaknesses of these types of approaches.

Such ideas remain important, but have been challenged by other ideas from at least two different directions. One is in the form of 'critical management studies' (CMS), a tradition that has emerged since the 1990s (Grey and Willmott 2005). Contributions to this tradition take many forms, but most share a critical stance to the dominance within management of ideas from the New Right and take a critical view on what is seen as the tyranny of managerialism. Also within this thinking is a strong interest in moving beyond Western management ideas in an era of globalization, and in opening up a set of reflexive methodological alternatives to scientific, positivist management research.

There are three common threads within critical management studies – de-naturalization, anti-performativity and reflexivity (Grey and Willmott 2005) – and are all of potential interest to NGO managers. *De-naturalization* refers to the need to challenge assertions about the existing order and its set of assumptions about 'how things are' in order to avoid forms of closed thinking sometimes termed There Is No Alternative (TINA). *Anti-performativity* refers to the idea of challenging the assumption that management – and other social relationships – are simply concerned with maximizing outputs from inputs. Instead, it seeks to bring more in-depth discussions of values, politics and ethics into management debates. Finally, *reflexivity* draws on thinking within the social sciences that seeks to understand the role of the observer or the position of researcher in the way in which knowledge is produced, rather than simply taking accounts of management and organization as objective or fixed.

For some critical management theorists, the work of Bruno Latour in science studies has also proved useful, offering as it does a view that 'redefines organisations as assemblages of ordering practices in perpetual transformation' (Brown 2011: 25). Latour's 'actor network theory' (ANT) has proved a useful approach within recent work on development as well, where different development actors – such as NGOs – are continually engaged in constructing order through 'political acts of composition' (Mosse and Lewis 2006, p.14).[21] This view of NGOs as 'brokers and translators' illuminates aspects of NGO management because it highlights the ways organizations operate within a world of hybrid interests and practices, in which boundaries between organizations and communities, for example, are never clear, and the messiness of everyday practices precedes the ideas and practices of development that are represented formally.

The postmodern perspective emerges as a third way of thinking about management. For example, Stacey *et al.* (2000) argue that 'chaos and complexity theory' provides a more appropriate conceptual framework with which to understand management dynamics. Here it is suggested that in the everyday world of organizational life there is little meaningful scope for predicting how managers and organizations will behave. Within this perspective, order and disorder exist side by side, and organizational 'success' is seen to come from an ability to manage the 'chaotic edge' between disintegration and ossification. Writers on management informed by the chaos and complexity approach argue that understanding ambiguity and paradox can offer important clues to understanding how organizations work and moreover has the potential to unleash creativity. According to Stacey *et al.* (2000: 8) the concept

---

BOX 3.4 USING SCENARIO PLANNING

A private sector technique known as 'scenario analysis' has come to be used by CARE, having reached the NGO sector during the past decade long after development of scenario planning within the commercial firm setting. It is useful for helping to confront unexpected possibilities in order to clarify NGO roles and objectives. In a case study of CARE's work in Sudan, the author explained how staff were organized in a three-day workshop to identify four alternative futures, each of which carried different levels of risk and hazard for the NGO's work. These then informed a 'strategic conversation' that moved from 'what will happen' to 'what if it happens'. This had the effect of shifting managers away from the temptation to simply continue with a 'business as usual' mode of operation towards a more proactive mode in which risks could be understood more directly, one that promoted discussion on the viability of specific options.

Source: MacDonald (2004)

---

of 'self-organization' is a key idea within the complexity approach to management because it implies analysis of a process in which: '... the power, politics and conflict of everyday life are at the centre of cooperative and competitive organizational processes through which joint action is taken'.

There is perhaps now less confidence among management theorists in traditional management ideas as earlier modern, rational paradigms of controlled, organized activity have gradually given way to views which place more emphasis on uncertainty, rapid change and an absence of measurable, objective practice.

Public management

Alongside the mainstream or generic management approaches that have focused mainly on the business sector, the organization of the public sector also constitutes another field of management activity. Known for many years as 'public administration', this focused for example on the nature and workings of bureaucracy, the challenges of decentralization and the nature of implementation and delivery of public services.

Its key thinkers and texts have been influential in public policy and project debates. For example, Albert Hirschmann's (1970) framework based around the ideas of 'exit', 'loyalty' and 'voice' as reflecting the range of people's choices when faced with authoritative intervention – such as in the case of a development project – have influenced thinking around the issues of people's participation, decision making and policy processes. Important ideas about people's participation in projects can also be traced back to Philip Selznick's influential public sector study of the barriers to public participation in the Tennessee Valley Authority. He identified these in the form of informal groupings within the organization and in the powerful vested interests that existed outside the project (Selznick 1966). Clay and Schaffer's work on the ideas of agency and 'room for manoeuvre' as a key concept in the public policy and planning process continues to inform work on these issues, as in the case of the Overseas Development Institute's RAPID programme that has engaged widely with civil society and advocacy issues (e.g. Court *et al.* 2006).

More recently, the field of public administration has come under challenge from mainstream management as neoliberal policy ideologies have taken hold around the world, and it has now been transformed into the field of 'public management' (de Haan 2009). What had become known during the 1980s and 1990s as the 'new public management' (NPM), began to draw on principles derived from the private sector, and favoured the use of markets as ways of allocating public resources more efficiently (Ferlie *et al.* 1996; Harris 2010). It also emphasized the use of private sector management techniques, downsizing and privatization (Polidano and Hulme 1999). It transformed the process of government – which came to be referred to more commonly as 'governance' – by arguing that government itself did not need to carry out more than a basic set of functions, and could be kept at arm's length, simply ensuring that other private and non-governmental agencies carried out specific tasks such as delivering services. Terms such as the 'mixed economy of welfare' and the 'purchaser provider split' opened the door for an increased level of contracting not only with business but also with the third sector.

Ideas and techniques from the public sector have over the years found their way into the world of development NGOs. For example, although commonly associated with NGOs, the use of approaches such as 'participatory learning and action' (PLA)[22] actually have their roots in the more forward-thinking sections of the public sector in certain parts of South Asia, where many of these ideas took shape among government agricultural research and extension institutions (Biggs and Smith 1998).

New technologies have begun to restructure some of the relationships between citizens and governments, and the limitations of new public management ideas have become more apparent. For example, problems emerged that included fragmentation of service providers and services, an insufficient supply of providers in many sector markets leading to insufficient competition, and a lack of policy coherence due to long chains between policies and their delivery. The result was a shift, at least in theory and in some contexts, towards more partnership and collaborative 'relational' approaches to public management, although most of the basic elements of 'new public management' (NPM) thinking still remain in place (Phillips and Rathgeb Smith 2011). Some now also argue that we are entering a new phase of 'digital-era governance' (Dunleavy *et al.* 2005). How might these changes and trends impact on NGOs? Should NGOs look to the public sector, where new management ideas have arguably provided a range of new concepts and practices for development?

Development management

Development management is also concerned with the way the public sector – alongside with the private and third sectors – organizes its work in the context of developing countries. It can therefore be viewed as another distinctive form of management. Unlike business management, it has a focus on the achievement of social goals outside the organization, rather than simply on the internal objective of making a profit. In the context of NGOs, development management is therefore fertile ground that needs to be explored. If NGOs are understood as third sector organizations concerned with the promotion of development objectives, then NGO management is clearly of great relevance. The key problem, however, with development management is the lack of agreement about how to define development itself (a question that is discussed in more detail in Chapter 5, and in Lewis and Kanji 2009) and therefore the precise question of what is actually to be managed.

In two influential articles, Alan Thomas (1996, 1999) explored the relationship between development and management. Thomas showed that while the term 'development management' refers crucially to people, it nevertheless also expresses ideas about authority and power. Development cooperation had primarily been an activity that took place between governments in the period up to the 1980s. Policy was seen in 'prescriptive' terms, in which governments simply took action to promote development. At the level of practice, early approaches to development projects were generally 'top down', in that they were based on the logic that 'development' was needed in a particular place, that the technical, spatial and administrative boundaries of its operation could be determined and that outcomes could be measured in what became known as the 'blueprint' approach (Gardner and Lewis 1996).

The rise of neoliberal development ideology, which places a central emphasis on the power of markets, led to an increasing disillusion with state-centred efforts to solve development problems through public action. This has also brought a new view of public policy as no longer simply being what governments do, but as a process that involves both governmental and private non-governmental public institutions (Mackintosh 1992: 1). This led to a decline in the old tradition of 'development administration', once a vibrant sub-field within the wider field of public administration, which was relabelled and reimagined as 'development management', just as public administration itself became relabelled as 'public management'. This reflects the principle that both public and private efforts at bringing about development are increasingly relevant, and the idea that 'management', rather than simply 'administration', is the matter at hand.

Thomas (1996) suggests that development tasks involve four distinctive elements: (i) the directing of efforts towards external goals as well as internal organizational ones; (ii) an emphasis on influence and intervention in social processes rather than simply using resources to meet goals directly; (iii) a lack of agreement on exactly what needs to be done leading to values-based debate and conflict; and (iv) the centrality of process and continuity, and not just task. The two views of management discussed earlier (top–down, instrumentalist as opposed to participatory, unpredictable) are not therefore mutually exclusive. In some circumstances the 'command and control' variant of management is an appropriate one, while in other situations the participatory approach makes most sense.

The model suggests three ways of approaching development management. The first is termed 'management in development', which is simply management in the context of long-term historical change. The second is 'management of development', which is management of the deliberate efforts at progress undertaken within more formal development initiatives. The third is 'management for development', and this third type, which is management with a specific development orientation, is not the same as just good management, because it is important to evaluate how well development tasks have been undertaken. In this way, both the instrumental and the expressive elements of management can be combined.

Nor does development management in this approach sit comfortably with managerialist discourse. Development management is essentially political and cannot simply be reduced to a technical formula since it requires 'the diagnosis of political contexts and organizational politics more than techniques' (Staudt 1991: 3). Development management is also complicated by the need to decide on and agree the development tasks and activities that need to be managed. These of course cannot easily be defined, because development tasks and activities cover a wide-ranging, highly contested territory that includes economic growth, social welfare, resource redistribution, political process, empowerment and human rights. As we will see, 'development' is a contested concept that is associated with different, sometimes contradictory, approaches to reducing poverty, building capacities and providing social welfare. For some NGOs the delivery of services will doubtless require a set of practices and techniques that could usefully draw upon public and private sector approaches. For NGOs involved in campaigning and networking, perhaps less of this material will be of value, and new approaches are needed.

The bundle of ideas loosely termed the 'new public management' (NPM) approach to administrative reform discussed above also subsequently dominated public policy in many developing country contexts. It has informed structural adjustment conditions imposed by the World Bank and the International Monetary Fund (IMF) on aid to recipient governments, included prescriptions for changing the way public sector management is organized, including the introduction of a 'purchaser/ provider split' in public service provision, the increased use of agency contracting in order to link performance and incentives, and stronger efforts to improve accounting transparency based on quantifiable output indicators. As these changes began to take effect, new roles were opened up for NGOs to become involved in service provision in the growth of 'contract culture' (Turner and Hulme 1997).

We turn in the following section to the field of third sector management, which constitutes another fertile area of enquiry from which to continue building our conceptual overview of NGO management.

Third sector management

As we saw earlier, NGOs have two distinct sides to their identities – as well as being development organizations, they are also part of the larger family of so-called 'third sector' organizations. Included in this larger family is a wide range of organizations that are neither part of the government sector, nor are they for-profit businesses whose *raison d'être* is the making of money. This third sector includes education establishments, pressure groups, religious organizations, trade unions, recreational clubs, community self-help initiatives and charitable welfare societies. There is a growing body of academic research specializing in the third sectors of Europe and North America (e.g. Powell 1987; Salamon and Anheier 1994) which has now broadened to include a more international approach (Salamon *et al.* 2003).

A significant part of this work is also concerned with organization and management issues (e.g. Batsleer *et al.* 1992; Billis 1993a and 2010; Hudson 1995, Anheier 2005). Such research has obvious implications for understanding NGO management, since almost all third sector organizations will arguably have at least some types of management issues in common. Researchers working on the third sector have arguably management issues in more depth than their counterparts working on development NGOs (MacKeith 1993, Lewis 1999a).

Third sector scholars have set about developing new theory, concepts and models to reflect the distinctiveness of management challenges in the third sector, based on new research. For example, Billis and Harris (1996: 6) stated, in a discussion of the application of knowledge to organizational issues in the British voluntary sector, that 'existing theories developed for other sectors went so far, but not far enough', and much of their work has been concerned with explaining this distinctiveness. Such work therefore draws on – but also challenges – areas of the 'mainstream' organization theory that was developed with reference mainly to the commercial and government sectors. One example is Billis' (1993a) model of organizational choice, where he argues that theories that imply an inevitability in the direction taken by organizational change may not always apply to the third sector, where there may be more room for manoeuvre.

What is the relevance for development NGOs? Comparatively little systematic work has explored this question, despite the rather obvious possibilities such a comparison would appear to offer. For example, the large quantity of research on the organizational implications of the growth of contracting relationships between voluntary agencies and local government in the provision of social services – the so-called 'mixed economy of care' – which took place earlier in Britain and the United States (e.g. Smith and Lipsky 1993; Kramer 1994) could carry lessons for those interested in how NGOs are increasingly taking over responsibilities for delivering services which were previously the responsibility of the state in developing countries (Wood 1997), and how NGOs become embroiled in 'partnerships' between the government and international donors (Lewis 1998b).

Since this third sector research literature is primarily concerned with Western country contexts, and with organizations engaged in welfare work and social service delivery, there will of course be significant differences in task and context. At the organizational level, different cultural norms and rules mediate organizational forms. The scale of need in an area of East Africa where there is severe poverty and malnutrition cannot be compared with the pockets of relative deprivation and social exclusion found in Northern Europe.

On the other hand, we suggested in Chapter 1 that the contextual challenges of NGO work do not any longer (if indeed they ever did) fit neatly into distinctions between 'developing' and 'developed', or 'North' and 'South'. For example, the hurricane which led to the disastrous flooding of the city of New Orleans in August 2005, and the inability of large numbers of its poorest residents to take action following evacuation warnings, provide a sobering example of the way in which the most vulnerable can be neglected even in the most 'developed' of country contexts.

John Gaventa (1999) has regularly made use of the idea of 'Norths in the South' and 'Souths in the North', because islands of 'Third World-like poverty' exist in parts of otherwise rich countries, and wealthy minority communities are increasingly common in many otherwise poor countries. Global capital has become highly mobile. The 2013 *Human Development Report* talks of changes within many developing countries within a 'rising south' that produces around a half of the world's economic output, around one third higher than 1990 (UNDP 2013). Furthermore, with the rise of the BRICs and the non-traditional donors, the distinction around developed and developing country contexts are increasingly open to question. The financial crisis in Europe is creating levels of hardship in a country such as Greece that could end up resembling those experienced in sub-Saharan Africa when the World Bank and the IMF imposed their 'structural adjustment' programmes of the 1980s and 1990s that impacted harshly on large sections of the most vulnerable in society (see Lewis 2014, forthcoming).

Alongside the generic organizational issues discussed in the previous section, we now turn to a brief discussion of some of these distinctive issues, which draws upon the emerging field of non-profit theory. Management guru Charles Handy (1988) suggested that third sector organizations are essentially 'value-driven' organizations and that this poses distinctive management challenges, because people work in these voluntary organizations from a variety of public and private motivations: a sense of altruism, an escape route from dominant ideologies, or increasing public status from being a member of a third sector board. This is not to say that such values may not be present in the private sector or the public sector, but they tend to be more powerful in defining identities in the third sector. At the same time, this may not *always* be true in the case of the NGO third sector sub-sector either. In some societies, NGO jobs may be highly prized since a job in a foreign-funded organization may bring an employee significantly higher material rewards than many other forms of employment that are available.

Third sector organizations also differ from the other two sectors in that there is no clear link between the providers of funds and the users of the services (Hudson 1999). In the private sector customers choose to select and pay for goods and services by comparing market prices, while in the public sector people can vote officials in or out of office. These elements of third sector distinctiveness generate distinctive management challenges such as difficulties in monitoring organizational performance, problems of managing multiple accountabilities, the need for creating intricate management structures in order to balance multiple stakeholders, conflicts between voluntarism and professionalism, the need to maintain sight of the organization's founding values and the tendency for third sector organizations to set vague organizational objectives. Research on NGO accountability, the role of boards of governors and the organization of staffing and volunteering, are all areas of management from which models and concepts developed in the wider third sector might be applied to development NGOs. There are, of course, limits to such exchange, and some dangers in importing and imposing yet more Western models in the name of development. As Baig (1999) showed in a study that reviewed the role of NGO boards in Pakistan using concepts developed in the UK, there may be only so far that one can go with such an approach.

Finally, research on the third sector has increasingly engaged with the idea of hybridity.[23] David Billis (2010a: 3) comments on the growth of blurred boundaries between the public, private and third sectors in the UK, and defines hybrids in the third sector as 'organizations that possess "significant" characteristics of more than one sector (public, private and third)'. This is not, he argues, simply a question of having a mix of different organizational features but is also about the existence of 'fundamental and distinctly different governance and operational principles in each sector'.

In Bordt's (1997: 80) study of women's organizations in the US third sector, the initial hypothesis was that the more politically radical women's organizations would begin to adopt non-hierarchical forms, while the less political and more professionalized types of women's organizations would use more traditional formal bureaucratic structures. Instead, a hybrid form was found to be the most common, in which organizations tried in novel ways to get the 'best of both worlds':

> Women's nonprofits in New York City that adopt a feminist ideology are not only thriving with the formal bureaucratic form but are also innovating by combining aspects of both bureaucratic and collectivist structures.

Third sector organizations with a consciously 'alternative' orientation concerned with radical, participatory social change were found to have successfully incorporated principles associated primarily with top-down management alongside alternative forms of organizing.

Should NGOs turn mainly to third sector or 'non-profit management' ideas? Many people argue that the sector requires a new set of specialized models and concepts to assist these distinctive types of organization improve their management (Bryson 1994). Or should development NGOs – as a diverse and increasingly multicultural group of organizations – seek to develop their own distinctive new management models, perhaps by exploring the possibilities offered by experimenting beyond the boundaries of existing practices, and outside primarily Western templates of organization?[24] These are not merely conceptual questions, and they have important implications for policy and practice.

Conclusion

Since development NGOs vary significantly in terms of structure, orientation and operations, this makes NGO management a complex topic. There is no clearly defined body of literature to which we can easily turn, so we have explored the need to work across subject boundaries and synthesize ideas from four different fields of research and practice – business management, public management, development management and third sector management. We have raised a set of important questions that need to be considered during the rest of the book. Should NGOs take management more seriously, and if so, what kind of management models should they be interested in? Do NGOs pay enough attention to the basic 'nuts and bolts' of mainstream management? What are the risks for the ways NGOs operate, and will a greater focus on management of all kinds move NGOs from being primarily value-driven and voluntaristic towards a more professionalized but less vital approach to their work?

4

CONCEPTS, HISTORIES
AND CONTEXTS

Although some observers seem to perceive NGO involvement as a late-twentieth-century phenomenon, in fact it has occurred for over 200 years. Advocates of a more extensive role for NGOs weaken their cause by neglecting this history because it shows a long time custom of governmental interaction with NGOs in the making of international policy.

Charnovitz (1997: 185)

Introduction

Before returning to the question of NGO management *per se*, the next two chapters further explore the background to the growth of development NGOs, and discuss concepts that are used to understand and analyze them. In our conceptual framework (Figure 2.1), we need to better understand the overall context in which NGO management can be located. We begin with a more detailed discussion of terms and definitions. The chapter then goes on to analyze wider context in terms of the histories of NGO in different parts of the world, the re-emergence of ideas such as 'civil society', and a set of wider policy changes within the context of neoliberal policy frameworks, including those of international development.

Terms, labels and acronyms

As we saw earlier, the term 'non-governmental organization', which tends to be applied mainly (though not exclusively) either to third sector organizations that work internationally or to those active in developing country contexts, has its roots in the UN system that was established after the Second World War. The designation 'NGO' was originally given to international non-state organizations that were awarded consultative status in UN activities. For the OECD's Development

Assistance Committee (DAC), an NGO is defined as 'any non-profit entity without significant government-controlled participation or representation' (OECD 2011: 6).

However, organizations that are termed NGOs in one country may be termed differently in another, often arbitrarily for no apparent reason other than that of history and tradition. For example, 'voluntary organization' or 'charity' are the terms that are widely used in the UK where there is a rich tradition of voluntary work and volunteering and a history of charity law which emphasizes Christian, and sometimes paternalistic, values. 'Non-profit organization' is more commonly used in the US, where the market rather than the state has long been the dominant institution, and where alternative forms of social organization can receive fiscal benefits if they can demonstrate that they are not commercial, profit-making entities.

There is no straightforward way to find a path through the terminological mire of the world's third sector organizations. But it helps to recognize that each of the above terms may be culturally generated, with usage historically traceable back to a specific social, economic and political context. This is more than just a semantic problem, because labelling has important resource and policy implications in terms of 'who is in and who is out', and 'who gets what'. In order to illustrate the terminological problem, Najam (1996b: 206) drew up a list of 48 different acronyms used for various kinds of NGO by practitioners and researchers all over the world, and even this list, as the author states, is far from exhaustive! I have added a few more in Table 4.1.

If each of these terms was used logically and consistently, then this might prove useful in providing a way of categorizing different types of third sector organization. But they are rarely deployed consistently. In Britain, the term 'voluntary organization' might typically be employed to refer to an organization working with the homeless in London, while a similar organization working with the homeless in India is likely to be termed a 'non-governmental organization'. In the United States, the term 'non-profit organization' covers many of the third sector organizations working domestically, but 'private voluntary organization' has traditionally been used within the USAID to refer to US non-profit organizations working overseas. Each term tends to be popular with some organizations but disliked by others. For example, some non-governmental organizations in developing countries resent the label 'voluntary' because they feel it detracts from the professionalized character of organizations that may not use volunteers, while others may dislike 'non-profits' because it makes them sound too business-like. Even the term NGO has become unpopular in some countries because it is associated with corruption. It is also often pointed out that one of the problems with the 'non-governmental' tag is that it lacks precision because it attempts to describe organizations by what they are *not* instead of by what they *are*.

The difficulty finding a workable and consistent terminology is complicated further by an enormous diversity of third sector organizations around the world. It is therefore common for the authors of many texts on NGOs to begin their writing with their own sets of definitions of different terms and types of organization. For example, Clark (1991) sets out six broad categories of NGO types based on the types of activities which they carry out: 'relief and welfare agencies' (e.g. Catholic

TABLE 4.1 The myriad of NGO acronyms and labels

AGNs	advocacy groups and networks
BINGOs	big international NGOs
BONGOs	business-organized NGOs
CBMS	community-based management systems
CBOS	community-based organizations
COME'n'GOs	temporary, improvised NGOs that follow funds
DONGOs	donor-oriented/organized NGOs
Dotcause	civil society networks mobilizing support through the internet
ENGOs	environmental NGOs
GDOs	grassroots development organizations
GONGOs	government-organized NGOs
GRINGOs	government-run international NGOs
GROs	grassroots organizations
GRSOs	grassroots support organizations
GSCOs	global social change organizations
GSOs	grassroots support organizations
IAs	interest associations
IDCIs	international development cooperation institutions
IOs	intermediate organizations
IPOs	international/indigenous people's organizations
LDAs	local development associations
LINGOs	little international NGOs
LOs	local organizations
MOs	membership organizations
MSOs	membership support organizations
NGDOs	non-governmental development organizations
NGIs	non-governmental individuals
NGIs	non-governmental interests
NGO	next government official
NNGOs	Northern NGOs
NPOs	non-profit or not-for-profit organizations
PDAs	popular development associations
POs	people's organizations
PSCs	public service contractors
PSNPOs	paid staff NPOs
PVDOs	private voluntary development organizations
PVOs	private voluntary organizations
QUANGOs	quasi-governmental organizations
RWAs	relief and welfare associations
SHOs	self-help organizations
TIOs	technical innovation organizations
TNGOs	transnational NGOs
VDAs	village development associations
VIs	village institutions
VNPOs	volunteer non-profit organizations
VOs	village organizations
VOs	volunteer organizations

Source: expanded from Najam (1996)

Relief Services and various missionary societies); 'technical innovation organizations' (e.g. Grameen Bank with its work with microfinance in Bangladesh); 'public service contractors' which work closely with Southern governments and official aid agencies (e.g. the US agency CARE); 'popular development agencies' which work with grassroots groups on self-help, social development and building grassroots democracy (e.g. BRAC); 'grassroots development organizations', which are membership organizations which may receive support from other organizations or may operate without external assistance (e.g. India's Self-Employed Women's Association, SEWA); and 'advocacy groups or networks', which are NGOs with no operational field projects but primarily exist to carry out education and lobbying (e.g. the World Development Movement in the UK). A functional definition such as this provides a very useful starting point, but it runs into problems because many organizations increasingly carry out a range of different types of activities.

Korten (1990) divides the third sector into four main categories of organization: 'voluntary organizations' (VOs) that pursue a social mission driven by a commitment to shared values; 'public service contractors' (PSCs) that function as market oriented non-profit businesses serving public purposes; 'people's organizations' (POs) that represent their members' interests, have member-accountable leadership and are substantially self-reliant; and 'government-organized NGOs' (GONGOs) that are creations of government and serve primarily as instruments of public policy.

Such categories are useful, because they tell us something about the origins and orientation of an NGO, but similarly they are not always very precise. Harsh *et al.* (2010) introduce another useful new descriptive term – the 'capital NGO', meaning the relatively powerful local NGOs that operate from the capital cities of developing countries:

> whose locational advantage is converted to a prominent position in development networks where they produce much needed employment, hosting for development tourism, and the accounts that are generally necessary for sustainability in return for resources.

One of the most prominent attempts to create a set of more analytical categories is the Johns Hopkins University Non-profits Research Project, which developed the 'structural operation' definition of the third sector organization discussed later in this chapter, and has in its research project on global civil society broken down NGOs into twelve different types.[25] The terminological muddle is a serious problem. It is more than a mere nuisance, as Vakil (1997) argues in a detailed article that seeks to analyze the range of different NGO taxonomies that is in use. The confusion creates difficulties for researchers attempting to develop theoretical work in relation to NGOs, and it impedes effective comparative analysis of empirical work on NGOs across different regions or country contexts. In practical terms, the lack of agreement may confuse the relationship between potential funders and recipients, it may make the task of government regulation more difficult, and it may also reduce the potential for NGOs to transfer knowledge and learn experientially.

Problems of NGO definition

NGOs have come to be seen as a specific sub-set of the wider family of third sector organizations. But scholars have long searched for more substantive ways to approach the subject of NGOs. Charnovitz (1997: 185) takes a very general view that 'NGOs are groups of individuals organised for the myriad of reasons that engage human imagination and aspiration'.

Within what he terms 'the international relations' definition he suggests that NGO is the term is usually left to refer to organizations that play an international role in environment, human rights or disaster relief. Charnovitz documents the emergence of NGOs primarily as organizational actors on the *international* stage from nineteenth-century anti-slave trade movements to peace groups in the League of Nations era, in the early twentieth century, and the growth of the formal NGO role as recognized by the UN Charter after the end of the Second World War.

Another approach is to focus more broadly on the idea that NGOs are third sector organizations that are concerned in some sense with social or economic change – an agenda normally associated with the concept of 'development'. This emphasizes the term 'NGO' as an agency engaged in development or relief work at local, national and international levels. Here NGOs may be contrasted with other types of third sector or non-governmental entities such as those engaged in sports, leisure or arts activities, or those that represent associations of business or professional persons. For example, Vakil (1997: 2060), in her still relevant comprehensive definitional discussions of NGOs draws on and adapts the work of the Johns Hopkins approach to suggests that NGOs are best understood as 'self-governing, private, not-for-profit organizations that are geared to improving the quality of life for disadvantaged people'.

Other writers situate NGOs firmly within the context of what has been termed the 'aid industry', discussed in Chapter 5 below. For example, Fowler's (1997, 2007) discussion of NGOs is linked closely to the world of international development assistance, and he sees the future of development NGOs in terms of their ability to break free of these links and gain more room for manoeuvre and independence. For some Southern writers too, NGOs are similarly seen in very specific terms that are linked to international aid. For example, Diaz-Albertini (1991) argues from Peru that Southern development NGOs should be seen as private, non-profit Third World organizations that implement development projects and programmes with the poor in their respective countries, as organizations predominantly formed and staffed by middle-class progressive professionals, and which receive most of their resources from North American and Western European non-government funding agencies. Yet not all NGOs choose to be part of the aid industry, as we have seen.

Is there a way out of this muddle? The originators of the Johns Hopkins approach have argued that there is. Salamon and Anheier (1992) suggested that most definitions of 'non-profit' organizations (their terminology and unit of analysis) have either been legal (focusing on the type of formal registration and status of organizations in different country contexts), economic (in terms of the source of the organization's resources) or functional (based on the type of activities undertaken by the organization). In place of these types of definition, they developed what they termed the 'structural/operational' definition of the non-profit sector, which they decided to base on the observable features of an organization. As the first third sector organizational definition to attempt a measure of cross-cultural rigour (it has been 'tested' in a range of countries around the world), this work undoubtedly moved forward the field. It can provide a useful starting point to define the organizations with which we are concerned in this book.

The Hopkins definition proposes that a non-profit organization has the following five key characteristics: it is *formal*, that is, the organization is institutionalized in that it has regular meetings, office bearers and some organizational permanence; it is *private* in that it is institutionally separate from government, though it may receive some support from government; it is *non-profit distributing*, and if a financial surplus is generated it does not accrue to owners or directors (often termed the 'non-distribution constraint'); it is *self-governing* and therefore able to control and manage its own affairs; and finally it is *voluntary*, and even if it does not use volunteer staff as such, there is at least some degree of voluntary participation in the conduct or management of the organization, such as in the form of a voluntary board of directors.

This definition, it is argued, fits quite well in general terms with the various types of organizations accorded non-profit status in different country contexts around the world (Salamon and Anheier 1997). I tend to agree with Vakil (1997: 2059) that out of all the definitions found in the literature, the structural/operational definition 'would probably be most useful in defining NGOs as well', and that although her assertion that NGOs are a sub-set of non-profit organizations concerned with 'social and economic development' is ambiguous, this definition can usefully be applied to development NGOs. The structural/operational definition is also useful in that it acknowledges the existence of broad voluntarist values even in the most professionalized organizations in the form of the voluntary governing body. As Levitt (1975: 63) pointed out, the existence of a formal structure and paid staff within a third sector organization 'does not disqualify it from Third Sector status'.[26]

The definition also allows that an NGO might generate income through profit-making activities while still stopping short of becoming a commercial business (i.e. by ploughing profits back into the organization and its activities), and it illustrates the fact an NGO cannot be part of, or organized by, the government (although an NGO must of course abide by the law and may register with government). Finally, the definition emphasizes that NGOs need to be autonomous in that they seek to manage themselves through their own structures and governing bodies.

The structural operational definition does have some limitations. One is that by focusing so strongly on the organization as unit of analysis, it downplays the importance of the organizational landscape and wider context. Another important limitation of the structural/operational definition is its insistence on a level of formality that might exclude small-scale community associations or mutual benefit organizations that in some societies may constitute the lifeblood of the third sector.[27] Similarly, by excluding cooperatives and mutual societies it can be argued that the definition excludes areas of socially focused entrepreneurship that have long characterized aspects of the history of the third sector, such as the friendly societies that were active in Victorian Britain in the development of social housing (Morris 1999). A third problem is that such a definition provides an essentially static picture that is unable to capture the ways that organizations change over time. Many NGOs have their roots in small-scale informal initiatives, but like all organizations tend to change, frequently drifting towards more formal or bureaucratic organizational forms (Billis 1993a).

In recognition of these terminological issues, throughout this book NGO is used broadly to describe third sector organizations concerned with development, human rights and social change. 'International NGO' (INGO) will be used to refer to organizations whose origins lie in the industrialized countries but which work overseas, while 'NGO' (NGO) generally refers to organizations that have developed autonomously in Africa, Asia and Latin America and work within their own country contexts. The broad definition of NGO used here includes organizations that are formally part of the 'development industry' (which consists of the world of bilateral and multilateral aid donors, the UN system and the Bretton Woods institutions) as well as those which are not and choose to work outside these structures. It includes those organizations sometimes termed community-based organizations (CBOs) or 'people's organizations' (POs) as well as those NGOs outside communities sometimes termed grassroots support organizations (GSOs), or intermediary organizations that seek to link and work with these community-level organizations. It includes organizations that in Tandon's (1996) distinction are functional NGOs that are simply 'conveying palliatives' as well as those that he terms 'thinking NGOs' which 'reflect on alternatives'. When necessary, different categories of NGO will be specified in the text that follows on the basis of their characteristics relevant to the discussion.

Theodore Levitt (1975), one of the originators and popularisers of the idea of the third sector, reminds us that there are many different roles played by such organizations: they may be campaigning or service providing; they may be membership or non-membership; they may be voluntarist or professionalized; and they may be charitable or non-charitable in nature. He also reminds us that third sector organizations constantly change. For example, they may evolve from temporary initiatives into formal organizations, or into looser 'social movements' focused around particular issues, e.g. the slave abolitionist movements of the mid-nineteenth century. David Korten (1987) outlined a framework that explained NGOs tend to evolve through a series of 'generations', from *ad hoc* relief agency in its early days simply seeking to meet the immediate needs of vulnerable people, to the more mature formal organization and eventually to a networked social movement organization that works in a more sophisticated way to also address wider structural concerns in a society (see Chapter 7 for a more detailed discussion of this framework).

The histories of NGOs

We have already noted that history and context is often overlooked in the effort to understand NGOs. While the rise of NGOs within development is comparatively recent, NGOs are far from new. Charnovitz (1997) traces seven stages to the evolution of NGO roles in international affairs, from 'emergence' in 1775–1918 through to 'empowerment' from 1992 onwards. This history begins with the rise of national level issue-based organizations in the eighteenth century, focused on the abolition of the slave trade and peace movements. By 1900 there were 425 peace societies active in different parts of the world, and the issues of labour rights and free trade were generating new forms of interest groups that were the forerunners of what we would now term NGOs. For example, in the US the first national labour union was the International Federation of Tobacco Workers, founded in 1876, and in the UK the Anti-Corn Law League campaigned for free trade against the system of tariffs between 1838 and 1846. By the early twentieth century, NGOs had generated associations to promote their own identities at national and international levels, so that at the World Congress of International Associations in 1910 there were 132 international associations present, and these were concerned with issues as varied as transportation, intellectual property rights, narcotics control, public health issues, agriculture and the protection of nature.

A growing level of involvement of NGOs continued during the League of Nations period during the 1920s and 1930s, a period Charnovitz terms 'engagement'. When the International Labour Organization (ILO) was set up in 1919 as part of the League of Nations, each member country sent four representatives: two from government, one from employers and one from worker organizations, which created a forum in which the three sectors – government, business and community – could each begin to influence international conventions on labour rights and standards. NGOs began to move from being outsiders bringing issues to the international agenda to insiders working with governments on international problems. After 1935, there was a 'routinisation' of activities within the League, and the growing hostilities that resulted in the Second World War contributed to the inhibiting of NGO participation and a period of 'disengagement' that lasted until the period of post-war 'formalization'.

In the post-war period, Article 71 of the United Nations Charter provided for NGO involvement in UN activities, and NGOs were active in the drafting of the Charter itself. Among the UN agencies, UNESCO and WHO both provided for NGO involvement in their charters. However, the reality was that Article 71 merely codified 'the custom of NGO participation', leaving NGOs with as few opportunities as they had enjoyed under the League. The period after the War was one of 'underachievement' in which, though active, NGOs did not contribute much more than 'nuisance value', hampered by Cold War tensions and the institutional weakness of the UN Economic and Social Council (ECOSOC), the body liaising with NGOs as set out in Article 71. It was not until the 1970s that there was an increased 'intensification' of NGO strength and activities, as shown by their growing presence at UN conferences such as the Stockholm Environment Conference in 1972 and the World Population Conference in Bucharest in 1974. NGOs played a key role in the drafting of the UN Convention on the Rights of the Child.

Since 1992, NGO influence at international level has continued to grow, as shown by the UN Conference on Environment and Development (UNCED) that saw NGOs active in both preparation and at the conference itself, which approved policy statements about the role of NGOs and suggested that the UN system should 'draw on the expertise and views of non-governmental organizations in policy and programme design, implementation and evaluation' (Agenda 21, quoted in Charnovitz 1997: 265). From only occasional mentions of the role of NGOs in the documentation produced by the Brandt Commission in 1980, we have now moved to a position in which the Commission on Global Governance in 1995 recommended that a Forum of Civil Society should be convened and consulted by the UN every year. Charnovitz has characterized this period since 1992 as that of NGO 'empowerment'. Indeed, Martens (2006) has argued that NGOs now form an integral part of the UN system.

Charnovitz's framework has been discussed at some length because it provides much-needed historical depth to the discussion of the NGO context, a perspective that is often lost within contemporary policy discussions.[28] However, it focuses exclusively on European and North American contexts and therefore tells only part of the story. Such 'NGO history' can also be written from the perspective of other parts of the world. In Latin America, the growth of NGOs has been influenced by the Catholic Church and the growth of 'liberation theology' in the 1960s, signalled by the Church's commitment to the poor, and to some extent by the growth of popular Protestantism (Escobar 1997).

The philosophy of the Brazilian educator Paulo Freire, with its radical ideas about 'education for critical consciousness' and organized community action, has also been influential (Blackburn 2000). Freire believed that illiterate people possessed a 'culture of silence' which could be challenged by a form of education which, rather than simply imposing the world view of the elite, could motivate the poor to question and build new liberating structures and processes for change. Freire's ideas continue to inspire and inform current approaches, such as the participatory planning processes pioneered in the city of Porto Alegre, Brazil (Guareschi and Jovchelovitch 2004). Freire's ideas have informed the philosophies and strategies of many NGOs in Latin America and beyond, such as Proshika in Bangladesh. At the same time, the tradition of peasant movements seeking improved rights to land, and the role of political radicals working towards more open democratic societies, has contributed to the rise of NGOs (Bebbington and Thiele 1993). Despite the radical origins of one key strand in the Latin American NGO community in the 1960s, the 1990s saw the crystallization of an increasingly heterogeneous NGO sector containing different approaches, which included professionalized careerist organizations close to donors and governments as well as organizations seeking radical alternatives (Pearce 1997).

Moving to the context of South Asia, Sen (1992) documented the rise of NGOs in India, which highlights the influence of Christian missionaries, the Indian reformist middle classes and the ideas of Mahatma Gandhi, who emphasized the role of voluntary action in strengthening Indian development. Gandhi's campaign for village self-reliance inspired local Indian organizations such as the Association of Sarva Seva Farms (ASSEFA), discussed in Chapter 7. Many of these NGOs have strong local cultural and historical roots that lie outside the Western 'aid industry'. Gandhi's ideas have also contributed to the 'appropriate technology' movement more widely in the North as well as the South (Thomas 1992). There are also long traditions of self-help in South Asia, such as the traditional rotating credit groups which can be found in countries such as Nepal where they are known as *dhikiri*, in which households as a survival strategy pool resources into a central fund and take turns in borrowing and repaying from the communal pot (1995). In India, there are many activists who have tended to abandon the NGO as a form of organizing in favour of looser informal networks and movements that place them beyond the regulation and scrutiny of the state (Kilby 2011). Such movements have long and complex roots that go back to the colonial era, as Guha's (1989) study of the Chipko movement centred on forms of resistance among forest dwellers.

Africa shares aspects of the missionary histories of Asia, where external organizations have interacted with local 'third sector' structures and ideologies. For example, Anheier's (1987) work in Africa highlighted the wealth of associational activity which underpins many African societies, while Honey and Okafor's (1998) work on home-town associations in Nigeria shows how community organizations have become increasingly important for mediating resources and relationships between local communities and global labour markets, educational opportunities and village resources. In Kenya, the 'harambee' movement of mutual self-help groups was a system based on kinship and neighbourhood ties, and was incorporated by President Kenyatta as part of a modernization campaign to build a new infrastructure after Independence (Moore 1988). It was seen as an alternative to top-down planning and as a way of sharing costs with local communities and, while briefly successful, its initial spirit of voluntarism was gradually sapped by bureaucratization. Box 4.1 explores a case of an African NGO shaped over time by a changing local and global context.

Within a particular country context, there are multiple and often contradictory influences with the third sector. In the UK, for example, the so-called voluntary sector is rooted both in traditions of 'charity', as well as in the radical activism of the 1960s, which emphasizes instead the 'empowerment' of disadvantaged groups and individuals. More recently, it has become common for activists to speak of the 'voluntary and community sector' in recognition of the tendency for policy makers to sometimes only emphasize the formal organizations in the sector (that they are interested in contracting for services) at the expense of the less formalized community-level organizations that see themselves as more closely linked to grassroots realities. This has become a politically sensitive issue in the current UK climate of the so-called 'big society' debate (the latest of a series of policy discourses around the third sector), in which more is being asked of the sector by a government seeking to roll back its direct involvement in social services (Lewis 2012).

NGOs and 'civil society'

During the last two decades, the concept of 'civil society' was revived from its eighteenth-century roots and applied to the field of development. These roots lay in

---

BOX 4.1 ACORD: SITUATING THE HISTORY OF AN NGO

The Agency for Cooperation and Research in Development (ACORD) began life in 1976 as an emergency response consortium of North American and European NGOs. It evolved over nearly five decades to become an African-led international alliance working for social justice. The network had begun originally with the simple aim of trying to work in the particularly difficult locations where few others tended to go, and operated at a time when local NGO counterparts were few. This led to early links with top-down government projects with expatriate staff, but the onset of structural adjustment changed the environment by reducing the state and expanding African NGO funding for service delivery. This next phase led to more work being undertaken outside government – doing local capacity building, empowerment and advocacy work and brought more African staff into ACORD.

By the early 1990s ACORD had become a progressive international NGO with a strong research and policy programme, but one that was becoming increasingly challenged by African staff to better reflect local and regional priorities. After its head office was moved from London to Nairobi, a more global and decentralized perspective around social justice and working with social movements gradually emerged, including a growing involvement with the World Social Forum. A new strategy for 2011–2015 is one that sets organization-wide priorities such as food security, and that takes a pan-African perspective on development. This has brought ACORD to undertake policy engagement with institutions such as the Africa Union, for example. The transformation was a complex, difficult and painful one. Between 2002 and 2006, a multi-level crisis brought near-bankruptcy and a breakdown in governance that almost destroyed the organization. The organization was saved by 'an enduring commitment to a set of ideals tempered by practicality' (p.10). Many developing country NGOs tend to 'evolve from models imported from abroad', and the history of ACORD may offer useful insights into this process.

Source: Fowler (2012)

---

the efforts of political scientists and philosophers to understand the relationship between states and citizens, and in particular what happens in the organized 'associational realm' that lies between the family and the state (Hadenius and Uggla 1996; Keane 1998; Glasius *et al*. 2004; Evers 2013). A revival of the idea of civil society took place within the development industry after the end of the Cold War, which saw support to civil society as a means to help move societies towards democracy (Box 4.3). It soon also became part of 'new policy agenda' debates around public participation service delivery, and campaigning and advocacy at the international level. It was also taken up by development agencies as part of the 'good governance' agenda (Van Rooy 1997; Lewis 2002a).

BOX 4.2 THE UK 'BIG SOCIETY' DISCOURSE

The idea of the 'big society' was launched by Prime Minister David Cameron as a central policy theme for the UK coalition government elected in 2010. The rhetoric claimed that the big society idea was about giving people more control over their own lives. It was presented with three main strands: (i) volunteerism and philanthropy – getting people to give up their time for free and setting aside resources to help others; (ii) localism and community empowerment – getting voluntary and community groups to take over the running of some public services (like sports centres, libraries and fire and rescue services); and (iii) public sector reform – cutting red tape and getting the public sector to be more innovative and entrepreneurial (e.g. promoting the idea of 'mutualization'), or floating off some units as 'employee owned' (such as in the model used by retailer John Lewis) to try to improve their job satisfaction and wider efficiency.

The idea can be seen to have origins in several intellectual traditions. First are US ideas about 'communitarianism', the 1990s call to restore civic virtues, get citizens to focus on their responsibilities as well as their rights and entitlements, and strengthen society's moral foundations to deal with social problems (see for example Amitai Etzioni's *The Spirit of Community*, 1993). More recently, Philip Blond's book *Red Tory* (2010) outlined a form of 'progressive conservatism', in which the idea of the 'market state' that had been at the core of the post-1945 consensus in the UK had been ended by the 2008 crash and recession. However, critics argued that the big society idea was a nebulous idea that merely provided a smoke screen for swingeing public expenditure cuts and the continuing privatization of public services (Ishkanian and Szretzer 2012).

Source: Lewis (2012)

While NGOs benefited from the new interest in civil society in terms of resources and profile, it also raised some issues and problems. While NGOs *do* form part of civil society, as we shall see, civil society is much broader. Some questioned the right of NGOs to speak on behalf of civil society. For a while, NGOs were regarded as a shorthand for civil society itself, and then later, as a reaction against this, civil society came to be seen as the wider third sector – community groups, local organizations, religious groups, trade unions, cooperatives – minus the NGOs. Many writers today still tend to point out that civil society should not be equated 'narrowly with NGOs' since civil society should be seen as a far more diverse universe of organizations, groups and values (Schulpen and Habraken 2013).

The idea of civil society goes back to the writings of the Scottish enlightenment thinkers such as John Hume and Adam Ferguson, as well as the German political philosopher G.W. Hegel, and resonates with other later classic works of political philosophy. The French commentator Alexis de Tocqueville talked about the

BOX 4.3 NGOs AND THE CONTEXT OF POST-SOCIALISM

It was only in the 1980s, during the period of *glasnost* (freedom) and *perestroika* (restructuring) that independent civil society groups and social movements began emerging in Russia, Eastern Europe and Central Asia. Following the collapse of the socialist regimes, democracy promotion was a central part of Western aid programmes and civil society was seen as critical for democratization and successful transition to a market economy. The expectation was that NGOs would take over most service provision from the state and build democratic norms and values. But civil society promotion was usually a top-down, donor-driven effort that led to an artificial but phenomenal growth in numbers of NGOs. In 1994 there were only 44 local NGOs working in Armenia, but by 2004 there were over 3,500 NGOs registered with the Ministry of Justice.

Some post-socialist countries, such as Czech Republic, Slovakia, and Poland, made a transition to democracy and capitalism and went on to join the European Union. But further east, former Soviet republics such as those in Central Asia and the Caucasus experienced a serious decline in living standards and poverty, social exclusion and social polarization. Rapid impoverishment followed the 'shock therapy' polices that were supposed to kick-start market economies and reduce the state services which had previously guaranteed – however imperfectly – access to education, healthcare and housing. Many are now identified as 'developing' countries, though poverty here has features that distinguish it from that in other developing regions. There is near universal literacy, high education levels and modern (albeit non-functioning) industries and social welfare systems.

For NGOs, there are distinctive challenges. NGO capacity remains weak and service provision fragmented. Many citizens still expect the state to provide services. Foreign development workers lack local knowledge since these countries were long closed to Westerners. Local knowledge may be devalued and seen as 'tainted' by communism. Projects and policies have frequently drawn too heavily on experiences from Africa or Asia, ignoring high local levels of education and urbanization. Few NGOs are membership-based or supported by wider citizenry, and the concept and role of civil society remains poorly understood by governments. Without strong local roots, and highly dependent on foreign support, NGOs in these contexts have often faced delegitimization. Much remains to be done to make NGOs more locally legitimate, accountable, and sustainable. As the EBRD's *2011 Life in Transition* report argued, there is a strong lack of public trust in NGOs that remains a major concern throughout Eastern Europe and the former Soviet states.

Source: Armine Ishkanian, personal communication

richness of associational life in the United States in his book *Democracy In America* (first published in the early nineteenth century) and he famously saw this activity as a source of democratic strength and economic power. In his *Prison Notebooks*, Italian activist and communist theorist Antonio Gramsci in the early 1930s wrote about civil society as a site for resistance to the exercise of hegemonic power in capitalist societies. Each of these thinkers presented different ideas about what the concept of civil society means, the ways in which it emerged in different parts of Europe and the analytical uses to which the concept might be put.

Since 'civil society' is a theoretical concept rather than an empirical one, an important challenge has been to try to apply it in the development field. As Van Rooy (1998) has shown, the concepts of civil society all too easily become conflated or simplified into an 'analytical hat stand' on which many different arguments are opportunistically placed. There has been a tendency among development policy makers to pick and choose among the many different understandings of civil society in order to operationalize the concept, with the result that 'a simplified set of arguments has been imported into Northern aid policy'.

Civil society is usually taken to mean a realm or space in which there exists a set of organizational actors that are not part of the household, the state or the market. These organizations form a wide-ranging group which includes associations, people's movements, citizens' groups, consumer associations, small producer associations and cooperatives, women's organizations, indigenous peoples' organizations – and of course the groups which we are calling NGOs. For NGO managers, the long philosophical roots of the concept are less important than the fact that there are perhaps two basic approaches to civil society, which can be termed the 'liberal' and the 'radical'.

In the liberal view, which is the one which has been most popular with governments and donors (and follows chiefly from de Tocqueville), civil society is seen as an arena of organized citizens and a collection of organizations that acts as a balance on state and market, as a place where civic democratic values can be upheld. In a normative sense, civil society is considered on the whole in this view to be a 'good thing', and a critique of state domination of society is implied. In the radical view, which is drawn mainly from Gramsci's work, rather than harmony there is an emphasis on negotiation and conflict based on struggles for power, and on blurred boundaries with the state. This view better acknowledges the reality that civil society contains many different competing ideas and interests, not all of which contribute positively to development. The liberal view has been particularly influential on development policy. For example, Bratton (1994b: 2) sees civil society as

> a sphere of social interaction between the household and the state which is manifest in norms of community co-operation (trust, tolerance, inclusion, joining), structures of voluntary association (citizens coming together into voluntary associations both local/national, formal/informal) and networks of public communication (pluralist media, personal access to communication technology etc.).

This view sees civil society as a source of civic responsibility and public virtue, and as a place where organized citizens – including NGOs – can make a contribution to the public good. The liberal tradition emphasizes the socializing effects of association, which helps to build 'better citizens'. The concept of civil society to which development agencies have been drawn is based upon the idea of an interdependent organic relationship between market economy, state and civil society (Archer 1994). In this model, there is a 'virtuous circle' between all three sets of institutions – a productive economy and a well-run government will sustain a vigorous civil society, a well-run government and a vigorous civil society will support economic growth, and a well-managed economy and a strong civil society will produce efficient government.

This logic was embraced during the so-called 'good government' theme within French and British foreign policies during the early 1990s. It was made clear to developing countries that a continuation of aid, particularly to Africa, would depend on new forms of conditionality. These conditions required a competitive, largely privatized market economy, a well-managed state (with good education and healthcare, just laws and protected human rights, and sound macro-economic planning) and a democratic 'civil society' in which citizens had rights as voters and consumers so that they could hold their institutions accountable. The conditions also required a free press, regular changes of government by free election, and a set of legally encoded human rights (Archer 1994).

Within this discourse, civil society was understood as overlapping with the market. This was evident particularly in the case of donor assistance given during the 1990s to the former Eastern Bloc countries, where the creation of capitalist market relations and the construction of a civil society were seen as being very closely linked. But there were also strong political elements in the new discussion of civil society within development. According to White (1994), the growth of civil society was seen to have the potential to make an important contribution to building more democratic governance processes, because it could shift the balance of power between state and society in favour of the latter. It could also enforce standards of morality, performance and accountability in public life, and act as a channel for the demands of organized citizen groups by creating an alternative 'space' – outside formal political structures such as political parties – for political representation and action. A good example of this can be seen in the Right to Information movement in India (Box 4.4).

The idea of civil society has led NGOs to seek greater involvement in advocacy, policy-influencing and alliance building roles that aim to open up political space for citizen voice in public affairs. By working as SCOs, NGOs aims to contribute to democracy building 'when groups (especially marginalized sectors of society) effectively participate in the marketplace of competing interests' as Covey (1995: 866) suggests. NGOs may try to broker relationships between the poor, the middle classes and elites, bringing the potential to both build civil society and enhance policy outcomes. Within such 'inter-sectoral problem solving', NGOs may try to shape alliance participants' awareness through 'bridging roles' (Brown 1994).

BOX 4.4 CONFRONTING CORRUPTION: AN NGO USES THE DELHI RIGHT TO INFORMATION ACT

In 2001, the State Government of Delhi passed the Right to Information Act, which made it incumbent upon government departments to publicly account for their actions and policies. Satark Nagrik Sangathan (SNS), a citizens' group disseminating information about food security entitlements in slum settlements of South Delhi, began actively using the Act to gain access to public records pertaining to the distribution of state-subsidized food and fuel meant for low-income households.

SNS concentrated their activities in five slum areas where low income residents had not received their food and fuel rations for over five years. The government-appointed distribution shops had refused to sell rations to designated ration card holders on the pretext that they had not received the rations from the state. Most of these card holders were from households who could not afford two square meals a day, let alone buying food and fuel in the open market.

SNS repeatedly approached the State Food and Civil Supplies Department at various levels, from the local public distribution system Inspector whose job it was to ensure ration distribution in the area, to the Food Commissioner, who sat at the head of the Department. When no action was taken, SNS applied for access to the records of two distribution shops under the Act, on behalf of the local residents. These records revealed that despite having regularly received highly subsidized foodgrain intended for sale to poor households, the shop owner had been selling it on the market for the past five years! Not only were the most vulnerable being deprived of their food entitlements, it was a loss to the system to the tune of several million rupees.

SNS therefore organized a *jan sunvai* (public hearing) to address the various issues they had uncovered. About 400 largely women slum dwellers gathered at a local Community Centre. The hearing was attended by the shop owners, the departmental officials, other NGOs, the Press and was presided over by a panel comprising members of the National Campaign for People's Right to Information and the Adviser to the Supreme Court on Food Security. The shop owner apologized publicly, but the people demanded legal action against him. They also demanded a departmental inquiry and action taken against the PDS Inspector and other concerned officials. The residents called for systemic changes such as the availability of rations at the beginning of the month, when salaries had been received, as well as the setting up of local vigilance groups to ensure proper distribution of rations.

This hearing was important because it voiced the concerns of vulnerable and marginalized people, and highlighted the positive role played by women in securing the household's food entitlements. Further, it provided a viable urban model for the *jan sunvai*, with a tightly knit and focused agenda and a time-bound schedule. Previously, such hearing in rural settings had often been lengthy and rambling affairs, involving multiple issues. Above all, the *jan sunvai* brought together antagonistic parties on a common platform and engaged them in a dialogue for systemic change.

Source: Yaaminey Mubayi, personal communication

Such work is extremely difficult. Diaz–Albertini (1993) shows how such bridging roles might function. Writing about the context of Peru, he outlined the twin need for NGOs both to strengthen civil society through grassroots empowerment work, and to seek to ensure the viability of the state as an apparatus that is capable of processing people's political demands and claims. He examined three ways in which NGOs have tried to institutionalize political practices and build bridges between the state and civil society in terms of welfare issues, each of which has distinctive advantages and disadvantages which need to be balanced and linked across three levels simultaneously. In the first, NGOs temporarily substitute for the state as service provider, creating higher quality services but leading to little sustainability. In the second, NGOs work to 'represent' the grassroots through lobbying work and political action, but this level of activity often tends to lead NGOs into becoming professional advocacy groups that gradually lose touch with real people at community level. This is a concern for some NGO commentators, who suggest that advocacy can sometimes be a distraction from an organization's main work in addressing the real needs of people who are poor and can therefore be an inefficient use of resources (Anderson and Rieff 2005: 36). At the third level, NGOs work with providing local community organizations with technical assistance, services and organizational support, but since few channels exist for presenting local demands to the state, NGOs can easily end up merely 'administering poverty' rather than working for structural change.

For many donors, the idea of 'strengthening civil society' became a specific policy objective. According to Brown and Tandon (1994), the strengthening of civil society requires attempts to improve the intellectual, material and organizational bases of the various actors within civil society. Although capacity building or organizational development (OD) has long been directed at strengthening the *performance* of organizations working in the public or the private sectors, different approaches are needed to support 'mission-oriented social change organizations' (see Box 2.1). Harry Blair (1997) has explored two main types of donor approaches to working with civil society: the first is reforming the system through working on the creation of an enabling environment by improving the rules of the game under which civil society operates.[29] The second is through support to sectoral agendas through working within the existing civil society environment by supporting specific organizations directly. A strong civil society is therefore seen as strengthening democracy by educating citizens to exercise their right to participate in public life, by encouraging marginalized groups to become more active in the political arena, and by helping to build overlapping networks. This also resonated with ideas about social capital (see Box 4.5), which is explored in more detail in Chapter 10.

A radical Gramscian of civil society sees it as the location for independent resistance to the state. Rather than the focus on balance and harmony embodied in the liberal view, MacDonald's work (1994) shows that civil society is in fact a zone of conflict. She draws attention in particular to the constraints of class and gender placed on people's actions, to the tensions between the state and civil society (and those which exist within civil society itself), and finally highlights the international political economy dimensions of the discourse of civil society in developing countries (see also Fernando 2011). In this view, the state is engaged in a struggle to control civil society. In addition to using its own formal state institutions to do this, the state also exerts its power through civil society institutions such as the media and the Church in order to maintain its authority.

BOX 4.5 INFORMAL SOCIAL SERVICES, NGOs AND 'SOCIAL CAPITAL'

In the south west of Uganda, where communities have been severely affected by the HIV/AIDS virus, many international NGOs have set up programmes designed to raise awareness about preventative health, to address the social and economic consequences of the disease through support to orphans to prevent them dropping out of school, and small loans to households to assist with income generation activities. At the same time, local rural communities were also seeking ways to adapt their own organizational structures and systems in order to deal with the problems. In some villages there was a tradition of 'munno mukabi', a form of self-help in which older village women clubbed together on an informal basis in order to help to arrange funerals for poorer households. With the spread of HIV/AIDS, the result had been an increase in the numbers of funerals and greater pressure on this informal system. It was also the case that many households now had family members who were sick, or with adult household members who were entirely bedridden. This arrangement was then adapted into a type of home visiting service, which made sure that people who were unwell did not lose touch with the rest of the village, and received food. This was a case of evolving local community self-help structures – a form of social capital – as an adaptive response to social welfare needs, and it was supported by an international NGO which began providing small amounts of credit to the 'munno mukabi' women – which was to be repaid via a profitable sideline providing catering to weddings and parties – which helped them to scale up their activities in the face of increasing need.

Source: author's own field notes

Such views emphasize the importance of understanding power, conflict and diversity within discussions of civil society, and not just harmony and balance. In this way, civil society can be seen not so much as an actor but as a context for action (Shaw 1994: 647). Civil society is a context within which a wide range of collectivities are formed and then interact, including formal organizations of a representative kind such as parties, churches, trade unions, professional bodies, formal organizations of a functional kind such as schools, universities and mass media, and informal networks and groups such as voluntary organizations, *ad hoc* activist coalitions and social movements. Civil society institutions are simultaneously located on the outer edges of the system through which state power is legitimized in society. At the same time, civil society is also an arena in which various social groups can organize in order to contest state power. In Gramscian terms, civil society can therefore be seen as the site of struggle between hegemonic and counter-hegemonic forces (MacDonald 1994).

The radical view of civil society recognizes that the conflicts over power and politics that take place in civil society may be important for formal political processes and cannot easily be separated from them. The capacity of NGOs to play civil society roles is contingent on the specific character and power of the state, and for developing countries in particular on the international political environment. In many countries, individuals may move between NGOs, the government and opposition political parties as the vehicles for political change. For example, after the change of government in the Philippines in 1986 that ended the authoritarian Marcos regime, there were many activists from the NGO sector who accepted jobs in the new administration because they saw government as a potentially more effective base for putting ideas into action (Borras 2001) (see also Box 10.5).

Donor support to civil society strengthening has often meant simply assisting service delivery NGOs rather than advocacy NGOs that might challenge government and donor policy (Kanji *et al.* 2000). In many contexts, when NGOs have become involved in political movements involving party or 'large P' politics, they have been criticized. For example, the participation of NGOs and other civil society actors in political struggles in Bangladesh during the 1990s led to criticisms that NGOs were getting 'too involved' in politics, but their supporters have argued that such involvements are not only legitimate, but form an essential part of NGOs' development role (Karim 2000). When some of the main NGOs joined the opposition political party and other groups to demand that a caretaker government be installed to preside over national elections in 1996, NGO leaders defended their actions by arguing that civil society organizations could not avoid involvement in vital political actions that had major implications for all citizens, and particularly the poorest people (Lewis 2010). Indeed, Chhotray (2008) suggests a useful distinction between 'small p' and 'big P' politics, while at the same time warning against too rigid a dichotomy between what are often overlapping spheres of activity.

Another set of radical criticisms of the liberal view of civil society is its normative character, which always assumes that civil society is a 'good thing'. Much has been made of the fact that civil society can include organized 'uncivil' groups of citizens, including religious fundamentalists, exclusionary nationalists or criminal gangs. Najam (1996b) points out that the racist Ku Klux Klan organization in the United States is in fact a civil society organization. In Latin America, Avritzer (2004) points to the extent of what he terms 'uncivil society' in countries such as Peru and Colombia which he contrasts with the more liberal forms of civil society that exist in Argentina and Chile. It does not make sense to conceptualize civil society in normative terms as always being positive in terms of social justice and development.

Most proponents of the liberal view also acknowledge that there are likely to be competing interests within civil society. The struggle between different interest groups can sometimes create a kind of paralysis. Blair (1997) points out that it is possible to have 'too much of a good thing' in terms of civil society action in the US: 'too much interest group influence over the state over too long a period may well lead to immobilism and a hardening of the democratic arteries or "gridlock" rather than to a rich and vibrant democratic polity'. The direct action taken by a range of civil society actors against the World Trade Organization (WTO) meeting in Seattle in 1999, or those actions against the attempts by private corporations such as Monsanto to introduce genetically modified crops in Europe, were highly visible and depending on one's point of view arguably effective engagements. But such actions raised as many questions about the accountability of the civil society actors involved as about the activities of the WTO and Monsanto. For whom were these groups speaking, and with what kinds of authority?

Alongside the liberal and the radical views of civil society, there is also what might be termed the 'relativist' critique (Box 4.6). Anthropologists have viewed the revival of the Western concept of civil society and its application to widely different cultures and contexts in different parts of the world with scepticism, pointing out the dangers of a new post–Cold War 'universalism' (Hann and Dunn 1996). Comaroff and Comaroff (2000) have also discussed the ways in which the construction of a 'civil society' was used as an instrument of exclusion by colonial rulers in Africa.

Clearly, civil society and its institutions may take different forms in non–Western contexts, as Brown (1994) has shown in Africa. Within this view, Africa is presented as possessing cultural and religious institutions which express collective identities, while new forms of third sector association have been created in response to adapting to urbanization and resisting colonization. In some countries, efforts by ruling elites to extend the state have sometimes met with resistance by groups such as lawyers and journalist associations in Nigeria, Christian church organizations in Kenya, and mineworkers' unions in Zambia. The concept of a national conference is a distinctive contribution to civil society. These conferences have been convened in more than a dozen francophone states, in which national elites and representatives of all major sections of society have come together, often chaired by a church leader, to discuss pressing political matters of the day. In both Benin and Congo, such assemblies met to demand the right to impeach a corrupt leader.

Western visions of civil society have come under criticism from theorists and activists in other societies where there may be civil society organizations that are based on traditional values of kinship and ethnicity and while not necessarily fitting the standard definition, may nevertheless carry out many of the other functions of a civil

BOX 4.6 HOW RELEVANT IS THE CONCEPT OF CIVIL SOCIETY TO NON-WESTERN CONTEXTS?

There has been a lively debate in recent years concerning the relevance of the civil society concept to societies beyond the West. Some argue that building civil society is a precondition for progress anywhere in the world, while others point out that efforts to build civil society often run up against local cultural obstacles. In relation to Africa, for example, four different possible answers can be identified to the question 'is the concept of civil society relevant?'. These can be summarized as follows:

Prescriptive universalism: civil society is a good thing, and needs to be built everywhere. This answer takes a positive, universalist view of the desirability of civil society as part of the political project of building and strengthening democracy around the world. There are many organizations and activists that explicitly embrace this view. For example, the global civil society network CIVICUS aims to '… help advance regional, national and international initiatives to strengthen the capacity of civil society' (see CIVICUS website: www.civicus.org).

Western exceptionalism: civil society was a specific product of Western history and culture and does not easily 'fit' with other contexts. The second possible answer is a clear 'no', based on the argument that a concept which emerged at a distinctive moment in European history can have little meaning within such different cultural and political settings. From this, 'civil society' is just another in a long line of attempts at misguided policy transfer from the West.

Adaptive prescription: a qualified 'yes', since the concept of civil society is very flexible, but it may not look the same or play exactly the same roles in non-Western contexts. For example, certain African kingship institutions may be included as a means of articulating relations between citizens and state. The concept will take on local, different meanings and should not therefore be applied too rigidly, either at the level of analysis or in the implementation of policy, where it cannot be deployed instrumentally in search of 'predictable' policy outcomes.

It's probably the wrong question to ask: it is more useful to focus on broader questions of democracy, politics and organization in any given context and leave the concept of civil society behind, especially since even in the West there are major disagreements about its meaning and relevance. In any case, the idea of civil society — whether explicitly recognized as such or not — has long been implicated in Africa's colonial histories of both domination and resistance, and in decisions over who is and who is not a 'citizen'. This view takes a broader perspective on social and political changes, and analyzes these in historical and cultural context, whether or not there is explicit reference made to 'civil society' concepts.

Source: Lewis (2002a)

society organization. For example, the Somali clan system simultaneously provides for the needs of the members of its communities, but at the same time contributes to the violence and hostilities that exist between different clans and factions (Edwards 1998). Van Rooy (1998) offers a realistic view in seeing the idea of civil society as both an *observable reality* in terms of an arena of conflicting organizations and interests, and a *normative goal* in that 'having a civil society, warts and all, is better than not'.

In some of the countries of the former Soviet Union, problems have also arisen when development donors have tried to support the emergence of civil society through funding local NGOs. For example, in Uzbekistan, the introduction of the concept of civil society has in fact become simply an instrument for local Russian-speaking anti-Islamic elites to construct a new power base far from the Western liberal civil society ideal (Abramson 1999). In the attempt to bypass corrupt government officials, there was a subsequent growth of new NGOs – many of which were controlled by the same elites as controlled the government – which merely led to the reproduction of corrupt and inefficient structures in the non-state sector. The attempt by donors to operationalize the concept of civil society arguably fails to address the pressing political and economic reforms that are needed to bring positive change. The problems of civil society building in Armenia and other former Soviet 'transition' countries highlight the special issues facing NGO managers in these areas. There are dangers in applying practical lessons on one context that have been learned elsewhere, since NGO management challenges always need to be addressed in context.

NGO roles in 'strengthening' civil society are only one of the ways in which the concepts of NGO and civil society have become intertwined. Another important issue for NGO management is the extent to which NGOs as organizations display characteristics of civil society within their structures and processes. To what extent does an NGO serve as a microcosm for the values and relationships of civil society? The very existence of NGOs with internal democratic processes is sometimes taken to be an indicator of civil society, since the values of participation, cooperation, trust and internal democracy may help to foster wider political processes by example. Writing about the US context, Abzug and Forbes (1997: 12) suggest that leaders within third sector organizations are not only 'guardians' of civil society with civic responsibilities outside their organizations, but are also 'responsible for expressions of civil society within their organizations'. For example, the level of independent trade union membership among the employees of an NGO may be one dimension of this internal civil society dimension.

The extent to which an NGO challenges oppressive gender norms and seeks to promote gender equity among its staff structures and relationships is another key aspect of civil society in terms of power and values (Goetz 1997). Howell and Pearce (2000) show that in Central America one of the criticisms made of donor preoccupations with supporting NGOs in order to 'build civil society' is that many NGOs have exhibited strongly hierarchical, less than participatory internal structures and processes. In Bangladesh, Wood (1997) has described the ways in which some NGOs may reflect within their own structures and processes the social and cultural norms of patron-clientelism, hierarchy and gender subordination that predominate more widely in society. Other NGOs have served to propagate alternative values and attempt to build a more gender-balanced alternative to mainstream organizational values (Kabeer and Huq 2010).[30]

Both liberal and radical conceptions of civil society can provide different perspectives on the roles of NGOs in political processes in helpful ways (Clarke 1998). In the Philippines, the liberal or de Tocquevillian view shows the ways in which NGOs have moved into territories previously occupied by political parties that found it difficult to adapt to the changing realities of human rights, environment, minorities and gender interests. But in the radical or Gramscian perspective it is also possible to use civil society theory to understand how NGOs have ultimately helped to institutionalize contested political interests in the Philippines. Radical militant social movements that developed under the Marcos dictatorship have become diffused in the post-Marcos era, and NGOs have contributed to the reduction of this anti-state pressure by absorbing activists into more legitimate 'development' and human rights concerns, and by ultimately strengthening the state. But the contradictions in the liberal view of seeking to strengthen NGOs as a proxy for strengthening civil society, and the dangers of taking an apolitical view, point to the need for NGOs and donors to pay more attention to radical ideas about civil society in seeking to explain and inform development action.

How do we bring together such a diffuse topic as civil society? In a valuable exploration of civil society in Central Asia, Charles Buxton (2011) usefully distinguishes three ways of thinking about civil society that helps to make sense of its complexity and multiple versions. First, the 'triadic' model reflects the idea of the three overlapping circles of the liberal version. Here donors and professionals work towards trying to create clearer rules for the third sector, improve its legitimacy and partnerships with business and government. Second, he describes the 'political/ rights' model of civil society that partly coincides with the radical versions of the civil society idea, where activists and dissidents try to influence the state. Finally, he identifies the 'arena' model of civil society, in which it is seen as a contested public space in which debates and contestation take place, and where family and clan groups form part of the discussion.

Global civil society

Until comparatively recently, civil society had been discussed only in relation to the nation state. However, it is now common to hear it argued that the nation state is in relative decline and that civil society increasingly seeks to represent itself across nation-state boundaries through the formation of global institutions, such as formal links between parties, churches, unions; and informal networks among women's movements, peace movements and global organizations such as Amnesty International and Greenpeace (Shaw 1994: 649). Global civil society activists are busy 'mobilizing resources, framing issues, and pushing agendas, by making entrepreneurial use of networks whether in the case of the anti-slavery movement or tax justice' (Anheier, 2011: 63).

Laura MacDonald's (1994) work on the links between 'international NGOs, national NGOs and popular organizations' in solidarity work around Central America during the 1980s highlights the rise of global civil society. In Nicaragua, for example, the US government's attempt to destroy an alternative form of democratic governance in the shape of Sandinistas led to local, and later international, resistance. International NGOs like Amnesty International, Greenpeace and Oxfam contributed to the emergence of 'transnational counter hegemonic networks', through forming wider coalitions with other sections of civil society:

> The potential long term impact of actors in global civil society lies not merely in their material resources but also in their ability to create new identities, to contest established ways of thinking, and to create new linkages between peoples in different parts of the globe.
>
> (Macdonald 1994: 277)

Clark and Themudo (2006: 50) argue that global civil society is now also increasingly being constructed and transformed by information technology in the form of internet-based 'dotcauses', described as 'cause-promoting networks whose organizational realm falls within internet space'. These organizations, concerned with issues as diverse as currency speculation or indigenous people's rights, but broadly linked with what has become known as the anti-globalization movement, has fed into debates about a range of issues, including the idea of 'global civil society' itself. Like most new concepts, the idea of global civil society also has its share of critics, such as Anderson and Rieff (2005), who argue that the lack of democracy within international relationships is perpetuated rather than challenged by the NGOs that make up much of the 'global civil society movement' and that there has been a 'severe inflation of ideological rhetoric' (p.26) around the concept itself.

Global civil society theory remains an important area for conceptual discussion and NGO-related action. It signals an optimism in some quarters about the role that NGOs, in conjunction with a wide range of other kinds of organization and networks, might play at a transnational level. For example, Kaldor (2003) argues that global civil society, which is 'both an outcome and an agent of global interconnectedness', brings a new form of politics that can 'supplement' democracy at the national level. It constitutes a realm of public debate and Kaldor suggests that in its 'activist' form (as opposed to other types or strands of global civil society which she analyses)[31] creates possibilities for democratizing and 'civilizing' the globalization process through demanding global rules and justice, including: (a) a strengthened framework of international humanitarian law; (b) a shift from military force to 'international law enforcement'; and (c) a stronger form of international policing in place of 'traditional peacekeeping'.

From civil society to 'third sector'

The rediscovery of the concept of civil society ran parallel to another conceptual discussion within organizational studies and public policy – the concept of the 'third sector'. This section takes the third sector concept as the entry point for considering NGOs as organizations before we move on later in Chapter 6 to discuss the various roles played by NGOs in development. There appears to be no precise moment of origin for the term 'third sector', which seems to date back to public policy discussions in the 1970s in the United States.[32] The US sociologist Amitai Etzioni (1972, 1973) is believed to have originally coined the term. Another important influence on third sector thinking was Theodore Levitt, a writer on marketing management at Harvard Business School in the 1960s and the person widely credited with popularising the term 'globalization' during the 1980s. Levitt's interest in the analysis of wider public policy was reflected in his book *The Third Sector: New Tactics for a Responsive Society* (1975) that recognized the emerging interest in the importance of the third sector. Finally, sociologist Daniel Bell in his book *The Coming of Post-Industrial Society* (1976) predicted the rise of the third sector as likely to become the most important institutional society in countries such as the US in the future. The idea of the third sector is useful to a discussion of NGO management because, while civil society provides an analytical framework for understanding the institutional arena in which NGOs operate, the concept of the third sector has its roots in the analysis of organizational difference and therefore draws useful attention to the ways in which NGOs and other third sector organizations are structured and motivated.

In his influential work on complex organizations, Etzioni (1961: 3) set about analysing why people become involved in organizations, and the different kinds of power relationships that determine organizational forms. What emerged was a conceptual framework that sets out three different basic types of organizational form. This is based around the concept of 'compliance' as a central element of all organizational structure that explains the relationship between those who have power and those over whom they exercise it:

> Compliance refers both to a relation in which an actor behaves in accordance with a directive supported by another actor's power, and to the orientation of the subordinated actor to the power supplied.

This determines commitment or alienation from the organization among those involved. Within most organizations there tend to be people with high levels of power who dominate, and those in subordinate positions with less power. Power relations differ in terms of the means used to achieve compliance, and usually take three forms: *coercive*, which is the application or threat of physical sanctions (such as pain or restrictions on the freedom of movement); *remunerative*, based on control over material resources and rewards such as wages or benefits; and *normative*, based on the manipulation of symbolic rewards and deprivations, the use of the power of persuasion, and on appeals to shared values and idealism.

While these types of power are not restricted to particular types of organization, one will tend to be the dominant force in any one organizational case, such that 'most organizations employ all three kinds of power, but the degree to which they rely on each differs from organization to organization' (Etzioni 1961: 6–7). Each type of power relation can then be equated with government, business and voluntary or third sector organization respectively. Following from this argument, Etzioni goes on to outline three kinds of involvement by people in organizations which he described as *alienative*, where involvement is kept to a minimum, such as among capitalists in foreign countries, prison inmates, enlisted recruits; *calculative*, where there is positive involvement of low intensity, such as business contacts and prisoners who have created relations with prison authorities; and *moral*, which indicates high-intensity involvement, such as devoted party member or parishioner in church, and followers and leaders in social organizations.

Although voluntary associations are highly diverse, Etzioni suggests that they chiefly use degrees of normative power to achieve compliance. They build commitment of workers, volunteers and members and compensate them primarily through symbolic reward. This line of thinking has led to the idea of a third sector as a loose category of organizations that are not government or for-profit businesses, but which are held together by the 'glue' of value-driven action and commitment. Najam (1996b) shows how Etzioni's schema of three different ways in which organizations mobilize resources – coercion and legitimate authority (the state), negotiated exchange in markets (business) and shared values in consensus-based systems (voluntary organizations) – can be used to argue that broad differences exist between the three sectors of institutional forms. Within policy circles, the discovery of the third sector has been seen as having several possible purposes – as another potential delivery system for services, as an area of 'private' activity into which government can shift responsibilities, and, as we saw earlier, the notion of an arena of 'civil society' in which individuals can organize social action.

There is another line of thinking that has led to the third sector concept based on the history of activist organizations. Levitt's (1975) book deals with the changes in the nature of protest and social movements in the United States, and represents another early documented use of the term 'third sector'. It seems possible that Etzioni and Levitt both began using the term around the same time. Levitt (1975: 7) traces the emergence of increasing forms of institutionalized social activism during the 1970s which was not just seeking 'specific reforms' as in the past, but was pressing for 'a more responsive society', with more 'benign behaviour' from government, business and educational bureaucracies than in the past. He suggested that 'these new organizations … demand our attention'.

Such demands centred on a greater emphasis of quality of life over material goods, a more equitable distribution of resources, higher levels of public participation in determining what is equitable, and through active interest groups and personal involvement rather than just through conventional politics. Levitt was writing in the context of the emergence of highly visible activism embodied in student groups, the Black Panthers, women's groups, environmentalists and the US New Left corporate responsibility movement. Levitt (1975: 8) claimed that

> To treat the Third Sector, its outcries and demands, its assertions and its tactics, simply as a brief though influential phase in the so-called American revolution

is to miss the possibility that fundamental new institutions are being created and new methods for achieving social change are being irrevocably manufactured.

The new ground which he identified took many forms, including challenging the 'safe anonymity' and controlling functions of large-scale bureaucracies in public and private sectors, a critique of normal bureaucratic 'professionalism', and the idea that government was unwieldy and unresponsive to people's needs.[33] Levitt points out that for too long policy makers and researchers have focused on only two broad sectors in a conventional taxonomy which divides society into public and private such that private is understood to be 'business' while 'public is presumed to be all else' (1975: 48–9):

> But that leaves an enormous residuum, which itself is divisible in many ways. … I have called this residuum the Third Sector … a bewildering array of organizations and institutions with differing degrees of visibility, power, and activeness. Although they vary in scope and specific purposes, their general purposes are broadly similar – to do things business and government are either not doing, not doing well, or not doing often enough.

There has always been a third sector, in the form of church groups, labour unions, sports clubs and music associations, but it was largely ignored by most social commentators. They have purposes, like all other organizations, but they differ chiefly in the tools they employ to get things done. Without any explicit reference to Etzioni's work, Levitt goes on to outline the different 'rules of the game' found in the different sectors. In business the main tool employed to get things done is that of exchange, rational calculation of competitive economics and market. In government the main tool is that of law, the power of compulsion, even if it is not explicit – the formal codification of legitimacy, whether real or contrived. Finally, for the third sector, things run on voluntarism, donations of time and money and quiet persuasion. Participation, Levitt suggests, is not usually motivated by income (although the desire to protect income may emerge), while resources are mobilized by an organization's ability to seek and attract them voluntarily.

The concept of the third sector can also be seen as a guiding metaphor (Wuthnow 1991) or a Weberian 'ideal type', which provides a comparative analytical framework for discussing organizational and institutional relationships, but which does not correspond precisely with realities on the ground.[34] Najam (1996b) suggests that Nerfin's (1986) framework of three systems of power – the 'prince, the merchant and the citizen' – provides a useful 'way of seeing' by contrasting government and economic power with the power of 'citizens and their associations'.[35] The resultant notion of a three-dimensional web of the institutional landscape of society shows both the blurred boundaries which exist (for example between private sector business and some NGOs) as well as a set of quite distinctive concerns, such as the building of organizations in the third sector based primarily on social vision. As a guiding metaphor, it is also important to realize that while the concept is relatively new, the organizations of the third sector are not, and the concept allows us to rein-terpret existing studies and data in a new light.

Economists have also attempted to explain the existence of the third sector as an institutional response to the meeting of certain kinds of human needs. A range of theories of the origins of the third sector have tended to focus on the issue of ser-vice provision and have frequently attempted to explain the general emergence of third sector organizations in terms of either market failure or state failure (Kendall and Knapp 1999). Within public goods theory, such as that of Weisbrod, third sector organizations emerge because there are unmet needs among sections of the population, either because there are minority interests which 'standardized' gov-ernment prescriptions tend to exclude (for example, the needs of people with highly specialized health problems) or which the private sector finds it unprofitable to address (such as the agricultural input needs of poor farmers on marginal or risk-prone lands). By contrast, other approaches such as Hansmann's theory empha-size the issue of *trust* in countries that provide tax incentives for 'not-for-profit' organizations (Anheier 2005). This 'non-distribution constraint' on third sector organizations (preventing them from distributing profits to shareholders as in the 'for profit' model) creates a situation in which the public is more inclined to trust 'non-profits' than for-profit businesses to do a good job in the provision of services, such as in the case of residential care for the elderly.

As Levitt (1975) points out, 'despite being ignored as a separate "sector", a vast literature arguing about its forms and taxonomies exists'. For example, research by Smith and Friedmann (1972), along with work by numerous anthropologists who have long focused on the organizational activity of communities in different parts of the world (Lewis 1999b), offers a relatively long and detailed history of thinking about what we have come to see as the third sector. It is useful to return to this work for historical perspective, even if such work does not present itself in the terms we have come to find familiar today.

With both mainstream and radical origins, the term 'third sector' is useful because it provides an analytical framework into which we can categorize NGOs as organi-zations based on a set of relatively clear conceptual distinctions in relation to gov-ernment agencies and for-profit business. These boundaries are in practice unclear and overlapping, and use of a simple three sector framework may only serve to obscure fundamental historical differences between states and regions (Tvedt 1998). Another perspective on the third sector developed by Evers (1995) sees it not as a clear-cut sector, but as an intermediate area between state, market and household. It is an area within a mixed system of welfare in which a range of different kinds of organizations, including hybrids and new types of partnerships, deliver services in new ways and challenge existing institutional arrangements.

Whichever third sector tradition is adopted, despite some limitations, a three sector model is a useful starting point for getting to grips with NGO management. In the face of the bewildering range of culturally specific and disputed terms within this field, the advantage of the 'third sector' idea is that it is relatively – though not entirely[36] – value- and culture-neutral.

The rise of NGOs in development

The end of the Cold War was associated with the emergence in the 1990s of what Mark Robinson (1993) termed the 'new policy agenda', and this heralded a period of heightened profile for NGOs. NGOs became identified as suitable vehicles for two new related areas of impetus within development policy: the idea of 'good governance', in which NGOs were viewed as public actors with key roles in supporting democratic processes in the political sphere; and the priority of 'economic liberalization', in which the *private* character of NGOs was emphasized, and they were seen as important market-based actors that could potentially deliver services more efficiently than the state (Edwards and Hulme 1995).

At the same time, there was a related set of policy agendas that saw NGOs as useful policy instruments for containing disorder after the collapse of the Soviet Union in newly unstable regions of the world, such as the former Yugoslavia and the Horn of Africa. NGOs had always been concerned with humanitarian relief and assistance work, but in some quarters NGOs now became seen – in Fowler's (1995) apt phrase – as 'ladles for the global soup kitchen'. At the level of global social policy a process was in place that heralded what Deacon *et al.* (1997) termed the 'residualisation of welfare'.

NGOs began to move into a more prominent position within development policy, often seen as the 'favoured child' of official development donors (Edwards and Hulme 1995). They were 'catapulted into international respectability' such that governments and multilateral institutions also suddenly began to see NGOs as useful, important actors in development (Brodhead 1987: 1). NGOs were attractive to both left and right, and were courted by those in the mainstream as well as those interested in alternative development ideas. Brodhead's (1987) assertion that NGOs are 'in one year, out the other' has generally held true within the development industry.

What explained the dramatic entry of NGOs into the development mainstream during the 1990s? There are four main interrelated clusters of reasons. The first can be linked to the theoretical 'impasse' within development thinking discussed earlier (Booth 1994). The macro-level theories of mainstream 'modernization' and radical 'dependency' that had dominated development ideas for two decades had begun to lose their appeal because they seemed to offer little in the way of practical utility to those interested in doing something about development problems. The search was on for new, alternative ideas and different kinds of development actor (other than governments). NGOs fitted the bill. Korten's (1990) ideas illustrate very well the way that theorists and practitioners from both the left and the right, who had become disillusioned with conventional ideas about development, became attracted by a set of new ideas about 'people-centred' approaches being offered by some NGOs.

A second set of reasons is related to the perceptions of many development agencies that governments had performed poorly in the fight against poverty. A search for alternatives to public sector action and 'government to government' aid became a matter of priority. The simple transfers of aid resources between governments were felt to have yielded poor results in terms of impact on poverty, and were believed have contributed to growing levels of bureaucracy and corruption. A pervasive argument was made, fuelled by the ideology of neoliberalism that was beginning to take root within Western public policy in the 1980s, that policy makers had overestimated the capacity of the state to initiate, implement and monitor appropriate development activities. Brodhead (1987) consequently suggested that the new policy interest in NGOs had little to do with any real understanding of the capacities or the potential of NGOs, but was instead driven primarily by a sense of disillusionment that more than 20 years of official overseas development assistance had apparently generated little in the way of measurable results. Many of those who wrote supportively about NGOs were critical of the state, such as Fisher (1998: 2), who in her book *Nongovernments* writes of the 'increasing inability of the nation-state to muddle through as it confronts the long-term consequences of its own ignorance, corruption and lack of accountability'. While some NGO supporters were driven by an anti-statist ideology, others were more pragmatic, and saw NGOs as a way simply to get more things done. For whatever reason, the aid industry 'discovered' NGOs and proceeded to invest them with a set of expectations, roles and agendas for improving the way development was to be undertaken.

While the rise of NGOs can be understood in terms of their 'discovery' by outside agencies, this was not the whole story. A third set of reasons centres on the ways in which NGOs themselves contributed to building up a new profile. As the traditional economic and political concerns of development have shifted in the 1990s to include debates about the importance of environment, gender and social development, a growing NGO presence and policy 'voice' became apparent. NGOs began to gain increased access to policy makers. They demanded that their ideas, views and approaches needed to be taken seriously. This was achieved through a combination of activism, campaigning and policy dialogue. For example, it seems unlikely that the influential UK 1997 *White Paper on International Development* would have placed so much emphasis on poverty reduction had not the NGO community advocated for a greater poverty focus in the British aid programme for many years (Gardner and Lewis 2000). NGOs also played their part in creating the momentum for the UN's Millennium Development Goals (MDGs). Today there is still a view of NGOs that sees them primarily as sources of development 'alternatives' in terms of both ideas and practices (Mitlin *et al.* 2005).

At the international level there are other reasons that might explain the rise to prominence of NGOs in international governance. Charnovitz (1997) lists four sets of reasons: the growth of inter-governmental negotiation around domestic policy brought about by integration of the world economy; the end of the Cold War, which removed the polarization of global politics around the two superpowers; the emergence of a global media system which provides a platform for NGOs to express their views; and the spread of democratic norms which may have increased public expectations about participation and transparency in decision making.

There is continuing interest in the roles of so-called 'faith-based organizations', a recently resurgent strand of thinking about civil society that has served to maintain policy attention on the world of NGOs. They are seen to add value to development work in terms of being long term and sustainable, reaching the poorest people, being legitimate in the eyes of those they serve, mobilizing motivated volunteers, and offering alternatives to secular views of development (James, 2010). One important element of this trend was linked to the discourse of 'compassionate conservatism' in the US that has been associated with the ideas of academic Marvin Olasky. The US$30m Compassion Capital fund was established in January 2002 by President George W. Bush (to whom Olasky was a close adviser) in order to provide contracts for services from local 'faith-based' welfare initiatives (Smith 2002). In addition to (mainly) evangelical Christian organizations in the US, humanitarian organizations informed by Muslim, Buddhist and Hindu values have also been recently gaining a higher profile in policy discussions about civil society and development (Mansour and Ezzat 2009).[37]

There is a sense in which NGOs can mean all things to all people, and that this may be another factor that helps to explain their ubiquity. As DeMars (2005: 2) put it, the NGO form 'has become so irresistible that a broad assortment of notables, missionaries, and miscreants are creating their own NGOs'. Indeed, NGOs tend to appeal to all sides of the political spectrum. For liberals, NGOs help to balance state and business interests and prevent abuses of the power these sectors hold. For neoliberals, NGOs are part of the private sector and provide vehicles for increasing market roles and advancing the cause of privatization through private 'not-for-profit' action. Finally, for the left, NGOs promise a 'new politics' which offers the chance of social transformation but presents an alternative to earlier radical strategies for capturing state power and centralization (Clarke 1998).

Making use of Najam's (1999) and Vakil's (1997) definitions of development NGOs, we find it useful to make a distinction between a *broad* definition (NGOs as an umbrella term for third sector organizations concerned with improved services and wider social change, whether part of the aid industry or not, including both public benefit and self-help) and a *narrow* definition (NGOs as donor-funded intermediary organizations which support community-level membership organizations). It is the broad definition that informs our approach in this book.

Conclusion

In order to take forward our exploration of NGO management, we have reviewed a set of definitional and conceptual issues around the nature of development NGOs, including the related concepts of civil society and third sector. A brief sketch of the history of NGOs at international level was also presented, and this history is shown to have far deeper roots than is often supposed. We considered the different regional and national contexts and influences on NGOs in different parts of the world, and diversity among various NGO traditions. Finally, the chapter discussed the wider policy context of the rise of NGOs and, more specifically, a set of changes within the development policy world that has helped to bring NGOs to greater prominence. In terms of our conceptual framework (Figure 2.1), we have therefore begun exploring the outer circle – the context in which NGO management must be understood. In the next chapter, we continue this exploration by examining the world of development, aid and its institutions.

PART II

The theory of NGO management

5

NGOs AND THE DEVELOPMENT CONTEXT

If the 1990s can be characterised as the decade of poverty reduction and good governance in international development, the 2000s have been defined by the aid effectiveness agenda.

Hayman (2012: 1)

Introduction

In this chapter, we turn to the overall context of the development system in which NGOs operate. We begin with a brief historical review of the ideas and practices of development, which began with an emphasis on economic growth and technology transfer but gradually evolved into a more complex set of ideas that also included human development, sustainability, participation and rights. This is followed by a discussion of the contemporary aid system, and its relationship with the world of development NGOs. NGOs are also active in the arena of humanitarian emergency and relief intervention, which is then briefly considered, and it is argued that these two worlds, though different, cannot be altogether separated. The chapter concludes with a discussion of the changing face of development, which has moved into an era in which effectiveness and results are now more strongly prioritized.

Understanding 'development'

Development as a concept has its origins in the experiences of Western countries, and in particular in the period of the Enlightenment in Europe during the seventeenth and eighteenth centuries. This was an era during which the prevalence of religious explanations about the world were gradually replaced by rational scientific perspectives that favoured the idea of 'progress'. These ideas were carried forward by European colonial powers during the eighteenth and nineteenth centuries and deployed both at home and in overseas territories in Africa, Asia and Latin America. After the Second World War, the modern concept of development became formalized as part of an international system put in place by the Western countries as part of a post-war international order that included the United Nations and the Bretton Woods institutions (the World Bank and the International Monetary Fund).

The idea of development is associated with that of 'modernity', a form of political and social order that is characterized by high levels of industrialization, urbanization and the use of high levels of technology. Following this, development has tended to be conceived primarily in material economic terms. It was argued that development could be measured through gross domestic product (GDP) per capita (dividing the wealth in the economy by the size of the population), making it possible to divide countries into low, lower-middle and upper-middle income countries. However, critics argued that such an approach created a predominant focus on growth rather than distribution, and on statistics rather than actual people.

Development was generally taken to mean positive change or progress, with the *Oxford English Dictionary* giving its basic meaning as 'a stage of growth or advancement'. As a verb development came refer to the activities required to bring positive changes about, while as an adjective it implied some kind of a value judgement, a standard against which societies could be compared. Development also implied a natural metaphor of organic growth and evolution. Some countries were seen as undeveloped or in the process of being developed, while others were viewed as having already reached a mature state of 'development'. Yet the concept of development is far from straightforward, and can be understood in many different ways, as we shall see below.

In their book *Doctrines of Development*, Cowen and Shenton (1996) famously argued that development can be seen as having two slightly different but interrelated meanings. In the first sense, development refers to deliberate attempts at progress through intervention, but in a second sense it also refers to the broader pattern of unfolding capitalist transformation and the efforts that people themselves constantly make to improve their quality of life. Following this distinction, Bebbington et al. (2008: 5) termed these two dimensions of development 'little d' development (unfolding patterns of capitalist change) and 'big D' development (deliberate interventions to promote positive change in the developing world).

Development as an idea therefore has meaning both at the level of theory, and that of practice. During the second half of the twentieth century, two main academic development theories – modernization and dependency – were in broad competition with each other, but by the start of the twenty-first century, debates about development had become more strongly focused around the worlds of policy and practice. As Thomas (2000) has suggested, while this brought a welcome connection with real world issues, it also arguably narrowed understandings of development to a set of narrow technical issues focused around the goal of 'poverty reduction' that was often defined in over-simplified terms.

For those who prioritize the transformative power of markets over structural change and redistribution, modernization theory embodied the idea that in order to develop poor societies needed to achieve economic take-off through capitalist growth, and free themselves of 'traditional' social and cultural impediments. The economic benefits of this growth would eventually 'trickle down' to those at the bottom of society, making this a development theory focused on more securing growth rather than on direct efforts to reduce poverty. Modernization theory has evolved and changed since its emergence in the 1950s, but can still be seen as informing mainstream neoliberal growth-centred views of development that still dominate today. On the left, modernization theories (there were several variants) were mainly challenged from the 1970s onwards by forms of radical 'dependency theory' that advanced a set of ideas influenced by Marxism. Proponents of this analysis argued forcefully that 'underdevelopment' was not an absence of development, but was instead the result of an active, unequal global process. In this view, poor countries did not lack resources but had been actively underdeveloped by their histories of direct colonization and then, after this had ended, by continuing unequal forms of international terms of trade. Development was not therefore possible without large-scale structural change, and only likely to be brought about by popular revolution.

By the 1990s, the field of development studies had reached something of an 'impasse', with both sides of what remained a mainly theoretical debate increasingly talking past each other, and relatively detached from issues of real peoples' lives on the ground (Booth 1994). Furthermore, those in the worlds of policy and practice who were interested in doing something tangible to challenge the increasing levels of poverty and inequality in the world found that neither of these theories had much to say to those who were committed to trying to find ways to contribute to positive change in actual communities in the here and now.[38] Some academics found that building links with the ideas and practices being discussed within the world of NGOs, such as empowerment and participation, offered a way out of this impasse.

In some quarters too within mainstream development agencies, some new ideas had been taking shape in the face of what were seen as increasingly irrelevant grand theories. One of the most significant was the concept of 'human development', devised by the United Nations Development Programme (UNDP) to provide the means to assess poverty and development in ways that went beyond the conventional reliance on measuring income and other economic criteria. It drew upon Amartya Sen's (1983) 'capability approach', which conceived of development in terms of the capacities of individuals to make choices that allow them to expand their 'quality of life'. Rather than simply seeing poverty as a state in which there was a material lack, this opened up new thinking on the non-material dimensions of poverty, and on the importance of viewing poverty not simply as a state but as a process.

A set of new ideas about vulnerability and sustainable livelihoods was also emerging. These implied a need to understand how individuals and households actually went about trying to make a living, and how they attempted to build resilience over time and protect themselves against crises and shocks. Ideas about quality of life and wellbeing expanded understandings of poverty to include non-material benefits such as political freedoms, equal opportunities and improved environmental and institutional sustainability.[39] Indeed, quality of life has subsequently become a one of the central new themes informing a wide range of development work (Kanji *et al.* 2012).[40]

Alongside this new thinking associated broadly with UN organizations, a set of ideas was also emerging among community-level development workers in the form of what can loosely be termed the 'participatory' or 'alternative' development paradigm. In contrast to government and mainstream development agencies, the emphasis was on 'bottom-up' rather than the 'top-down' approaches. New ideas around participation, empowerment, local action, indigenous knowledge and sustainability were the hallmarks of this new paradigm. Furthermore, wider practice now came to be seen in terms of process – as non-linear, unpredictable and operating with complex, open systems (Ebrahim and Rangan 2010). Doing development work required a much fuller appreciation of the need for participation of the subjects of development in planning interventions, in information gathering and in the bridging the gap that existed between research and practice. Some of this new thinking was influenced by work of development NGOs.

An influential advocate of change has been academic and activist Robert Chambers, who has emphasized the need to change the personal behaviour and attitudes of those working within development organizations and governments. Chambers' argument for a 'reversal' of the conventional order of things, so that rather than imposing their knowledge on those being 'developed', outside 'experts' should instead listen and learn from local people, has inspired many people. Chambers saw a need to stem and reverse what he saw as longstanding trends of outsider dominance in development, through taking action to make personal-level changes among the individuals in power who determine policies, procedures and organizational cultures. Issues of power and gender were given particular priority (Chambers 1983, 1994, 2005).

Such thinking also drew upon the ideas of anthropologists and sociologists of development, whose work emphasized more field-level engagement than had been common among economists and political theorists of development. For example, feeding into this trend was a new interest in 'actor-oriented' accounts of social change, an idea that was associated with rural sociologist Norman Long's research work in Mexico. Long's approach to rural development aimed to go beyond the modernization versus dependency stalemate to explore the ways that change was, or was not, *actually happening* through people's own efforts on the ground. It drew both on anthropological traditions of ethnographic fieldwork and on Anthony Giddens' theoretical writings on the complex interaction between individuals and structures (Long and Long 1992). Meanwhile, other new theoretical developments were also underway. Postmodern ideas about development began to emphasize diversity, the primacy of localized experience and the colonial roots of development policy discourses (Escobar 1995; Gardner and Lewis 1996). These suggested that there were no generalized answers and solutions to development problems, and that there should be an emphasis instead on strategies rather than solutions.

NGOs within changing development thinking

How did NGOs fit into all this? Development NGOs have been connected with development at both levels, within both 'big D' and 'little d' understandings of development. Many NGOs are focused on making interventions and prioritize working directly with people, by setting up projects that can provide goods and services to people in need. Some also offer new ideas about how to do this effectively, such as by using participatory approaches. Other NGOs place less emphasis on doing 'big D' development in a direct sense and focus instead on 'little d' issues to support better regulation of the economy, fairer trade rules and the protection of human rights, sometimes joining with government or with people's movements to do so. Yet the overall profile of NGOs within the changing landscape of ideas and polices around development has varied. In Figure 5.1, the main development theories are outlined, alongside the level and type of attention that they give to the role of NGOs. Different ideas about development have tended to represent the role of NGOs in different ways.

Earlier thinking about development during the 1970s and 1980s, such as modernization and dependency, had paid relatively little attention to NGOs. But as newer and sometimes alternative development ideas took shape, NGOs began contributing to wider debates about empowerment, gender and participation. NGO perspectives were often driven by practical experience, and were written up into articles, manuals and policy documents.

NGOs therefore became associated with the rise of a deeply practice-focused, people-centred or 'alternative' development paradigm.[41] In the wake of earlier grand theory, a 'development as empowerment' approach was seen as a new way to link theory and practice (Black 1991; Friedmann 1992). Empowerment referred to efforts to change the power relations between different sections of society and the various actors in development processes. It was seen as a grassroots process with psychological and organizational dimensions, and emphasized support to collective self-help by people to assert greater control over their environment. Some mainstream agencies also began to take notice. For example, The World Bank's (2002) 'sourcebook' on empowerment listed four key elements as access to information, inclusion within decision-making, accountability of organizations to people, and local organizing capacity to resolve problems of common interest. However, as ideas about empowerment became taken up within mainstream worlds of development, they were often broadened beyond original more radical meanings (Kilby 2011).

Institutionalists were also discovering the third sector, and some saw NGOs as important new actors that could play useful roles alongside states and market actors within new models of public management. Many also saw NGOs as potentially *innovative* organizations, capable of developing new approaches to problem solving, based on their organizational flexibility and their closeness to local communities. According to Poole (1994: 105), NGOs can function as

> alternative providers of such services, financed by the state, and/or by international donor agencies where the state is economically too weak. Besides

making a unique contribution to agricultural development, the NGO sector can supply other benefits. Diversity in the provision of agricultural technology and services is likely to promote efficient competition, and to stimulate the process of institutional and democratic evolution that are themselves dimensions of national development.

TABLE 5.1 NGOs in the context of changing development ideas

Development theory	Main development idea	Role of NGOs
'modernisation' (key author: W.W. Rostow, 1960)	transition from pre-capitalist conditions to modern capitalist growth and change	NGOs are rarely mentioned
'dependency' (key author: A. Gunder Frank, 1969)	underdevelopment as a continuing condition of subordination after colonial exploitation of third world 'peripheries' by Western 'core' countries	NGOs are rarely mentioned, but 'social movements' often seen as positive forces for liberation and revolutionary change
'institutionalism' (key author: E.A. Brett, 1993)	only by improving structural relationships and economic incentives will optimum conditions for development be achieved	NGOs are seen as one of the three main institutional sectors; with the 'right' rules and incentives in place, and in optimum circumstances and contexts, NGOs can have comparative advantages over the other two sectors in providing services
'neo-liberalism' (key author: J. Sachs, 2005)	making globalization work for the poor: market mechanisms are the key to unlocking the potential of developing countries to develop economically	NGOs are flexible agents of democratization and private, cost-effective service delivery
'alternative' development (key author: J. Clark, 1991)	grassroots perspectives, gender equality empowerment and bottom-up participation are the key to sustainable and equitable development processes	NGOs are critical actors in terms of their closeness to the poor and their ability to challenge top-down mainstream development orthodoxies
'post-development' (key author: A. Escobar, 1995)	the idea of development is itself an undesirable Western imposition on the rest of the world – we therefore need to abandon it	NGOs are agents of modernization destroying local cultures and economies, only local social movements constitute useful sites of resistance to these processes

Source: Lewis and Kanji (2009)

In this type of argument, the respective roles of public, private and third sectors should be determined by weighting up the comparative advantage of each. Ideas about the comparative advantage of development NGOs continue to inform the rationale among Western donors for giving support to NGOs. For example, a recent OECD report stated that NGOs are considered valuable development partners by OECD countries because of their proximity to beneficiaries, ability to deliver humanitarian aid quickly, and their capacity to promote democracy and innovate (OECD 2011).

Other ideas in development also made connections to NGOs. For example, the work of NGOs chimed with the growing academic and policy interest in the concept of 'social capital' that became popular around the turn of the millennium, where the idea of strengthening community-level relationships and trust became seen as an important objective for democracy and social stability (see Chapter 10, and Box 4.5). Within social capital theory, the creation of new cross-cutting social ties and networks that went beyond traditional kinship, religious or ethnic identities were viewed as contributing to improved possibilities for collective action and increased levels of democratic participation (see Putnam 1993; Bebbington *et al.* 2006). Alongside social capital, the concept of 'social exclusion' also gathered attention, since it claimed to address issues of marginalization and inequality in ways that went beyond conventional definitions of economic poverty (Bhalla and Lapeyre 1997).

Finally, NGOs also became strongly associated with rights-based approaches that have steadily gained ground in development (ODI 1999; IDS 2003). This was a response both to progress at the international level in terms of new legal rights frameworks, and to the work of local-level activists and movements around the world that are using and adapting rights frameworks as means for claiming social justice. The shift to a rights-based approach has brought issues of economic, social and cultural rights centre-stage, alongside existing concerns with civil and political rights. In fact, this new interest is better seen as a 'revitalization' of an older development and rights discourse that had emerged with the first UN World Conference on Human Rights in 1968 (Molyneux and Lazar 2003). The rights perspective has proved useful in linking poverty reduction efforts with citizenship, laws and accountability and, in the case of humanitarian intervention, highlighted the need to build local dialogue around protection of the rights.

The international aid system

The concept of development became one of the dominant ideas of the second half of the twentieth century, embodying a set of aspirations and techniques aimed at bringing about positive change or progress in the countries of the 'third world' (Africa, Asia, Latin America).[42] International aid became a prominent element within international relations during the period after the Second World War, and was primarily conceived in terms of a set of relationships between rich and poor

---

BOX 5.1 RIGHTS-BASED APPROACHES: IMPLICATIONS FOR NGO PRACTICE

Increased transparency: the need for an NGO to be explicit in relation to its principles and values in when it deals with other development actors and local people. A key area is making partnerships with other agencies more accountable and responsive.

Shifting from beneficiaries to partners: seeing people with whom an NGO works as active citizens rather than as voiceless recipients of assistance.

The analysis of power relations: NGOs require a sophisticated understanding of how local institutions operate within a given context and the complexities of local politics.

Building new skills in political analysis and diplomacy: since the right-based approach is one that implies a deeper engagement with local laws, social norms and political systems it brings with it a high level of sensitivity and added risks of allegations of interference.

An emphasis on working with the poorest: the rights-based approach draws renewed attention to people who remain hidden or 'to whom no-one listens' in their local struggles for justice on the broader landscape of development activities.

Engaging more fully with legal systems: this can provide NGOs with the means to help build people's awareness of their rights, through for example legal aid provision and rights awareness training.

Encouraging better accountability between governments and citizens: examples here would include supporting the right to information, for example.

From the point of view of Oxfam International, Jeremy Hobbs has recently suggested that rights-based approaches has increased the complexity of organizations, since they now have to focus not just on managing service delivery, grants and technical projects but also on building political alliances and bridging across both developed and developing country contexts to get at the structural constraints that hold back change, such as trade rules and unequal access to the world's resources.

Source: IDS (2003), Hobbs (2013)

---

country governments. Aid was channelled predominantly into large-scale, top-down, government-organized projects located in the developing world.

An international system was formed in support of these goals. What some have termed the development industry has become a powerful and complex system of public and private agencies channelling international development assistance. Its main institutional actors include multilateral institutions such as the World Bank, the inter-governmental agencies of the United Nations, the bilateral donors such as DFID and USAID. As de Haan (2009) suggests, aid can be understood as having multiple motives: its helps to structure international power relations, reflects collaboration between states, and embodies a set of norms around improving the quality of life – and 'its principles always reflect a combination of motives, and aid practices tend to create their own dynamics' (p.3).

As we saw in Chapter 4, NGOs had received little in the form of official international aid in the early days of development. During the 1950s and the 1960s official donors and NGOs had tended to pursue different development agendas, remaining largely disinterested in each other's activities and occasionally suspicious of each other's agendas (ODI 1995). NGOs were generally seen as organizations that were only useful in emergency work rather than as serious actors in development. It was in the late 1980s that they became the focus of new attention. The aid industry acquired a raft of specialized, development-focused international third sector organizations channelling funds from governments and publics into different kinds of development and relief work. As a result, for many people the concept of 'NGO' has become inseparably linked with the business of international development, even though there are NGOs that do not receive official development funding, and those that are highly critical towards or oppose the mainstream world of development aid.

When Western donors began paying more attention to development NGOs, it was because NGOs were perceived to offer at least three 'qualities' that official aid was seen as unable to provide. The first was that NGOs were believed to engage more effectively than governments with citizens in the developing world, particularly people living in poverty, women or minorities normally excluded from economic and political participation within existing institutional structures. The second was that NGOs appeared to be less tied to the geopolitical interests of states (heavily polarized in the Cold War period), and were seen as more independent in the development agendas that they were able to pursue. The third was that NGOs offered ordinary citizens in the North opportunities to engage more directly with issues of poverty and social justice – as supporters, volunteers or contributors to organizations and campaigns (Little 2003).[43] Donors had previously worked with NGOs in relief settings, but now proceeded to increase their funding to NGOs for development work. NGOs were claiming to reach people more effectively than traditional government-led development projects, and donors had become more aware of evidence of generally poor performance of such projects.

The new interest in NGOs was also deeply ideological. As we saw in Chapter 2, the 1970s saw the emergence of a new set of neoliberal policy prescriptions that favoured less intervention by governments in markets and a stronger role for private institutional actors. The economic breakdown created by the oil crisis and the rise of 'stagflation' had led to a loss of confidence in dominant Keynsian economic principles and created a ready audience for the market-led, individualist ideas central to the ideology of neoliberalism. In the development field, the World Bank and the IMF began propagating these ideas heavily.

In what was soon termed the 'new policy agenda' of governance reform and liberalized markets, NGOs were assigned key roles in new service delivery models (Robinson 1993; Edwards and Hulme 1995). NGOs were favoured because they offer effective service delivery (of education, shelter, credit, healthcare the rapid disbursement and utilization of project funds, an assurance that ~~funds would~~ be handled and spent honestly, a sense of 'ownership' of an intervention among its beneficiaries leading to improved sustainability, and a private identity as non-state actors in service delivery that signalled a move towards privatization.

By the 1990s, development NGOs had become fully part of the development system and began to receive a higher proportion of international aid. Yet perhaps surprisingly given the regular outbreaks of public concern about the volume of resources NGOs control (see Box 1.1), the vast majority of official development assistance still does not go to or through the NGO sector. According to Little (2003: 178), NGOs in fact control only 'a meaningful but small share' of the word's assistance to developing countries, which in 2009 was around 13 per cent of aid provided by the OECD DAC countries (OECD 2011).

Official funding for NGO projects and programmes has tended to follow several different routes. One is the demand-side model where NGOs themselves put forward specific projects and programmes and then receive funding for this work from donors. NGOs may also negotiate a block funding partnership agreement with a donor, and then use it flexibly to support a range of agreed activities. The second (and increasingly dominant) model is that of 'contracting', a supply-side model where NGOs are engaged by donors to undertake specified tasks within the pre-planned programmes devised by donors or governments. There are different forms of contracting arrangement, but in most, donors sub-contract projects to NGOs and provide the funds required to carry them out, within increasingly tightly specified administrative margins, the latest of which is the 'payment by results' system.

One claim often made by NGOs is that they use official aid to do things other agencies cannot do. Yet the argument that funding through NGOs makes it possible for official aid to reach people and places it would not otherwise reach has been contested by one of the few detailed quantitative studies of NGO funding patterns carried out by Koch and Dreher (2008). Based on data from 62 of the larger international NGOs in 13 OECD donor countries, the authors found that rather than complementing official aid by working in environments that were difficult or 'out of the way', most NGOs tended to followed the country choices of their donors, cluster by following the choices made by other NGOs, and choose to work in countries with continuities with their own cultures, religion and past colonial histories.

Challenges within the NGO relationship with donors

Closer links with the development industry created a dilemma for NGOs, often summarized by the old proverb 'he who pays the piper plays the tune'. The growth of 'contracting' relationships, in which NGOs were paid to carry out predetermined work on behalf of donors or governments, has by definition implied a loss of autonomy and independence even as it has created opportunities to expand and reach more people. Rapid growth has sometimes led NGOs into scaling up their activities too quickly, or narrowing their activities unnecessarily. Rather than setting an agenda, NGOs were now instead left implementing the agendas of others.

A further set of problems for NGOs involved with the aid industry centred on what Ian Smillie (1994) and others called 'the tyranny of the project'. The project was a basic building block of development management that made it possible for donors to control an intervention using a logic model of planning. But according to Campbell (1994: 3) such an approach also often 'prevents the community from effectively managing its own programmes', because it is difficult to build local ownership of externally driven activities. Furthermore, dependency by governments on NGOs to provide basic services, which are themselves dependent on foreign donors, sometimes served to undermine the basic accountability rights of citizens to demand services from governments, since the resources underpinning such services became controlled from outside the country (Wood 1997).

This led to a wide range of associated concerns. Some NGOs feared negative impacts on long-term local organization building work, as donors have favoured more rapid results to show their constituencies at home (Edwards and Hulme 1995). A focus on short-term outputs and outcomes also inhibited learning and reflection, with implications for the capacity of NGOs to generate new ideas (Carroll 1992: 18). Finally, with donors usually unwilling to cover core costs, NGOs found themselves struggling to cover administrative costs. This contributed to the view that NGO became valued by donors as a cheap way of getting things done, and not because of any other creative characteristics.[44]

A final area of controversy was the changing relationship between international and national or 'Southern' NGOs. By the late 1990s, international NGOs found themselves operating in a changing policy environment (Lewis 1998c). There was a steady shift from international NGOs' direct implementation of projects and programmes towards the idea of constructing partnerships with local implementing organizations. Another trend was an increase in the 'direct' funding by donors of local NGOs that in some cases began to bypass the international NGOs who had become used to acting as intermediary organizations for donors. There was an 'identity crisis' among international NGOs that found themselves caught between 'one country's concern and the problems of people in another' (Smillie 1994: 184). This began to give some international NGOs an uncertain, hybrid character, since they are part of the third sector of the North, but work predominantly in the South.[45]

What seems clear today is that the relative independence of NGOs as development actors has gradually become more tightly circumscribed within the modalities of the aid industry in the twenty-first century. Tina Wallace and her colleagues (2013: 16–17) speak of 'a perfect storm' that has occurred within the NGO environment that has combined managerialist donor thinking on logic models, results, targeting and value for money, an increasing role for the private sector and its values in development, and a tendency for international NGOs in particular to grow and adopt more professionalized, corporate identities. First and foremost, they argue, this perfect storm has negative implications for people affected by poverty. But at the same time, it is changing the overall climate of NGO work:

INGOs started out, in the main, as independent players in development and humanitarian aid, working with local partners and communities ... concepts such as solidarity and accompaniment were common in many organizations, and the space for critiquing and challenging dominant norms existed, though it was often not a comfortable space to occupy, something experienced by many gender staff, for example... This was not a 'golden age' for NGOs ... But for us what is important is that there was *space* for discussion; in many INGOs debates were fierce and strong, critiques existed and people were not afraid to speak. This contrasts with the fear of openly questioning strongly presented narratives of aid that exists in many organizations now.

The context of humanitarian relief

Although our concern is primarily with the development roles of NGOs, we cannot overlook the related field of relief and emergency work. Indeed, as we saw in the context of David Korten's schema of NGO generations, NGOs often have their original roots in people coming together to meet needs after a disaster.

In contrast to the longer-term challenge of development, relief work was commonly seen simply as an immediate response to natural or man-made disasters in terms of the relatively unproblematic challenge of distributing resources to those in need in the form of goods, services and technical assistance. Disasters were often understood as interruptions in the linear process of development, after which 'normal' longer-term development work could be resumed (Macrae and Zwi 1994).

In this model, the concept of 'rehabilitation' formed the bridge between relief and development. As understandings of social change and instability grew more sophisticated, linear views were abandoned in favour of those encompassing issues of complexity and process. The emergence of the term 'complex political emergencies' during the 1990s signalled a recognition that there are areas of the world where insecurity, instability and disorder are more or less permanent conditions (such as in Somalia or Afghanistan) and where conventional thinking about making a distinction between 'development' or 'relief' interventions was of limited value.

The idea that relief work was less problematic for NGOs than development work also turned out to be largely illusory (Abdel Ati 1993). New thinking about relief has problematized it in three ways. The first is that relief is increasingly understood as not – as was once believed – politically neutral, because political factors limit access to resources, and aid itself becomes a political resource. The second is the recognition that even after a problem or hazard has passed, the capacity of communities to access resources may be impaired and people may remain vulnerable. The third is the idea that relief and development tend to have different objectives, with the former concerned with physical survival and the latter aiming at sustainability and the building of appropriate social, political and economic systems.

Like development, relief work increasingly also challenges the simple dichotomies of North and South that were once common. Hurricane Katrina in the United States revealed the inequalities and 'third world' levels of emergency response found

BOX 5.2 NGOs AND THE TURKISH EARTHQUAKE

On 17th August 1999, an earthquake shook the eastern edge of the Marmara Sea, an industrial region some 80 kilometres from Istanbul, claiming over 17,000 lives and leaving half a million people homeless. The early aftermath witnessed an unprecedented mobilization of NGOs and other civil society actors who were hailed as heroes able to provide crucial early response. Among the NGOs, Arama Kurtarma Dernegi (AKUT), which means 'Search and Rescue Association' and was previously concerned with mountain rescue, became a favourite with the public and the media having rescued over 200 people from the rubble. In the days that followed, a group of 40 NGOs coordinated their activities by forming a 'Civil Society Earthquake Coordination Committee', in order to construct and manage a city of 2,000 tents providing temporary homes for the victims. This contrasted starkly with the efforts of the government and the military, who appeared completely unprepared and took two weeks to coordinate their response.

However, despite the political capital gained by their activism, the network of organizations was simply too loose to transform to an effective movement and civil society remained 'less a "society" than simply thousands of volunteers' (Kubicek 2002: 40). Gradually the state took over the humanitarian operations related to the earthquake and regained control of the agenda. NGOs managing the tent cities were asked to leave, the reluctant ones being persuaded with threats to turn off water and electricity supplies. NGOs reacted to attempts by the state to limit their activities by taking a proactive stance. A manifesto was published in all the major newspapers, appealing to the state not to over-centralize relief efforts and to recognize the value of the NGO contribution to the relief effort. This manifesto, signed by over 100 NGOs, represented a highly significant and unusual initiative that challenged prevailing norms in Turkey. Despite these efforts, however, by the end of the year the Turkish state had taken over the running of the tent cities and the NGOs were forced to take a less prominent role. At the same time the subsequent service provided by the state in the tent cities were more efficient and of improved in quality, suggesting that NGO pressure had played a role in setting a standard for the state to meet.

On the one hand, NGOs in Turkey demonstrated their ability to provide an effective practical response, and successfully challenged the state to raise standards. On the other hand, events suggest that civil society still lacks the political edge that would enable it to become more than an array of activists and organizations each with their own particular agenda. While some described this unprecedented mobilization as the 'coming of age' of the Turkish NGO sector, this was ultimately short-lived.

Sources: personal communication from Markus Ketola; Jalali 2002; World Bank 1999; Kubicek 2002.

in areas of the American South. The Kobe earthquake in Japan was a disaster that required massive emergency efforts and generated an unprecedented response from and profile for the Japanese 'third sector' (Kawashima 1999). The Turkish earthquake had a similar galvanizing effect on citizens and civil society and shifted people's expectations about third sector roles, and, just as importantly, the responsibilities of the state itself (Box 5.1). More recently, in March 2011, the earthquake and tsunami that devastated areas of northeast Japan has brought home the vulnerabilities located within even the wealthiest societies.

After the 9/11 attacks in 2001, US foreign policy shifted to include what it began to call the 'war on terror'. This brought changes within wider Western aid policy that in some cases reduced the capacity of development NGOs to maintain their room for manoeuvre. While strong and growing links between conflict and poverty had been observed and documented throughout the 1990s, this relationship has become more widely acknowledged and translated into new aid policies. One result has been what Harmer and Macrae (2003) call the increased 'securitisation of aid', which has included the following trends: (a) renewed engagement by the US with 'failed states' to reduce security threats (as opposed to previously mainly investing in states that were willing to embrace reform); (b) an increased linking of military, political and humanitarian responses to instability; and (c) the closer intertwining of military and welfare roles within some radical Islamic groups with the wider third sector. In Iraq, food aid in particular was viewed as an integral part of the reconstruction and stabilization process requiring arrangements for engagement with occupation forces.

This securitization of aid framework became overlaid on the neoliberal framework that had been growing in strength during the 1990s. It changed the priorities and contexts of international development assistance, particularly in relation to NGOs, civil society and development issues. Reflecting on the impact of the so-called war or terror on civil society, Howell (2006b: 126–7) writes

> the global war on terror has led to the constriction of civil society space, a clampdown on NGOs with a concomitant othering of Muslim organizations, the unsettling of an overzealous embrace of civil society by donor agencies, and the undermining of the principles of neutrality, impartiality and independence amongst humanitarian agencies.

Aid was further instrumentalized and seen as a politicized tool of governance that could be used to resolve conflict and secure order in troubled areas of the world (Duffield 2002).

Although there had been attacks on NGO staff before, another consequence of the policies that followed 9/11 has been the targeting of local and international NGOs and their workers as agents of Western power and influence by militants. In areas such as Afghanistan and Somalia, humanitarian workers have long been identified as legitimate targets by armed groups pursuing political objectives (Stoddard *et al.* 2009). The situation worsened in May 2011 when the CIA's search for and subsequent attack on Osama bin Laden's residence in Pakistan was undertaken by agents who had used a bogus NGO polio vaccination campaign in the local area as cover for preparing their mission. In January 2013, in a revenge attack, seven staff of a health education NGO called Support With Working Solutions, which runs a school and a dispensary in Swabi district northwest of Islamabad were attacked and killed by the Pakistan Taliban as they drove home in their vehicle. The US alliance of NGOs InterAction had previously put out a statement saying that the CIA's approach had compromised the global perception of NGOs as independent organizations and put aid worker lives at risk.

The post-2003 reconstruction effort in Iraq helped to usher in a new era in which humanitarian organizations will in the future compete within a new private 'humanitarian industry' working in infrastructure and services such as health education and water, based on for-profit provision (Harmer and Macrae, 2003). Both development and humanitarian actors now face a more complicated operating environment, and may need to make increasingly difficult judgements about the legitimacy and legality of struggles and conflicts if 'universality, impartiality and neutrality' principles are to be maintained. NGO efforts in relief continue to attract more and more criticism in the media, and divide observers and participants, as Box 5.3 shows in the context of Haiti.

The managerialization of official development assistance

The aid industry has always been characterized by a rapidly changing set of ideas, approaches and terms (Lewis 2009). The narrow emphasis on economic growth and technology transfer that had characterized the 1950s and 1960s had evolved and diversified by the 1990s. In a brief period of optimism after the end of the Cold War it looked as if alternative paradigms might be gaining ground, but development has gradually become more and more infused with managerialist ideology that has gained influence across many other areas of public life, in the form of new systems of performance measurement, accountability and audit. Not without justification, the world of development aid began to face 'increasing internal and external critique, and a growing need to show results for tax payers' money' (de Haan 2009: 173).

There has been a new emphasis on performance indicators, most noticeably in the form of internationally agreed targets for poverty reduction. The UN Millennium Development Goals (MDGs), agreed by 189 nations in September 2000, put in place a set of eight poverty reduction goals and 18 targets, including halving poverty and hunger, creating universal primary education, and halting and reversing HIV/AIDS. The MDGs carry the ultimate objective of reducing by half the number of people living on less than US$1 per day by 2015.

The MDGs have provided a reasonably solid basis for organizing around common basic themes and have undoubtedly helped to bring a much-needed focus to international efforts at global poverty reduction. Yet the MDGs were open to the criticism that they ignored the structural causes of poverty and the question of social inequality and exclusion. Concerns were also raised about whether or not the

BOX 5.3 TWO CONTRASTING VIEWS OF INTERNATIONAL NGO EFFORTS IN POST-EARTHQUAKE HAITI

Since Haiti received around $US5 billion in international support for relief and reconstruction after the devastating earthquake of 2010, there have been multiple opinion pieces that in some ways have signalled a turning point in earlier optimism about the effectiveness of humanitarian relief (see Box 1.1). The truth may be more complex.

Among many issues, NGOs have been strongly criticized for failing to coordinate their efforts in Haiti, for not responding to basic rights and obligations owed to citizens, and for basic lack of effectiveness in the work that they have done. In one of many strongly critical articles in the international media, Michael Jennings (February 9, 2012) wrote: 'not enough has been done to transform temporary shelters into permanent homes, or to provide access to drinking water and sanitation services. In some camps run by NGOs, people were still dying from cholera a year after the disaster struck'.

Others have taken a more positive view. In an article that aimed to redress the balance (entitled 'There is hope for Haiti, despite what the critics say') Christian Aid's Prospery Raymond (January 10, 2013), motivated by the large amount of outside criticism, wrote on the same blog: 'The aid Haiti has received has generally been used to support a society left devastated by the massive damage the earthquake caused, and to give a degree of strength and resilience to the country's already fragile economy. Without this kind of support the situation would be far worse than it is.' Citing work by the NGOs' local partners to provide cash grants for people to start local businesses and create jobs, the building of solidarity among Haitians to reconstruct their society, and the efforts to build sustainability and resilience through agriculture and forestry. While problems of coordination, public administration systems and government capacity remain, 'civil society has remained in touch with the needs and demands of local people and a lot more Haitians are now far more capable of addressing emergencies'.

Sources: Jennings (2012); Raymond (2013)

targets may obscure important qualitative criteria, such as gender and social attitudes, or the quality of schooling in a particular education system. Questions were also raised about who was involved in setting and measuring the targets. There were also concerns that in seeking to achieve maximum impact in meeting the goals overall, donors reprioritized their efforts towards areas of the world where the largest concentrations of poverty are found – mainly Africa and South Asia – at the expense of substantial minorities of people in middle income countries that remain poor and marginalized.

Since 2005, *effectiveness* has become a new watchword, applied both to aid and development. The formalization of a new set of principles on aid effectiveness took place at a series of High Level Forums. The 2005 Declaration on Aid Effectiveness, usually known as the Paris Declaration, was the first landmark agreement and was signed by 35 donor countries, 26 multilateral donors, 56 recipient countries and 14 civil society observers. It set out new principles for the relationship between donors and recipient governments based on the pillars of *harmonization, ownership, alignment, mutual accountability* and *results*. This was followed by the Accra Agenda for Action in 2008 which built on these principles further, around additional themes that included commitments to improved planning and predictability within aid processes, more use of country systems to deliver aid rather than donor systems, less rigid conditionality, and the relaxation of tied aid restrictions (Mawdsley 2012). In late 2011 the OECD's 4th High Level Forum on Aid Effectiveness (HLF-4) met in Buzan, Korea to review progress and agree priorities for the future, based on the two continuing priorities of implementing the Paris principles for reform, and improving value for money through investing aid resources more cost effectively. The outcome was the Buzan Partnership for Effective Development Cooperation that built further on earlier principles and for the first time agreed a framework for development cooperation that encompasses traditional donors, those involved in South–South cooperation, private funders and the BRICs, and civil society organizations. It remains to be seen where the Buzan Partnership will lead.

As part of these trends, there has been a new emphasis on 'results' and 'value for money', in line with a need to better quantify the difference that development efforts were making. In the past, it had often been felt that impact evaluations were costly and difficult to carry out, and there was usually political sensitivity around any findings that suggested poor results. This has brought some important changes in the way aid is delivered and assessed. One trend is the increasing use of experimental studies that compare change in an intervention area with a control location. For example, the use of randomized control trials (RCTs) has become a popular method to build better knowledge and evidence about 'what works', and has been popularized by Banerjee and Duflo (2011) in their bestselling book *Poor Economics*. Another is the idea of 'payment by results' (PBR), a form of contracting in which those who commission services only pay the provider once 'a pre-determined result has been achieved and independently verified' (Eyben 2013: 15).

The trend towards measurement, effectiveness and value for money has been part of a broader reorganization of public life in many Western societies, as discussed by Michael Power (1997: 44) in his book *The Audit Society*. One element of this reorganization is a set of new arrangements put in place based on the need for tax payers to know that their money is spent economically, efficiently and effectively (the three 'Es') and to challenge what the author calls 'cosy cultures of professional self-regulation'. The problem with this, as Power argues, is that while no one could argue with the logic of trying to improve public accountability systems, the technologies that tend to be deployed to achieve this remain uneven, and tend to be better suited to demonstrating that efforts are in place rather than actually contributing to positive change.

While all this emphasis on demonstrating results and impact is to be welcomed as a means for ensuring that those who plan and implement development interventions need to think more rigorously about what they are trying to achieve, it also raises concerns about what is being measured and why. As one senior staff member in a leading UK NGO recently put it:

> In a positive way, this is helping us to be more thoughtful and more systematic in the way we allocate funds, and helping us develop clearer frameworks about the difference we are making. But the downside is that it is effectively tying funds up to specific kinds of activities, and it reduces our flexibility and our ability to support projects that may be at a very early stage, and fairly high risk. What we may end up doing is going for the safe things...[46]

The changing face of donorship

The twenty-first century has seen the landscape of international development change in other important ways. The power and influence of Western aid is in decline and new or re-emerging country donors are becoming more prominent, within a realignment of broader global power. For example, China has provided extensive assistance particularly to Africa in recent years (an estimated US $18 billion in 2007). Aid is now also provided through a range of other 'non-DAC' nations including the Gulf States, South Korea and South Africa. Russia, Poland and the Czech Republic all have aid programmes, as does Thailand and Turkey. There has also been an expansion of new private sector development philanthropy, in the form of agencies such as the Gates Foundation with an endowment of more than US $30 billion.

Countries such as China, India and Brazil are beginning to speak a new development language of South–South cooperation. They often claim to promote an anti-imperialist ideology, contrasting their language of partnership and self-reliance with that of former Western colonial powers who offer charity with one hand and conditionality with the other. There is a new prioritization of building infrastructure among many of the Eastern aid donors, such as China (Glennie 2012). Some argue that this restructuring of the aid system provides welcome alternatives for recipient countries, while others remain suspicious of new donor motives and fear that the modest gains brought about by international aid may be put at risk (Mawdsley 2012).

The changing global context raises a set of new questions about how international aid will look in the future. There are fewer poor countries, with the majority of the world's poorest people now found in the middle-income countries. For Sumner and Mallett (2013) this means that the old international aid system is no longer fit for purpose and that a shift is required from thinking about aid as 'resource transfer' to a much more equitable form of aid as 'global development cooperation'. They advocate moving from what they term Aid 1.0 to Aid 2.0, in which addressing poverty is seen as a global problem requiring collective action. The global financial crisis that began with the 2008 banking crash has further reduced the capacity of many Western governments to provide international aid.[47] These changes, combined with the rise of non-traditional aid donors, have prompted new questions about the future of development assistance beyond the MDGs, and even the prospect of moving towards a world without aid in the not too distant future.

For US economist Dani Rodrik, the future of the international development system depends on finding ways to ensure that rich countries take their responsibilities more seriously by adopting 'do no harm' approach. He suggests that the coming policy priorities should include carbon taxes that can help reduce the impacts of climate change, more work visas to make it possible for people from poor countries to find work, tighter controls on arms sales to developing countries, increased sharing of financial information to reduce opportunities for money laundering and tax evasion, and less support for repressive governments (Rodrik 2012). Taking a not dissimilar approach, Sumner and Mallett (2012) identify four principles for a new approach to aid. First, aid should be catalytic in the sense that it should identify spaces in which to support change already happening from within, and focus on local forms of resource mobilization such as domestic taxation. Second, there should be a stronger focus on the use of global public goods to manage risk. Third, research and knowledge transfer needs to take centre-stage, not in a one-way North–South way as before but within multiple systems and feedback loops that include flows between low- and middle-income countries as well as rich countries. Finally, they emphasize the need for policy coherence so that trade, migration and environmental policies are enacted in ways that are in line with global development priorities.

The challenge of developing the post-2015 UN Development Agenda got underway in January 2012 with representatives from more than 50 UN agencies tasked to develop a review of the MDG lessons and generate ideas for a new agenda. The report noted the need in future for a more holistic approach based on four key dimensions: inclusive social development, inclusive economic development, environmental sustainability, and peace and security. As Deacon (2012: 2) argues, there has been useful space opened up for moving towards 'the issue of inequality and equity rather than just poverty … and engaging in policy recommendations and not just targets … and a reordering of priorities other than economic growth'. However, it remains to be seen how far such changes lead to meaningful action in the years to come. At the time of writing, the new objectives being discussed to replace the MDGs after 2015 build further on these targets but bring in the idea of ending absolute poverty, giving more priority to social protection, women's rights, and ending conflict.[48]

New aid modalities and implications for NGOs

The 'good governance' agenda of the 1990s evolved further during the 2000s into a more tightly coordinated effort by development donors to influence recipient governments, and create a greater sense of ownership of agreed – or sometimes imposed – agendas for policy reform.

This process of a partial 're-governmentalization' of aid brought some important implications for NGOs. Hinton and Groves (2004: 4–5) suggested that there was recognition among donors that the new policy agenda had not done enough to increase living standards in poor countries:

> There has been a dramatic shift from a belief in the importance of projects and service delivery to a language of rights and governance. Among policy-makers there has been an evolving sense of the need to involve members of civil society in upholding their rights and working to promote transparent, accountable government … Donors are emphasising the need to work in partnership with national government rather than create parallel structures for service provision. The 1990s witnessed a gradual increase in the flow of aid delivered through governments, as support for democratic national processes grew.

Yet this apparent move back towards a focus on the state was deceptive, since it was taking place within the same neoliberal policy framework that had earlier advocated a reduced role for the development state through policies of privatization and structural adjustment.

The clue was in a new set of mechanisms that donors were using to work directly with government. On one level these seemed to offer a more central role for government, but in practice they often provided more powerful means to influence policy making and implementation in indirect ways. Moving away from the previous emphasis on projects, there was a move towards what became termed 'upstream aid', as Beall (2005: 4) observes:

> While projects remained tenacious, from the 1980s onwards they increasingly gave way to programme aid, usually directed at particular sectors such as health and education or public sector reform … Currently there is a growing trend towards the delivery of aid through Direct Budget Support (DBS), where financial support is channelled directly to a recipient government, usually through a ministry of finance, in a context where conditionality is arguably less oppressive and negotiated in advance in the context of policy dialogue and development partnerships.

Alongside DBS, other new policy tools were designed by the World Bank and other funders in order to promote more coordinated donor support of governments. These included Poverty Reduction Strategy Papers (PRSPs), Sector-Wide Approaches (termed SWAPs), and methods for improving accountability between civil society and government using tools such as Participatory Poverty Assessments (PPAs). For example, SWAPs aimed to bring donors together into a single unified funding mechanism in support of a country's health or education policies, and aimed to provide consistency throughout the policy making and implementation process. In a similar vein, PRSPs were intended for government, private sector and civil society to work together to develop a single national development plan to tackle poverty across all sectors. The stated donor aim was that these tools made it possible for policies to be more strongly 'owned' by recipient governments and their citizens. The move by many development donors away from free-standing projects or programmes towards broader support for budgets and policy reform within recipient governments – sometimes seen as part of what has been termed 'the new architecture of aid' – seems set to continue.

This re-governmentalization of aid has nevertheless taken place alongside continuing donor interest in NGOs and civil society. Development NGOs have continued to be seen primarily as service contractors, but also as part of wider civil society that could serve to drive wider social, political and economic change alongside the state. For example, a DFID White Paper on aid (2009: 132) stated

> These organizations can and do often deliver basic services where states cannot or will not. They challenge governments to ensure that policies benefit ordinary people, including the poorest. And they can help citizens hold their states to account.

Rebuilding a role for NGOs in the post-2005 world

The importance of NGOs and civil society had been recognized in passing by the Paris Declaration, but many in the international NGO community also now felt that their role had not been properly acknowledged:

> The Paris declaration provides only a limited picture of development cooperation, of the various players involved, and how those players need to relate to each other in order to secure sustainable development results. CSOs consider that the Paris Declaration failed to recognise them as agents of development and change in their own right, whose priorities might not always mesh with those of governments.
>
> (OECD, 2009: 12)

There was also a concern that an emphasis on harmonization set out by the Paris meeting might result in a loss of diversity and autonomy for civil society, since the richness of civil society depends on range of multiple voices and approaches coexisting with each other in any given setting (Pratt, 2009).

Following from these concerns, the *Better Aid* document drawn up by the Advisory Group on Civil Society and Aid Effectiveness for the 2008 Accra follow up to the Paris meeting aimed to create more space for NGOs to participate in and shape aid effectiveness discussions. It restated and updated the importance of CSOs (the term now used in place of NGOs) as being effective at reaching the excluded, at mobilizing community development efforts, and delivering humanitarian aid. It reminded the development community that NGOs were often major service providers, 'drawing strength from their diversity and capacity for innovation', and that they 'help to enrich policy discussions by bringing different, sometimes challenging, perspectives to policy dialogue and public accountability' (OECD, 2009: 14).

Changes to NGO funding pathways

The new aid architecture impacted upon NGO funding in several ways. First, the new emphasis on reducing donor transaction costs meant that NGOs were required to compete for funds and adapt to new funding models. Funding to NGOs in particular, especially when large numbers of smaller organizations are concerned, can require enormous amounts of donor staff time to disburse and monitor. This has led to the growth of competitive tendering in which donors contract a for-profit or non-profit agency to manage a programme. NGOs have had to learn new skills such as auditing, oversight and monitoring because they may be competing with private sector companies – such as PricewaterhouseCooper, which now has many DFID contracts for example – within a more commercialized aid setting. Bilateral donors such as DFID are now tendering the management of large country- or sector-level programmes. Christian Aid for example is now delivering a civil society programme in India worth £25 million.

NGOs have also seen the growth of the local fund model. Donors seek to reduce costs by disbursing large lump sums to be managed by an NGO or a mixed consortium of organizations on behalf of the donor, and packaged into grants for local organizations based on criteria set by the donor (Box 5.4). Although often described as partnerships, these may take the form of contracting in which an NGO is given responsibility for an agreed set of tasks that contribute to DFID's overall objectives in a particular country or sector for a specific time period (Wallace *et al.* 2006).

Opportunities and constraints for NGOs

These changes may have narrowed the room for manoeuvre for NGOs in several ways, but they have also brought opportunities. Back in the 1990s, Riddell and Robinson (1995) coined the idea of the 'reverse agenda' in the relationship between NGOs and the donor community. NGOs have not simply been acted upon, they argued, but have also helped to shape aspects of the donors' own thinking. Issues that had previously been seen mainly as NGO concerns are now far more deeply entrenched within mainstream official donor activities – issues such as the concept of participatory planning, the gender dimensions of development, and environmental concerns. Rights-based development, discussed above, is another example of a successful influencing of the wider development agenda in part by NGOs. While many donors included NGOs in the implementation of their projects, it has slowly become more common for them to consult NGOs on policy issues. NGOs are becoming more tightly institutionalized into government and donor systems, but both NGOs and these wider systems do not remain static (Nelson 2006). For example, the Busan agreement adopted in December 2011 was the first such

BOX 5.4 CHANGING DONOR APPROACHES TO NGO FUNDING: MANUSHER JONNO FOUNDATION, BANGLADESH

Manusher Jonno – which means 'for the people' – began life as a small consortium of local and international agencies coordinated by CARE and funded by DFID to the tune of £13.5 million. DFID wished to fund a wide range of innovative human rights and governance work in Bangladesh but wished to avoid incurring the transaction costs of funding large numbers of often small civil society organizations that would deliver this kind of cutting edge work. Instead, DFID tendered for the management of the project in order to find the most cost effective and decentralized way of working. In 2002 MJ began work, establishing a small secretariat in Dhaka, developed its administrative systems and a set of criteria for funding and advertising for project proposals. MJ was immediately deluged with applications from all kinds of organization for a wide range of type of project and at first found it difficult to cope with the demand. In particular, there were many applicants whose proposals did not fit within MJ's brief – since human rights and government work was a relatively new framework for many local NGOs – and large amounts of time were needed to better inform applicants about MJ's objectives and to provide capacity building to NGOs around human rights and governance themes. By late 2005 MJ had developed robust operating systems for dealing with applications and monitoring the progress of more than 120 partners. A key lesson nonetheless was the severe underestimation of the massive administrative workload that was passed down from DFID down to the decentralized MJ secretariat. MJ achieved the status of an independent, local trust separate from both DFID and CARE in 2006, but by 2012 it was still mainly relying on DFID for the bulk of its funding. MJ foundation nevertheless serves as an important local funding point for organizations in Bangladesh seeking support for human rights and governance work.

Sources: author's own field notes; Beall (2005)

partnership agreement to be negotiated 'with strong input from developing countries, from new donors and from civil society' (Hayman, 2012).

Writers such as Michael Edwards (2008) and Alan Fowler (2008) regularly suggest that more NGOs need to free themselves from the world of aid funding if they are to offer genuine alternatives. They argue that NGOs should be aiming to move towards a non-aided future, in which they can form closer ties with the people they seek to represent. At the same time, some argue that more could be achieved if aid agencies provide the right kind of support to the right kinds of organizations. For example, David Satterthwaite (2005: 2) has argued that development aid has 'provided too little support to' the numerous local organizations that benefit and represent poorer groups, which remain largely 'invisible to development assistance'.

Conclusion

A central aspect of NGO management is the capacity of an organization to operate effectively within the constantly shifting context of development ideas, policies and practices. This chapter has provided an overview of the development context – including both the idea of development and the emergence of an international aid system – from the point of view of development NGOs. For many, the idea of an NGO is more or less synonymous with the world of the aid industry, but this is not necessarily so. While there *are* clearly a great many NGOs which depend on international development assistance, there are others that seek to 'go it alone', relying instead on the voluntary labour of their staff or members, on contributions from the local or the international community, or on using the market for other sources of income. The importance of foreign aid and formal development agencies is arguably declining in a world in which private resource flows between individuals (such as the growth of remittances), and the effort to create new forms of organization outside the aid industry (such as the 'my NGO' phenomenon) are increasing. As the middle classes grow across previously poor societies, new forms of social solidarity with those living in poverty, perhaps involving new NGO forms, may also emerge. Nevertheless, the aid system remains important to NGOs as both a source of funding, and as a powerful set of institutions that development NGOs are seeking to influence.

6

NGO ROLES IN DEVELOPMENT

NGOs are seen to have a central role in development practice, but the question that remains unanswered, and probably never can be answered, is: what role (or roles) should this be?

Kilby (2011: 1)

Introduction

We move now from a discussion of the general context in which NGOs operate to consider the organizational roles they play in development work. The following section focuses on what development NGOs actually *do*, and argues that what they do can be summarized broadly in terms of three main overlapping sets of roles: those of *implementers*, *catalysts* and *partners*. Of course, each role is not confined to a single organization, since an NGO may engage in all three groups of activities at once, or it may shift its emphasis from one to the other over time, and as context and opportunity change.

The *implementer* role is defined as the mobilization of resources to provide goods and services, either as part of the NGO's own project or programme or that of a government or donor agency. It covers many of the best known tasks carried out by NGOs and includes the programmes and projects that NGOs establish to provide services to people (such as healthcare, credit, agricultural extension, legal advice or emergency relief) as well as the growth of 'contracting', in which NGOs are engaged by government or donors to carry out specific tasks in return for payment. The role of *catalyst* is defined as an NGO's ability to inspire, facilitate or contribute towards developmental change among other actors at the organizational or the individual level. This includes grassroots organizing and group formation (and building 'social capital'), empowerment approaches to development, lobbying and advocacy work, innovation in which NGOs seek to influence wider policy processes, and general campaigning work. The role of *partner* encompasses the growing trend for NGOs to work with government, donors and the private sector on joint activities, as well as the complex relationships that have emerged among NGOs, such as 'capacity building'. The new rhetoric of partnership now poses a challenge for NGOs to build meaningful partnership relationships and avoid dependency, co-optation and goal displacement.

NGOs as implementers

Service delivery is the most visible implementation role carried out by NGOs. An NGO can be engaged in providing services to its clients through its own programmes, it may be contracted by government to deliver services that were formerly provided by the state, or it can be contracted by a donor to provide services within a project. For example, NGOs were brought into the World Bank's 'structural adjustment programmes' (SAPs) during the 1980s to provide a social 'safety net' to vulnerable sections of the population (Box 6.1). They may also be engaged by private corporations to do community-level work, as in the case of the Chevron oil company developing its gas fields in north east Bangladesh (Gardner 2012). NGOs do not always provide services directly to community-level groups or clients, but may also provide training or research services to government or private sector, or to other NGOs.

The service delivery role remains an important and often successful one for development NGOs. For example, in agriculture NGOs may be engaged in the delivery of services to people in 'unreachable' areas such as the fragile, complex or risk-prone lands for which government outreach is poor (Chambers 1987; Bebbington 1991; Kaimowitz 1993). Such work may also make it possible for NGOs to go on to strengthen wider systems of delivery through training, research and innovation. For example, the work of the Baptist Rural Life Centre (BRLC), in Mindanao in the Philippines, centres on the identification of soil fertility problems with poor upland subsistence farmers in communities that were ignored by government extension service workers more interested in richer farmers growing cash crops. The NGO developed a simple but effective technology that would allow farmers to make the soil on sloping lands more secure and productive as well as providing a varied yield of essential foodstuffs throughout the year. Once this sloping agricultural land technology (SALT) had been tried and tested, the NGO then set about working to ensure it was utilized by other organizations and by government through demonstration events and training work (Watson and Laquihon 1993).

Some NGOs choose service contracting because they become tired of surviving at the financial margins, or of fighting against established interests; a sense of obligation to improve job security for staff; a belief that contracting will eventually bring more funding and opportunities to go back to earlier approaches. It also brings greater susceptibility to Northern policy priorities of shifting public to private responsibility. Service providers therefore tend to be criticized for becoming

---

BOX 6.1 THE GROWTH OF NON-STATE ACTORS IN HEALTH SERVICE DELIVERY IN AFRICA

NGO service provision can take two main forms – *direct service provisioning* and *self-help from below*. During the 1980s and 1990s the adoption of structural adjustment policies by many African governments led to drastic cuts in the provision of social services, with the result that various types of NGO or third sector organizations have attempted to fill the resource gap. Church-based NGOs have been particularly prominent in providing health services. In Zimbabwe, church missions provide 68 per cent of all hospital beds in rural areas, while in Zambia the third sector – which is mostly church-based – provides 40 per cent of health services in rural areas. Self-help initiatives have emerged as citizens have addressed the resource shortfall themselves. For example, in Kenya the *harambee* self-help movement (which was originally established by President Kenyatta) has helped to create a network of health infrastructure in rural areas, though grassroots involvement in construction and maintenance later declined. In Uganda, self-help initiatives in the health sector have emerged from below in recent years, while many rural schools are being managed and funded by parent-teacher associations, despite being still nominally under the control of the state.

Source: Robinson and White (1997)

---

non-profit private sector businesses rather than value-driven NGOs, and running the risk that they may be deflected from their original broader, value-driven goals by concentrating only on delivering services (Carroll 1992). However, some observers are uncomfortable with the NGO implementation role and see it as essentially non-developmental. For example, David Korten (1990) suggests that an NGO that is a 'public service contractor' has lost autonomy, become instrumentalized and shaped by the agendas of government, far from the creative NGO ideal. Korten's argument is that although public service contractors may be well managed and efficient, it has lost autonomy, and is at risk of becoming a proxy for government under privatization agendas.

Another reason for criticism is misgiving about the accountability and the sustainability of NGO service delivery work. A key issue is the relationship to government and whether NGO services are supplementing, undermining or replacing public services. Where NGOs may be dependent upon foreign development assistance, it is not desirable for basic services to pass into the hands of NGOs whose lines of accountability are not clear. Carroll's (1992) view is that NGOs 'should emphasise capacity building or viability upgrading services, not routine services'. Evans (1996) argues that rather than NGOs and government merely complementing each other's work, a more useful 'synergy' can be created if the relationship is a mutually reinforcing one based on a clear division of labour and mutual recognition and acceptance of these roles. Robinson and White (1997) provide a useful framework in which to analyze these relationships, based on three basic processes within the public–private relationships around service provision – the *determination* of which social services are to be supplied, the *financing* arrangements for these services, and their actual *production*.

Some of those who advocate an increased level of NGO contracting for essential service delivery have taken on board such criticisms and instead advocate a 'pragmatic' involvement by NGOs. This stresses a limited time scale, and the ultimate goal of having the state (or the private sector) take over provision once new skills and approaches are acquired and resources mobilized (e.g. Poole 1994). Carroll (1992: 66) suggests that while there may be good short-term reasons for 'gap filling' in public provision, the value of NGO service delivery should ultimately be judged on its developmental impact:

> while service delivery has a strong intrinsic value, it should really be evaluated on the basis of its instrumental value as a catalyst for other developmental changes.

For optimists, the increasing profile of NGOs as service providers is seen as part of the growth of 'civil society', which will strengthen wider democracy and ultimately improve the efficiency and accountability of the state. In Africa, for example, Semboja and Therkildsen (1995) outline a scenario in which, following economic growth and 'successful' structural adjustment, the state will create an appropriate 'enabling environment' to allow the NGO sector to prosper, with the result that the quality and sustainability of services increases. However, the same authors also outline a pessimistic (and perhaps more realistic) scenario, in which it is not always clear who or whose values NGOs represent, and where NGO links with donors, elite and state patrons create ambiguity as far as their role in democratization is concerned.

There are two main sets of issues for NGOs in terms of longer-term thinking about implementation questions. For those emphasizing pluralism, the growth of NGOs as service providers increases choice. For example, Brett (1993) points out that NGOs, alongside the state and private sector, exist within a pluralistic organizational universe, which will expand the range of social choice and potential as relatively autonomous agencies existing within an open society. The challenge is for NGOs to achieve accountability and performance levels comparable with the other two sectors. However, for those stressing the role of NGOs in promoting development and change, there is concern that NGO potential strengths might be underused. After all, even when the quality of services is high, most NGOs offer limited, piecemeal or patchy provision which can never compete with the state in terms of coverage. One future possibility is the increasing specialization and differentiation between two types of organization – between contracting NGOs and organizations with a more developmental focus (Edwards and Hulme 1995). For Carroll (1992), the key question is whether service delivery is a 'means' or an 'end' for development NGOs: a question which leads us on to a discussion of the NGO role of 'catalyst'.

NGOs as catalysts

One of the dominant views of what NGOs are all about is the idea that their *raison d'etre* is to try to make things happen. Grant and Crutchfield (2007: 40) write:

> These organizations and the people who lead them want to solve many of the biggest problems plaguing our world: hunger, poverty, failing education, climate change. They aspire to change the world. They don't want to apply social Band-Aids. They seek to attack and eliminate the root causes of social ills.

For many development NGOs, a key strategic choice is between what David Korten (1987: 6) calls 'the output vendor versus the development catalyst'. This section discusses what the development catalyst role might mean for NGOs. It includes empowerment (addressing local power relations), advocacy (seeking to influence policy in favour of marginalized groups), and innovation (developing new and better ways of doing things).

At the community level, many development NGOs speak of 'empowering' their clients or beneficiaries. The word 'empowerment' has come to acquire several meanings, from the radical transformative educational ideas of Paolo Freire to the personal 'self-improvement' sense common in management and self-help books.[49] Alternative development approaches may seek empowerment of households and their individual members. For example, Friedmann (1992: 31) shows how households are concerned with three different kinds of power: social (access to information, knowledge and skills, participation in social organizations, financial resources); political (access by individual household members to decision-making processes singly or in groups, e.g. voting, collective action, etc.); and psychological (an individual sense of power and self-confident behaviour, often gained from successful action in the other levels).

Rowlands (1995) points out that empowerment in a development sense is best seen as a process that includes becoming aware of the power dynamics in one's life, developing skills and capacity for greater control, exercising that control without infringing rights of others, and supporting empowerment of other people in the community. In this view, the process involves moving from insight to action, and from individual to collective action. Activists and researchers have used empowerment-centred approaches to explore gender and power in development. For example, Moser's (1989) view of empowerment rests on a generative view of power, linking empowerment to problems of exclusion and participation. It emphasizes bringing in people who are usually outside the decision-making process, as well as going beyond the formal institutions of political and economic power into the dynamics of oppression in the personal sphere. Moser's ideas also show that alternative development approaches, if they focus on the household, need to recognize that unequal access to decision making and resources exists *within* households as well as between them.

Freire's ideas of 'conscientization' placed emphasis on the role of an outside, professional facilitator who played an educational and ultimately catalytic role in creating the conditions for action towards change to take place. For some NGOs, this role is played by its staff who organize and educate people before later withdrawing. Case studies of the early work of the Bangladesh NGO Proshika illustrated the different ways in which this approach helped generate local efforts to act collectively to bargain for higher wages from landowners, to occupy land intended for redistribution to the landless but occupied by local elites, and for action to be taken by local police to support women's rights (Kramsjo and Wood 1992). However, NGOs may find the withdrawal stage difficult to achieve, especially when their clients come to rely on the relationship.

Alan Thomas (1992: 121) provides a useful example of empowerment with the Indian NGO ASSEFA (Association of Sarva Seva Farms) that draws on both Freirean and Gandhian ideas. Formed in 1969, ASSEFA develops land given to the landless through the Gandhian Bhoodan 'land gift' movement. It initially worked on settling communities on this land, but now works for rural industries, education and health and works in five states.[50] Its field staff worked for many years with communities on 'empowerment' before moving on and leaving villagers to address their own problems in their own ways, having altered the balance of power. One previously landless villager remarked:

> We have gained recognition in the village. Other castes, who were our masters earlier, now not only listen but pay attention to what we say.

In the context of Bangladesh, Kabeer *et al.*'s (2012) work describes how Nijera Kori's (NK) social mobilization approach to working with landless rural people has shown that a combination of economic, political and social barriers exist to hold people back. In response, NK and its members have evolved an approach that innovatively combines different forms of support to prevent the problem that arises when an NGO focuses too narrowly on forms of *either* economic *or* political support. Without livelihoods support, people are unable to sustain social mobilization, while without political support, people will be unable to engage with poor governance and citizenship rights at the local level. Such radical NGO approaches have generally become less common in Bangladesh. In general, NGOs have moved towards more market-based versions of empowerment, through economic activity rather than through political activism. This has often been linked with microcredit, which carries an empowerment narrative that has been questioned in some quarters. For example, some studies question how far women's decision-making power within the household is affected in the Grameen Bank's approach (Goetz and Sen Gupta 1996).

The second key catalyst role is advocacy. Jenkins (1987: 267) defined policy advocacy as 'any attempt to influence the decisions of any institutional elite on behalf of a collective interest'. Advocacy is also about influencing *outcomes* in relation to decisions relating to public policies and resource allocation 'in ways that directly affect people's lives' (Cohen *et al.* 2001: 8). Advocacy is often associated mainly with attempts to influence government or sometimes also the private sector, but it can be seen more broadly as being about trying to influence all types of wider social, political and economic 'systems and institutions' that have a bearing on people's wellbeing. Michael Edwards (1993: 3) identified some additional specific aspects of development NGO advocacy as

> an attempt to alter the ways in which power, resources and ideas are created, consumed and distributed at global level, so that people and their organizations in the South have a more realistic chance of controlling their own development.

The aim is to improve access and voice in decision-making processes, and to challenge and change power relationships in ways that meet the goal of greater social justice and lead to institutional change.

There are different forms of advocacy, as well as different approaches to its practice. Cohen *et al.* (2001) distinguish *ideological* advocacy (groups seeking to make their values and beliefs dominant); *mass* advocacy (the airing of grievances in order to confront power holders); *interest-group* advocacy (making demands around a specific set of issues important for certain groups); and *bureaucratic* advocacy (the idea that think tanks and academics present findings in official processes as 'experts'). NGOs may try to influence policy by working 'outside the tent' (by mediating between informal networks and providing evidence to influence the policy process) or 'inside the tent' (sitting around the table as formal participants in policy processes), as Pollard and Court (2008) have described.

By the mid-1990s, advocacy had become widely acknowledged as an important NGO activity, not only for shaping wider policy, but also as a means for NGOs to improve their effectiveness and impact, and as a potential strategy for 'scaling up' their work. For many NGO writers such as David Korten (1990), advocacy can be seen as a mature and developmentally sound NGO activity, particularly for international NGOs, because it addressed the structural roots of poverty rather than the symptoms, and because it moved international NGOs away from direct implementation in the South and towards engaging with power structures based closer to home (Box 6.2). Yet results, as Edwards (1993) pointed out, were often disappointing. Its potential was often found not be fulfilled due to the absence of clear strategy, the failure to build strong alliances, an inability to develop alternatives to mainstream orthodoxies, and the dilemma of relations with donors. For some development NGOs more used to service delivery, advocacy also presented new organizational challenge requiring a reorientation of the organization.

The efforts of NGOs at UN global summits have presented a more positive picture, showing how NGOs have achieved influence through lobbying, particularly in the base of 'low salience' policy issues such as environment, gender and poverty, as opposed to 'high salience' policy issues such as military spending, human rights and economic reform (Van Rooy 1997). Successes have also included the instituting of a baby milk marketing code, the drafting of an essential drugs list, and the removal of restrictions on international trade for some items, for example on the textile

BOX 6.2 NGOs AND INTERNATIONAL ADVOCACY ROLES

NGOs contributed to the campaign for the abolition of the slave trade in the nineteenth century, to the rise of international humanitarianism in the form of the Red Cross movement, and to the emergence of international human rights law, such as the UN convention on the rights of the child. Advocacy work by Northern NGOs has been part of the post-cold war development policy agenda that has aimed to help build democratization processes within both the developing and 'post-communist' worlds. Advocacy has also become an important activity for Southern NGOs too, where environmental campaigns such as that against the Narmada Dam in India have been built by local organizations with international links. The efforts of NGOs from both North and South at the UN global summits such as the Rio Environment or Beijing Women's Conferences indicated growing NGO influence through lobbying work on policy issues such as environment, gender and poverty.

In the global environmental arena, NGOs also have a history of playing important roles, from the 'green' perspectives of the 1970s to the sustainable development paradigm of the 1993 UN Rio Conference. More recently, the emergence of codes of conduct for national and international business is one such strategy pursued by NGOs in conjunction with social movements, religious groups and investors. For example, the Coalition for Environmentally Responsible Economies (CERES) in 1989 established a 10-point environmental code of conduct for corporations based on what were termed the Valdez principle after the Exxon Valdez oil disaster of that year. However, progress with cooperative and voluntary strategies for engagement with the corporate sector were dealt a severe blow by the failure of some countries, and in particular the United States, to endorse the Kyoto Protocol on climate change.

In the field of conflict and disarmament, NGOs played a key role in the International Campaign to Ban Landmines (Scott 2001). This was a coalition of NGOs that mobilized campaigning across the world that led to a 1997 convention signed by 122 states in Ottawa, Canada that banned anti-personnel landmines, later adopted as a treaty within the United Nations. It showed growing power of NGOs within international politics, leading to tangible results within the space of just a few years of action. But it also showed the diversity of interests among the NGO community since the US National Rifle Association – also an NGO – put up considerable resistance to the attempt to control international arms flows.

Such NGO advocacy roles seem set to grow, as shifting frameworks of global governance increasingly allow space for non-governmental actors to build stronger voices for local and global citizens.

Source: Lewis (2006a)

quotas from Bangladesh, which helped create new women's employment during the 1990s (Clark 1992). National level campaigns such as that against the Narmada Dam in India have been established by local organizations with international links. In 2005, the Make Poverty History campaign supported by NGOs such as Oxfam GB achieved a high profile in relation to the building of a social movement seeking to influence the G8 countries, the European Union, the IMF and the World Bank in relation to fairer trade, debt cancellation and increased levels of international aid.[51]

Advocacy work also raised new challenges for NGOs of assessing impacts. In her discussion of four NGO case studies in the Philippines and Mexico, Covey (1995) assessed the effectiveness of advocacy not just in terms of achieving the desired policy impacts, but also in terms of the process itself, which is seen as making a contribution to a healthy civil society. This is connected to ideas about building 'social capital' advanced by Putnam (1993) and with ideas under the new policy agenda to build democratization processes within the South. As we saw in Chapter 4, the results are not necessarily developmentally sound, and a form of interest-group 'gridlock' can be the results of an active civil society meeting a weak state (Blair 1997). NGOs can balance power in multi-organizational alliances by playing a 'bridging function' (Brown 1991) which links grassroots level and national or international action, and different kinds of organization. Covey (1995) concluded that NGOs need good links with the grassroots for an advocacy strategy to work, along with a stable and responsive government with which they can develop a dialogue.

Finally, NGOs have long been seen as innovators, able to bring new ideas and approaches to solve development problems. For Brown and Korten (1991: 65) a key NGO strength is that of being able to 'find innovative solutions to novel problems and to support successful innovation in government programmes', and their capacity to do this stems from their 'small size, administrative flexibility, and relative freedom from political constraints'. The topic of NGO innovation will be returned to in detail in Chapter 9.

NGOs as partners

The concept of 'partnership' has become central to policy makers and practitioners (Wallace 2006). Much of the early interest in development partnerships was focused on building better links between the work of government agencies and NGOs in development projects (Farrington and Bebbington 1993). Brown and Ashman (1996) suggested that cooperation between government and NGOs needed to span gaps of culture, power, resources and perspective if it was to be successful. In broad terms, the creation of partnerships is seen as a way of making more efficient use of scarce resources, increasing institutional sustainability and improving beneficiary participation. At a more general level, creating links between government agencies and NGOs may have implications for strengthening transparency in administration and challenging prevailing top-down institutional culture, both of which may contribute to the strengthening of the wider 'civil society' and fragile processes of democratization (Lewis 1997). On the other hand, the increased interest in NGOs as vehicles for service delivery is strongly linked to demands for privatization within the new policy agenda. Models of partnership have been transferred from rich country contexts to developing country or transition contexts with mixed results (Box 6.3).

The idea of improving relationships between NGOs and the private sector came somewhat later, but has now blossomed into a dynamic area. NGOs saw opportunities both to influence social issues and increase their profiles by experimenting more with working with private companies, for example in the diamond, mining and clothing industries. Around the issue of child labour, for example, international NGOs were seen to pursue multiple strategies with the private sector, such as by talking informally with companies to address problems 'quietly' (and perhaps protect the vulnerable livelihoods of children) while simultaneously undertaking high-profile campaigning on child rights (*'Alliances between companies and non-governmental organizations attracts varying degrees of enthusiasm'*, Financial Times, 29 November 2002).

BOX 6.3 THE PURSUIT OF PARTNERSHIP BY INTERNATIONAL NGOs: POWER, FUNDING AND THE DILEMMAS OF 'AGENCY CREATION'

International NGOs have increasingly worked 'through' local NGOs to undertake development activities within partnership arrangements. One study examined relationships between four international NGOs and five local NGOs working on urban poverty in Nairobi, Kenya. It found that the international NGOs followed a number of strategies to secure their own objectives, such as encouraging their local partners to try new approaches and activities through simple requests or on occasion as a requirement for the continuation of funding. A further strategy that emerged in the course of the study was that of 'agency creation'. Three of the international NGOs had been directly involved in founding new organizations, and two others had sponsored local activities that have resulted in new organizations being formed. These internationally sponsored local agencies have Kenyan board members (for the most part) and employ Kenyan staff.

A number of reasons for agency creation emerged. In one case, an international NGO initiated the establishment of a network to share information and lobby for policy change. The network promoted a local identity but was managed and funded by the instigating NGO. The second case of agency creation occurred when an international NGO withdrew from an area of work that it had supported within its own operational activities, and its programme staff then decided to form a local NGO to carry on the work. Staff of the international NGO then provided informal support. A third example occurred when a local voluntary group providing professional legal services formalized and modified their work and created a specialist local NGO. This followed an offer of funds from an official development assistance agency (which was rejected) and then from an international NGO. A further reason for establishing new agencies that occurred in two cases was to promote areas of development work that the NGOs considered not to be taking place; and in a further case it was to replicate work that was not judged to be of an adequate standard.

International NGO influence remains strong in these newly created development agencies. One staff member for the network noted that: 'All proposals have to be approved by [the international NGO] in Kenya and the head office'. A second donor agreed that the founding agency 'has a strong direction on the programme'. An international NGO staff member, reflecting on one more such effort, argues that the international NGO is '... likely to be too prescriptive'. But others are more supportive of such work. Two of the local board members spoke of their appreciation of international NGO support: '... it was good for [the NGO] to give it direction in the early phase, or it might not have got off the ground'. The strategy of agency creation has wider implications for relationships between international NGOs and local NGOs. First, it demonstrates the ways international NGOs use their power to modify the nature of the local NGO sector. Second, in creating new NGOs, international NGOs may reduce solidarity and create more competition between local NGOs. Third, the strategy may enable international NGOs to pursue agendas with less consideration given to the perspectives of the South.

Source: Diana Mitlin, personal communication

Partnership tends to mean different things to different development actors, and there is in practice a wide gap between rhetoric and reality. We can use the term 'partnership' to refer to an agreed relationship based on a set of links between two or more agencies within a development project, usually involving a division of roles and responsibilities, a sharing of risks and the pursuit of joint objectives, in this case between government agencies, NGOs, donors and farmers. The term 'linkage' is used to refer to specific points of the partnership at which activities are shared between different agencies and stakeholders at different levels of the project. A project that involves partnership is likely to have a range of inter-agency linkages at various levels. The use of the word 'partnership' covers a wide range of different relationships between agencies that may have either an *active* or a passive, *dependent* character, and this is discussed further in Chapter 10.

Active partnerships are those built through ongoing processes of negotiation, debate, occasional conflict, and learning through trial and error. Risks are taken, and although roles and purposes are clear they may change according to need and circumstance. Dependent partnerships, on the other hand, have a blueprint character and are constructed at the project planning stage according to assumptions about comparative advantage and individual agency interests, often linked to the availability of outside funding. There may be consensus among the partners, but this often reflects unclear roles and responsibilities rather than the creative conflicts that emerge within active partnerships.

The origins of the partnership (such as compulsion, agreement or financial incentive) may hold the key to its success or failure, and may limit the scope for subsequent process monitoring. For example, agencies may enter into relationships in order to gain access to external resources which are conditional on partnership. Agencies can drift into partnerships without adequately considering the wider implications. For example, new roles for staff may have to be created in order to service the partnership properly, or management systems may be required to monitor the progress of new activities. NGOs in particular are vulnerable to being viewed instrumentally, as agents enlisted to work to the agendas of others as 'reluctant partners' (Farrington and Bebbington 1993). Partnership may bring extra costs which are easily underestimated, such as new lines of communications requiring demands on staff time, vehicles and telephones; new responsibilities for certain staff; and the need to share information with other agencies. Building partnerships is likely therefore to be difficult.

While partnerships between different actors are usually seen by development agencies as essentially positive, there is a view, particularly among some NGOs, that 'partnership' may be becoming a degraded term. Clearly, any new thinking on forms of partnership is to be welcomed. In particular, mechanisms are needed for monitoring how the partnership is measuring up once the linkages are in place, and developing the means to achieve appropriate 'course corrections' when necessary. Many partnerships begin with a dependent character but can be made more 'active'. Essential to any notion of the value of deploying partnership as a tool for achieving project objectives is the idea that agencies acting together are able to achieve certain objectives which they would be unable to manage singly. This idea is the key to 'measuring' the success of any partnership.

Linking management challenges and roles

If we return to our conceptual framework (Figure 2.1) it is possible to link all of these roles with each of the three interlocking circles of the NGO management challenges in terms of *organization*, *activities* and *relationships*. For example, acting as a catalyst in relation to community empowerment will require an NGO to manage an appropriate set of internal organizational arrangements, to design a set of appropriate activities to meet the goals of the intervention, and to negotiate suitable relationships with relevant people and organizations.

Effectiveness: are NGOs any good at what they do?

The case for NGO effectiveness essentially rests on four main sets of arguments. The social argument suggests NGOs can facilitate participation and can reach those sections of the population that are bypassed by conventional public services (Anheier 1987). The economic argument emphasizes efficiency, arguing that NGOs can provide services more cost-effectively than government, due to lower labour costs and incomplete pricing (Smith 1987). The political argument is that NGOs may be less vulnerable to capture by established political interests, or patron–client networks, and may offer people alternatives to the status quo. Finally, cultural arguments assert that NGOs may be more embedded in local contexts and therefore sensitive to meeting needs. International NGOs may also achieve this closeness when they support local organizations as an alternative to building new ones. Each of these arguments can be shown to have some merit, but none can be taken for granted or assumed, and it is necessary to pay careful attention to specific cases and contexts. However, there is surprisingly little strong data about the effectiveness of NGO work. What we find in the literature is a set of writings that tends to take either a 'pro-' or 'anti-' NGO case based on limited generalized evidence, or a specific narrow case.

One of the earliest examples of the pro–NGO case was Michael Cernea's (1988: 8) influential report for the World Bank. Cernea argued that NGOs' main potential contribution to development was their ability to strengthen local organizational capacity. He noted that 'the NGO priority on first organizing the people embodies a philosophy that recognizes the centrality of people in development policies and action programs and the importance of self-organization'. In this view, NGOs can organize people to make better use of local productive resources, create new assets and services, promote equity and alleviate poverty, influence government action, and establish new institutional frameworks to sustain a more people-centred form of development. This gives NGOs a 'comparative advantage' over government agencies that rests on four main strengths: reaching people in remote areas where government is ineffective; operating at lower cost due to the voluntary nature of their activities and lower technological overheads; promoting local participation by working with community groups as partners, emphasizing self-help initiatives and local control of programmes; innovating and adapting to local conditions and needs. Cernea's analysis serves as a useful benchmark against which the claims on behalf of NGOs can be assessed.

Other literature offers a comprehensive critique of the capacities of NGOs. An early piece that received widespread attention was Judith Tendler's (1982) analysis of donor evaluations of 72 NGO projects from around the world. This report found that many NGOs were often top-down rather than participatory in their decision making, that most villagers were marginally (if at all) involved in NGO project design; that local elites often influenced or controlled NGO programmes; and finally that NGOs tended to introduce known techniques into new areas rather than actually 'innovate' themselves. This study was influential in acting as a counter-weight to the strongly idealistic pro–NGO literature that developed during the 1990s. Since then, many other writers have been critical of the attention which NGOs have received, and have pointed out that very little documentation from the field exists with which the pro–NGO lobby can support their claims.

To this has been added a range of other critiques. First, it has been argued that in the aid industry there is too much overlapping of vested interests (donors, international NGOs and development idealists) to allow for honest analysis (Sanyal 1991). Second is the suggestion that NGOs are far from creating real movements of the poor, but simply create groups of people brought together around provision of resources from outside and are therefore themselves 'patrons' (Hashemi 1989, McGregor 1989). Third, NGOs may serve as a palliative, reducing the possibility for genuine radical action aimed at structural change by people who are poor. In this view, people are kept just above the poverty line, offering short-term relief but making peoples' position worse in the long term (Arellano-Lopez and Petras 1994). Fourth, NGO efforts are too small and piecemeal to make a difference. Only government has the coverage – and mandate – to reach people across a whole country. Finally, one of the most hard-hitting critiques of NGOs centres on the problem of accountability failure. In NGOs, accountability tends almost always to be stronger 'upwards' to funders, staff and governments than 'downwards' to the people the NGO is claiming to serve. NGOs are seen as relatively unaccountable to local citizens, and their receipt of increasing amounts of foreign funds conflicts with the sovereignty of the state (Sogge *et al.* 1996; Wood 1997; Tvedt 1998).

Other criticisms of NGOs have been concerned with efficiency and cost-effectiveness. Although there has been little systematic research on this issue, Ellis (1984) suggested that NGO projects often have poor cost-benefit ratios, are not sustainable in the long run, and lack wider replicability. Many NGOs actually spend more delivering services per capita than governments. If government had these levels of funding, according to this line of reasoning, they would manage the same level of success. The new fashion for using experimental evaluation tools such as RCTs as a means for establishing whether and how interventions work in specific local contexts offers a set of new insights into the circumstances under which NGOs may offer effective use of resources (see Chapter 5).

A brief summary of NGO strengths and weaknesses suggests that what may be seen as NGOs' 'positive' and 'negative' qualities may often simply be different sides of the same coin (Annis 1987). For example, an approach that is considered flexible and spontaneous by some may be viewed as amateurish by others. Those who argue that it is useful to make intrinsic comparisons between NGOs, for-profit organizations and governments are perhaps missing the point. Brett (1993: 298) argues that NGOs need to be seen alongside government and private sector organizations in a 'pluralistic organizational universe', and therefore selected for specific tasks on the basis of some common criteria for performance judgement:

> Significant similarities exist between the three kinds of organization, which enable us to apply theories developed across the whole range; but real differences in philosophy and practice still remain between them, and this makes it possible for each to solve particular kinds of problems more effectively than the others. Thus, providing support selectively to all of them is likely to

produce a pluralistic organizational universe which will expand the range of social and individual choice and potential.

Michael Edwards (1999a) evaluated four organizations in South Asia in a revealing and balanced study that seeks to identify the criteria that contribute to successful NGO initiatives in terms of impact, sustainability and cost-effectiveness. The results uncovered a large variation in all three criteria, which can be understood as the result of the interaction between the context in which the NGOs operate and *the external influences* on their work, and a set of *internal influences* based on the organizational choices that NGOs make. Although the contexts of, for example, the Indian state of Orissa and that of rural Bangladesh offer different levels of opportunity and constraint, the high variation in NGO performance was attributed more strongly to the different strategies selected by the NGOs, such as the ability of an organization to combine clarity of purpose with a sustained, long-term commitment to its work, a balance between material provision and community organizing, good organizational learning and communication, and the use of strong external linkages for leverage and ensuring resource flows.

The point is not only that NGOs deserve to be seen alongside a range of other actors in development, but also that it makes little sense to generalize about organizations which vary enormously within and between contexts. Fisher (1994: 139) writes:

> Despite the remarkable similarities among NGOs in different parts of the Third World, the time for 'feel good' generalised discussions of 'North-South partnership' is past. Country-specific field research on 'who is doing what where' is an urgent necessity, given the global need for sustainable development.

This is perhaps true of more than just partnership issues between North and South, but also of the entire discussion on NGOs. However, it is also wise to keep in mind the critics of NGOs such as Tvedt (1998) who argue that the diversity of the NGO community is often exaggerated (if it existed at all). There may be an isomorphic trend towards routine NGO service delivery – and credit delivery in particular – that may narrow the wide-ranging array of activities usually claimed for NGOs by their supporters.

Conclusion

This chapter has considered the organizational dimensions of NGOs and their roles in development. It is possible to outline the main NGO roles, seen here as implementation, catalysis and partnership. It has also considered different views of the effectiveness of NGOs in these roles. These roles can be linked back to the conceptual framework of NGO management (Figure 2.1) that was set out in Chapter 2, since each element of the management task – organization, activities and relationships – is likely to involve combinations of these roles. The high level of diversity of development tasks, as well as of NGOs, necessitates against setting out a general blueprint for either understanding or managing an individual NGO and its activities. Instead, NGO management requires synthesis and improvisation. This diversity is central to the creative ideas, insights and approaches that NGOs have the potential to bring to development.

7

ORGANIZATIONAL THEORY, AMBIGUITY AND NGO MANAGEMENT

> (NGOs) are not mere passive recipients ... they actively translate and reshape some of these practices in order to align them with the local cultural values, norms and beliefs.
>
> *Claeyé (2012: 212)*

Introduction

Following from our discussion in Chapter 5 of the ways that we can draw upon different areas of management (private sector, public and non-profit) to help understand the specific field of NGO management, we turn now to examine two further areas of research and theory: organization theory and the anthropology of organizations. Both of these fields can help open up important additional areas of insight in relation to the specific management challenges faced by development NGOs. In particular, they allow us to examine in more detail how organizations grow and change, how NGOs attempt to learn, how leadership systems function, and overall highlight the importance of ambiguity in the organization of NGO identities and activity. The concept of ambiguity, defined as the coexistence of two or more meanings within a single subject or entity, is a particularly important element in the complex puzzle that NGO management represents, and is explored in the second half of the chapter. It gets to the importance of values in the work NGOs do, and leads us to the argument that NGOs require a humanistic form of management that is sensitive to people, place and complexity.

Organizational theory

Organizational studies is concerned with understanding the structures and processes that underpin decision making 'in the systematic collective pursuit of specified goals', and has its origins in rational models found in work such as James G. March and Herbert A. Simon's influential 1958 book *Organizations* (McAdam and Scott 2005: 7). The field of organizational theory offers a set of contrasting theoretical perspectives on organizations – such as modernist, symbolic-interpretative and postmodern – each of which can provide different kinds of insight into how organizations work. Specific models and theories, such as resource dependence, institutionalism and organizational life-cycles, can be applied usefully to development NGOs, even though such models were mostly developed in relation to other types of organization.[52]

While most organization theory has its roots in the business sector, many of its ideas are relevant to NGOs. At a very basic level, organization theory allows us to break down an organization into its constituent parts. Hatch (1997) presents a conceptual model of 'the organization', represented as the interplay of four interrelated elements: culture, social structure, physical structure and technology, and suggests that all of these are 'embedded in and contributing to an environment'. Such frameworks have become part of the discourse around the organizational strengthening of NGOs (see for example Sahley 1995, Fowler 1997). Like all research fields, organization theory is a far from unified body of work, and different approaches and traditions compete with each other for explanatory power.

Hatch describes multiple, often contradictory perspectives offered by three main research traditions within organization theory by summarizing these as *modernist*, *symbolic-interpretative* and *postmodern* traditions (Box 7.1). This framework is useful to analyse how NGOs work as organizations. These three traditions are not mutually exclusive, and a 'multiple perspectives approach' can allow each one the potential to illuminate different aspects of organizational life. This fits with a view of development NGOs as highly complex organizations working with a high degree of ambiguity within an increasingly diverse and rapidly changing environment. For example, a modernist perspective is at the heart of Max Weber's ideas about bureaucracy that have informed third sector scholar David Billis' (1993a) theory-building in relation to voluntary sector organization, while the symbolic-interpretative tradition tends to inform much of the work on organizational learning within the NGO sector. Postmodernist ideas have come to the forefront in relation to organizational change processes within NGOs, and in relation to understanding the contested, multiple viewpoints that emerge in relation to the work NGOs do.

Institutionalism and resource dependency

One of the dominant areas of organization theory in recent years has been neo-institutionalism, which carries elements of both modernist and symbolic-interpretative perspectives. Neo-institutionalists (a term used to distinguish it from earlier political science approaches that focused on the comparative study of formal institutions of government) argue that organizations that share a similar environment are likely to engage in similar practices and begin to take on similar characteristics as each other. They come under pressure to legitimize themselves by taking on a set of

BOX 7.1 RESEARCH TRADITIONS IN ORGANIZATION THEORY

Modernist organization theory has its roots in several thinkers from the first part of the twentieth century. The sociologist Max Weber's theory of rational-legal authority exercised through an objective and impersonal bureaucracy is a cornerstone of modernist organization theory. The ideas of F.W. Taylor and his notions of 'scientific management', and Henri Fayol's theory of the rational administration of organizational activities, both of which emphasized structure, hierarchy and control, have also been influential. Later, open systems theory brought with it the idea of organic growth and development of organizations, their different levels of activity and the interconnectedness of organization and environment.[53]

The *symbolic-interpretative* perspective emphasizes the subjective realities of organizational life and shows how organizations are built from negotiations and understandings of the world. In this view, organizations are seen as socially constructed and can therefore be changed, assuming we can become more aware of our participation in organizational processes. The importance of ambiguity is recognized as being both a source of power and creativity, as well as perhaps an area of danger and confusion. The anthropologist Clifford Geertz's (1973) concept of culture as socially constructed and open to continuous change has been used to explore how people within organizations create and maintain 'organizational culture' through the use and interpretation of symbols.

More recently, the *postmodern* perspective on organizations evolved as a critique of the modernist quest for universal explanations for organizational life, and concentrates instead on complexity, fragmentation and contradiction. For theorists within the complexity and management field, for example, the focus is on the disjuncture between what managers feel they ought to be doing and what they actually find themselves doing, and point out that: '... life in organizations is essentially paradoxical. Managers are supposed to be in charge and yet they find it difficult to stay in control. The future is recognisable when it arrives but in many important respects not predictable before it does. We sense the importance of difference but experience the pressure to conform ...' (Stacey *et al.* 2000: 5). In the postmodern view, organizational change is becoming less predictable as information is exchanged more rapidly and more frequently, and organizations themselves are becoming more informal, flexible and participatory in response to uncertainty. At the same time, the radical critique of power in organizations within the postmodern approach had led to the need for self-reflexive organizations and for means through which 'voice' can be achieved for those who are marginalized or excluded within organizations.

Sources: Hatch (1997); Stacey *et al.* (2000)

institutionalized ideas and practices that help them to understand and operate in the wider context of the social world. They become shaped by an institutional logic that requires them to signal to different stakeholders, referents and constituents that the organization is legitimate (DiMaggio and Powell 1991). Within this approach therefore, understanding how organizations fare does not only depend on examining conventional performance factors such as efficiency and reliability, but also on understanding social dimensions of organizational performance such as accountability and legitimacy. This opens up a new perspective on how and why organizations change, for example. Proponents of neo-institutionalist theory famously argued that organizations tend to change primarily in order to be more like each other – pressured, for example, by the state and other institutions to conform to accepted practice – and they termed this process 'isomorphism'.

Another area of organization theory that has proved attractive to NGO researchers is the 'resource dependency perspective' (Pfeffer and Salancik 1978). This is based on the idea that instead of seeing organizations as relatively autonomous, it is instead necessary to focus on the environment as a strong constraining influence that limits an organization's room for manoeuvre. All organizations must depend on the environment for the resources they need, whether money, people, ideas or information. Different organizations may be more or less autonomous than each other, but none is ever free of these pressures. Environmental contingencies help to determine internal management factors, such as the availability of staff and the processes of leadership succession. Asymmetrical exchange processes between organizations and their environment reflect differential power relationships, such as those between NGOs and donor agencies. As a result, organizations face uncertainty when those controlling resources in the outside environment are undependable, as in the case of changing donor funding policies, or the reduction of public contributions to NGOs during an economic downturn. Since organizations are always in a state of interdependence with their environment, they are 'torn between their desire for autonomy and their need to control uncertainty created by dependence on the environment' (Hudock 1999: 24). In order to manage volatility in their wider environment, organizations must therefore continuously engage in negotiation and exchange. They may, for example, try to reduce their dependency on their environment by controlling the flow of information about themselves to outsiders, or try to diversify the places from which they try to access resources.

Within this perspective, the function of management becomes the need to direct an organization towards a more favourable relationship with its environment through three kinds of management action – symbolic, responsive and discretionary. *Symbolic* management refers to those actions that make little or no difference because outcomes are in reality determined mainly by the context, such as replacing a leader. This may only alter appearances, but on the other hand if people believe that a new leader has some power (even if they don't in practice) then this may relieve the pressure. *Responsive* management refers to those actions taken by managers that do make a difference, even though they are undertaken within the various constraints created by the environment. Finally, the *discretionary* role is the successful balancing of these constraints in the interests of the organization, based on good 'scanning' of the environment for information.

Hudock (1995) was one of the first researchers to show how this theory can be useful when applied to development NGOs that are highly financially dependent on donors. Hudock's research found local NGOs to be locked into asymmetric forms of interdependence with their international NGO partners. She showed in a series of case studies how local NGOs in West Africa are therefore extremely vulnerable to 'goal deflection' and 'unplanned structural change', because they are subject to a struggle to meet the external demands of their funders. Yet resource dependence theory is not without its critics. As we saw earlier, David Billis (1993a: 213) suggests that the resource dependency perspective is unhelpful for depicting organizations 'at the mercy of powerful and almost uncontrollable forces' and instead suggests that organizations have choices if they can better understand what is happening to them. This perspective is also supported by research by undertaken by Dechalert (2002) among NGOs in Thailand, and by Themudo (2003) in Portugal and Mexico. Both researchers identified the ways in which different organizations in otherwise similar contexts do nevertheless take on very different forms based on the decisions and choices that they make. Decision-making processes within organizations can and do produce different outcomes across different organizations, despite the similarities that may exist within their wider resource environments.

Evolutionary theory and organizational life cycles

Life-cycle theories have a long history in organizational studies, and allow reflection on organizational change not just in terms of values and approaches, but also in terms of changing structures. They form part of an evolutionary perspective on organizations, which focuses on how organizations change over time. This is relevant to NGOs because it helps us understand how they are initiated, how they change and grow, and the problems that some NGOs face when their founder leaders move on and there are leadership succession issues.

Larry Greiner's (1972) work is foundational within life-cycle theory. He was concerned with understanding and managing the organizational crisis that tends to occur when an organization can no longer be sustained by its initial creative burst of energy, and when its increased complexity becomes too challenging for its original leadership. Greiner used the metaphor of the human life-cycle to help understand the structural changes experienced by organizations, setting out a series of five phases through which most organizations will pass. He termed these the entrepreneurial, collectivity, delegation, formalization and collaboration phases. In this perspective, each phase is dominated by a distinctive focus, and Greiner suggested that transition to the next stage was usually triggered by a serious crisis that threatened the very survival of the organization. The reasons for each crisis was seen to follow a sequential pattern which started with a leadership crisis, followed by one of autonomy, control, red tape, and finally by a crisis of renewal. In this way, according to

Hatch (1997: 177), 'every stage of an organization's development contains the seeds of the next crisis'.

Life-cycle theory has been linked with NGO management in different ways.[54] The best-known example is David Korten's (1987) influential framework of three NGO 'generations' (introduced in Chapter 2). Korten suggested a model of organizational evolution through a series of stages of development based on incremental learning. This leads to a chain of increasingly sophisticated approaches to working with people who are poor in terms of increasing use of ideas about sustainability, self-reliance and participation. In the 'first-generation' NGO, the priority is to meet needs through relief and welfare work, but this may change once those needs are met or once an organization begins to learn and grow. In the second generation, a growing awareness of wider 'development' ideas and the influence of outside agencies such as aid donors may promote a new set of objectives that go beyond meeting immediate needs to build small-scale, self-reliant local development initiatives. Following from this, there may be a new preoccupation with creating more sustainable changes in the 'third-generation' organization, along with a desire to seek changes in the wider institutional and policy context through campaigning or advocacy. The 'fourth-generation' NGO – an extra level added later in a 1990 publication that revisited the idea – aims to support wider social movements for action on a national or global level to bring about wider change on issues such as gender, environment and conflict resolution.

The different NGO generations were according to Korten also associated with changes in programming strategy based on a growing awareness of possibilities gained through experience and learning. In the first stage, an NGO is the 'doer' and there is a largely passive role for 'beneficiaries', and the main management needs are skills in operations and logistics management in the delivery of welfare services. Meeting immediate deficiencies among beneficiaries for food, healthcare or shelter means that most first-generation NGOs are mainly concerned with temporary alleviation of the symptoms of poverty but without addressing root causes. The second-generation NGO approach of small-scale, self-reliant local development sees NGOs seeking to transform themselves into development agencies and focus on 'community development' work aimed at creating self-reliance and sustainability of projects. As time goes by, the growth of donor support to NGOs brings about a need to focus more strongly on the development of improved project management skills and systems. At the same time, an NGO moves from being primarily a 'doer' towards working as a catalyst trying to make something happen, such as training and mobilizing people. The problem that then emerged was that many NGO efforts proved unsustainable after the organization withdrew, and its services provided merely to be 'handouts in a more sophisticated guise'. This led to new thinking and a subsequent focus on sustainable systems development as the third-generation stage.

At this point, an NGO may begin to look beyond the immediate context and community to also engage more fully at the institutional and policy levels in an attempt to create an 'enabling' environment in which greater local control and initiative is possible. The NGO realizes that local gains made still depend on the continued NGO presence and donor funds, but that acting on its own only local, piecemeal impact can be achieved in the long term. Links with larger institutions, such as collaboration with a business or a link with a government agency, may lead to provision of services on a more sustainable basis. In this model, the NGO gradually moves from being primarily a service provider to becoming a catalyst, seeking to gain leverage over policy discussions in favour of poverty reduction and 'bridging' between local community-based initiatives and wider development actors. In 'fourth-generation' strategies NGOs experiment further with this idea by creating wider alliances with social movements and subordinating their organizational identities within these wider social forces.[55]

Such strategies result from the refusal by many development NGOs to be simply engaged in 'patching up' wider development problems, and instead they reach for alternative development paradigms. By turning towards social movements NGOs can create changes in public consciousness that can mobilize forms of voluntary action on a national or global scale – such as landless movements, women's movements, peace movements or environmental movements. The 2005 Make Poverty History campaign was an example of NGOs and other civil society actors building such a movement. But as Korten pointed out, such movements may also become institutionalized once they lose their initial energy. He gives the example of the Chinese Mass Education movement started by James Yen in the 1920s, which took on a momentum of its own, with several hundred volunteers teaching literacy to five million villagers around the country. When it was later identified by outsiders as a successful venture, and given public funding and US support it lost its vibrancy. By the time the communists came to power in China, the original spirit of voluntarism had gone. Development NGOs often recognize the challenge of the fourth generation idea, which is for the NGO 'to coalesce and energise self-managing networks over which it has no control' (Korten 1990: 127), but they tend to find it difficult to put into practice if it means a loss of control.

Korten's concept of life cycle differs from Greiner's in some respects. What drives the changing orientation of these organizations, according to Korten, was not necessarily a series of organizational crises, but a combination of the growing awareness of local community needs and a clearer definition of the NGO's own 'purpose and distinctive competence'. He draws on the notion of the human family, in which new generations take their place alongside the older ones. Korten also sees an evolution from relatively simple to complex multi-stranded activities and aims, ultimately leading towards the 'catalyst' role. Although these different approaches may each be present within the wider NGO community at any given time (or even within one single organization), Korten (1990: 147) presents the framework in terms of an evolutionary schema based on 'an underlying direction of movement that makes it appropriate to label these orientations as first, second, and third generation'.

Korten's schema is useful because it shows that NGOs, like most other organizations, rarely stand still, and it illustrates how organizations may combine several roles or activities at any one time. It seeks to explain how NGOs emerge, change and manage a variety of tasks. Although Korten is not very specific about how these changes take place, it seems to imply 'evolution and adaptation to the socio-economic context' (Senillosa 1998: 46) as a result of a combination of internal and external forces. Indeed, Korten ends the article with a set of comments about the need for NGOs to improve their management systems and structures in order to improve their effectiveness. The generation framework has been influential and has been widely cited by writers on NGOs (e.g. Clarke 1998; Vakil 1997). A version of the theory also underpin's Taylor's (2010: 198) idea of the phases of organizational development in which an NGO passes through a life cycle from pioneer phase, through differentiation and integration towards 'full and conscious maturity'. It is clear that the generation concept remains an attractive one: the idea of 'creating the next generation NGO' provides the subtitle for Ronald's (2010) book on the future of international NGOs.

There are also some caveats needed with the life-cycle and generation approach. First, Korten's generation theory should not be taken to imply that all NGOs pass through these stages. Second, the theory can also be seen to carry an Asian bias, which means that while it may fit with, say, BRAC's history in Bangladesh, but it may not fit with the life history of an NGO in another regional context. Senillosa (1998) is critical of the 'generation' idea, pointing out that several different generations can coexist within one organization. This renders the concept rather imprecise, and suggests some of the different ways in which NGOs may evolve in different contexts. For example, at a workshop in Nigeria which I attended in 1999, several education NGOs were discussing the need to move away from solely concentrating on advocacy work (their original purpose) towards service delivery through which real and immediate needs could be met, and which many felt would give organizations more credibility both with local communities and with policy makers. Finally, despite the argument that an increasing sophistication among NGO approaches moves organizations further towards 'fourth-generation' strategies over time, funder pressures may instead tend to push development NGOs towards service delivery approaches rather than ones where NGOs act as catalysts (Atack 1999).

We also need to remember that organizations make active decisions and are not necessarily trapped by life-cycle logic (Billis 1993a). Different outcomes emerge from different choices that are made by managers. They suggest that organizations do not change along predefined paths and have drawn attention to the importance of the environment, structures and the human resources of organizations in determining patterns of change. There is also a problem of normative subjectivity in the generation idea. There is an implicit assumption that as it evolves, the NGO becomes 'better'. This becomes apparent in that while Senillosa states that there need be no hierarchy in the different generations of NGOs – 'the first generation is no worse than the fourth' (1998: 46) – he is at the same time making the claim for fourth-generation NGOs that they hold the key to the future. Like much of the writing on NGOs, the theory contains an at-times-difficult combination of subjective tone (which seeks to identify an 'ideal' path along which NGOs might move) alongside an explanation of how NGOs as organizations change over time.

Leadership: charisma or contingency?

Organization theory draws attention both to what goes on inside the organization and its relationships with the environment. Ronalds (2010: 118) suggests that the quality of leaders and managers is 'the single most critical element in these organizations effectively responding to the increasingly complex and unpredictable challenges they face'. NGO leadership has received comparatively little attention from researchers, perhaps because NGOs have been reluctant to face up to the fact that in many cases their leadership systems are so highly personalized (Hailey and James 2010).

It has been widely observed that NGOs tend to be formed by charismatic, entrepreneurial individuals who remain, at least in the early years of the organization, the main driving force. Max Weber originated the sociological concept of charisma, meaning an extraordinary quality akin to a 'gift of grace', in relation to his general theory of authority. Individual charisma was seen as a form of power that was derived from the special qualities of an individual (in contrast to the charisma of office, which was derived from the nature of the position). For example, in his account of Amnesty International's organizational development, Stephen Hopgood (2006: 54) recounts a description by an early associate of its founder as an 'evangelist with a divine spark'.

Strong founder-leaders create a strong sense of shared values and internal organizational discipline, while also using their contacts to mobilize resources and manage the political environment in which their organizations operate. Founders often 'retain charismatic control over the organization as it grows' and may monopolize contacts with other agencies and with the government (Wood 1997). Only after being 'tested' by a leadership crisis (in Greiner's sense) in which a founder-leader is successfully replaced, can an organization be seen as fully mature. This is a point to which Amnesty, which went through a leadership crisis for several years after its founder-leader barrister Peter Benenson stepped down due to ill-health in 1964, and countless other longer-established NGOs, can testify. The concept of 'leaderitis' is used by Watson (2001) to describe the affliction of overbearing NGO leadership that, while providing a strong resource for the organization, tends to make it difficult for leadership succession to take place.

NGO founders can also be seen as 'social entrepreneurs', to use a term that has become popular in recent years. The economic concept of the entrepreneur as an innovator and risk taker can be applied to creative individuals engaged in value-driven social change processes. The key characteristics of a social entrepreneur as defined by Kickul and Lyons (2012: 22) can perhaps be seen as analogous to those of a charismatic NGO founder:

> Prospective social entrepreneurs may have instilled into them strong beliefs about what is right and wrong. They likely have learned empathy for those who are less fortunate. They often have a strong sense of justice. This causes them to be altruistic, morally outraged by injustice, and sensitive to issues of equity.

According to Leadbeater (1997), social entrepreneurs frequently draw on private sector business ideas and methods. They may also operate on the margins of the third and the public sectors: for example, A.H. Khan in Pakistan was originally a civil servant who initiated the public sector Pakistan Academy for Rural Development in the 1960s (now BARD in Bangladesh) and later established the influential NGO Orangi Pilot Project in Karachi during the 1980s (Khan 1999). The founder of BRAC, Sir F.H. Abed, was an executive in an oil company before leaving to return to Bangladesh and set up an NGO, and he has drawn upon aspects of this earlier experience in another sector.[56]

Though it would seem from casual observation that the 'charismatic' leader is a vital component of many an NGO, particularly in its early years, there are increasingly cases where leaders have stepped down and the organization has continued. Wood (1997) points out that charismatic NGO leaders may use personal networks and extended kin ties as management tools, often producing strong centralizing tendencies in which even comparatively trivial decisions need to wait for decisions from the top. While such practices may raise problems of nepotism and inefficiency, they can also nevertheless be seen more sympathetically as organizational adaptations to a frequently hostile institutional environment. Edwards' (1999a) study of South Asian NGOs found that the more successful NGOs tended to have 'inspirational but not overbearing' leadership, which was able to guide the organization through crises and provide a clear sense of direction while allowing room for initiative and ideas from throughout the organization and its clients.

Writing in the general organizational literature, Bryman (1992: 157) shows how understandings of leadership in organizations have repeatedly returned to an idea of the charismatic leader. However, an emphasis on 'heroic individuals' may unhelpfully underplay the many contextual factors that influence leadership, such as organizational structures and systems. Instead, Bryman argues that 'contingency' theories of leadership, which stress context rather than any innate human qualities of leadership, are also useful. This view is also supported by Henry Mintzberg (2010) who argues that development organizations especially need to move away from US-influenced heroic models of leadership to those that emphasize 'engaging management' in which the task of managers is to 'help others to be important' and 'bring out their energies', thereby earning trust and respect.

This approach to understanding leadership can also be seen to be important for NGOs. In the Bangladesh context, for example, some of the major NGO leaders are clearly charismatic individuals supported by their class background, social status and levels of education. Others draw some of their power from contextual factors such as having been student activists in the pre-Independence period, while others were returnees who came back to their country from overseas in order to put into practice humanitarian or development-oriented programmes. Indeed, in John Hailey's (1999) work on South Asian NGO leaders, both types of approach to leadership are given equal weight. The study highlights the 'chameleon-like' qualities displayed by successful individuals who operate using different kinds of 'intelligence', which they need to continuously combine if they are to maintain their position and their success (see the discussion below on ambiguity). Hailey characterizes these main four forms of intelligence as aspirational, rational, environmental and interpersonal.

Ronalds (2010: 119) also argues that NGO work is distinctively challenging, requiring leaders who are equipped to deal with additional complexities that go beyond the traditional leadership competencies in the business world. Identifying the challenges of complex governance and diffuse structures of power that operate within NGOs, he argues that legislative, people-centred leadership is the key to success rather than the executive leadership found in the corporate sector. The NGO leader must rely on 'persuasion, political currency, and shared interests' to create conditions under which good decisions can be made.

Despite the general lack of studies of NGO leadership, some recent work points to some interesting if potentially contradictory observations. First, the idea that international NGO managers place a higher importance than managers in other sectors to the centrality of values and purpose is borne out by recent data from *People in Aid* (2012) who surveyed 1,518 managers across sectors and found NGO managers 'on average slightly more engaged than their public and private sector counterparts reflecting the values based nature of work in this sector', and that 'the collective sense of purpose for INGOs is very strong and almost 70% of managers report it as high, compared to 52% of other not for profits, and just over 30% of private sector organisations'.

At the same time, Dickmann *et al.* (2010) in a case study of 'humanitarian leaders' in three leading UK development NGOs found that these organizations were yet to give leadership issues the priority they required to build effectiveness. The evidence that they present indicates that the NGOs still need to identify and develop 'critical leadership competencies' in order to attract the most suitable people, and that a more 'participative culture' was needed in which leaders engaged other staff more fully.

Like many other organizations, some in NGOs have come to recognize the value of 'enabling' models of leadership (in contrast to the charismatic hero style of leadership), in which managers seek to create a suitable environment for learning, sharing and thinking systemically. Management theorist Henry Mitzberg (2010) argues that this enabling approach is particular important for all types of development work. A key challenge then for the NGO context is to move beyond the 'one best way' tendency and accept that there is no single approach to effective NGO leadership, as contingency theory convincingly shows (Bryman 1992: 157).[57] Does the leadership succession question raise important questions about the future of NGOs? Or will such conflicts be negotiated in ways so far unidentified? Leadership problems, after all, have been successfully negotiated by older NGOs such as Amnesty International or Oxfam, where the profile of the actual organization has long since superseded that of its leader at any particular time.

Organizational learning: a failure to learn from failure?

The importance of organizational structures for organizational effectiveness is emphasized within the open systems approach to organizations (Hatch 1997;

Ebrahim and Rangan 2010). This approach is an area of organization theory that has been enthusiastically embraced by many NGO writers. The pioneering work of Chris Argyris and Donald Schön (1978) showed how people in organizations face contradictory pressures on their behaviour that produce unhelpful 'defensive routines' that tend to inhibit learning and lead them to resist change. For example, a control system in an organization can generate a paradox in which staff may be encouraged to take initiatives and risks, but at the same time told not to violate rules and regulations, creating a profound tension between the need for stability and the need for change. Approaches to strengthen 'organizational learning' have blossomed into a wide-ranging area of theory and practice.

Within mainstream management, Peter Senge's (1990) *The Fifth Discipline* remains one of the most influential texts on organizational learning. It argued that organizations need to develop a range of key skills if they are to survive in a rapidly changing world, but are normally held back by a set of 'learning disabilities'. These disabilities include the tendency to learn only from their own experience when it is also necessary to learn indirectly from the experiences of others, and for the inability of individual staff to see the whole picture above individual concerns with only their particular part of the organization. Senge set out five key skills, which he called 'disciplines', that managers needed to acquire: (i) personal mastery (the need for staff to learn self-discipline and self-awareness); (ii) flexible 'mental models' which avoid the pitfalls of stereotyped thinking and reveal an openness to new ideas; (iii) the building of a shared vision about what the organization wishes to achieve; a commitment to team learning in which people overcome the tendency to simply defend their own 'patch' and learn to share and cooperate; (iv) a form of systems thinking which takes into account both long- and short-term outcomes of decisions; and (v) an awareness of the complex interrelationships between different levels of organizational activity and the need to address root causes of problems rather than symptoms. Together these skills, according to Senge, could be developed in order help to build a 'learning organization'.

Following from the priorities of critical management theory, the idea of reflexivity is both important to organizations, and to researchers who try to make sense of what they do. The concept of organizational learning made a considerable impact among researchers and practitioners concerned with NGOs and management. Probably the most authoritative and theoretically informed study of organizational change and learning in relation to development NGOs is that by Ebrahim (2003). Drawing on work by James March and others, he distinguishes three ways of learning: *learning by doing*, as a trial and error process; *learning by exploring* which involves a more open-ended process of search and experimentation; and *imitation*, which involves mimicking the behaviour of another organization.

Organization learning was also central to Brown and Covey's (1987) study of US NGOs, which identified four kinds of core organizational activities: attracting resources, empowering beneficiaries, undertaking public education and doing advocacy work. The authors analyzed four areas of NGO management in which the NGOs undertake these activities. The first was the NGO's mission and its implications for management, particularly as its mission began to shift from relief to development. The second was the linkages established by the NGOs with diverse constituencies and the complex environments in which they operate, i.e. funders, beneficiaries and other stakeholders. The third was the nature of the organizing mechanisms used to regulate behaviour, such as leadership, formal structures, informal cultural mechanisms and values. The fourth and final area was in the realm of organizational dynamics, such as strategic planning and decision-making. The authors argued that to be effective, NGOs needed to play *bridging roles* between different constituencies.

The need to learn lessons when things go wrong is one of the most important prerequisites for organizational learning. The experience of some level of 'failure' is a common one for managers, but evidence suggests that there is a high level of reluctance among NGOs to fully engage with it. From studies of public management, there is evidence that 'sharp thinking' is far more likely to result from a confrontation with perceptions of failure than 'reasoning about "how to create value" on a blank page' (Hood 1998: 23). In the NGO world, Smillie (1995) identified a 'failure to learn from failure', suggesting that 'there are few reasons to disseminate the positive lessons of development, and many more powerful reasons to conceal and forget the negative ones'. These days, the managerialist emphasis on results-based management within the aid industry has dramatically increased the pressures on NGOs to project success and conceal failure. In the third sector literature, Helmut Anheier (2005: 254) too suggests that many non–profit organizations may remain locked into a kind of 'stalemate' 'state of hidden failure' since there is little or no pressure from the market or from voters to provide a system check on NGOs' organizational performance. In the NGO world, some small steps forward have been taken. The need to confront and learn from failure recently gained widespread attention with an initiative of Engineers Without Borders to break the silence (see Box 7.2).

Alan Fowler (1997: 64) points to a reality where many NGOs in practice find it difficult to become 'learning organizations'. He identified development NGOs' inability to learn as a key management problem, with serious implications for their effectiveness and survival:

> An almost universal weakness of NGDOs is found within their often limited capacity to learn, adapt and continuously improve the quality of what they do. This is a serious concern ... if NGOs do not learn from their experience, they are destined for insignificance and will atrophy as agents of social change. NGDOs urgently need to put in place systems which ensure that they know and learn from what they are achieving – as opposed to what they are doing – and then apply what they learn.

There appear to be many reasons why NGOs in practice seem to find learning particularly difficult. Britton (1998) identified a set of internal and external barriers such as stiff funding competition, the pressure to show low rates of administrative overheads, poor incentive systems, and an activist culture that values focusing on the

---

BOX 7.2 ENGINEERS WITHOUT BORDERS AND WWW.ADMITTINGFAILURE.COM

Canadian NGO Engineers Without Borders challenged the tendency for organizations to ignore or conceal failure by publishing what must have been one of the first publicly available NGO 'failure reports'. In the 2010 Failure Report different staff began to own up to various things that had gone wrong in the course of their work. For example, one staff member in Malawi wrote about a water project where he mistakenly prioritized tangible activities when there were deeper problems of sustainability as a result of low levels of government resources. Another manager in Zambia found that efforts to support local small enterprise by providing equipment were neglecting the longer-term problem of replacement parts availability in the area. The NGO has followed this by establishing a web site on which other development NGOs are invited to write up their failures so that others can learn from them. As Madeleine Bunting, writing in *The Guardian* newspaper put it:

'So are we ready for a grown-up conversation about what NGOs do? Are they the force for good portrayed in their marketing? Or are we all colluding in wanting to believe their wild promises ... saving babies' lives for a fiver?... This is brave stuff. Anyone who has ever worked in aid projects will recognise all of it. The confidence with which aid workers can think they know what they are doing, plunge in and make countless mistakes. But this is the knowledge that NGOs keep well clear of their marketing departments. It's an ugly dishonesty that runs through almost all aid work, a painful underbelly to the very obvious idealism and good intentions.'

Source: Bunting, M., *The Guardian*, 17 January 2011.
See also http://www.ted.com/talks/david_damberger_
what_happens_when_an_ngo_admits_failure.html

---

present over planning for the future. One of the key problems NGOs face is the development of effective information systems that can allow all staff to access the information they need about monitoring and impact (See Box 7.3). A further problem was that much of the information and knowledge within NGOs (particularly in smaller organizations) tends not to be written down, instead remaining locked up within particular individuals' heads. This creates a problem of information flow in the day-to-day running of an organization, and an even bigger one during the long term as staff leave and move on. For example, during an evaluation by the author of an international NGO working in Uganda, it became clear that as senior expatriate staff came and went from the organization every two years or so, similar mistakes were repeated because local middle-level managers did not have an opportunity to share what they knew with the incoming senior managers. This is linked to the problem that Sogge (1996: 16) once termed 'the continuity of discontinuity', in which the world of development is characterized by constant disruptive change.

BOX 7.3 LEARNING AND INFORMATION MANAGEMENT

Two main kinds of information exist within NGOs. The first is *product data* that is easily measurable (e.g. financial progress reports, narrative reports, annual budgets, work plans and baseline data). The second is *process data*, which is qualitative, context specific and more effective at capturing gradual change (e.g. information generated by participatory rural appraisal, process documentation, field diaries, community meeting notes). Ebrahim found NGOs ready to share product data with funders, but shared process data only so far as it related to 'success story' case studies. Less straightforwardly positive experiences were withheld, either for practical reasons (product data can be more quickly read and analyzed) or political expediency. NGOs therefore come to pay disproportionate attention to the collection of product data. Because it is available and manageable, it becomes central to decision making. Process data, if it exists, comes to play a secondary role. It was found that the dominance of product data has a depoliticizing effect overall, since it decontextualizes NGO work away from social and political dynamics.

This pattern is compounded by donor information requirements. Focusing on a European Community grant aimed at supporting more systematic data collection within NGOs, Ebrahim shows how a heavy emphasis was placed on financial progress documentation and baseline impact data through standardized reporting formats. This was by no means a bad thing, since one NGO involved had no prior experience with target setting, and gained new, more efficient ways of planning and budgeting. But it produced a systemic rigidity that tended to limit information management within certain prescribed formats, such as the logical framework tool. In the log frame, objectives, purpose and results are hedged by 'assumptions', so that uncertainties are sometimes assumed away. This then tends to reinforce the exclusion of process data. In one case, an NGO agreed to measure 89 different indicators. Many indicators were useful in terms of justifying their work to the funders, but of little value to the NGO itself. And the large scale of the data collection that was required ended up restricting the NGO's capacity to focus on other work.

Ebrahim concludes that funder demand for information may strengthen NGO information systems, but at the cost of process data. It emphasizes forms of information that enable easily quantifiable valuations of success and failure, and these forms then come to feature disproportionately in decision making. At the same time, NGOs may consciously attempt to avoid excessive funder influence by the 'symbolic' generation of information to satisfy funder needs, selective sharing of information and the use of outside professionals to enhance the legitimacy of the information provided. The above combination of funder demands for information, NGO resistance to external interference and bias towards more manageable forms of information, all serve to further entrench existing information systems.

Source: Ebrahim (2003)

Most NGOs also want to demonstrate to their donors and supporters that the work they do is effective, and admitting that not all of it is effective may threaten future funding and cause reputational damage to the organization. At the same time, the culture of action that exists within many NGOs may lead staff to focus on trying to get the work done, rather than considering how well it is being done. Yet the work undertaken by most development NGOs is incredibly difficult, and it is reasonable to assume that it is not always going to be effective. Furthermore, the emphasis on the idea of innovation that informs the current policy and funding climate depends on the idea of taking risks and learning from error, since this is essentially how innovation takes place.

Anthropological perspectives on organizations

There has been a long tradition of studying organization life within the discipline of anthropology, in what has been termed the 'anthropology of organizations' (Wright 1994) or the 'ethnography of organizations' (Gellner and Hirsch 2001). Anthropology offers at least three distinctive areas of contribution to the understanding of NGO management. One is in its insistence on the value of studying organizations ethnographically, based on 'participant observation' fieldwork during which the researcher engages with people as intensively as possible, sharing their lives and conversing with them in an open-ended way. Recent years have seen the emergence of detailed anthropological studies of NGOs such as Erica Bornstein's (2005) ethnography of Protestant NGOs and morality in Zimbabwe and Stephen Hopgood's (2006) study of Amnesty International. The second is the capacity of anthropology to bring a comparative cross-cultural perspective to bear that seeks to challenge the ethnocentrism of research that takes for granted categories and ideas used in the researchers' own society. This is particularly important when we bear in mind that most NGO work is undertaken in non-Western contexts, and that development interventions frequently take the form of cultural encounters that take place at both the level of the organization and the individual. Finally, the anthropology of development is a vibrant sub-field of anthropology offering distinctive critical perspectives on the world of NGOs (and development organizations more widely) and the contexts in which they undertake development work (Lewis and Mosse 2006; Murray Li, 2007).[58]

Social anthropology (or cultural anthropology, the comparable term used in the US) can also enrich the study of the third sector by generating ethnographic data about organizations and the contexts in which they work, and in bringing distinctive theoretical and methodological approaches (Lewis 1999b). Anthropology has traditionally been associated with the study of 'traditional' or non-Western communities, particularly those that were subordinate, marginalized or geographically remote. There are rich ethnographic descriptions of non-Western third sector organizations such as grassroots associations that are contained in anthropological monographs that go back many years.

Organizational ethnography treats organizations and their relationships as units for research using participant observation. A good ethnography according to S.P. Bate (1997) has the following characteristics: it conveys to the reader a strong sense of 'being there'; it offers unexpected details and conclusions based on asking open-ended research questions; it reflects multiple voices; and finally makes a contribution to understanding by offering some kind of a model, or a set of new theoretical insights. Ethnographic research is a way of thinking and way of writing which can also enrich our understanding of culture and organizations, frequently undermined by the tendency to essentialize the concept of culture in organizations in the search for quick-fix management solutions.

The anthropology of organizations has also evolved through links with organization theory researchers working closer to home than the non-Western societies where most early conventional anthropologists carried out their work. For example, the General Electric Company's Hawthorne studies were carried out in Chicago by George Elton Mayo during the 1920s and became important in contributing to the development of the 'human relations' school of management. Mayo's work challenged the dominant management orthodoxy of the time (informed by F.W Taylor's notion of the worker as motivated solely by rational self-interest) by generating new insights into the importance of social relationships in the workplace. The study found that productivity increased when specific groups of workers were paid attention to, given benign supervision, consulted about targets, and generally allowed to create a social atmosphere away from the coercion of top-down management systems. Gradually, organizational anthropological research of this kind broadened to focus on community relationships within wider policy issues of education, health and bureaucracy, and later also with international development institutions (Wright 1994).

Anthropological approaches to power

While anthropology is often associated in the public imagination with the study of exotic cultures, it has long been focused on a far wider range of subjects and contexts. Gledhill (1994: 7–8) in his book *Power and Its Disguises* argues that the distinctive contribution of anthropology to social science is primarily one that

> attempts to examine social realities in a cross-cultural frame of reference. In striving to transcend a view of the world based solely on the premises of European culture and history, anthropologists are also encouraged to look beneath the world of appearances and taken-for-granted assumptions in social life in general. This should help us to pursue critical analyses of ideologies and power relations in all societies, including those of the West.

Significant numbers of anthropologists have gradually moved away from earlier preoccupations with marginal or remote peoples to 'study up' instead, by focusing also on the powerful and more mainstream subjects such as governments and corporations (Gardner and Lewis 1996).[59]

At the same time, anthropological work that had its origins in non-industrialized settings has turned out to have enormous value for analyzing aspects of modern life. For example, the theory of 'the gift' that was initially outlined by Marcel Mauss, showed the ways that apparently irrational gift giving was important for the structuring of social relationships because it created the obligation of reciprocity. This theory has been more recently used to explore the world of development aid and highlights both the underlying power relations within development assistance and aid relationships, where power is asserted by development agencies over those in the receiving group that they are ostensibly seeking to help (Stirrat and Henkel 1997).

Anthropological critiques of managerialism and development

Like critical management theory's preoccupation with the idea of denaturalization, an anthropological perspective also offers a critique of the 'one best way' tendency implicit in mainstream management thinking – whether in its top-down or enabling forms – that often serve to extend Western cultural hegemony through the co-optation of local value systems (Marsden 1994). What anthropology may be able to do is open us up to the possibilities of the roles which might be played by indigenous management styles and local understandings of 'organization' and 'development' as appropriate foundations for development efforts (Marsden 1994: 35). For example, in one well-documented case the Philippines Irrigation Authority (PIA) managed to restructure an inefficient top-down bureaucracy by decentralizing water provision to locally developed irrigation management structures, by drawing upon the capacity of organized groups of local farmers to manage their own community irrigation systems (Korten and Siy 1989).

Cross-cultural study of organizations has long been an area of increasing interest to organizational anthropologists (Hamada 1992). One obvious area in which anthropological research can contribute to NGO management is in the study of the cross-cultural encounters that are created through the work of international NGOs (Wright 1994). For example, what are the management challenges and organizational implications of deploying expatriate NGO staff to work in non-Western country contexts? What is the consequence of conflicts between different cultures and values? Where NGOs are seeking to work with partners in a development setting, how should they manage the tension between their values and culture and those of the partner organization?

A small but growing literature is beginning to address these types of questions. A study by Mukasa (1999) carried out in the context of international and local staff within an international NGO working in Uganda raised a fascinating set of issues around frequent changes of expatriate staff, a tendency for local staff knowledge to be undervalued, problems of cultural sensitivity and awareness, lack of clarity in overall staffing policy, and tensions around differences in lifestyles and living standards. Kaufman (1997) provides some useful insights into the career paths of some UK NGO staff, while Biggs (1997) examined the 'coping strategies' used by development agency personnel as they go about their work. Fechter and Hindman (2011) have explored the moral ambiguities of aid workers in their personal worlds. Baillie Smith and Jenkins (2012) have explored the lives of Indian NGO activists using life history narratives to reveal their 'intermediate' status as strategic cosmopolitans negotiating space between the wider aid industry and local lives. Finally, Scott-Smith's work (2013) offers a challenge to development organizations to overcome the tendency for aid workers' lives to continue to be insulated (through lifestyle, language, formalism and economic relationships) from local realities where they remain a distinct class embedded in a developmentalist ideology.[60]

Anthropological work at the same time challenges the simple dualisms that run through our accounts of NGOs and their work. For example, there is the danger of creating over-generalized or mechanistic characterizations of the cultural encounter between organizations and communities, or development workers and beneficiaries. As we saw earlier in the context of the brokers and translators approach to understanding development organizations ethnographically, such dichotomies are problematized using ethnographic accounts of the interpretative and transformative work that is carried out by social actors in intermediary roles throughout such interactions. Drawing on the tradition of actor-oriented anthropology and Bruno Latour's work in science and technology studies, development interventions can be unpacked ethnographically in terms of the complex roles, relationships and representations that structure processes and outcomes.

Despite their association in the public mind with the concept of 'culture', anthropologists too have problematized the instrumental use of this difficult concept. Particularly problematic is the way it has become used as an explanatory variable within some areas of organization theory in the normative writings of some management gurus. For example, John Van Maanen (2001: 244) describes the concept of culture as 'a rather well-worn accounting device' that is increasingly used to explain all manner of things, with the consequence that it loses its value:

> It can be and is used to explain if not justify such matters as sterling or poor organizational performance, the success or failure of mergers and acquisitions, or the presence of absence of harmony among members.

Such explanations cannot of course be taken at face value, but require careful contextualization and interpretation along with all other aspects of organizational life, as we will explore in Chapter 8.

The concept of ambiguity

An anthropological approach is also useful in engaging with the concept of ambiguity, which has also increasingly attracted attention from management theorists. The management of ambiguity is often seen as a key to understanding the challenges faced by organizations in the postmodern world, and as providing an alternative perspective to and contrast with the earlier 'rational scientific' theories of management (Peters and Waterman 1982; Morgan 1997). For anthropologists, ambiguity is often central to explanations of how cultures, ideas and activities are constructed, negotiated and reworked through processes in which both tension and creativity may be present (Wright 1994; Curtis 1994). For example, an emphasis on managing shared meanings in organization theory highlights the challenges of managers to clarify and project their organization's desired future identity and image in order to guide effective organizational change (Gioia and Thomas 1996). Martin and Meyerson (1988) show how ambiguity can be double edged: it can facilitate innovation and creativity as well as confusion and paralysis within an organization. Ambiguity can therefore be seen both as a source of both creativity and danger.

The idea of ambiguity is also important in the context of countering managerialism within a more humanistic value-driven idea of management. Ambiguity can be defined as the coexistence of two or more meanings within a single subject or entity. Ambiguity pervades the subject of NGO management at two levels. First, as we have seen, there is a conceptual ambiguity around what type of management might be appropriate for NGOs to draw upon. Second, when we consider NGOs as real world organizations we find that they are themselves ambiguous organizations whose identities and activities are always open to multiple interpretations. In literary theorist William Empson's famous book *Seven Types of Ambiguity* (1930) he suggested that the quality of ambiguity, when it is held together in coherent ways, may lend a subtlety, richness and power to a piece of writing – an idea that can also be applied to the world of organizations. This positive view can also be linked to the concept of *productive ambiguity* used within the arts in which multiple perspectives bring new insights.

Some third sector researchers, influenced by both the anthropological and the organization theory traditions, have also been drawn to the concept of ambiguity. For example, drawing upon the work of the anthropologist Edmund Leach, Billis (1993a) has argued that organizations may exhibit a set of organizational problems created by the existence of an ambiguous zone between the bureaucratic and associational 'worlds', which tend to operate through very different sets of rules (discussed in more detail in Chapter 11). For example, the 'bureaucratic world' operates according to the rules of hierarchy and role specialization, while by contrast the 'associational world' is characterized more by face-to-face egalitarian relationships and multifaceted, informal roles. Many third sector organizations as they grow become caught in the ambiguous zone between the two, bringing confused roles and identities. There is danger in the ambiguity, but also potential creativity, since an organization that is able to hold on to its values and principles even as it develops forms of bureaucratic structures will find that it can maintain a competitive edge.

Helmut Anheier (2005) summarizes four sets of tensions that arise from what he sees as the common ambiguities that are in play within non–profit organizations: between structures that allow predictability but that also need to be able to improvise and be creative; between a technocratic culture that emphasizes performance and outputs, and one that focuses on people; between the structures of hierarchy and centralization, as opposed to ones that facilitate bottom-up decision-making and decentralized networks; and finally between 'outer-directedness' (reacting to and adapting to events and opportunities in the outside environment) and 'inner-directedness' (focusing on the organization's own objectives, values and worldview as the main source of strategy).

The idea of ambiguity has also been applied to the analysis of the sector boundaries between state, business and third sectors (Billis 1993b). Carroll (1992: 138) shows that 'socially-oriented businesses' are under constant tension between their profit-making and their equity-promoting selves. A study of 'community trade' work undertaken by The Body Shop, a UK-based 'social' business in collaboration with South Asian NGOs, alternative trading organizations and producer groups, illustrates the relevance of the concept of ambiguity in understanding the complex management challenges involved for both NGOs and business when attempts are made to link poverty reduction objectives to the action of commercial market forces – on the boundary between the for-profit and non-profit sectors, as we will see in Chapter 10.

The management of development NGOs is riddled with elements of both ambiguity and paradox: for example, the challenges of combining directive management styles with participative ones, of engaging well-paid professionalized personnel (alongside volunteers in many cases) to meet the needs of some of the world's poorest people, and the challenge of accommodating the 'cognitive dissonance' that inevitably emerges in the course of making necessarily small efforts to bring about change when large-scale needs remain unmet.

In his recent biography of ACORD, an organization that began as an international initiative but is now an African NGO (see Box 4.1), Alan Fowler (2012: 127) concludes that the organization's transformational journey has been characterized by the struggle to control ambiguity and paradox within the organization:

> How paradoxes are recognised and 'managed' matters in shaping an NGO's moral behaviour and, hence, its identity and reputation. ACORD's aspiration for solidarity with marginalised communities, while relying on foreign-funded professionalism, has invited tensions and ambiguities, often with negative effects on staff that are picked up by stakeholders. NGOs thus have to make many decisions on how to address the paradoxes that affect their development work and its public projection ...

The central tension that needed to be resolved was between the identification with vulnerable people, and working effectively as a professionalized organization with international donor funding.

Conclusion

This chapter has explored the idea that both organizational theory and areas of anthropological work can provide useful and potentially complementary insights for NGO management. There is still comparatively little research available on many of these themes in relation to the NGO world. More empirical research will be therefore needed if we are to gain a better understanding of the ways in which development NGOs can build and maintain their influence in a rapidly changing world. Organization theory provides a fruitful approach to analyzing important aspects of NGO management, from organizational learning and change through to organizational life cycles and leadership. The anthropology of organizations offers another, related perspective on NGO management that draws on both on conceptual insights and on ethnographic approach to understanding the lived realities of those involved in organizations and within their development encounters. Finally, we have explored the centrality of ambiguity in the ways that NGOs need to manage a wide range of complex value-based challenges.

8

CULTURE AND ORGANIZATION

... we take seriously the idea of a culture of aid work that shapes the world of development professionals as much as other cultures, and yet like all cultures, is rarely singular or simple.

Fechter and Hindman (2011: 2)

Introduction

In this chapter we explore issues of organizational structure and culture that are important in the analysis of NGO management. Social structure is concerned with the social relationships that exist within an organization, while culture refers to the shared ideas and values that people bring to these relationships (Jones 1996). A cultural perspective on organizations invites us to understand organizations in a bottom–up way, drawing on human experience. It requires us to understand culture in two interrelated ways – in terms of the wider societal cultures in which organizational activity takes place, and in relation to the 'organizational culture' that is created within particular organizations and those people with whom they interact. It also brings insights into the interactions that take place at the interfaces of NGO work, and the hybrid systems and cultures that emerge from such interactions.

Culture, management and globalization

The study of management in recent years has been characterized by the recognition that economic, social and technological change at the global level has dramatic implications for the management of all types of organization. As Barbara Parker (1998: x) puts it:

> The world increasingly resembles a global market place where integration
> across 'traditional' borders is evident in almost every dimension of life. ...
> Increasingly a world with fewer boundaries calls for organizations able to
> transcend vertical and horizontal boundaries and create hybrids that are both
> cost effective and responsible to local, regional, domestic, international and
> global communities of interest.

One important area of reduced boundaries is in the tendency for crossing traditional borders of space, time and cultural assumptions. This means that new relationships are being constantly generated both within and between organizations, often
with hybrid outcomes both at the level of organizations and at the level of ideas and
practices. Third sector organizations are now facing more and more internal diversity in human resource terms, and are developing new and more intense cross-
cultural relationships and linkages across shifting global landscapes.

At the same time, a focus on structure can sometimes draw attention away from
cultural issues relating to an organization's people and its values. For example, there
is growing awareness that formal strategies for organizational change need to be
supported by a strong focus on culture and values at the individual and the organizational level. As Owusu (2004: 108) observes, from the perspective of many years
of experience of practice and reflection within the NGO sector:

> Change must begin from within development organizations themselves and
> must go beyond just restructuring when things appear not to be working.
> Often development organizations are quick to embark on restructuring in the
> belief that adjusting organizational structures is enough to solve underlying
> problems. But new structures do not, in themselves, herald new dawns. Rather,
> it is the attitudes, behaviours, values and commitment that underlie these
> structures that hold in them the seeds of success or failure.

Of particular relevance to NGO management then is the need to reflect on
organizational culture and cross-cultural issues. Many development NGOs seek to
build, and put in place, ways of working that can reflect, and are appropriate to, the
values of strengthening social justice and achieving poverty reduction in the particular contexts where the work is being undertaken. For example, some have
argued that one of the strengths of Grameen's approach to microcredit and social
business is its rootedness in Islamic values that seek to tame uncontrolled economic
growth with social goals and humanistic values (Mansour and Ezzat 2009).

Development organizations often also work at 'interfaces' between different cultural settings – the most obvious being one between development workers from
one society working in another. NGOs, perhaps more than any other type of organization, are seeking to manage complex cross-cultural encounters both *within* their
organizations as staffing becomes more diverse, and *between* themselves and their
clients, since organizational success depends on working closely with communities,
individuals and institutions with which they may often be unfamiliar.

However, such difference should not simply be conceived in terms of a polarity between Western and non-Western contexts. For example, a study by Olie (1996) shows a surprisingly high level of cultural variation in relation to management practices *within* Europe. Furthermore, there is a high level of diversity within cosmopolitan cities such as London or New York, which we would expect to be increasingly reflected within organizations working in such cities.

The management of cross-cultural encounters

While there may be tensions between different approaches to management, issues also arise based on different cultural contexts in which NGOs operate, and different sets of values within cross-cultural encounters that inform management practices. Dichter (1989a) notes that both the top-down and the enabling approaches to management are derived essentially from the Western private sector, though development NGOs may show varying levels of awareness of this. While NGOs need to pay attention to basic management principles, it is important to consider the different contexts in which NGOs operate. For example, Campbell's (1987) framework for understanding NGO management emphasizes cultural difference as a key element.

Of course, these issues are not entirely new for international NGOs. There is a long tradition of international agencies going to work in the countries of the South, where they encounter differences in both culture and context (Box 8.1). The development industry has long been characterized by such cross-cultural encounters between Western developers and (usually) non-Western 'developees'. There has periodically been concern voiced around this topic, such as the work of Jaeger and Kanungo (1990: 1) that describes encounters that have often been characterized by imposition of ideas and practices, lack of sensitivity to difference and by misunderstanding.[61] They make the case for thinking more deeply about the need for 'indigenous' management in developing countries, a line of thinking that is particularly appropriate for NGOs, arguing:

> Uncritical transfer of management theories and techniques based on Western ideologies and value systems has in many ways contributed to organizational inefficiency and ineffectiveness in the developing country context.

The basic premise is that the external environment in many developing countries is different to that of the developed countries, where certain development ideas and techniques are developed, and that the process of 'transfer' of ideas, techniques and practices is therefore misguided. Yet these are not issues that only affect international NGOs, since cultural differences can also be important *within* countries. The encounter between a middle-class urbanized Southern NGO staff member and a rural villager may also be characterized by difference, misunderstanding and complexity. At the same time, there are these days 'Southern NGOs' working transnationally in some areas of the world. BRAC has worked in Afghanistan since 2002, and has since gone on to establish development programmes in several sub-Saharan African countries (Smillie, 2009).

BOX 8.1 ISSUES IN THE 'INTERNATIONALIZATION' OF NGO MANAGEMENT

International NGOs continue to evolve. A decade or so ago, there were two main trends: NGOs which began in one country expanded to new ones in a process of 'going international' (such as Action Aid or BRAC); forms of transnational NGOs were specifically formed with representatives from more than one country (such as Civicus). This led to distinctive organizational challenges and structural responses: 'ethnocentric' structures based on tight control of subsidiary offices by centralized headquarters, and 'polycentric' structures with a high degree of decentralized local control and interconnectedness. The structure that an NGO adopts needs to maximize proximity of decision-making processes to its constituent groups wherever they are. It needs to balance structures with members' and core values, to sensitize structures to cultural and regional diversities, and to create communication methods to allow participation. One strategy is that of the rotating headquarters: the International Association for Volunteer Effort's (IAVE) original HQ was in the US, but moved to Colombia for four years when its president was from that country, and then to Australia.

More recently there have been growing examples of mergers, federations and international NGO families as organizations seek to build economies of scale and critical mass, or need to respond to resource pressures. There are also new demands on professional staff within INGOs, who need to have an international outlook, multicultural sensitivities and the ability to remain as neutral or objective as possible in discussions based on different cultural, national and political difference. Today, NGO managers in the UK report a need to learn new skills to operate within the new donor 'development effectiveness' agenda, including the acquisition of private sector style tendering skills, and the development of new organizational systems than can adequately measure results and impact.

Sources: Koenig 1996; INTRAC 2013; author interview notes

Organizational culture

The concept of 'organizational culture' is important for understanding a range of NGO management issues, from organizational learning to managing change processes. In early work on this subject in relation to the third sector, Handy (1988: 85) pointed out that the concept of 'organizational culture' had been held back within management studies by the predominance of what he termed the rational or 'engineering model' of management, which tended to conceptualize organizations as machine-like and similar to each other. He offers a simple common-sense definition of 'organizational culture':

If organizations are communities, mini-societies, rather than machines, then it is natural to expect that each community will have its own taste and flavour, its own way of doing things, its own habits and jargon, its own *culture*.

Culture, as Van Maanen (2001: 244) argues, tends in the main to be 'inchoate, contested and ambiguous', but its identification as part of organizational life is useful because it helps to reveal organizations not as the logical, rational machines characterized by means-ends thinking that many economists would have us believe, but as complex social constructs characterized by ceremony, custom, ritual and myth like any other community. For example, Box 8.2 discusses how norms around gender relations are constructed and managed within organizations and in relation to their activities and work.

Handy's (1988) particular contribution was to distinguish four main organizational cultural styles that help categorize the ways in which people within organizations believe they should work. Within 'power culture' there tends to be a dominant central leader and an emphasis of individuals over roles and procedures, as might be found in a small company or a trade union. 'Role culture' is present where an organization is essentially bureaucratic and specialized according to specific roles rather than individual people, and such organizations are secure and predictable, such as a tax office. The third type is 'task culture', in which judgements are made by results based on the power of experts. Here an organization often makes use of a relatively flexible team culture, such as a consultancy team, but this approach may often be quite hard to manage in practice. Finally there is 'person culture', in which an organization exists mainly for the good of people within it and has no particular goal beyond this one. Here, management is attempted by securing mutual consent. Handy suggests that there are many third sector organizations that display this type of organizational culture.

An understanding of these four styles of organization culture has been influential in both business and development management fields, and can be used to help analyze what goes on within NGOs (Lewis 2002b). For example, in the case of some small-scale informal organizations, or those at an early stage of development, a 'person culture' may dominate and lead to a situation where the staff may feel that although they are getting something out of the NGO there are questions to be asked about its overall effectiveness. In the case of a more bureaucratic, formalized NGO, the dominance of 'role culture' may inhibit learning and creativity within the organization. For NGOs that retain a strong charismatic leader or a founder-leader, the price of a dominant 'power culture' may be an inhibition of the abilities of other staff to play an effective role in the organization. The challenge may often be the building of a 'task culture' which allows NGO staff to work flexibly in the context of their specific competencies, within work teams in a more satisfying and stimulating environment which in the end will produce better results (Maxwell 1997).

Such analyses draw heavily upon the symbolic-interpretative perspective outlined above by Hatch (1997). But postmodern perspectives have also been influential in the analysis of organizational culture. For example, Alvesson (1993) outlines

BOX 8.2 GENDER AND ORGANIZATIONAL CULTURE

The social science definition of 'gender' distinguishes the *social* from the *biological* construction of differences between men and women, focusing on the rules, traditions and norms which help determine the values and attributes which are considered 'feminine' and 'masculine', and the ways in which power is allocated and used differently by women and men. Fowler (1997) reviews the ways in which roles and power are divided along gendered lines within NGOs, and the degree to which 'female' and 'male' principles are reflected and valued in an NGO's organizational culture. Many NGOs have paid little attention to gender inequalities within their own organizations, and have preferred to see the importance of gender in their sectoral work. NGOs have an 'immediate sainthood', but often the culture of masculine exclusiveness and sexual harassment are as common in NGOs as elsewhere (Ashworth 1996). Some NGOs have 'gender units' but these are often marginalized or used as 'alibis'. Recognizing this, some NGOs such as ACORD are working hard to develop a gender policy, but with mixed results so far (Hadjipateras 1997). In the North, there is often discussion of 'equal opportunities' (Osborne and Homer 1996). Liberal and radical perspectives can be contrasted here. The Western management literature is increasingly focusing on women and business leadership and the challenge of increasing women's 'presence' (e.g. T. Morgan 1994). Wallace (1998) documents efforts to 'institutionalize' gender within some Northern NGOs' structures as well as within their programmes, finding that male trustees and directors still dominate the organizational culture, even if there has been some success with programmes and staffing. Preconditions of success of building a gender policy include: leadership should not be actively opposed; resources must be allocated, activities must not be seen as an add-on; responsibility for change management must be allocated and indicators of progress agreed (Fowler 1997). In the South, research on gender issues within BRAC is beginning to appear. Rao and Kelleher (1995) analyze BRAC's Gender Quality Action-Learning (GQAL) programme, which seeks to sensitize its field staff to gender issues. The research highlights tensions between the twin tasks of 'lending money' and 'empowering women' that BRAC undertakes. Goetz (1997) examines the issues of 'gendered time and space' within BRAC and its implications for men and women staff. Some writers have suggested that NGOs may have 'a feminine development approach and masculine organizational culture' (e.g. Fowler 1997: 79) in which cultures of action and control take precedence over cultures which value communication and participation.

the debate as to whether or not organizational culture – a shared, unifying system of values, meanings, understandings in the Geertzian sense – is the binding force in organizations, or whether, we should focus more on the concept of 'ambiguity' as playing the central organizing role through an organization's need to manage contradiction and confusion. An interesting example of the use to which the post-modern perspective can be put in the third sector context can be found in the work of DiBella (1992), who showed how planned organizational change did not take place within an international NGO due to the existence of a range of persistent 'sub-cultures' existing throughout the organization that were based on fragmentation and difference. This created a kind of 'organized anarchy' as the basis for the organization, which while relatively stable showed itself largely resistant to change.

Indeed, culture itself turns out to be a difficult concept in that the idea of a single unifying shared culture rarely applies to organizations any more than it does to most societies. Multiple cultures are likely to exist within an organization, and in an NGO this might for example be between those who are concerned with mission and values, and those preoccupied with bureaucratic tasks such as basic administration. Alvesson (1993: 118) argues that neither a sole emphasis on a unitary culture, nor one simply on the organizing power of ambiguity is adequate. Instead he suggests a 'multiple cultural configuration view', which sees organizational cultures as mixtures of cultural manifestations at different levels and of different kinds. In this view, different cultures and sub-cultures overlap in an organizational setting with profession, gender, class or ethnic group. Box 8.2 examines these issues in relation to the concept of gender.

One of the few studies to focus on this issue was Brown and Covey's (1983) analysis of an NGO as a 'microcosm' of its environment, containing diverse cultural perspectives in a way that internally reproduced ideological conflicts characteristic of the wider society. The authors highlight the 'ideological negotiation' that took place within a US-based third sector organization working in development education, project management and government lobbying. For example, tensions between staff from different ethnic groups (with white males dominating senior management) and between clerical workers and managers (the former with low salaries and little input into decision making) were found to be basically ideological conflicts, also rooted in the racism located in wider society. Brown and Covey (1983: 246) concluded that

> organizations cannot be efficiently co-ordinated without recognizing and managing ideological diversity rooted in the cultural origins of organization members.

The authors argue therefore that the challenge is to build values and ideologies that appeal across cultural boundaries and encourage constructive ideological negotiations. However, the challenge of building and sustaining common ideas and meanings is not just a difficult challenge within organizations, it is also made more complex by the rise of partnerships and multi-agency development projects. As Lewis *et al.* (2003) have shown in relation to inter-agency World Bank projects, combinations of non-governmental, public and private actors can create projects which become fragmented through tensions over issues of meaning, culture and power among different perspectives within and between different types of project actors.

Organizations and wider societal culture

A key challenge for mainstream management has been to find ways of relating ideas about wider cultures with the concept of organizational culture (Box 8.3).

Tayeb (1988) undertook a study that compared India and Britain in order to explore the relationship between national cultural contexts and organizational culture. In an analysis of the main approaches to the cross-national study of organizations, he shows that a set of different factors helps to determine the structures and activities of organizations, within which culture is just one. First, a 'contingency perspective' is important, since it focuses on securing a fit between structure and context that is fundamentally necessary for any organization's survival. Second, a 'political economy' focus is needed in order to examine the social and economic structures that also help determine aspects of the organization. Finally, the 'cultural perspective' highlights the ideational process in which attitudes and values of individual members help determine the organization's structure. For NGOs, all three levels are important for cross-cultural management.

The study of relationships between culture and organizations in the management literature is dominated by the work of Geert Hofstede, a Dutch social psychologist, who in the 1970s undertook a massive study of the US-based multinational IBM, which was then operating in more than 40 countries. Hofstede argues that 'organizational cultures', the set of values and norms that are constructed within organizations, may be more malleable than national cultures and can be drawn upon within organizations to build bridges between different national cultures through the acquisition and deployment of intercultural communication skills.[62]

The study explored the work-related values held by employees working for the corporation, and found wide-ranging national cultural differences in its offices around the world (Hofstede 1991). These variations led Hofstede to build a theoretical framework in order to analyze the contours and dynamics of these different 'national cultures', suggesting key differences along four sets of general variations: power-distance (the distance staff feel from their superiors); uncertainty-avoidance (the ways in which staff deal with novelty and risk); individualism (the level of integration of individuals into collectivist groups); and masculinity (the valuing of performance and ambition compared and contrasted with the valuing of quality of life and role flexibility).

Different cultures were then mapped across these four dimensions, and Hofstede argued that we should not assume that management prescriptions operate in the same way in different national contexts. One useful example discussed by Hofstede is the history of 'management by objectives' (MBO) that was developed in the United States in the 1960s as a planning tool.[63] This example shows the potential pitfalls for NGOs of applying a management tool developed in one cultural context to an organization within a different cultural setting. Hofstede shows that this particular Western-designed piece of management technology requires low 'power-distance' and 'uncertainty-avoidance', since it requires that subordinates negotiate forcefully with their superiors, and that risks must be accepted by all levels of staff if it is to operate effectively.[64]

The evidence he presented suggests that MBO was introduced far more success-fully in Britain than in France, where power-distance and uncertainty-avoidance were found to be higher. Jaeger and Kanungo (1990) make the point that if MBO is used in the 'wrong' context, then it may actually be *dysfunctional* because it can create distrust between senior and junior staff. It is not difficult to see why Hofstede's work has received wide circulation within organizational studies, as Hatch (1997: 210) suggests:

> The importance of Hofstede's work is not only that it identified specific cul-tural differences between nations, but Hofstede also showed that organiza-tional culture is an entry point for societal influence on organizations.

Hofstede has many critics. Some researchers within the organizational studies field have been critical of his both his methodological approach and some of his assumptions. For example, McSweeney (2001) argues that despite the large volume of questionnaires deployed overall in this massive study, Hofstede's samples in many countries were in practice extremely small. The research was also restricted only to employees of the IBM corporation, so that any generalization derived from the characteristics of this self-selecting sub-group to those of the larger national popula-tion of an entire country may be open to criticism.

Recent work by Frederik Claeyé (2014) provides a valuable analysis in the con-text of South African NGOs that helps move us to beyond static discussions of the NGO cultural encounter to one that embraces more fully ideas about agency, power and hybridity, and reflects the complexity of NGO management practices. Drawing on Norman Long's (2001) concept of the 'interface' as a locus of interaction between structures and agents where worldviews and cultural paradigms are produced and transformed, and on critical management and development perspectives that ques-tion mainstream understandings and practices and emphasize power and resistance, he argues that alternative approaches to managerialism are needed if cross-cultural encounters around NGO work are to be effectively attuned to local needs.

Claeyé argues that Hofstede's analysis is flawed by a culturalist approach that assumes that difference is simply about the values that people hold in different soci-eties rather than power and relationships. Using a critical, cross-cultural perspective he examines how the global and the local come together in the formation of man-agement ideas and practices through processes of both imposition and resistance. When faced with ethnocentric and narrowly defined discourses of Western devel-opment management used by their funders and partners (and which they are essen-tially forced to 'mimic'),[65] South African NGO managers are shown to be engaged in practices of both mimicry and contestation that allows them to construct, with varying degrees of stability, a hybrid form of management that reflects local condi-tions and contexts. In particular, they combine elements of a managerialist, technical accountability and results focused agenda with humanist ideas rooted in the Ubuntu tradition that emphasizes social solidarity, interpersonal relationships and reciprocity. Claeyé (2014) writes of the resulting hybrid management system:

BOX 8.3 ICEBERGS AND HIPPOS: ORGANIZATIONAL DEVELOPMENT (OD) EXPERIENCES IN MALAWI

Rick James (2003) documented his own international capacity building work with NGOs in Africa and provides a set of valuable insights into the realities of organizational change. One is the importance of understanding context. History and politics in Malawi created an environment in which the authoritarian style of Banda's 30-year dictatorship (itself following on from a long era of colonial domination) brings certain distinctive organizational implications. Hierarchies are strong, interpersonal trust has been eroded and sensitive disputes between staff in organizations are resolved behind the scenes rather than in public. Relationships between staff and outside 'experts' are extremely complicated. Western-style participatory management styles and OD techniques are not easily transferable. But this does not mean either that the concept of OD is irrelevant or inappropriate.

James uses an ethnographic approach to try to understand the structures, relationships and ideas within African NGOs *on their own terms*. For example, he finds that democratic decision-making in organizational change processes are differently structured, focused on private one-to-one conversations more than plenary discussions. He also shows that the language of Western OD needs to be adapted if it is to be understood locally. For example, trainers often speak of an organization as an 'iceberg' with the bulk of its structure hidden out of sight. This is a metaphor of limited relevance to the everyday life of people used to a tropical climate, and suggests a better image of an organization as a 'hippo' similarly partly submerged. Going deeper, James explores how local counterpart ways of thinking about organizational change have long existed in these communities. These range from a tradition that accepts the need for outside facilitation to solve organizational problems ('the stranger brings the sharper blade') to the recognition of the need for cooperative problem solving ('one finger does not squash a tick'). These ways of thinking about organizations are in many cases much older than Western discourses of organizational change, and outside 'experts' need to learn from them. Methods and tools are different too, with storytelling as a method for addressing organizational problems favoured within James' data. In the West, the importance of storytelling as an important method for business management and participatory learning and action in development is often under-recognized (Denning 2000).

James shows the ways in which concepts of OD can be translated and interpreted between 'Western' and 'African' contexts, if this is attempted with openness and sensitivity. But James also implicitly questions the principles of simple 'technology transfer' embodied in much of NGO capacity building literature and its associated practices by drawing attention to the existence of important 'counterpart traditions' of participation and organizational change in other contexts. The possibilities for a more genuine 'two way learning' within international development relationships, he argues, is thereby opened up.

Source: James (2003)

the discourse of Ubuntu … provides participants with a set of guidelines for interpersonal behaviour that shapes the way in which the notion of NPO management is constructed. Emphasising the community and the reciprocal relations and obligations of the members of the organizational community, Ubuntu's humanist orientation might be seen as an antidote to the economic rational mindset underlying managerialism and its shift towards becoming more business-like.

Examples of these practices include the use of informal, storytelling, writing poems and picture drawing in eliciting evaluative feedback from community members with whom the NGO works, and the favouring of open door policies in which managers and staff interact freely and share problems based not only on professional concerns but also derived from distinctive locally rooted ideas of compassion and survival ('getting through it together'). Hybrid management systems such as this that emerge are not necessarily stable or conflict-free, but they may contribute to 'culturally appropriate ways of managing' (Claeyé 2014).

Conclusion

In this chapter, we have discussed the importance of linking ideas about wider culture within an understanding of the ways in which organizations are managed. In the increasingly complex global and local settings in which NGOs work, certain management assumptions embodied in Western business school training are increasingly under challenge. This of course is not only the case with NGOs, but also within the wider corporate world as well. Some companies are increasingly operating using new hybrid models of management, for example combining Western-style accounting systems with non-Western team structures, and with authoritative leaders who nevertheless give their local managers a high degree of autonomy and flexibility (Parker 1998: 25).

PART III

The practice of NGO management

9

SERVICE DELIVERY, ADVOCACY, INNOVATION AND EVALUATION

> ... NGOs are only NGOs in any politically meaningful sense of the term if they are offering alternatives to dominant models, practices and ideas about development.
>
> *Bebbington, Hickey and Mitlin (2008: 3)*

Introduction

In this chapter, we turn once again to the main activities that are undertaken by development NGOs. First we discuss service delivery, and ask to whom should such services be provided, and at what cost? How should the NGO manage relations with other service providers, such as the state? The chapter then moves on to consider the catalytic role of advocacy, in which NGOs seek to influence wider policy. Advocacy requires specific skills such as identifying appropriate issues, maintaining accountability to stakeholders, and managing information. Next we consider the issue of innovation, a less tangible, but for many an equally important, NGO activity. Some argue that this is a special strength of development NGOs, but how innovative are NGOs in practice? Finally we discuss evaluation. NGOs need to develop the means to assess how well they are doing, but many have neglected this activity in the past. Since it is both in an organization's own interests to evaluate effectively, as well as a requirement that is increasingly imposed by funders, NGOs need to manage their evaluation processes as effectively as possible.

Service delivery: means or end?

Tom Carroll (1992) pointed out long ago that service delivery is perhaps the most directly observable and clearly visible role that NGOs play in development work. In this role, goods and services that are wanted, needed or otherwise unavailable to people are provided by NGOs. Sometimes the NGO itself takes a decision to provide services to meet hitherto unmet needs, while in other cases an NGO may be 'contracted' by the government, often taking over delivery of services formerly provided by the state. This makes service delivery by NGOs a highly political issue. The most common sectors for NGOs' provision of services are health, education and rural development. While NGO service delivery is normally thought of in relation to people who are in need, we should also remember that services can also take the form of training, research or conflict resolution services to other sections of society, such as government, private sector or other agencies.

There are three main roles NGOs can play, which can be briefly illustrated with reference to agriculture and development. The first role is as an *implementing* agency that actually delivers the services to people. An example of this is an NGO that works with farmers in remote, difficult-to-reach areas who may be farming fragile, complex or risk-prone lands for which government outreach is poor (Bebbington 1991). In undertaking this kind of work, NGOs may draw on the use of local field staff whose knowledge may bring a better 'fit' with the everyday realities of local people than can be the case using outside professional experts. The second role is that of *strengthening* already existing public delivery systems by providing new insights into unmet needs, and perhaps also developing innovative responses to delivery challenges. These might include developing new approaches, or carrying out wider training. It might also include, as Guijt (2008: 164) argues, 'cultivating values of trust, dignity, culture and identity' to build 'mutually respectful' relationships in the delivery of services to marginalized people. The third is that an NGO can work with its clients in the community to assist them in *generating pressure* or 'demand pull' so that people can themselves claim better services from government and hold it more accountable. Such an approach links the idea of citizenship entitlements to basic services with the developmental challenge of claiming and realizing rights, and defining their needs.

NGOs can serve as 'bridges' between clients or beneficiaries and other service providers (Brown 1991). For example, this is an approach used by PDI in the Philippines in its efforts to keep pressure on government to maintain implementation of its agrarian reform policy, while at the same time assisting farmers with practical help in taking possession of and commencing cultivation of the new land that they receive (Box 9.1).

As we have seen, some theorists and policy makers argue that NGOs may have a specific organizational comparative advantage' in service delivery, based on qualities such as flexibility, value-driven commitment and cost-effectiveness.[67] Carroll (1992) found in a survey of 30 Latin American NGOs engaged in rural development activities that all appeared to show an outstanding capacity to implement projects compared with other kinds of agency. In contrast to many of the public and private service providers at the time, activities were typically completed efficiently – so that seeds, tools or fertilizer were distributed before planting, requests for credit were processed in a timely manner, and demonstrations to farmers of new techniques were effectively organized.

BOX 9.1 THE WORK OF PDI IN THE PHILIPPINES: COMBINING ADVOCACY AND SERVICE DELIVERY

The Project Development Institute (PDI) was founded in 1990 with a vision of building and strengthening local people's organizations (POs) in support of poverty-focused agrarian reform. The government of the Philippines has been committed in principle, since the late 1980s through the Department of Agrarian Reform, to redistribute agricultural land from rich to poor.[66] However, the process has so far been slow, its procedures top-down and little progress has been made, particularly in relation to indigenous people who are often the most marginalized section of the rural population. The Rural Empowerment through Agrarian/Asset Development (READ) programme has been developed to follow PDI's policy of securing 'genuine' land reform through combining provision of social and economic support services to farmers alongside active lobbying and negotiations with DAR and the government to maintain pressure to secure asset redistribution. At the forefront of this process are the POs of peasants and indigenous people, which PDI has helped to strengthen and build through provision of organizational and financial support services. For example, the institutionalization of regular negotiation meetings between public officials and POs has helped to reduce the gap between bureaucrats and farmers in the area. By the time of an independent evaluation undertaken in late 2003, the READ programme was found in two years to have established 59 POs in the Central Luzon area and PDI to have built a credible partnership with DAR in the implementation of agrarian reform. By October 2003, 2953 hectares of agricultural land had been successfully transferred to 985 low income peasant households, with another 2000 hectares soon to follow. Furthermore, PDI had also managed to build a stronger understanding amongst the POs of the Agrarian Reform law and of their rights under it.

Source: Evaluation of the READ programme, PDI, Manila, January 2004

How was this achieved? Evidence indicated that certain organizational characteristics made it possible for NGOs to achieve this and that these derived from their effective internal management systems as compared to other actors: relatively 'flat' (as opposed to hierarchical) organizational structures with smaller gaps between the office and the field than was typical in other types of agency; participatory modes of decision making which reflect the ideas of both managers and field staff; a strategy of 'organizational learning' which incorporated feedback from the field and distilled the lessons learned from success and failure to improve future performance; and finally, finding a distinct niche for an NGO's work that could allow it to develop a specialized role where it then build a comparative advantage.

There is also some evidence in the literature about the cost advantages of NGO service delivery. The example of Bharatiya Agro-Industries Foundation (BAIF) illustrates that NGOs can be more cost-effective than government in performing certain service delivery tasks. It is not often possible to make straight economic comparisons between NGOs and government, but BAIF's efforts to produce cross-bred dairy cattle in six states of India were in this case compared with a similar government programme in Tamil Nadu, and the overall costs of developing inputs came out as 66 per cent those of government, due probably to lower labour productivity in the government sector (Satish and Prem Kumar 1993). In today's development policy environment, a renewed emphasis on 'value for money' is once again highlighting the idea that NGOs may have advantages in cost-effectiveness, but it is also arguably putting pressure on organizations to work in areas or tasks where they can show relative low costs rather than those where good work cannot be done cheaply.

However, there have long been critics of what we might term 'the comparative advantage view' of development NGOs. First, it is often difficult to find rigorous evidence to support the idea, and the diversity of NGO forms seems to mitigate against making such generalizations. Second, Biggs and Neame (1995) suggested that it may often be the *relationships* between NGOs and other types of organizations that generate effectiveness rather than organizational characteristics within the NGOs themselves. For example, evidence from north east Brazil highlighted the importance of synergistic combinations of different actors including central government, local municipal authorities and civil society groups in improving healthcare services (Tendler 1997). Indeed, for every case of the effective NGO it is usually possible to point to many others with high administrative overheads, poor management systems and lower levels of effectiveness. Nor are such characteristics fixed: Seckinelgin (2005) has argued that while some HIV/AIDS NGOs have been drawn into donor-funded interventions in Africa based on their closeness to local communities, it is precisely this closeness that soon becomes lost once the organizations become institutionalized within international systems.

Despite the many positive stories about NGO service delivery, critics have also argued that it undermines the state, creates problems of citizen accountability, and may be unsustainable (Fowler 1997). When NGOs simply become 'public service contractors', they tend to be 'driven by market considerations more than values, lose their original value driven character, and are therefore more like businesses than voluntary organizations' (Korten 1990: 102). There are certainly many documented examples of NGO service provision being characterized by problems of quality control, limited sustainability, poor coordination and general amateurism (Robinson and White 1997). Therkildsen and Semboja (1995) painted a mixed picture of NGOs and service delivery as it emerged in East Africa during the decade of the new policy agenda. There may also be a tension between what Korten (1987: 6) calls 'the output vendor versus the development catalyst'. Trends in the aid industry towards budget support means that a greater proportion of donor funds than ever before go directly to governments that then fund NGOs in service delivery roles through local 'contracting' arrangements.

A key dilemma for NGOs is therefore the question of whether service delivery is a *means* (to provide people with services to meet immediate needs, but with an eye on influencing and improving wider delivery systems so that the NGO's role is essentially a temporary, transitional one) or an *end* in itself, in which NGOs as private providers become one set of actors among many who are contracted to deliver services. Carroll (1992: 42) argues that while many development NGOs can simply remain as efficient service providers, most usually also seek to do more, such as promoting participatory values or supporting democratic principles. As services are scaled up, these other activities may become squeezed out 'services that were intended as a means frequently become an end'.

Furthermore NGO service delivery is often carried out as part of a particular project, which by definition will have a finite end. The question becomes how services will then be made sustainable: through the imposition of user fees, community ownership and operation on a voluntary basis, or by government or the private sector taking over. As a result, Carroll (1992: 66) argues that the effectiveness of NGO service delivery should be judged on its developmental impact:

> while service delivery has a strong *intrinsic* value, it should really be evaluated on the basis of its *instrumental* value as a catalyst for other developmental changes.

Finally, the issue of citizen accountability provides a key dilemma. If government delivers services, there is at least in theory a system of redress available when things go wrong. The rights of citizens to challenge officials may be difficult to operationalize in practice, but they exist. In a private market system, service users can also, in theory, choose another provider, if there is one. But with NGO service delivery, there is little possibility of complaint or redress. For example, in Bangladesh, where NGOs funded by bilateral and multilateral donors are taking over key services from the state in health, education and agriculture, the concept of the increasingly privatized 'franchise state' was coined by Geoffrey Wood (1997) to illustrate this danger. Citizens may no longer be able to exert pressure on government for improving public services, but instead become dependent upon NGO intermediaries and the international donors that fund them. This is an increasing problem in both developed and developing societies where neoliberal NGO 'contracting' cultures have taken root.

In an extreme example of where dependence on NGO service delivery can lead, the case of Somalia is particularly tragic. At the time of writing, it was announced that Medecins Sans Frontieres (MSF) had decided to close its operations in Somalia, where its efforts have for 22 years constituted the main healthcare service for people across the country. The decision was taken based on the rise of violent attacks on its staff of more than 1500 people across the country, which the extremely fragile government has been increasingly powerless to prevent.[68]

Service delivery as empowerment and participation

Returning to our earlier discussion of the instrumental and expressive dimensions of management, another key question is exactly *how* services are delivered by an NGO. If an NGO implements service delivery in ways that are empowering, this may serve as a catalyst for other forms of longer-term change. This will depend not only on the approach taken, but also on the ways an organization develops its own staff. Many NGOs speak of building empowering and participatory management styles in which operating staff are seen as the starting point for action, as a source of skills and capacities, and are encouraged to take initiative in solving problems (Holcombe 1995).

The concept of empowerment has multiple origins: in Western counselling and social work theory (Solomon 1976), in Freire's (1972) radical educational work on 'conscientization', and in Gandhian ideas in India (Thomas 1992). Empowerment arose as a tool for understanding what is needed to change the situation of poor and marginalized people – a process which involves a process of personal development, moving from insight and understanding to action, individually and then collectively (Rowlands 1995). What is common to these ideas – which do not in practice really form a coherent ideology or set of practices – is an emphasis on process, with a movement through a series of developmental stages: becoming aware of the power dynamics in one's life, developing skills and capacity for greater control, exercising control without threatening other people's rights, and then going on to support the empowerment of others in the community.[69]

In order to understand empowerment, we need first to analyze the concept of *power*. Rowlands (1995) argues that it is useful to distinguish 'power over' (control or influence by some people over others, such as men over women, dominant caste over low caste) from 'power to' (a generative view of power in which people stimulate activity in others and raise morale). She argues that genuine empowerment implies gaining 'power to' in order to resist and challenge 'power over'. This process has three dimensions: personal, with the growth of greater self-confidence; relational, in the ability to renegotiate close ties and gain greater decision-making power; and collective, in building links to work together and cooperate with others locally or nationally.

The concept of empowerment became central to alternative development theory and practice. Friedmann (1992) identified three different kinds of power: *social* (access to information, knowledge and skills, participation in social organizations, financial resources); *political* (access by individual household members to decision-making processes singly or in groups, e.g. voting, collective action, etc.); and *psychological* (individual sense of power and self-confident behaviour, often from successful action in the above domains); each of which is necessary for building an alternative approach to development which focuses on more than simply material wellbeing (Friedmann 1992). An example of this is the progress made in local governance in Porto Alegre, Brazil. Participatory healthcare interventions in the city have been assisted by a greater recognition of the 'psychosocial' dimensions of poverty, such that locally marginalized people have gradually become empowered to better state their needs and ideas within a more open local public sphere (Guareschi and Jovchelovitch 2004).

Moser's (1989) discussion of empowerment and gender links empowerment with the concept of 'participation'. The act of bringing in people who are outside the decision-making process can lead to a focus not only on the formal institutions of political and economic power, but also on the dynamics of oppression in the personal sphere. The concept of participation became very widely used in development and, like 'empowerment', has both a development sense (the involvement of beneficiaries in development programmes) and a management sense (in which staff and partners are involved in decision-making processes). Within NGO service delivery strategies, the level of participation can influence both the quality of the service that is being provided and the likely outcome in terms of empowerment and sustainability.

The origin of the concept of 'participation' was in part a reaction to top-down statism during the 1960s and 1970s, when dissatisfaction among development personnel grew at government's inability to take responsibility for promoting social development (Midgley 1995: 60). This failure was due in part to the creation of large bureaucracies, the selection of wasteful projects and the involvement of corrupt politicians. In the prevalent top-down approaches of the time, projects did not involve people in the processes of their design and execution. A view emerged that 'development' could be better fostered through community participation in which

> ordinary people are mobilised to establish projects that serve their local communities and ... are actively involved in these projects.
>
> (p.60)

These ideas, at least in their more radical form, were also associated with activist writers such as Freire. However, as Cornwall and Brock (2005) have suggested, participation quickly became a broad catch-all term (what they usefully term a 'development buzzword') covering both mainstream ideas about involving people as well as more radical ideas about collective action, negotiation with the power structure and building self-reliance.

There have been many critics of the ways in which the concept of participation has been used. Rahnema (1992) argues that the realization in the 1960s that growth did not reach the poor led to a reassessment of top-down strategies, with an incorporation of ideas about participation as a means of merely involving people in activities that had already been initiated by the state or by development organizations. As a result, Rahnema argued that the idea of participation lost its threat and became a potentially contradictory concept that can sometimes be perversely used to actually rob people of their ability to act together in their own best interests. In this view, participation can be used to import into communities ideas that become attributed to those communities to secure the token involvement of people in order to display a level of participation to outside agencies, and as such it can be cynically used merely for the legitimization of outsiders' decisions.[70] A collection of critical papers by Kothari and Cooke (2001) echoed and extended this critical view by speaking of the 'tyranny' of participation in relation to the ways in which participatory development has become a technical approach that serves to downplay the role of power and politics.

Sarah White's (1995) conceptual framework for thinking about participation helps unpick the complexity. Participation initially arose as a form of protest, but became mainstreamed and lost its political meaning, which now needs to be recovered. There are two levels to the politics of participation. The first is 'who participates?', given that most communities are not homogenous; and the second is 'at what level?', since implementation is not enough and some power over decision making is also needed. White suggests four forms of participation. The first is *nominal*, such as when government-formed groups are created, but their main purpose is a tokenistic display. The second is *instrumental*, and this can be a way of providing labour under resource shortfalls created by structural adjustment, which then counts as a cost to local people. The third is *representative*, where, for example, a certain group within the community gains some leverage within a programme or project by gaining access to the planning committee and is able to express its own interests. The fourth and strongest form is *transformative*, in which people find ways to make decisions and take action, without outsider involvement and on their own terms. Only this final form is truly 'empowering' in a political sense. But top-down interests in participation are different from bottom-up interests, and participation is therefore a 'site of conflict' that might have positive or negative outcomes for the poor. Like empowerment, participation is also a process, and people may stop participating if they do not feel their interests can be met.

Can participation survive as a credible concept? Hickey and Mohan (2004: 5) suggest that it can, so long as a focus is maintained on the political rather than just the technical dimensions of participation:

> understanding the ways in which participation relates to existing power structures and political systems provides the basis for moving towards a more transformatory approach to development; one which is rooted in the exercise of a broadly-defined citizenship.

The link between participation and citizenship allows for the concept to be both broadened and focused, and connects participation more explicitly with the new emphasis on rights-based development in which development can be seen as seeking to increase people's agency, status and capacity to increase their control over social and economic resources.

Managing the dilemmas of service delivery

The wider environment in which NGOs work, as well as internal factors arising from the organization's own dynamics, may produce pressures towards what is termed 'goal deflection' in the organizational literature, when NGOs move away from their original objectives and concentrate on other, often less ambitious, goals. In particular, these isomorphic pressures on NGOs may diminish the creativity and diversity of the NGO sector as a source of ideas and alternatives (cf Mitlin *et al.* 2005). The classic example of this is the gradual homogenization of relatively diverse NGO sectors into ones that over time have narrowed to become predominantly concerned with service delivery, often focused on credit services.[71]

According to Korten, these pressures may be the result of becoming tired of surviving at the financial margins and struggling for funding, the frustrations for activists of long-term struggles against established interests, the sense of obligation which emerges over time to improve job security for staff, and finally the belief that service contracting can buy time, bring more funding, and therefore eventually opportunities to do other work. They may also come from external pressures from donors who want NGOs to comply with a wider policy towards building a privatized contract culture, or because they want NGOs to undertake work that allows them to show quick, measurable results rather than messier, less quantifiable activities such as empowerment or awareness raising about citizens' rights. Many NGOs are dependent on official international funding, and may become subject to the influence of wider neoliberal policies for redefining the nature of public and private responsibility in society, reallocating delivery of what were previously publicly funded services to market or non-market providers, and 'contracting out' services.

Pressure towards doing service delivery may also come from the local community level. For example, one NGO known to the author in Bangladesh reported that while it had originally been its policy to go into communities with a social mobilization approach rather than one based around the delivery of material resources, pressure from local people gradually persuaded the NGO to begin operating a credit programme because that was what they felt was needed. Of course, from another perspective, this could also be taken more positively as an example of an NGO responding in a participatory way to community needs.

In the light of these different perspectives on NGO service provision, Poole (1994) makes a 'pragmatic' case for NGOs to get involved in service delivery in contexts where services are in short supply, where the needs of the poor are not being met, and where privatization policies leave very little in the way of other options. But there is increasing acknowledgement that there are limits to NGO roles in service delivery. North (2003: 17) writes in relation to NGOs and poverty reduction efforts in rural Ecuador:

> It is states and global forces that set the parameters for development ... To be sure, NGOs can still play important roles. For example, NGO assistance was critical in the construction of infrastructure and the provision of services in two of the cantons ... but NGOs do not have the resources to finance such programs in all of Ecuador's poor rural municipalities. Only the Ecuadorian state can do that.

Instead, as Guijt (2008: 166) has argued, the challenge for NGOs 'lies in articulating clearly the interconnectedness between their service delivery function and that of more structural change-of-power relations, or the advocacy function'.

NGOs and advocacy: strategies for structural change

The second main activity for which NGOs are widely known is that of advocacy, as we saw in Chapter 6. For Lindenberg and Bryant (2001: 173)

> Advocacy work entails moving beyond implementing programs to help those in need, to actually taking up and defending the causes of others and speaking out to the public on another's behalf.

Advocacy calls for changes in policy that can address 'the root causes of problems' and 'not simply speaking out to alert people of a problem in order to raise funds to support operational work'. It can be distinguished from policy 'implementation', since it involves the articulation of a set of demands or positions in relation to policy, but not necessarily the enactment of such policies. However, advocacy cannot be separated from questions of implementation. From the point of view of NGO management, advocacy therefore brings us back to our conceptual framework in which activities, organization and relationships are set within a broader context.[72]

Writing from the context of the United States, Jenkins (1987) argues that many non-profits see themselves as having legitimacy to represent the non-commercial interests of the general public as opposed to the special economic interest groups within the rest of society, such as commercial businesses, or governmental elites, which left to themselves, might work against the public interest. Advocacy therefore also brings us back to the liberal conception of 'civil society' in which organized groups of citizens challenge and check the excesses of state and market. It also links with wider questions of social change, such as the role of social movements. Some NGOs can be seen as organizational components of social movements that are seeking to connect with institutionalized systems of decision making (McCarthy and Zald 1977; Dechalert 1999). NGOs may become advocates of issues that have yet to generate social movements in a particular context, such as child rights or consumer rights, by acting as the 'advance guard' for sentiments on behalf of a certain part of the population. There are also some interesting examples of NGO/social movement hybrids such as the IBON Foundation in the Philippines (Box 9.2).

Michael Edwards (1993: 3) has suggested that international NGO advocacy is a distinctive and complex activity, with ambitious aims and objectives. The rise of tax fairness as an advocacy issue in development (Box 9.3) serves to illustrate this point. Objectives are tied in with INGOs' two-fold efforts to build partnerships in the countries where they work, and to change the 'rules of the game' in their own countries:

> [advocacy] …. is an attempt to alter the ways in which power, resources and ideas are created, consumed and distributed at global level, so that people and their organizations in the South have a more realistic chance of controlling their own development.

Such action may have two forms: first, influencing global processes such as world trade, or bringing about lifestyle changes among their own supporters and constituents; and second, influencing specific policies or projects. The former may be relatively public and confrontational – and therefore quite difficult to achieve – while the latter is less so and may be based on dialogue and information provision. Both

---

BOX 9.2 IBON FOUNDATION AS A HYBRID NGO/SOCIAL MOVEMENT ORGANIZATION IN THE PHILIPPINES

During the years of the Marcos dictatorship, people in activist organizations, radical church groups and people's movements came together to establish an NGO in 1978 as an autonomous research and information collection initiative. It became an important actor in local, national and international information and activist networks around key social political and economic issues. It has managed to build and maintain a reputation for engaged and rigorous work, along with a commitment to a set of values that means its work is always driven by people's needs, and has maintained strong ties with popular grass-roots movements such as the Kilusang Magbubukid ng Pilipinas (KMP) peasant movement and the Kilusang Mayo Uno (KMU) trade union centre. Their 'hybrid' form makes it possible to access funding from foundations and other donors. Since democracy was restored in 1986 in the country IBON has also worked as a capacity development organization around knowledge building in the education sector. It has created the IBON Partnership in Education for Development (IPED) to meet the demand in the formal education sector for new ideas to help revitalize the curriculum, with more than 200 partner schools currently subscribing its education materials service. IBON is accredited as a service provider with the Professional Regulatory Commission (OECD 2009). IBON has evolved in interesting ways while always maintaining a radical edge.

Sources: Africa 2013; OECD 2011; author interview notes

---

of these activities are complementary, according to Edwards, but he suggests that many NGOs have failed to realize this and have been unable to build on available opportunities to combine local, national and international work.

Advocacy and the policy process

The advocacy role also requires an NGO to form an understanding of the policy process. Building on the original insights of Harold Laswell during the 1950s, who argued that policy development could be best understood as a sequence of steps in a process of decision-making, it has become common to conceive of the policy process in terms of a 'stage model' or cycle that leads from 'agenda setting' to 'policy formulation', 'decision making' and 'implementation', to be completed by a final stage of 'policy evaluation' and reconceptualization in the light of experiences (Howlett and Giest 2013). However, other social scientists question this linear rational model of policy making, arguing that it is a far more complex political and social phenomenon that needs to be understood in different ways and at different levels. For example, Charles Lindblom (1959) wrote of the importance of incrementalism in policy making, which he famously labelled 'the science of muddling

---

BOX 9.3 NGO ADVOCACY ON FAIRER TAXATION

As part of the lobbying effort to influence the post-2015 MDG agenda, and its ongoing research, Action Aid has been attempting to get the issue of reforming the rules that make tax avoidance and evasion possible. In a recent briefing paper, 'Bringing taxation info the post-2015 development framework', the NGO has argued that the strengthening of tax collection capacities and the reform of international rules remain pressing and key issues for securing progress on development and social justice. Action Aid's Clare Coffey is quoted as saying:

We have seen from our work in Africa and South Asia how international tax rules support tax avoidance, and what that can mean in terms of lost revenues and thus lost public services. Our recent investigation in Zambia found that just one subsidiary of the British multinational Associated British Foods has avoided enough tax via tax havens to pay for 48,000 children to go to school each year.

Action Aid is now arguing for international tax agreements to provide a stronger safeguard for the rights of developing countries to collect taxes, to reduce unhelpful tax competition between countries, and illuminate tax operations of multinational companies, including their use of tax havens. The campaign is focused on the idea that it should be possible for developing countries to raise tax revenues to 25% of GDP by 2030, and to reduce the corporate tax gap by 20%.

Source: http://www.actionaid.org.uk/news-and-views/actionaid-calls-for-post-2015-development-panel-to-address-domestic-taxation
(accessed 5 August 2013)

---

through'. In this view, policy makers tended not to devise and implement grand plans, but compromised and 'made do' with whatever options were expedient and to hand.

Anthropological accounts have also sought to challenge tendencies among both researchers and policy analysts to insist on rational linear models of the policy process despite the evidence that exists to the contrary. For example, David Mosse's (2005) work challenged the rational linear model by finding in his research that rather than determining a set of practices, policy did many other things, such as legitimizing practice, securing political support, and maintaining stability in the ways interventions are represented. In this view, policy does not simply drive practice. Yet although the linear model is 'patently far removed from real life', as McGee (2004: 7) points out, 'it is surprisingly alive and well in policy, development and political circles and even in policy actors' own accounts of what kinds of process they themselves are involved in'. Instead it makes more sense to recognize 'the complexity, ambiguity, and messiness of policy processes' (Wedel *et al.* 2005: 44).[73]

When considering how NGO manage advocacy work, Adil Najam (1999) identified three stages of the 'policy process', which he sees as the process of conceiving,

BOX 9.4 NGOs, RESEARCH AND GRASSROOTS CAMPAIGNING

India's Centre for Budget and Governance Accountability (CBGA) is a non-partisan, non-profit research and advocacy organization based in New Delhi. It promotes transparent, accountable and participatory governance, and a people-centred perspective in fiscal policies (www.cbgaindia.org).

CBGA conducted a study to assess the constraints affecting fund utilization in government social sector programmes. The study attempted to understand better the underlying reasons why state governments were unable to spend fully, leading to lower allocations in subsequent years as the government blamed state level authorities for poor fund utilization. The study flagged three key concerns: first, the absence of effective decentralized planning meant that there was no link between communities and planning processes. Second, critical bottlenecks in budgetary processes and institutional arrangements meant that a large share of spending came in the final two quarters of the fiscal year, and was focused on easy to disburse outputs at the expense of much-needed investment in quality of service (training, information, communication). Third, neglecting provisioning for non-negotiable, fundamental requirements of infrastructure and human resources meant that most of what was being spent was ad hoc and failed to bolster weak infrastructure. The result was that those states already possessing capacity constraints and poor infrastructure are unable to spend, making it likely that they receive fewer funds next time round. States with better governance of services receive more. The study brought the spotlight back onto the Union government and argued for greater devolution of financial powers, increased spending and more flexibility to factor in state-specific concerns.

The findings are now being applied by the People's Budget Initiative (PBI), a coalition of over 400 organizations with the aim of promoting people's voices in the policy making processes that determine priorities in government budgets in India. CBGA forms the Secretariat for PBI, providing CBGA with a strong grassroots link. Eleven civil society organizations across various states are now adopting a similar framework to track fund flows and spending in critical development schemes up to the district level. They are working towards developing a a methodology that will enable organizations at the grassroots to track funds and utilization patterns to be able to demand for improved budgetary processes.

Source: Pooja Rangaprasad (see CGBA/UNICEF India 'Budgeting for Change Series', 2011, http://cbgaindia.org/publications_working_papers.php

designing and implementing public action: *agenda setting* (the agreement of priorities and issues), *policy development* (making choices among possible alternatives and options) and *policy implementation* (undertaking actions to translate policies into practice). Najam usefully suggested a model with four potential NGO roles within the 'policy stream': *service providers* (acting directly to do what needs to be done);

advocates (prodding government to do the right thing); *innovators* (suggesting and showing how things could be done differently); and finally *monitors* (trying to ensure that government and business do what they are supposed to be doing). He characterizes NGOs as 'policy entrepreneurs' balancing and combining elements of some or all of these roles in the pursuit of social change.

Advocacy organizations may involve the use of routine political channels, or they may adopt more confrontational direct actions such as marches or demonstrations. Bratton (1990: 95–6) argued that NGOs seeking to gain a 'voice' on behalf of the poor in policy making through non-confrontational means tends to be a more useful strategy for African NGOs than mobilizing people against the power structure (which may be too confrontational) because it allows the NGO leaders

> to identify openings in the administrative system and to cultivate non-adversarial working relationships with the politically powerful.

Bratton's model gives NGOs the task of articulating many of the under-represented demands and needs of the poor to policy makers more effectively. In this way, the policy environment can be 'influenced' even if it cannot be 'controlled' (de Graaf 1987). But in order to be successful at advocacy in achieving policy impact, NGOs need both technical and managerial competence on the one hand, and political clout (i.e. a political constituency that can be mobilized) on the other (Bratton 1990: 93). The experience of PDI in the Philippines within the agrarian reform process (Box 9.1 above) shows the way in which an NGO can make progress if it is able to combine service delivery and community organizing with an advocacy strategy that is based on carefully negotiated and managed partnerships with both government and local organizations.

Managing relationships between advocacy and service delivery activities

Although many NGOs specialize in either service delivery or advocacy, the two roles are not mutually exclusive in practice and may be often combined within one NGO. For example, Kanji *et al.* (2002: 32) found in a study of NGO advocacy work in Kenya and Mozambique over land issues that 'service delivery is often important, not only in itself, but as a way of gaining legitimacy and as an entry point for advocacy'.

This makes the question of managing different tasks in combination a crucial one for NGOs, a point that lay at the heart of Alan Fowler's (1997) overview of NGO management issues as 'striking a balance'. The strategy of providing services to a section of the community that is otherwise excluded from government service provision, for example, while simultaneously exerting pressure at the policy level for improvements in provision in the longer term, is one such balanced strategy. Another type of strategy is entering into a formal contract with government to provide a specific service for an agreed length of time in order to build trust between NGO and government, and create opportunities for influence. On the other hand, there are some NGOs that find that the balance is not sustainable, and that entering into a contract with government simply robs them of their spirit and their independence.

Service delivery and advocacy activities may be mutually reinforcing in terms of effectiveness and impact. In their study of twelve high-impact non-profits, Grant and Crutchfield (2007: 35) found that

> High-impact organizations may start out providing great programs, but they eventually realize that they cannot achieve large-scale social change through service delivery alone. So they add policy advocacy to acquire government resources and to change legislation. Other non-profits start out by doing advocacy and later add grassroots programs to supercharge their strategy. Ultimately, all high-impact organizations bridge the divide between service and advocacy. They become good at both. And the more they serve and advocate, the more they achieve impact. A nonprofit's grassroots work helps inform its policy advocacy, making legislation more relevant. And advocacy at the national level can help a nonprofit replicate its model, gain credibility, and acquire funding for expansion.

The organization of advocacy

The organizational implications of NGO advocacy work remain relatively unexplored. Young (1992) examined the activities of international NGOs based in the United States. The study suggests that an increase at the international level in advocacy as opposed to service delivery has been facilitated by, first, the growth in perceptions of the global nature of problems such as pollution, disease and poverty, which therefore require cooperation across national boundaries; and second, the emergence of improved communications and transportation technology.[74] Organizations are increasingly opting for decentralized and federated structures as those most suitable for international advocacy work.

Young discussed three international NGO case studies: Nature Conservancy, International Physicians for the Prevention of Nuclear War and the Institute of Cultural Affairs. All have their roots in the US but work internationally, and each has formed a loose 'federal structure' with networks of relatively autonomous units (analogous to a 'multi-headed hydra') rather than a formal, monolithic hierarchy. This helps balance coherence and unity, and maintains local autonomy and diversity. Each NGO was found to depend heavily on a 'charismatic leader' at the early stages of its formation, but to be moving towards the replication of dynamic and visionary leadership at the local level in order to carry on the work. The organizations relied on a set of common values and beliefs about conservation, development and peace as the 'glue' which binds the organization together, and an organizational culture which values collegiality rather than material reward as the main incentive for staff performance. The levels of internal democracy in these organizations in terms of membership was found to be not particularly high, with quite low levels of participation and a certain amount of 'free-riding'. Instead, the NGOs tend to have 'privileged member' groups upon whom they relied for a disproportionate amount of the support and work.

Michael Edwards (1993) has long been critical of international NGOs' 'patchy' record of achieving influence with power holders and in educating their publics. Many of the results have been disappointing due to the absence of clear strategy, a general failure to build on strong alliances, an inability to develop suitable alternatives to current orthodoxy, and the problem of 'room for manoeuvre' created by the relations with official donors which exist for many international NGOs. A tendency was noted by Andy Norrell (1999) for some UK NGOs to drift from service delivery into advocacy work, bringing a range of organizational tensions and problems, including tensions between operational and policy staff, and an inadequate appreciation of resource allocation issues for undertaking advocacy work. Nevertheless, John Clark (1992) points out that international NGOs have found some success with efforts to establish a baby milk marketing code, drafting a list of essential drugs and removing restrictions on trade for some items in favour of poor producers in developing countries.[75]

The Jubilee 2000 campaign arguably tells a brighter story, since this multi-sectoral alliance of church groups, NGOs, trade unions and other civil society groups has succeeded in generating considerable awareness among policy makers and publics about the problem of Third World debt, but ultimately failed to generate more than a small impact on the overall scale of the problem, which remains vast. Nevertheless, it created momentum built upon by the Make Poverty History Campaign that secured further commitments to debt reduction. Edwards (1999b) later became more optimistic about international NGO advocacy work around the success of campaigns dealing with subjects such as 'sex tourism' and landmines in recent years because, unlike subjects such as environmentalism and women's rights, it has become possible to present these subjects powerfully both to the public and to policy makers and link them to practical solutions.

More recently, new approaches to catalyzing change have been gaining attention. For example, there has been a steady rise of interest in the idea of multi-stakeholder, inter-organizational change networks that Waddell (2011) has termed global action networks (GANs). This concept does not just refer to NGOs and community organizations, but to links with government and business as well. He gives the example of the Climate Group as an example, which bridges traditional boundaries between government, business and NGOs not through lobbying or policy influencing but by creating experimental projects on the ground using LED technology to improve street lighting, with the participation of all three sectors. These new configurations are portrayed as innovative and pioneering, and as attempting to build new synergies that go beyond existing forms of practice such as 'the advocacy traditions of NGOs that focus on telling others what to do' (p.xiv).

Innovation and NGO management

An ability to innovate is often claimed as a special quality, or even as an area of comparative advantage, that is held by NGOs over other kinds of organization, especially government agencies. Innovation is central to claims that NGOs can provide alternative approaches to development (Mitlin *et al.* 2005). While there are some NGOs that do not see innovation as part of their activities, many do claim to offer innovative solutions to problems, and it is common for donor agencies to emphasize innovation as a key criterion for receiving funding. There is certainly some evidence to support the claim that some NGOs have been able to develop alternative ideas and approaches. For example, innovation may include the development of new technologies (such as the SALT technology in the Philippines referred to earlier), creating new management practices (such as the Grameen Bank's credit and savings model with its tightly structured village-based group system), or devising new consultation and approaches to learning (such as participatory approaches and tools) (Box 9.5).

BOX 9.5 AN NGO INNOVATES A POST-HARVEST PROCESSING SYSTEM FOR SMALL-SCALE INDIAN HILL FARMERS

One form of innovation undertaken by an NGO working in India has involved combining research and intervention in ways that seek to combine continuous organizational learning with a recognition of institutional change in order to build improved sustainability. International Development Enterprises (IDE) was established as an NGO in the late 1970s with an interest in appropriate technology. However, what made it different was that it remains dedicated not just to developing appropriate technology but also combining it with a business approach that would ensure users were able to adopt it sustainably within viable livelihood systems. Farmers in the North Indian state of Himachal Pradesh were searching for ways to market their tomato crop in high value urban markets and identified post-harvest packaging as a key constraint. IDE was able to play a flexible role in researching potentially useful alternative packaging forms both internationally and locally though its partners and contacts, a trail that led to both public research institutes, a local NGO and private companies. A successful project was able to replace inappropriate wooden boxes with a locally produced cardboard packaging system in a way that has provided a sustainable low-cost solution to farmers' business problem. IDE played 'a role that fall somewhere between the conventional mandate of public and private sectors, creating the initial conditions needed for the market to take over and provide services to rural households' (p.1856). IDE's approach is therefore to try to support the emergence of new 'innovation systems' through a process of trust building and exchange within the wider system in which farmers and NGOs operate. IDE seeks to bring to the table skills in critical reflection and learning, facilitation and trust-building, as well as team-building and relationship-creating capacities.

Source: Clark *et al.* (2003)

How are some NGOs able to manage an innovative approach? Clark (1991: 59) argued that they may be less constrained by orthodox ideas and structures than are mainstream aid agencies and governments. He found evidence that their staff had considerable flexibility to experiment, adapt and try out new approaches to problem solving. There are several reasons for this in Clark's view: they may be smaller in scale, with fewer staff and formal structures, which can mean that decision making is a relatively straightforward process; local officials will not be very involved, which can reduce the level of administrative red tape; the level of outside scrutiny and regulation may be very low; and an ethos of 'voluntarism' may encourage individuals to develop their own ideas, experiment and take risks. In the 'reluctant partner' research project collected among agricultural NGOs in South Asia, it became apparent that NGO innovations are rooted in a problem- or issue-oriented approach to agricultural change: responding to opportunities and constraints identified by the rural poor (Farrington and Lewis 1993). The case study in Box 9.5 below highlights the continuing role of NGOs in supporting innovation systems that can address local development challenges in poor communities.

There is comparatively little conceptual research on the issue of NGO innovation.[76] For some leads on this it is therefore necessary to turn to the business and non-profit literatures. In the business literature, Amendola and Bruno (1990: 419) have argued that innovation is 'a learning process which concerns both the firm and its environment and that results in deep changes for both of them'. In the non-profit literature, the British writer Perri 6 (1993: 6) has defined innovation as 'the introduction of changes in the production of goods and services' and presented a useful framework that distinguishes invention, innovation and diffusion as distinct parts of the innovation process.

Drawing on the US literature on non-profits, Kanter and Summers' (1987: 161–2) classic paper explored innovation in organizational terms:

> Innovation is a crucial element of an organization's effectiveness because it addresses the organization's potential to meet future demands, to take advantage of opportunities and resources within the environment, and to use resources (both human and material) to generate new products and services.

The authors present a case study of a US non-profit healthcare service organization, and show that innovation within an organization can be measured by conducting an audit of the organization's capacity to develop and implement new policies, new services, new organizational structures and new working methods. They also suggest a number of organizational factors which are likely to either encourage or constrain innovation, such as support of middle managers by senior managers and the existence of appropriate rewards and incentives for experimentation and risk taking; collaborative mechanisms which can facilitate exchange and learning with other organizations; support from experts and other contacts outside the organization; and systems which can facilitate participation from beneficiaries and the wider community. They also identified factors that tend to discourage innovation, such as active or passive resistance from colleagues, powerlessness in the form of an inability to command the necessary resources or technical information, and lack of reward for experimentation.

This has led to a strong emphasis on innovation as a management challenge and to a set of high expectations about what NGOs can achieve. Hudson (1995: 238), in his introduction to management in the UK voluntary sector, sees the encouragement of innovation as a key task for managers, going almost far enough to suggest that successful innovation is the key to third sector survival:

> Chief executives have to encourage innovation: they have to ensure that the organization is constantly moving forward and finding ways to campaign and deliver services that meet new circumstances. It means searching for new ideas, sometimes from other countries, sometimes from local branches and sometimes from organizations in other fields. It means putting staff time and money into new ideas and acknowledging that while many will fail, a few will become the engine for the organization's future development.

A key indicator of successful innovation is whether ideas and practices are taken up elsewhere, spread or replicated (Chambers 1992: 46). For example, PRA has been adapted and further developed by NGOs such as MYRADA in India by inviting people from government and other NGOs to participate in field training meetings. Good ideas and experiences, says Chambers, tend to travel very fast, such as the idea of using farmers as informal agricultural extension agents that was pioneered by the US NGO World Neighbours (Bunch 1985). As Chambers (1992: 46) has argued, this approach has been adopted very widely across the world by a variety of agencies:

> This points to methodological innovation and the sharing of innovations as NGO activities which can have a very wide impact indeed. An NGO which develops an approach and method which then spreads can count that spread among the benefits from its work. A small NGO can, in such a manner, have a good impact vastly out of proportion to its size, especially if it shares open-handedly and builds in self-improvement. Indeed where small NGOs have successful innovations, they should consider their strategies to stress dissemination.

However, there is increasing recognition of the idea that development NGOs need to do more than just focus on generating new ideas. Mitlin *et al.* (2005) argue that there is a need for NGOs to focus more strongly on building relationships with other progressive actors, such as political parties and social movements in order to maintain pressure for alternative outcomes in the face of an increasingly orthodox policy environment.[77] For example, in the Philippines, the IBON Foundation is a research organization with its origins in social movements and radical church groups and it today provides services in the form of research and education materials for use in campaigning by people's movements locally, regionally and internationally. It has links in the Philippines with a range of civil society groups including the national democratic left, peasant movements and trade unions (Africa, 2013). The relationships that NGOs need to build and manage are discussed in more detail in Chapter 10.

The concept of innovation is of course drawn from the private sector. During the past decade, the private sector has come to play a higher role in development work than previously, and innovation has become central to the work of the Bill and Melinda Gates Foundation, as well as social businesses working on technological development solutions such as one laptop per child, white LED lighting, and solar powered energy equipment. In many sectors today, NGOs increasingly face competition from the private sector in the form of 'social entrepreneurs and tech firms that are pushing the envelope with innovative ways to assist communities even in the remotest corners of the globe' (Cooper 2012).

The idealism of the 'NGOs as innovators' approach has inevitably generated scepticism in some quarters. As Clark (1991: 59) points out, the claimed special strengths of NGOs in innovation capacity, such as voluntaristic style and small scale, is really doubled-edged, because the same points can be used to make the case for NGO amateurism, since it

> fosters idiosyncrasy, lack of continuity and poor learning abilities. It should also be said that many NGOs are far from innovative, but prefer to apply well-tested approaches to new constituencies.

Some analysts have argued that far from being inherent, NGO innovativeness may derive instead from an organization's relationships with other agencies and with professionals working in other institutions (Kaimowitz 1993). It is clear therefore that innovation is not a prerequisite for success, and nor can it be regarded in any general sense as an innate characteristic of all NGOs. Policy pressures on NGOs to come up with novel solutions to complex problems may lead to unrealistic expectations and the 'magic bullet syndrome' (Vivian 1994). Problems of poverty and development are not new problems and many individuals and agencies have long struggled with them. As Biggs and Neame (1995) also suggest, it is often the collaborative process that drives the appearance of innovation, rather than any inherent capability of NGOs themselves. Waddell's (2011) work on global action networks (GANs) seems to recognize the limitations of NGOs and other traditional organizational forms to argue that genuine innovation is more likely to arise when individuals step out of these contexts into potentially creative new form of inter-organizational configurations and relationships.

Innovation has become a major policy 'buzzword' in relation to the wider third sector and social enterprise worlds (Cornwall and Brock 2006). Others increasingly play down the idea of innovation. A constant focus on innovation, particularly on the part of funders seeking a quick fix, may unhelpfully draw resources away from important everyday challenges involving tried and tested approaches (Lewis 2012). For example, Seelos and Mair (2012: 49) concluded that innovation has become overrated. It may be unhelpfully viewed as a shortcut to success and it may sideline other more valuable core routine activities. Furthermore, there are important issues of culture and power to be considered. In the world of development, many innovations are drawn from 'recipes developed in the Western world and involving ... technical support from consultants ... who have limited understanding of local contexts'. They suggest that innovations often fail when transferred to other, riskier environments, while at the same time the potentially valuable lessons that might accrue from 'failed' innovations often remains undervalued. In short, they argue that the difficulties of undertaking successful innovation are rarely appreciated fully:

> unless leaders engage in an honest and critical diagnosis and evaluation of negative organizational factors and innovation hurdles, the well-meaning recommendations provided by the innovation literature may not have much impact.

Evaluation

Despite the increased profile of the NGO sector and the growing resources it consumes and generates, the overall NGO contribution to reducing global poverty through service delivery and advocacy remains small and largely unproven. In this section, we move on to discuss the ways in which NGOs have attempted to assess progress and improve effectiveness. They have used techniques for performance monitoring and evaluation, and they have attempted to increase impact through strategies for 'scaling up' successful work (Edwards and Hulme 1992).

There is a long history of approaches which have sought to measure the effectiveness of development projects, from the mainstream planning tool of traditional cost-benefit analysis long used by the public and private sectors to the more recently fashionable 'stakeholder analysis' approach developed by some development institutions (Gosling and Edwards 1995; Eade and Williams 1995).[78] Yet there are arguably two quite surprising features of the NGO evaluation scene that become apparent from a reading of the literature. The first is the relative lack of attention which has been paid among NGOs in general, until quite recently, to the importance of evaluation as a tool for improving performance through learning and as a means of ensuring accountability. Instead, evaluation is frequently viewed as something that has been imposed upon NGOs by a funder or a government agency and therefore undertaken with reluctance or even resisted. As Smillie (1995) points out, many NGOs have been reluctant to undertake evaluations because they lack the necessary tools or time, because they are not secure enough to face up to negative outcomes, or because evaluations are imposed by donors. The result has been a frequent 'failure to learn from failure' among the NGO community.

The second is the fact that when NGOs have either undertaken or been subjected to evaluations, the information about their performance which has emerged has often been rather less flattering to the NGOs than many would assume from current received wisdom and public perceptions. Nor has NGO evaluation been studied much as a subject of research.[79] Lindenberg and Bryant (2001: 237) in an analysis of twelve prominent international NGOs' engagement with organizational transformation remark: 'it was striking to see how little is actually known about monitoring and evaluation systems in NGOs'.

What is meant by evaluation? Evaluation is the term usually given to describe the process of assessing performance against objectives, and it can be contrasted with the activities of monitoring, which usually refers to the regular collection and analysis of data about the organization's ongoing activities and the process of appraisal, which is the assessment of a proposed project or programme. As Riddell and Robinson (1995: 44) point out:

> At their best, evaluation techniques should be able to assess performance results against objectives, and benefits against costs, and in so doing identify strengths and weaknesses in a way which can have a positive impact on the effectiveness of projects and programmes.

Pressure for improved evaluation comes from internal and external sources. As bilateral and multilateral donors have increasingly funded development NGOs since the 1980s (Fowler 1997), there have been more stringent contractual demands placed upon NGOs for financial accountability and for the realization of agreed impacts. There is also a set of pressures that comes from inside the NGO. Riddell and Robinson (1995) argue that evaluation is in the interests of NGOs because practical lessons can be fed back into decision making in order to improve future performance, and because by showing that funds are well spent, support can be strengthened and funding can be made more secure. Evaluation is the key to the 'learning organization' approach favoured by Korten (1990) and other writers on organizations.

Evaluations can operate at three different levels, as Marsden and Oakley (1990: 12–13) have outlined. The first is at the level of the donor agency (a NNGO or a funding agency), which is usually an 'external evaluation' in which evaluators are not themselves involved in the project implementation. The second is undertaken by the implementing rather than the funding agency (such as an SNGO) and this may take the form of a 'joint evaluation' involving both external evaluators and project staff. The third is the idea of the 'self-evaluation' which is undertaken by the so-called 'beneficiaries' themselves, usually with the participation of project staff, and perhaps drawing upon the services of an outside facilitator (Sen 1987). Evaluating the impact of service delivery can be relatively straightforward if data is collected on goods and services received, and on the numbers and types of people who are able to access and use them satisfactorily.

Assessing the impact of advocacy may be more difficult. Work towards developing a new approach to assessing the impact of advocacy work was explored by Lewis and Madon (2003), drawing on case study material from an NGO in Bangladesh that has long been involved in advocacy work. A framework was generated during discussions with NGO staff and other stakeholders through which different levels of impact from advocacy work could be assessed according to a set of criteria

(Table 9.1). Four types of impact were identified in this study: (i) the immediate outcome in terms of whether the overall aim of the campaign was met; (ii) whether there were deeper rooted changes in the process of policy making over the longer term (such as a commitment to consult more broadly) or whether the result achieved was merely 'one off' in nature; (iii) the results in terms of an NGO's own learning about approaching its future advocacy work; and (iv) whether wider relationships for future action amongst civil society actors has been strengthened, regardless of whether the campaign had been a success in terms of meeting its immediate goals.

According to Riddell and Robinson (1995: 50) judging NGO performance has always been more of an art than an exact science. The main reasons for this are, first, the difficulty of measuring 'social development' as opposed to economic development in that qualitative achievements cannot be evaluated objectively (Marsden and Oakley 1990; Harding 1991); second, the difficulty of building into evaluations the idea of 'process', because there is no 'correct' time at which assessment should be made (during the project, five years after?); and third, the attribution problem created by the fact that the changing wider social and economic context in which NGO activities take place can make it difficult to make an objective judgement about whether the NGO or some other factor has brought about an observed

TABLE 9.1 A framework for assessing NGO campaign impacts

Activity	Immediate policy outcomes	Process policy outcomes	Organizational learning outcomes	Civil society outcomes
Campaign to remove dangerous illegally imported pesticides from the market	High	Low	Medium	High
Campaign to introduce wider consultation into national budgetary planning	Medium	Medium	High	High
Campaign to change forestry policy in favour of the rights of minority forest dwellers	High	High	Medium	Medium
Participation within a donor employment and business support project to try to shift the project towards a stronger poverty focus	Low	Low	High	Low
Participation within a civil society initiative to examine the poverty impact of World Bank structural adjustment policy and thereby influence the Bank	High	Medium	Medium	Medium

Source: Lewis and Madon (2003)

change. Fowler (1997) therefore suggests a way forward by assessing NGO performance as 'combined social judgement' in which the uniting principle can be the structural engagement of multiple 'stakeholders'. Evaluation should therefore be seen as part of the NGO learning process, not as an externally imposed burden and as part of a continuous process, not as an isolated event (Marsden and Oakley 1990).

Two main trends in NGO evaluation tend to dominate. The first is the managerialist approach. Here, the use of a logic model tool such as the log frame (see Box 3.1) offers the means to measure progress by charting indicators against the objectives agreed before the beginning of the project or programme. In this perspective, evaluation is seen primarily as a means of control to ensure accountability for the responsible management of donor funds, and to confirm that the agreed activities have actually been undertaken. Donors or government may undertake such evaluations as part of a funding relationship or contract. Other tools that may be deployed within such evaluations include cost-benefit analysis, staff and beneficiary interviews, and financial audit. The overall purpose may be the need to confirm that funds have been used properly, or to make a decision as to whether funding should be renewed for another period. This perspective on evaluation seeks to form an objective view of events that have taken place, and tends to assume that given the 'right' approach to gathering information a relatively clear picture can emerge.

The second is more of a bundle of approaches, inspired by the participatory learning and action (PLA) movement (Chambers 1994) (Box 9.6), by open systems approaches to performance measurement that recognize that it is a 'contested terrain', (Ebrahim and Rangan 2010: 20), and by the Romantic tradition of management philosophy (Gulrajani, 2010). Working within a more interpretive view of organizations, these approaches tends to see evaluation findings less as objective facts than as a combined judgement that reflects the different perspectives of the different stakeholders involved. They also work with a relatively long-term process view, instead of aiming for a 'snapshot' view of a particular moment. The 'appreciative enquiry' approach, for example, seeks to create positive conversations around building on the best of 'what is' to imagine the best of 'what can be', and argues that an overly strict emphasis on a problem-solving approach to management limits the imagination and creativity of managers (Cooprider and Srivastva (1987; Postma 1998).

Participatory approaches became popular in recent years, but have become increasingly squeezed out by the 'results' agenda that has come to dominate the world of official funders (see Chapter 5). At the same time, participatory evaluation lends itself to criticism in two main areas: it can easily be co-opted into the top-down paradigm, and it can all too often mask differences of power, class and status.

Recent work by Ebrahim and Rangan (2010) offers what they term a contingency approach to performance measurement that draws on a wide range of different approaches and ideas across different traditions of evaluation, including open systems theory, organizational ecology and theories of change. Recognizing that organizations need to use both simple linear theories of change and more complex multi-causal ones, they suggest a contingency framework for measuring results in

---

BOX 9.6 THE RISE OF PARTICIPATORY MONITORING AND EVALUATION (PM&E)

The importance of taking local people's perspectives into account, the rise of organizational learning and the pressures for greater accountability have all contributed to the rise of PM&E as a means to improve the effectiveness of development intervention. Advocates of this approach suggest a radical rethinking of conventional monitoring and evaluation work based on four broad principles: (i) opening up design and implementation to those affected (participation); (ii) discussions with all stakeholders about data collection and analysis (negotiation); (iii) using the evaluation as the basis for improvement and course correction (learning); and (iv) responding to changes in the overall group of stakeholders and the environment (flexibility).

An extensive toolbox exists for doing this, ranging from the use of conventional questionnaires and mapping techniques, to the more open-ended and experimental collection of personal histories and the use of video for the presentation and discussion of ideas and viewpoints. Indicators for identifying and monitoring change are essential to PM&E, and this is a complex task that needs to balance local relevance with wider comparability, the involvement of stakeholders with the time available, and tangible with intangible changes (e.g. increased income as well as increased self-esteem). There are many problems that can arise, such as the different interests between stakeholders that lead to conflict, and the struggle that managers and community members may face in seeking to be open to different points of view. In this approach, it is often necessary to work with informal forms of data collection and imperfect information, based on the idea that information only needs to be 'good enough' for the task at hand. In some situations, PM&E can be used alongside more conventional forms of M&E in order to supplement it.

Source: Guijt and Gaventa (1998)

---

which there are four broad types of result. Institutional results refer to complex changes at the societal level that might include policies and rights and require measurement of outputs and influence, while niche results refer to simple causal results such as delivering basic emergency services in which inputs, activities and outputs can all be measured. Ecosystem results refer to results in the wider field of actors and processes, such as collaborative development, in which outcomes and impacts can be measured. Finally, integrated results refer to more complicated forms of service delivery in health or education in which aggregate outputs, outcomes and sometimes impacts can be measured. The authors conclude that 'it is unlikely that managers will find singular or unambiguous measures of performance' (p.41) and must combine tools and approaches, and balance organizational goals with the wider environment in which they work.

Scaling up

In keeping with the traditions of alternative development paradigms such as that popularized by Ernst Friedrich Schumacher (1973), some NGOs have been content to take a 'small is beautiful' view in their work. Yet the small scale of NGO programmes may generate criticism of low level impact. Thomas (1992) discusses the case of the Association of Sarva Seva Farms (ASSEFA), a Gandhian NGO in India that develops land given to landless low-caste households through the Gandhian *bhoodan* 'land gift' movement. It aims to build more self-reliant communities through provision of credit and supply of agricultural, industrial and health services alongside organization building and awareness raising. Yet at present rates of activity it will take the NGO several hundred years to develop the 1.3 million acres of *bhoodan* land that has already been distributed. Cases like this have created growing awareness of the limitations of the piecemeal approach to large-scale problems. NGOs are vulnerable to criticism from development policy makers that all they do is tinker at the edges of the problem of poverty, which has led to what has become known as strategies for 'scaling up'. This refers to attempts at 'increasing the impact of grassroots organizations and their programs' (Uvin 1995: 927).

A conceptual framework for scaling up is provided by Edwards and Hulme (1992), who argue that there are three main types: the first is 'additive', in which an organization seeks simply to increase its size and the overall coverage of its programmes; the second is 'multiplicative', in which an organization attempts to gain more leverage and influence by ensuring that its ideas are put into practice by other development actors and therefore reach a greater number of the target population; and the third is 'diffusive', in which the NGO tries to transfer or spread its approaches beyond the organization's own immediate sphere of influence. Four main strategies for achieving scaling up can be identified: working with government (Parry-Williams 1992); linking the grassroots with lobbying and advocacy efforts in order to move beyond mere service delivery (Constantino-David 1992); advocacy work to change the broad institutional and public frameworks in which resource allocations are made (Clark 1992); and finally, organizational growth (Howes and Sattar 1992).

Just as NGO evaluation has sometimes been complicated by donor relationships in which methods have been imposed on NGOs, hazards have also been identified on the road to scaling up. Dichter (1989b) has discussed the dangers for NGOs of what he terms the 'replication trap' – unrealistic pressure from donors or governments to develop easily replicable projects – and he emphasizes long-term institutional learning as the prerequisite for a successful scaling up strategy. The best documented cases of scaling up come from Bangladesh, where the founder of BRAC, Sir Fazle H. Abed set out to counter the Schumacherian view with the challenge that 'small is beautiful, but big is better'. BRAC's growth into one of the largest NGOs in the world seems to bear out the view that scaling up can be achieved under careful leadership and stringent planning (Smillie 2009). Another well-known case is the Grameen Bank, which took a different approach to spreading its ideas outside the country. Rather than growing any larger as an implementing organization, it has encouraged replication and adaptation of its original micro-credit delivery model around the world. Hulme (1990) likens this to 'institution breeding', rather than replication, since it has worked best when the model has been carefully adapted by users to suit local conditions, rather than simply transferred wholesale from one context to another.

Service delivery and advocacy roles each require NGOs to develop appropriate structures that can both 'get the work done' as well as conforming with the NGOs' own values and priorities. NGO management is also concerned with the questions of improving performance, which requires both evaluation and working to increase impact, and which has led to strategies for 'scaling up'. For example, the BRAC worked hard to try to develop a 'flat organizational structure', as Lovell (1992) has outlined, as well as striving to put in place structure and culture that would facilitate a process of organizational learning.

Conclusion

This chapter has reviewed the main activities undertaken by NGOs, and explored how these have been managed. Drawing on both the research literature on NGOs and their management as well as on work from other fields, we first explored the two main activities of service delivery and advocacy, and noted the relationship that needs to be managed between them. Turning to innovation, we explored its centrality as well as how far this role may have sometimes been overstated. We then examined the question of evaluation, along with the strategy of 'scaling up' that offers NGOs another option for improving effectiveness. The focus has been on the challenge for NGOs of managing activities within the complex changing organizational and political environment in which a set of pressures from donors and governments create a difficult environment that development NGOs will need to navigate.

10

NGOs AND THE MANAGEMENT OF RELATIONSHIPS

> The essential challenge in NGO management lies in maintaining and exploring the fine balance between recognition and change, between sufficient integration with its environment to be efficient and sufficient distance from it to be effective.
>
> *de Graaf (1987: 297)*

Introduction

In this chapter, we examine NGO relationships with local communities, with government, with business and with other development agencies. NGOs should not be seen as closed organizations with clear boundaries around them but instead as open systems or entities that are interdependent with and shaped by resources, events and actions of other actors in their environments (Fowler 1997). Relationships are not only important for the sustainability and effectiveness of development NGOs, but also for their organizational wellbeing and creativity which as Biggs and Neame (1995: 39) point out also depends on their participation in 'formal and informal networks and coalitions'. In keeping with the conceptual framework presented in Figure 2.1, our argument is that relationships need to be understood in relation to a broader context. Though an oversimplification, the institutional triangle of state, market and civil society is useful in a general sense for understanding the management of NGO relationships (Brown and Tandon 1994; Turner and Hulme 1997; Wood 1997). However, the approach will clearly need to be located within specific political, institutional and historical contexts. For example, the civil society space China, where the state is dominant and strong, is a far smaller and more constrained one than India where there are longstanding traditions of public association and protest.

Understanding NGO relationships

If we return to the basic conceptual framework presented in Chapter 2, we find that it is necessary to further unpack the relationship between an NGO and its environment. One useful way of doing this is to draw upon de Graaf's (1987: 285) 'strategic management' framework. He draws upon ideas from organization theory developed by Smith *et al.* (1980) to show that NGOs, in addition to managing events and processes within the boundaries of their own organizational set-up, need also to understand and influence the wider organizational environment which lies beyond their immediate field of operation:

> The environment is crucial for NGOs because unlike commercial organizations which can measure their success in terms of activities and their immediate results (i.e. production, sales and profits) NGOs must perceive and assess the implementation of their plans within the context of external dimensions.

An NGO's environment can therefore be seen as having two dimensions: one which consists of factors which lie largely within the span of an NGO's control, while the other consists of processes shaping the wider environment over which an organization has proportionately less control.

This idea can be represented using the three concentric circles set out in Figure 10.1. The first contains those factors that can be broadly *controlled* by the NGO such as staffing, budgeting, planning specific activities, setting objectives or choosing an organizational structure. The second circle encapsulates elements of the environment that can be *influenced* or even changed by an NGO, by processes of persuasion, lobbying, patronage, co-option and collaboration. These include, for example, elements of government policy, the activities of an international donor or the agenda of a UN summit meeting. The third circle contains elements that can – at a particular moment – only be *appreciated* by the NGO, such as wider political structures, the macro-economic system, the technological environment and the international dimensions of context. This is not to say that aspects of the third circle can never be open to change by an NGO (or by a movement in which an NGO may take part), but the model expresses the idea that NGOs need to prioritize strategies based on opportunities and constraints if they are to be effective. This final circle can also be understood to include the processes and relationships that may need to be 'read' by an organization, but which cannot easily be predicted (Kaplan 1999).

The practical value of such a model is that it allows an NGO to develop a strategic approach to management in which priorities can be set and resources allocated, while still keeping a watchful eye on the 'big picture' within which the NGO operates. For example, Pratt (2010: 165) sets out an agenda of strategic issues and priorities that he argues now face development NGOs in the coming years, including structures and identities, pressures of commercialization, improvements to governance and management systems, clarifying appropriate roles in development, and making a transition from 'an aided to an unaided development sector'. Each of these can be understood and planned for within this type of conceptual framework.

Furthermore, it offers a dynamic framework in which NGOs can both seek out opportunities to influence change, and react to shifts in wider economic and political processes. Development NGOs both influence, and are influenced by, their wider environments. For example, an NGO which is normally engaged in service delivery may, based on its reading of the environment, decide at a particular moment – such as after a change of government, the appointment of a new minister or during a period of media publicity relating to a particular issue – to exploit an opportunity to lobby the government over a particular issue. At other times, the environment itself may alter as a result of wider political or economic processes, which may then allow more opportunity for an NGO that is alert to begin to exercise greater influence, or conversely, the 'closing off' of the organizational and political space in which NGOs work. The Philippines in 1986 is an example of new ground opening up for NGO activity after the fall of the Marcos dictatorship (Box 10.5). The boundaries around these three areas are neither permanent nor clear-cut, but will change from time to time.

Indeed, the NGO environment rarely stands still for long. For example, the Russian Human Rights Research Centre, one of Russia's oldest NGOs established in 1990 immediately after the fall of the Soviet Union, was by 2006 facing a crackdown by the government which fears that human rights NGOs have become a front for political opposition and foreign interests.[80] Today, as Ronalds (2010) argues, the twenty-first century context in which NGOs operate has been changing rapidly (including reduced food security, climate change, increased urbanization, political instability and volatility) requiring NGOs both to upgrade their skills and competencies and to approach their work in a 'more sophisticated and politically sensitive way' (p.191).

De Graaf (1987) was critical of what he saw as a common NGO failing in that many organizations tend to concentrate disproportionately on the factors under their control rather than those over which they have less control or simply need to gain more appreciation. Leaders and managers may prioritize decisions about or implementation of internal plans, personnel, budgets and procedures at the expense of monitoring and evaluation, for example, which also have enormous importance for NGO programmes and activities. The success or failure of a development NGO therefore depends as much on its ability to appreciate outside forces correctly and if possible to exert influence over its environment by devoting as much attention as it does to the implementation of its programmes. Yet some NGOs, facing increasingly complex and turbulent environments, may respond by ignoring the outside world and turning inwards, seeking to bring their beneficiaries under their control rather than supporting people's efforts to gain access to wider resources and build greater levels of self-sufficiency and autonomy. Alan Fowler (1997) warns NGOs against falling into 'romantic isolation' and suggests that an organization achieves greater 'leverage' when it builds links with other actors that can help it make sense of the context, such as think tanks and universities. More recent research such as Grant and Crutchfield (2007) continues to support such a view.

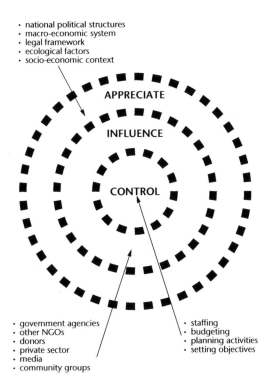

- national political structures
- macro-economic system
- legal framework
- ecological factors
- socio-economic context

APPRECIATE

INFLUENCE

CONTROL

- government agencies
- other NGOs
- donors
- private sector
- media
- community groups

- staffing
- budgeting
- planning activities
- setting objectives

FIGURE 10.1 A framework for strategic NGO management

Accountability relationships

Accountability is the key practical concept around NGO relationships. It has come to be understood as both a potential strength and a source of weakness for NGOs. Accountability, as Edwards and Hulme (1995: 9) defined it, 'is generally interpreted as the means by which individuals and organizations report to a recognized authority (or authorities) and are held responsible for their actions'. Accountability is strength because it enables an organization to work effectively and signals legitimacy. Yet a common criticism of NGOs is that while they may work towards upwards accountability towards the authorities and funders, they pay less attention to the 'downwards' accountability required in their relationships with their clients or beneficiaries, or 'sideways' to other development actors working alongside them. For this reason, accountability is sometimes seen as the 'Achilles heel' of the NGO movement (Hulme and Edwards 1997).

An actual or perceived lack of accountability of NGOs has become a factor in the 'backlash' against NGOs that has occurred in many societies. Citizens may come to see NGOs as either the instruments of donor or foreign government interests, or as the vehicles used by local unscrupulous individuals to pursue their own self-interested agendas. Yet in one sense accountability is a fairly straightforward technical question because most development NGOs are accountable to some kind of voluntary body (a board of trustees or governors) that is supposed to derive no financial gain from the organization and have no ostensible financial interest. Those NGOs that are membership organizations are of course directly accountable to their members, who elect a governing body. At the same time, NGOs are also accountable under the relevant laws of a particular country where they operate, and in theory at least, the state has powers to intervene if they transgress laws relating to accounting, rules of bureaucratic procedure and registration obligations.

However, the reality of managing accountability is rarely very simple for development NGOs because they have multiple 'stakeholders' and are accountable in different and complex ways to a variety of different groups and interests. Edwards and Hulme (1995) show that NGOs face demands for two principal types of accountability, the first being *functional accountability* (short term, such as accounting for resources, resource use and immediate impacts), and the second *strategic accountability* (accounting for the impacts that NGO actions have more widely, and those made on other organizations). This duality makes accountability a particularly complex challenge for NGOs, as it does for the third sector more widely.

Indeed, it has come to be widely acknowledged that third sector organizations have far more complex problems of accountability than do private sector or public sector agencies (Rochester 1995). For example, Diana Leat (1988) outlines three levels of accountability; *full*, *exploratory* and *responsive*. The first, 'full accountability' is where there is a right to demand an account from an NGO and then impose a penalty if it is not forthcoming, such as the withdrawal of funding. This type of accountability has become a dominant feature of the NGO world because funders wish to ensure that NGOs use resources efficiently and for the purposes agreed. This trend has drawn criticism, however, because this primarily financial type of accountability is only one element of the complex 'bundle' of accountabilities to which an NGO must respond.

A second category is that of explanatory accountability, which means that an organization needs to respond to a call for account with information and explanation, but the only sanction applicable if this is not forthcoming is one of disapproval. This is the type of accountability that an NGO might face when it seeks to work with local authorities within a loose framework of informal cooperation and coordination. A third type is that of 'responsive accountability', where there is no formal sanction at all but which runs instead on trust and good faith. When, for example, an NGO claims to be accountable to the wishes of a particular section of the community, the truth of such a claim depends on the willingness of the agency to take this into account, rather than on any real ability of the community to exercise effective power over the organization.[81] NGO claims to legitimacy are often based on the strength of their accountability to people who live in poverty, but the reality for many NGOs is that this area of 'responsive accountability', which lacks sanctions or accountability mechanisms, may be the weakest link of all. Box 10.1 explores one NGO's efforts to manage these difficult contradictions.

BOX 10.1 ACTION AID'S ACCOUNTABILITY LEARNING AND PLANNING SYSTEM (ALPS)

In 2000 Action Aid International launched its Accountability Learning and Planning System initiative, known as ALPS. In response to criticisms of time-consuming and linear reporting systems, ALPS was an ambitious attempt by the NGO to better align its planning, reporting and monitoring systems with its values. It aimed consequently to challenge the typical power relations that led to accountability that faced upward to donors, rather than downward to intended beneficiaries. The third and latest version of ALPS has four components: (i) policies and processes that are the practical ways in which Action Aid's work is planned and monitored, such as strategies, reviews and audits; (ii) principles, such as transparency and a commitment to learning, help determine how these processes are conducted; (iii) in line with these principles, attitudes and behaviours of Action Aid staff and partner organizations are key; (iv) the fourth component in the form of the programming approach was added with the 2011 version of ALPS to highlight that the human-rights based approach is the foundation of Action Aid's work.

Action Aid has been lauded within the development NGO community for the formulation of ALPS. Indeed, many of the policies and processes have been innovative and progressive, such the Participatory Review and Reflection Processes and the Open Information Policy. However, implementation of these policies and processes with the principles, attitudes and behaviours envisioned in ALPS has not proved easy. Despite notable 'islands of excellence', in countries with strong civil society traditions (such as in South Asia and Latin America) reviews in 2004 and 2007 showed disappointing levels of intended ALPS values and implementation. Despite the fanfare, ALPS had run into similar problems as other participatory initiatives that aim to transform power relations. For instance, Action Aid and partner staff may not be willing to work in ways that undermine their own power. Furthermore, in an aid system that increasingly seeks fast results, it is difficult to argue for the time or the resources that would need to be invested if deeply entrenched power relations were to be seriously tackled. Or could it be that the problems are more fundamental? Is Action Aid setting itself an impossible task: to be consistently accountable to poor and marginalized people who do not have power, while remaining accountable to agencies from whom they acquire resources? After twelve years of ALPS implementation, the time has perhaps come to ask that question.

Source: Sinead Walsh, personal communication

The UK's Commission on the Future of the Voluntary Sector in 1997 led to the establishment of the sector's first Code of Practice. Its main points included stating an organization's purpose clearly and keeping it relevant to current conditions; being explicit about the needs an organization intends to meet and the ways this will be achieved; managing and targeting resources effectively and 'doing what we say we will do'; evaluating effectiveness of work, tackling poor performance and responding to complaints fairly and promptly; agreeing and setting out all those to whom an organization is accountable and how it will respond to those responsibilities; being clear about the standards to which work is undertaken; being open about arrangements for involving users; having an open and systematic process for appointing to the governing body; setting out the role and responsibilities of the governing body; having clear arrangements for involving, supporting and training volunteers; ensuring policies and practices do not discriminate unfairly; and recruiting staff openly and remunerating them fairly (Ashby 1997).

There have been several efforts of this kind designed to improve NGO self-regulation in recent years in the form of such codes of conduct. The Philippines Caucus of Development NGO Networks (CODE-NGO) network established in 1991 was one of the first attempts to create a development NGO code of practice at the national level, setting out a clear set of principles for NGO accountability and transparency (Sidel 2005). Other initiatives of this kind have come from the NGO humanitarian context, such as the Code of Conduct for International Red Cross and Red Crescent Movement and NGOs in Disaster Relief (IFRC 1997), the People in Aid Code of Best Practice in the Management and Support of Aid Personnel (ODI 1997), and the Sphere Project Humanitarian Charter and Minimum Standards document (www.sphereproject.org/). Many governments, donors and NGOs consider such codes to be a valuable step forward. But it remains difficult for such codes to be enforced across all organizations. The development of appropriate sanctions mechanisms is one possible response to this problem. For example, Box 10.2 summarizes an initiative by One World Trust that explores the need for complaints procedures systems as a mechanism of last resort for accountability within NGOs, for the benefit of staff and clients.

There have also been larger-scale attempts to regulate organizations, such as the American Competitiveness and Corporate Accountability Act of 2002, commonly known as the Sarbanes–Oxley Act. This was passed in part in response to corporate scandals in the United States such as that of the Enron energy company. The act sets out strengthened measures to safeguard auditors' independence from their clients and creates a new entity that can enforce audit standards. It also makes it a crime to destroy litigation-related documents, and affords new protection to whistle blowers. Although this Act is primarily concerned with the regulation of for-profit businesses and only applies to publicly traded corporations, some argue that its principles of new governance standards may also serve as 'a wake-up call to the entire non-profit community'.[82] According to the GuideStar website (www.guidestar.org), many non-profit organizations in the US have voluntarily begun implementing elements of Sarbanes–Oxley by creating new audit committees and procedures.

Accountability, like evaluation, may be viewed by some NGOs as a requirement imposed upon them from outside rather than an organizational asset. While this is a common experience (and it is of course necessary for an organization to be externally accountable), an organization needs to establish its own *internal*

BOX 10.2 IMPROVING ACCOUNTABILITY THROUGH SELF-REGULATION: COMPLAINT AND REDRESS MECHANISMS FOR NGOs

Work at One World Trust to establish a Global Accountability Framework has identified four main areas of NGO accountability: transparency, participation, evaluation and 'complaints and redress' (C&R). This latter dimension has to date received very little attention in the NGO world. While other more familiar mechanisms will ensure accountability under normal circumstances, C&R is identified as an important mechanism of 'last resort' which can ensure that both internal and external stakeholders can ensure that any complaints about an NGO's operations are reviewed and acted upon. As such it is an important element of NGO self-regulation. But a review of existing procedures found that even in NGOs where there was a C&R mechanism there was a lack of clarity on what constituted a complaint 'against whom' or 'against what standards', and second on the procedure for filing and processing such complaints. The resulting guidelines developed by One World Trust for this purpose suggest a new framework for a workable C&R policy. Five principles which are set out are (i) the need for complaints to be made confidentially, (ii) assurance that the complainant will not be retaliated against, (iii) making information about the procedure readily available to all stakeholders, (iv) making it straightforward for a complaint to be filed and (v) ensuring that any learning from the complaint is fed back into the organization. Significant challenges include the capacity to determine relevant or valid complaints, making the mechanism as independent as possible from the organization and ensuring access to the mechanism for the weakest and most vulnerable stakeholders.

Source: Commonwealth People, published by the Commonwealth Foundation, April 2005. Further details of the initiative can be found at www.oneworldtrust.org

---

accountability systems. This is vital for the health of any NGO, as Edwards and Hulme (1995) point out:

> Performing effectively, and accounting transparently, are essential components of responsible practice, on which the legitimacy of development intervention ultimately depends.

Essential to this process is the need for NGOs to manage their 'multiple accountabilities' rather than to have these accountabilities eroded by allowing only certain lines of accountability – such as to funders – to dominate above others within the accountability 'bundle'. In the balancing of multiple accountabilities, every NGO faces organizational tensions that require effective management if over- or under-accounting is to be avoided in key areas of NGO relationships.

There will probably never be perfectly accountable NGOs. Fox (1992), for example, has shown that in both public and private agencies it is common for both leaders and subordinates generally to try avoid accountability. But when accountability falls below a certain level, the likelihood of ineffectiveness or illegitimate actions is likely to increase (Edwards and Hulme 1995). In a political climate in which corruption of NGOs has become a widely perceived problem, developing new approaches to achieving and demonstrating better accountability is a priority. It should not just narrowly defined in terms of financial scandal, but also more broadly terms as a gradual drift away from an NGO's original vision and stated mission for the wrong reasons. In the 1990s, the policy environment of the 'new policy agenda' may have offered considerable opportunities to NGOs, but there were also associated dangers of co-optation and goal deflection. Such problems became even more acute in the post 9/11 era of 'the war on terror', when some Western governments began demanding specific loyalty to foreign policy objectives as a condition of funding (Howell 2006b).

In a wide-ranging review of regulation and accountability issues, Mark Sidel (2005: 835) considers both imposed formal accountability systems and self-regulation initiatives, and identifies problems common to both approaches. He warns that there are dangers both from both over-zealous self-regulation by NGOs, and from intrusive forms of government regulation such as schemes for certification or accreditation. Meeting a heavy level of bureaucratic top-down accountability criteria could easily draw NGO energies away from their work, and sap their potential for innovation and creativity:

> best practices or 'weak codes' may in fact be all that is needed to keep most nonprofits on a straight and narrow path, along with a stronger backbone on the part of key nonprofit and philanthropic umbrella organizations to criticise clearly inappropriate activities of their peers, and perhaps a stricter set of rules reserved for those organizations receiving substantial government funding or those engaged in clearly quantifiable and rankable activities. In seeking to forestall or ameliorate government's occasionally strong impulses towards stricter regulatory plans, we must take care that the harder forms of self-regulatory solutions do not do nearly as much damage as well.

The accountability problem is one that has persisted and appears intractable. Some writers such as Ebrahim (2010) have begun asking whether simply asking for more and better accountability – the wider trend within the current managerialist regulatory policy environment – is in fact a fruitful approach to addressing NGO accountability problems. Instead, he asks whether it would be better for leaders and managers simply to 'prioritise among competing accountability demands' in clearer and more transparent ways – about to whom an organization should be accountable, and for what. There are a set of specific tools that are available to NGO managers for making this work in a strategic way, including evaluations, disclosure, self-regulation, participation and adaptive learning.

NGO relations with communities

Many development NGOs seek to build sustainable development interventions by forming direct relationships with sections of local communities. For example, an organization may deliver services to a marginalized group of people (such as landless rural women), or it may attempt to build the organizational capacity of a neighbourhood organization. Some NGOs seek a less direct relationship with local communities but attempt to represent their interests in undertaking advocacy work, or attempt to work within broader definitions of the public interest. Whichever the approach, most NGOs claim to be accountable to wider communities, and claim legitimacy on the basis of this accountability.

One of the main problems with the concept of community is that it is imprecise and masks the social differences that are important to understand in the context of NGO work. For example, during the 1980s the Bangladeshi NGO BRAC undertook a detailed study of the rural local power structure of ten villages and produced *The Net*, a report that challenged the myth that villages were socially cohesive and relatively egalitarian communities (BRAC 1983). This was important because it challenged conventional wisdom. Development efforts by the government to organize 'farmers' cooperatives' in rural areas had quickly become dominated by the rich and excluded the poor. BRAC found that NGO efforts (including their own) to provide material and organizational resources for low-income households had also been systematically undermined by local elites who 'captured' these resources and made it difficult to reach people living in poverty directly.

The 'myth of community' also came under attack from feminist scholars and activists who argue that the concept is unhelpful because it masks in most societies important areas of difference in gender and power (Guijt and Shah 1998). *The Net* study was influential in that it helped influence many NGOs to develop more selective grassroots group-based approaches that bypassed elites and identified women as a key target group.[83]

The concept of 'social capital', which generally refers to cross-cutting ties based on trust and reciprocity between organized individuals, has potentially useful implications for the ways NGOs manage community relationships (see Box 4.5 on the case of informal social services in Uganda). NGOs may aim to strengthen local organizational structures in the form of group building, and sections of communities may seek to organize themselves into membership NGOs. As James Coleman (1988: 19), one of the originators of the concept writes, social capital

> exists in the relations between persons. ... For example, a group within which there is extensive trustworthiness and extensive trust is able to accomplish much more than a comparable group without that trustworthiness and trust.

Social capital can therefore be seen in terms of trust-based connections between people which help to facilitate participation in civil society, either through direct and focused action towards political change, or through membership of welfare, cultural or leisure associations which help focus people further towards public responsibility. Indeed, the concept of social capital widens the issue of participation in civil society, beyond political participation and towards other forms of social participation, such as through welfare support networks.

Donor interest in social capital drew mainly on Robert Putnam's (1993: 167) argument (based on a study of democratization in Italy) that social capital embodies relationships of trust and civic responsibility that can be built up between members of a community over a relatively long period:

> Social capital ... refers to features of social organization, such as trust, norms [of reciprocity] and networks [of civic engagement], that can improve the efficiency of society by facilitating co-ordinated actions.

He suggested that where citizens take part in associational life and informal networks, an awareness of the greater good develops that has positive implications for local democratic processes. In this view, civil society is strengthened by the growth of horizontal non-kinship ties between citizens. For Putnam, social capital is the opposite of what Banfield (1958) called 'amoral familism', a phenomenon observed in more traditional rural communities where the self-interest of family and kin dominated social life at the expense of other community members and wider norms of trust and cooperation. Putnam's ideas also suggested that strong cross–cutting social capital could reduce the destabilizing effect of single interest religious or ethnic groups within a culturally diverse context.

Other theorists such as Coleman (1990: 300–2) however included kinship structures within the definition of social capital:

> Social capital is the set of resources that inhere in family relations and in community social organization and that are useful for the cognitive or social development of a child or young person ... it is not a single entity, but a variety of different entities having two characteristics in common: they all consist of some aspect of social structure, and they facilitate certain actions of the individuals who are within the structure ... social capital is productive, making possible the attainment of certain ends that would not be attainable in its absence.

Social capital is an ambiguous concept that has been understood differently by various theorists.[84]

The concept of social capital is not without its critics, since, despite being taken up enthusiastically by agencies such as the World Bank, it may overplay the potential of local organization at the expense of the importance wider structural political and economic change (Bebbington et al. 2004). Some critics also suggest that there is a 'dark side of social capital' (Putzel 1997) and that organized local action is not always a force for 'good'. Some grassroots organizations, for example, may be exclusionary and may reflect precisely the kinds of subordination, narrow self-interest or intolerance that an NGO seeks to challenge. Nevertheless, the value of the social capital concept, as Bebbington (2004: 6) has suggested, is that it represents 'an attempt to understand the social and cultural dimensions of development processes'.

NGO roles in supporting local sustainable development initiatives may centre on attempts to strengthen local social capital. For example, there many be traditional rotating credit groups (sometimes termed ROSCAs) that have long existed in many societies, in which trust between members makes possible the undertaking of group savings and loan schemes as a form of self-help initiative (Chhetri 1995). These may in turn be supported by outside NGOs and can be used as the basis for new work, such as skills training. There are many NGOs, such as the Grameen Bank or BRAC, which seek to build new groups, forms of social capital, which will provide a stable and accountable set of local structures for micro-credit provision and other services.

However, there is a whole raft of problems that have been raised in connection with development NGOs' attempts to build relationships at the community level. Carroll (1992) highlighted the problem that some NGOs overstate the extent to which they can build sustainable structures among communities. Arellano-Lopez and Petras (1994) have argued that in Bolivia, where outside NGOs have linked with local free-standing grassroots groups and movements, NGOs may have actually weakened the structures for local action and autonomy by bringing people into donor-funded 'poverty alleviation' activities. Some NGOs are criticized for holding on to groups for too long and reducing the chance of sustainable, autonomous group action (Carroll 1992: 113; Lewis and Siddiqi 2006). As a result, Howes (1997) argues for the need for NGOs to promote membership organizations that can be self-sustaining after an NGO withdraws, but he also notes the rareness of this actually taking place.

There are also some positive examples of politically minded development NGOs that have successfully widened the democratic participation and citizenship of people living in poverty. In Bangladesh, NK is an NGO that has since 1980 single-mindedly pursued a social mobilization approach despite the wider donor and government pressures that have moved the NGO sector as a whole towards service delivery, and microfinance in particular. Since the 1970s, the organization has prioritized working with the landless poor with an agenda that focuses on rights, solidarity, mobilization, training and education. It has resisted the market-centred, individualized development agenda implied by the more neoliberal philosophy of microfinance. It makes a clear separation between itself and the federated village level groups that it has formed and continues to support. A randomized study undertaken by Kabeer et al. (2009) found evidence that NK members possessed higher levels of political awareness and participation than non-members, as well as a set of material benefits that included more diverse diets, higher levels of economic activity, and more asset ownership. Most interestingly, higher levels of political consciousness were found to translate into lower levels of trust in local public institutions and the workings of the local power structure. The grassroots organizations make their own decisions and provide the basis for a highly democratic organizational structure in which both staff and members have equal representation.

In terms of the strategic management of NGO advocacy, there are a number of useful lessons that emerge from Covey's (1995) work. In order to achieve success in changing policy, a coherent campaign strategy must be combined with adequate resources, and it is necessary for NGOs to 'frame' the issue in such a way that it must appeal to grassroots groups and local communities, and also limit the opposition's ability to organize. The representation of issues may become a battleground. For example, in one case, a ban on logging was portrayed effectively by opponents as a threat to local jobs and livelihoods. In order to achieve impact at the civil society level, the case studies reveal the value of building international support networks among a range of different kinds of third sector organizations, and the need for local grassroots groups to have voice within the alliance, without which they will 'exit', as did a group of Mexican Indians in one case when they found that they were not being listened to by more powerful environmental NGOs.

NGO relations with government

Government attitudes to NGOs vary considerably from place to place. They range from friendly policies that emphasize forms of partnership to active hostility in which governments interfere in the affairs of or even dissolve NGOs (with or without good reason). Some NGOs may cooperate with such courtship, while others may fear co-optation. Some governments have attempted with varying degrees of sincerity, to bring NGOs into the implementation of policies, and occasionally, into wider discussions of policy choices and options. At the same time, within the changing frameworks of international aid, NGOs have become important components of the forms of international governance that has become 'dispersed' beyond the nation-state within a shifting transnational framework of actors, aid flows, policy prescriptions and institutional relationships (Mosse 2005). Some therefore see NGOs as *de facto* extensions of the neoliberal state and as crucial to the ways in which such states now operate.

John Clark (1991) asserted that NGOs 'can oppose, complement or reform the state' but they cannot ignore it. They can choose from several possible strategies in relation to government. First, they can seek to maintain a low profile by working in the 'spaces' that exist in government provision, sometimes with tacit government acknowledgement or letting government take credit for what is achieved by the NGO. This gap-filling role may bring short-term benefits, as we saw in Chapter 9, particularly when resources are severely limited, but can also raise problems of sustainability and accountability in the longer term. Second, NGOs can engage in selective collaboration with certain government agencies, which may be restricted to a particular sector, or may be based on individual relationships between personnel or local level links that may not have formal government backing. This strategy has the merits of pragmatic thinking, but may lead to haphazard inconsistencies in policy and implementation. The final stance that NGOs may take is that of policy advocacy, in which the organization acts as a pressure group in support of the interests of certain groups, or demonstrates alternatives to the government's own approaches along the lines suggested earlier by Adil Najam (1999).

Most NGOs realize that their impact will be limited unless they form some kind of relationship with government. As de Graaf's (1987) conceptual framework suggests, the management of relationships with the state is an important element of overall strategy for most NGOs. Yet this often poses difficult challenges. One collection of writing about development NGOs in Africa characterized NGOs working in countries such as Kenya, Tanzania, Zimbabwe as essentially being caught 'between a rock and a hard place', between the governments who feel threatened by their activities on the one hand, and by the development donors with their changing priorities and unrealistic expectations on the other (Igoe and Kelsall 2005).

BOX 10.3 AFGHANISTAN: CONCERNS ABOUT PERFORMANCE-BASED HEALTH PARTNERSHIPS

A World Bank proposal for an experimental performance-based partnership model for rebuilding health services in Afghanistan has come under criticism for its unproven assumptions and a set of ethical concerns. The proposal is one to subcontract the delivery of health services to NGOs, according to the NPM principle that governments should increasing move from actually doing things to instead 'making sure that things get done'. The problem is that in Afghanistan the state is virtually non-existent, and therefore an assumption of the relative strengths and weaknesses of public and non-governmental agencies of the kind made in some Western countries is highly problematic. Since the state will be unable to manage performance-based partnerships effectively, it is argued that the result will be the complete privatization of health services and the further marginalization of a state that already lacks the confidence of many of its citizens. Evidence from earlier schemes in Ghana and Thailand showed important limitations in the way contractors monitored progress and results, while in South Africa evidence indicated that contracting out produced lower cost provision of some services but was found to conceal high transaction costs for the state. The introduction of user fees (suggested for Afghanistan) has been shown in several contexts to be an inequitable way to finance health services since it excludes the poorest. On an ethical level, there are also concerns voiced that the proposed policy experiment will be funded as a pilot using donor loan money that will eventually have to be repaid, in part by those citizens who may be disadvantaged if things go wrong.

Source: Ridde (2006)

The state also tends to take an interest in NGOs from the perspective of ensuring financial control and accountability, particularly if there are foreign funds being channelled to the NGO sector. As Bratton (1989) shows, the state can use at least four different strategies to define their relationships with NGOs: *monitoring* (keeping track of what NGOs are doing and, if necessary, restricting registration of organizations it does not like); *coordination* (seeking to spread NGO activities more evenly across geographical areas and sectors in order to avoid duplication); *co-optation* (in which the state seeks to 'capture' NGOs and steer them away from potentially threatening roles into the kind of work which the government wants); and finally *dissolution* (in which the state develops mechanisms which give it absolute control over NGOs which gives it the power to delay approval for their activities, limiting their scope or ultimately closing down the NGO if considered necessary).

Many NGOs therefore find themselves with an ambivalent attitude to the state. If NGOs decide to work together more actively with the state, the risk is that they could themselves become less effective (because they may enter into more bureaucratic ties and arrangements) and that the relationships 'downwards' to their community-level groups will be damaged. Those organizations that were formed under conditions of political repression may find it difficult to trust or work with government, even when it has changed. On the other hand, NGOs that had their roots in struggles against repressive states, such as in South Africa or in Palestine, may then find that their roles are less clear once a more accountable, democratic government has been installed.

There have been a number of broader approaches to understanding the role of state within the study of development and social policy. A 'public interest' view of the state was prevalent in the 1950s and the 1960s, in which it was believed that society has a set of common interests that can be identified and served by the state. Mackintosh (1992) has argued that this view has long been in decline. The critique from the left argues that there is a lack of identifiable common interest in society due to the fragmentation of interests produced by class, ethnicity, gender and age, and that the state mainly exists to serve the interests of the middle class and of commerce. On the right, the neoliberal critique of the state centres instead on the likelihood of officials to act in their own, rather than common, interests, and the tendency of bureaucratic structures to obstruct rather than facilitate development initiatives and implementation of policy change.

In his work on development and participation, Robert Chambers (1994) advances a reformist view of the state based on the need to 'reverse' the conventional relationships that exist between professionals and clients, age and authority, and masculinity and femininity. The idea of building an 'enabling' state is key, where the government carries out the essential tasks of maintaining peace and the rule of law, basic infrastructure and services, and manages the economy effectively.

Yet states may also see NGOs, or NGO-like agencies, as flexible tools for maintaining or extending their power (Fisher 1997). The increasing use of NGOs to deliver services through contracting arrangements has already been discussed. The creation of government-organized NGOs (sometimes known as GONGOs) is also a well-documented practice in many countries, allowing government access to possible funding opportunities as well as offering a tool to help it keep control over sensitive community-level issues and politics (Fowler 1997).

However, in recent decades, governments have been losing power and influence under the wider processes of globalization, and under neoliberal processes of state restructuring. Although many may oppose it, NGOs are often themselves implicated as part of these neoliberal state restructuring processes. As Ferguson and Gupta (2002: 990) have suggested:

> The outsourcing of the functions of the state to NGOs and other ostensibly nonstate agencies, we argue, is a key feature, not only of the operation of national states, but also of an emerging system of transnational governmentality.[85]

Moving into a closer relationship with the state can also bring identity problems and organizational tensions within the NGO, particularly if earlier opposition to government was a key plank of its strategy. In Chile, Bebbington and Thiele (1993) describe how some NGOs have moved from an oppositional stance to the roles of constructive critic and innovator, and they have shown how the contracting relations which emerged between NGOs and a demilitarizing state led NGOs to take on many new staff, some of whom did not share the ideological commitment of the founders or supporters recruited during the years of repression. Even when the state is democratic, social and economic work by NGOs implies criticism of the state's own shortcomings, which can continue to generate tension between government and NGOs (Box 10.4). Bratton (1989: 585) has suggested that

> government-NGO relations are likely to be most constructive where a confident and capable government with populist policies meets an NGO that works to pursue mainstream development programmes ... and most conflictual where a weak and defensive government with a limited power base meets an NGO that seeks to promote community mobilisation.

Rather than seeing government and NGOs as being in competition, Evans (1996) has instead pointed to the need for building synergies between different kinds of public and private agency – an issue discussed in more detail in the section below on partnership and contracting.

The effort of NGOs to try to improve the accountability of government to citizens has taken an interesting turn in parts of India with the rise of the 'right to information' movement. For example, the potential for NGOs to strengthen accountability between communities and public officials is well illustrated by an unusual group in the state of Rajasthan in India. Activist group *Mazdoor Kisan Shakti Sangathan* (MKSS) has been working to improve the right of access of ordinary citizens to information held by public officials in rural areas. In particular, the organization began to address problems in the public distribution system that prevented government-subsidized essential goods and public works schemes benefiting the people for whom they were intended.

BOX 10.4 GOVERNMENT REPRESSION AND GRASSROOTS CONTESTATION IN FORMER COMMUNIST SETTINGS

In the second decade after independence, while NGOs are becoming more professionalized, established and confident, their relations with the state often remain tense. Following the Rose and Orange Revolutions in Georgia and Ukraine respectively, wary governments attempted to further curtail NGO advocacy and public activism. In Russia, this crackdown on NGOs intensified with the return of Vladimir Putin to the presidency. Putin supported the passage of a law in July 2012 that requires all foreign-funded NGOs involved in political activity to register as 'foreign agents' in Russia. This crackdown on NGOs is accompanied by the rise of state-supported, 'loyalist' NGOs throughout the former Soviet countries. The best-known example of these is the Russian NGO *Nashi* (Ours), which uses Western models of activism, but is highly critical of the Western models of democracy and human rights.

However, NGOs in the former Soviet Union have come a long way since the 1990s and are now beginning to assert their rights to participate in their countries' development and transformation. They continue to push for sustainable development, good governance, and respect for human rights. Their work is bolstered in part by the emergence of new grassroots civil society groups that began to emerge since 2008 and have used direct action to raise awareness of important social, political and environmental issues. The numbers and influence of these groups began to grow more rapidly in 2011, inspired in part by the global anti-austerity (e.g., Occupy Wall Street, the *Indignados* in Spain, etc.) and pro-democracy movements (e.g., the demonstrations in Tunisia, Egypt, etc.). Similar to their global counterparts, new civil society groups and movements in various former Soviet countries including Russia, Georgia, Ukraine and Armenia, address economic inequality, corruption, human rights abuses, and authoritarianism. The relations between these new civil society groups and established NGOs are fluid and complex.

Source: Armine Ishkanian, personal communication

By gaining access to public records through petitioning a small number of sympathetic public officials, MKSS was able to begin to match stated resource allocations with actual sales and distribution, and uncovered levels of fraud ranging from $2,500 to $12,500 per village in 'missing' resources. The organization has successfully organized 'public hearings' in which detailed information is read out to villagers and elected government officials are invited to attend and account for any discrepancies. In a few cases, resources have been returned to villagers by shamed officials. More significantly, by involving sympathetic members of the Indian administrative service in exposing corruption in this way, the pressure for state government reforms to provide better access to information in order to improve transparency and accountability in relation to public goods is gaining momentum (Jenkins and Goetz 1998). (See also Box 4.4.)

In some countries, the boundaries between state and NGOs may not be clear-cut, as in the case of Judith Tendler's (1997: 146) documentation of successful development in northeast Brazil that was based on a three-way dynamic between central, local government and civil society. She noted the movements of key individuals between different sectors such that 'the assumed clear boundary between government and non-government is actually quite blurred'. In recent work in the Philippines, movements of people from NGOs into government has provided opportunities for civil society reformers to move into certain government departments to attempt to pursue change from the inside (Lewis 2012). In the 'polities approach' set out by Peter Houtzager, there is an emphasis on the idea that civil society can only be fully understood in relation to the activities of the state.

At the same time, boundaries between the three sectors of government, business and third sector may be becoming increasingly blurred, with important implications for NGO management. Cooper (2012) quotes the CEO of Mercy Corps who

---

BOX 10.5 SIDEWAYS STRATEGIES: SECTOR BOUNDARY CROSSING AS A STRATEGY TO INFLUENCE GOVERNMENT

In some country settings, individuals from civil society cross over into government as part of reformist strategies when opportunities arise in the wider political environment. For example, in the Philippines there has been a succession of such 'crossover' activists since the fall of the authoritarian government of President Marcos in 1986. It has become common for elected governments to bring in a range of people from civil society (along with the more traditional individuals from the world of business) to pursue agendas for reform in areas such as social services, housing and agrarian reform. The experiences of such people have been mixed, as have the impact of such 'sideways strategies' on these particular reform agendas. Civil society activists inside government have been credited with helping to provide expertise and pressure to drive through new land reform laws that have the potential to reduce the large-scale inequalities that continue to plague the country. Efforts on the *inside* to drive through policies on land reform also create opportunities for NGOs on the *outside* to work towards the proper implementation of reforms over the longer term. At the same time, such experiences may have helped to strengthen the capacities of civil society people by providing people with a clearer understanding of how the public sector works and how policy processes operate. The boundary between NGOs and government is not as fixed as is sometimes assumed, and boundaries are constantly being crossed and remade within the micro-politics of activism.

Source: Lewis (2013)

recently stated: 'I think you are going to see more experimentation around blurring for-profit and not-for-profit business models'.

If we return to the three-sector model set out in Chapter 4, we find that relationships with the state (and the market) may create tensions and challenges for NGOs through the creation of ambiguity. Writing in the third sector literature, David Billis (1993a) draws upon the work of anthropologist Edmund Leach and argues that certain organizational problems may arise as a result. These are created by the existence of an ambiguous zone between the bureaucratic and associational 'worlds' that normally operate through very different sets of rules. For example, the bureaucratic world relies upon hierarchy and role specialization, while the world of associations is characterized by face-to-face, egalitarian relationships and multifaceted, informal roles. This idea has also been applied to the analysis of the boundaries *between* sectors (Billis 1993b).

NGOs and the business sector

Today, there are NGO partnerships with business in many arenas, including energy, finance, information technology and health. This is quite a turnaround from the days when NGOs tended to campaign against the activities of international corporations around issues such as child labour or infant formula. A longstanding distrust of the private sector among many UK NGOs for example has given way to the view that while retaining the wish to criticize when necessary, in the words of one manager of a UK development NGO, 'You are not going to solve poverty without the private sector'. Cooper (2012) quotes Justin Forsyth, the executive director of Save the Children Fund UK, who remembers how the NGO once used to picket the pharmaceutical company GlaxoSmithKline (GSK) at its annual meeting to protest against their drug policies. SCF has recently formed a partnership with the company to invest in new health workers to administer vaccines. Forsyth goes on to praise GSK: 'they are at the forefront of finding new solutions to illnesses such as diarrhoea and pneumonia, [and] investing in a malaria vaccine'.

Philanthropic relationships between NGOs and business go back a long way. The concept of 'philanthropy', defined in general terms as 'the ethical notions of giving and serving to those beyond one's immediate family', has long existed in different forms in most cultures, often informed by different religious traditions (Ilchman *et al.* 1998). Examples include the Ford Foundation in the United States, which owes its endowment to the philanthropic activities of the famous car company and which now funds a range of third sector activities (among other types of organizations). Another is the Tata Foundation, funded by the large Indian industrialist family. Newer approaches sometimes termed *philanthrocapitalism* or *impact investing* have begun to transform traditional forms of philanthropy. This refers to private developmental investment for socially viable returns that may produce below market returns but offer significant social benefit. Since the financial crash in 2008, this has become more attractive to investors faced with excessively low interest rates in conventional markets.

In earlier editions of this book, relationships between NGOs and the business sector were found to have been relatively unexplored in the literature, but this has been changing for some years. One of the striking changes encountered when talking to international development NGOs in the course of writing this third edition is a sense of increasing rapprochement with the private sector. Cooper (2012) speaks of a 'paradigm change' and writes:

> Relations between the corporate and non-profit sectors have never been easy. But in recent years, many within the NGO community have gained a 'pragmatic comfort' with the business world.

The realization that no single type of agency can tackle large-scale problems effectively is one driver of the rise of new public-private partnerships, with development donors also pursuing closer linkages with the private sector. One early example of this was The UK Ethical Trading Initiative, established in 1999, as an alliance of NGOs, trade unions and companies concerned with improving labour standards within international supply chains (Forstater *et al.* 2002).[86]

Some NGOs see this as a 'win win' situation in which they gain access to additional resources while at the same time exerting greater influence over the international value chains of big companies (Box 10.6). Consumers also tend to respond well to the messages of ethical consumption. There is a blurring of organizational boundaries between business and NGOs that some argue will be good for both sides and lead to creativity and innovativeness and that such 'interactions are important, relevant and vital to a thriving social and business sector, and worthy of study and analysis for years to come' (Yaziji and Doh, 2009: 182). Others are not so sure, pointing to the unequal partnerships that may also characterize such NGO relationships with the private sector. The increased links with the private sector also brings many risks. Gomez and Helmsing (2010: 391) suggest it may be difficult for many development NGOs 'to balance their broad goals with playing a for-profit game', and that they will need to put in place appropriate government structures to ensure that they do not lose their 'moral essence' as they become more closely linked to for-profit worlds and the market economy.

Engaging with the market to promote development

NGOs may engage with support to business activity as a developmental strategy, such as small enterprise building. NGOs have long been involved in small business development, through providing training and capital. Dignard and Havet (1995) present a series of case studies to show that the funding of micro- and small-scale enterprises carried out by women has become a popular development strategy, because these activities can accelerate overall levels of economic activity and can contribute a more equitable distribution of development benefits than male borrowers. At the household level, gendered management and investment strategies often mean that women expand their enterprises to kin networks (i.e. social

---

BOX 10.6 BUILDING MANAGERS WITH EXPERIENCE ACROSS SECTORS

The importance of finding practical ways to bridge the gap between the third sector, the government and business is increasingly recognized in the form of new thinking about developing individuals with a stronger grounding in practical experience of how each of the three sectors actually works. A recent article in Harvard Business Review suggested that 'tri-sector leaders' carry with them a mind-set that is powerfully different from those staff only familiar with one of the sectors. They know how to balance competing motives, and are good at acquiring transferable kills, translating ideas and skills across contexts, maintaining intellectual consistency on a subject, building integrated networks, and being mentally well-prepared to deal with diverse challenges. Lovegrove and Thomas give the example of Coca-Cola appointing Jeff Seabright to address the company's growing problems around increasing NGO and community criticism of its unsustainably high levels of water consumption in its Indian manufacturing plant. With extensive development agency and government experience Seabright was new to the private sector. But using his experience of mapping water stressed areas and water risk analysis from other sectors, he has helped the company create a more sustainable water stewardship policy that is helping to reduce water consumption. According to the authors '[t]oday the company uses only two litres of water to produce a litre of Coke. It is 52% of the way to meeting its 2020 target for water neutrality and is regarded among NGOs and international governments as an industry leader in this area' (p.48). In terms of practical ways forward to build managers with experience across sectors, the authors make three concrete recommendations: (i) for organizations to consider more arrangements for personnel exchanges to take place across sectors, particularly for mid-career staff (ii) for more energy to be devoted to within staff development thinking and training within organizations, and (iii) that 'tri-sector issues' need to be made more fully part of academic and executive training.

Source: Lovegrove and Thomas (2013)

---

priorities) rather than growth and profits, by creating 'multiple enterprises' (Downing 1991).

Many NGOs have also moved significantly towards the private sector in relation to the delivery of microcredit programmes. Providing these kinds of financial services requires both a sound knowledge of banking management practices, and a close understanding of local business opportunities in the community. The Grameen Bank, with over 7 million borrowers in Bangladesh, and many other microfinance providers have focused on the power of women as effective borrowers and economic agents. During recent years, however, microcredit has lost its shine somewhat.

A series of empirical studies have called into question its effectiveness as an anti-poverty strategy, and some of the organizations that have promoted it, particularly those from the for-profit sector, have been discredited. Critics such as Aneel Karnani (2007) has argued that while microfinance 'yields some noneconomic benefits, it does not significantly reduce poverty', and favours the creation of jobs as the best way to tackle problems of poverty. For other critics, the apparently irresistible drive among NGOs to move into the microfinance field has also reduced the diversity and creativity of the NGO sector, by pulling organizations away from their social origins and values and slowly turning them into private sector organizations (Dichter 1997).

An increased interest at the global level among NGOs in what have come to be termed 'social business' activities (such as the Grameen family of organizations) is associated with a questioning of the morality of a market ideology that has grown in influence since the 1980s. This has grown more pronounced since the financial crisis of 2008. In the longer term, it has also been linked with a renewed engagement with the concept of the 'social economy', which according to Reifner and Ford (1992) can be defined as 'a market economy in which asocial market forces have been socialized'. This idea has its roots in the work of Karl Polanyi (1957), which explored the ways economies of pre-industrial societies were socially embedded with important norms of social reciprocity and mutual aid, but which became steadily weakened by the rise of modern industrial consumer capitalism.

Contracting with private sector

There are growing 'service ties' between NGOs and business, in which a company contracts an NGO to carry out a certain social function. In what are sometimes called 'social action partnerships', a private company works with an NGO as part of a wider multi-agency development programme on a social or environmental issue, or a partnership in which a business contracts an NGO with specialized skills. For example, oil companies in Nigeria have used NGOs to provide water and health-care services to remote communities living in oilfield areas as part of their corporate social responsibility (CSR) activities. In Nepal, a private company has worked with local NGOs around the issue of 'fair trade' (Box 10.7). Within fair trade partnerships, NGOs and businesses seek to harness win–win outcomes in relation to trade and social justice. Supporters of fair trade argue that it serves the multiple purposes of securing better prices for developing country producers, educating consumers to demand social, economic and environmental business standards, and generating revenue for an NGO from the market. Others point to the contradictions that are involved in the idea of trying to create 'an alternative ethical space [that] is incorporated into the commercial strategies and practices of producer organizations' (Luetchford, 2006: 128).

Fair trade may have the potential to generate more sustainable alternatives to conventional development assistance and project-based interventions, but it may also blur the boundaries implied by the three-sector model if organizations within

---

BOX 10.7 INTERNATIONAL AND LOCAL PRIVATE SECTOR SUPPORT TO AN NGO IN NEPAL THROUGH 'FAIR TRADE'

In Nepal during the 1990s, a major UK company (the Body Shop) built a trading relationship with a local socially and environmentally aware paper business and a local NGO, funded through profits generated by this 'fair trade' link. The small family-owned enterprise makes hand-made paper for the local market, and like the Body Shop sees itself as a socially aware business with a set of environmental, social and economic objectives. Under the trade link, the size and scale of its operations increased considerably. From a turnover of only a few thousand pounds based only on domestic sales, a move into exports through the Body Shop increased turnover rapidly to over £250,000 within a few years and the local market was abandoned. Staff quadrupled in number, working conditions were improved way beyond local standards, and paper production was made environmentally sustainable through the use of innovative recycling, renewable energy and organic dyes. A local community-based NGO (established by managers and friends of the local business) was able to fund itself using the innovative method of taking a share of the trade profits, made possible by the payment of a 10 per cent premium by the Body Shop, over and above the agreed price paid for the paper products. The NGO initially worked on credit and literacy programmes with the local community around the factory, including employees and their families, but later broadened its activities to include other nationally identified priorities such as HIV/AIDS awareness raising and education work. However, rapidly changing consumer tastes in the North had gradually led to falling sales, creating a funding problem for the NGO and difficulties for the paper company itself. With renewed efforts at diversification, and a late re-entry into the local market, many problems have been solved and the NGO and the business remains active. Expectations, which became confused by the ambiguities between 'business' and 'social' objectives, were eventually scaled down to more realistic levels on both sides.

Source: Lewis (1998a)

---

fair trade partnerships are forced to operate beyond the rules of their usual 'known' environments. An *ambiguous* zone may arise around the relative priorities of 'business' and 'development' objectives, which can create 'distinctive problems' for organizations of both types engaged in fair trade partnerships. This is because fair trade explicitly mixes profit-making with the objective of social or environmental development and change. Such ambiguity creates both opportunities and constraints for NGO management strategies. In the case of The Body Shop's community trade partnership, new opportunities and creative ideas were found to be highly vulnerable to the changing tastes of Western consumers and difficult to sustain.

Companies increasingly work with NGOs to implement CSR initiatives. For example, the US oil company Chevron contracts with local NGOs in northeast Bangladesh, where a gas field has been established in a densely populated rural area. Working with a local NGO, two diagnostic medical clinics have been set up and operated by the NGO in the area as part of the company's community partnership programme (Gardner 2012). This may provide NGOs with a useful source of funding and may allow companies to channel resources into useful social projects.

However, CSR has proved controversial. One of the strongest critiques is that CSR mainly serves the company's interests and helps it consolidate its power more by signalling its social responsibilities than actually changing its operations in more deep-rooted ways. This is the argument of a detailed anthropological study by Dinah Rajak (2011) of Anglo American's mining activities in South Africa. CSR has taken the place of government funding for many NGOs in the post-apartheid era. Without state funding, NGOs have been compelled to become 'social entrepreneurs' in order to generate resources. For example, they must now compete with each other for funds from mining businesses engaging in CSR, and NGOs have become disproportionately concentrated around mining areas in the hope of accessing some of this new privatized funding. Rajak (2011: 189) argues that CSR is taking the place of the idea of a grassroots civil society that had been idealized in the 1990s rather than contributing to it. Drawing upon anthropological theory of 'the gift', Rajak describes a form of 'veiled' partnership created by conditionality and asymmetric power:

> the NGO is trapped between the impossible demands of the company, and the inability to voice their discomfort due to a fear that their funding will be taken away and that, after all, they are indebted to the company for this 'free gift'.

This offers a caution against the enthusiasm for CSR found in some quarters of the development community. Some emerging research on CSR points to the importance of trust building, and suggests that the relationship with NGOs is likely to be more successful once a company has a mature and well-developed CSR strategy (Yaziji and Doh 2009).

Engagement with the private sector on behalf of communities

NGOs may seek to represent local community interests and protect their rights within wider processes of negotiation around securing informed consent in relation to natural resource extraction. For example, Buxton and Wilson (2013) provide a contemporary example from Papua New Guinea (PNG) in which indigenous people's rights have been established in international conventions for 'free, prior and informed consent'. Under international law, members of local communities are entitled to seek an agreement for compensation and benefits if proposed activities by oil, gas and mining companies is likely to impact significantly upon local people and the environment. Some companies are open to the business case for creating what is termed a 'social license to operate', because this signifies that the proper procedures have been carried out to ensure legal compliance and socially responsible practice. In negotiations among different stakeholders in PNG, NGOs that were agreeable to all sides were brought in by mediators during consultation processes in order 'to represent the interest of those who may not have such a strong voice' (p.41). The mediation company had been employed to design a process for renegotiation waste from the Ok Tedi gold and copper mine flooded local land and destroyed local livelihoods (Buxton and Wilson 2013).

NGOs have also been involved in trying helping to make company-led grievance mechanisms work between companies and communities. To get disputes resolved or remediated, local civil society groups and NGOs have for example helped local communities to access available dispute resolution channels. For example, the Accountability Counsel's work in relation to Maple Energy's oil activities in the Peruvian Amazon is a case in point. This is being attempted at two main levels: the first is about linking local people with existing mechanisms such as the US Overseas Private Investment Corporation, and second involves undertaking higher level advocacy in order to try to get such mechanisms and broader systems to work more effectively (Wilson and Blackmore 2013).

Engaging with the market to generate resources

NGOs have also engaged directly with the market for their own organizational purposes in some cases. The market has become a potential source of income for NGOs seeking to reduce or eliminate their dependence on foreign donors or the government. For example, NGOs have developed relationships with local businesses in order to gain not just financial resources in the form of donations or sponsorship, but also information and advice as well as donations in kind, such as the use of office furniture or equipment. Some NGOs have formed their own businesses, such as BRAC in Bangladesh, which established various businesses including a network of department stories and a printing press, the profits from which are ploughed back into the NGO.[87] This preserves the status of the organization as a 'not-for-profit' organization, even though a part of the organization is engaged in profit-making activity, and this and other business ventures, along with the service charges administered, has helped to reduce the NGOs' reliance on foreign funding to less than one-third of the overall budget.[88]

Another example of this is for NGOs to build *governance linkages* with the private sector. It has been common practice to invite representatives from the business sector to serve on the governing bodies of some NGOs, either to lend respectability to the organization or to provide specialized skills and knowledge that can contribute to strengthening the NGO's work.

NGOs and international development agencies

As we saw in Chapter 5, the aid system is a set of institutions and organizations concerned with the funding of international development. While not all NGOs are necessarily funded by international aid, for many this relationship is one of the most critical for maintaining their organizational wellbeing. The relationship is an inherently difficult one for NGOs to navigate, partly because, as we saw in Chapter 5, the world of aid is characterized by frequent and rapid change, and partly because NGOs tend to be the junior partner in an unequal relationship around funding. Brown and Covey (1983) highlighted a set of tensions inherent in the external relations of NGOs, and NGOs have begun to develop distinctive techniques for managing the donor dimensions of their relationships more effectively. For example, the evolution of the 'donor consortium', in which NGOs receiving funding from a number of different donors (each of whom may have different disbursal methods and reporting criteria), is one such response (Smillie 1988; Wright 1996).

In this model an NGO works with the donors to form a group that can standardize procedures and timetables and establish a single point of contact and communication working with donor consortia. Some of the major NGOs such as BRAC in Bangladesh have found this an improved way to organize their relations with donors, although in the case of Sarvodaya in Sri Lanka in the 1980s, a donor consortium led to unnecessary administrative centralization, an increased workload for staff and the loss of the bottom-up culture of participation within the organization (Perera 1997). Schmidt and Zeitinger (1996) argue that donors often still do not know enough about many of the NGOs they support, and that more genuine partnerships are needed, rather than just instinctive trust.

One of the main issues in the management of NGO relationships within the 'aid industry' has been the unequal relationship between international NGOs and their partners. By the 1990s, many international NGOs had moved from implementing projects themselves to forming 'partnerships' with local organizations that carry out the work. Donors also experimented with new ways of working with NGOs, such as 'direct' funding of local NGOs instead of funding them through international NGO intermediaries. Such changes have had profound implications for the international NGO community, which has increasingly found itself in the midst of a rapidly changing aid environment and international context. Some have argued that it has led to a sharpening of purpose and useful questioning of roles, while others suggested a growing 'crisis of identity' (Smillie 1994).

One study has analyzed changing relationships in the context of Sida NGO support in Bangladesh (Lewis and Sobhan 1999). It compared the effectiveness of the 'direct' route via the donor's office in Dhaka with the more familiar 'indirect' route in which Sida's headquarters in Stockholm-funded Swedish NGOs, who then worked with Bangladeshi NGO partners. The study found the two routes to be essentially complementary, since direct funding reduced the costs of the international 'intermediary' NGO and allowed a direct dialogue with local leaders and organizations, while indirect funding maintained a useful link and a dialogue between the government's aid programme and the Swedish public. It also created opportunities for Swedish NGOs to undertake development education work at home informed by their work overseas. However, the research found arguments for direct funding were more compelling as a means for channelling resources to the most effective local NGOs. Some of the Swedish NGOs, particularly those which were from the more conservative missionary backgrounds, tended to be involved in routine, operational, less sustainable NGO activities such as running clinics and schools.

The increasing numbers and scale of NGOs have also highlighted the need for more effective coordination with each other, which has not proved a straightforward challenge. Carroll (1992) argued that coordination between NGOs is a key to improving performance, but that in practice 'competition' is more common, which brings us back to the subject of resource dependence, since NGOs may wish, due to limited funding sources, to protect their funding source information and to maintain a distinct activity niche which they can then use to maintain access to resources. The attempt to coordinate NGOs may come from NGOs themselves, which is more likely to succeed, or it may be imposed from outside usually by government or donors. Coordination may take the form of a formal structure, such as the national NGO council which was established and documented in Simukonda's (1992) case study from Malawi, which was ultimately an unsuccessful venture, or it may be informal in nature, such as the flexible grassroots network in Thailand discussed by Korten (1980), in which NGOs came together around a specific campaign, in this case against a proposed dam project. Another recent trend is the growth of NGO families, affiliates or federations – such as those around Oxfam or Save the Children (INTRAC, 2013). Working in these groupings has required NGOs to learn the techniques of 'matrix' management, working alongside partners in ways that allow coordination, autonomy and coherence across porous organizational boundaries. Matrix management has become seen as a frame of mind as well as a multiple set of reporting lines across organizations that makes it possible to manage across as well as within organizational groups (Barlett and Ghosal 1990).

All third sector organizations tend to be highly resource dependent and may require diverse sources of funds for their survival (Bielefeld 1994). This may lead to a range of organizational problems. For example, when an organization accepts a higher level of official funding, it may become more vulnerable to changing donor fads and fashions (Smillie 1995), or face decreased legitimacy in the eyes of some of its other stakeholders (Bratton 1989). Rapid growth may create structural pressures, such as the transition from the associational world to the bureaucratic world of formal structures and hierarchies (Billis and MacKeith 1992). There may be the hazard of what organization theorists term 'goal deflection', as funders favour certain approaches or sectors over others, such as services over empowerment (Hashemi and Hassan 1999).

The discourse of 'partnership'

This chapter concludes with a discussion of 'partnership', a key policy concept that has been increasingly deployed in the context of NGO relationships. Partnership is the term often used to refer to the funding and capacity building relationships between international and local NGOs, to the contracting relationships with NGOs that may be created by government, and to forms of linkage between NGOs and the private sector. Calls for partnership (along with other related terms such as 'collaboration', 'accompaniment', 'coordination', 'cooperation' and 'complementarity') have now become a familiar part of development discourse. For example, the DAC members 'consider NGOs to be valuable partners because they have important comparative advantages', including closeness to beneficiaries, capacity to provide humanitarian assistance quickly, ability to work in the context of 'fragile states', and capacity to promote democracy and innovate (OECD 2011: 17).

The discourse of partnership may be used to refer to relationships in which there is useful complementarity and co-production between organizational actors, or it may conceal elements of inequality and coercion between actors with different levels of power in the relationship. Inter-agency partnership arrangements in practice are rarely subjected to detailed scrutiny (see Box 10.3 on Afghanistan for an exception).

Research undertaken within an inter-agency project in Bangladesh (Lewis 1998b) identified a distinction between 'active' and 'dependent' partnerships. In many aid-dependent contexts, it is common for partnerships involving NGOs to have a *passive* character, either because the idea of partnership has been imposed, or because agencies have brought themselves into partnerships only in order to gain access to external resources. The study focused on the differing perceptions and expectations of agency staff engaged in a fisheries project involving many partnerships at different levels between government agencies and NGOs. It also attempted to identify what value, if any, such partnerships had added to the project's work, in terms of ideas and implementation. Partnership was found to be a changing evolving idea that had both passive and active elements over time, and at different levels of the project. In some cases (although not by any means all) partnership linkages had contributed to useful changes of approach within the project, with benefits to the project's 'target group', in this case low-income rural households engaged in small-scale aquaculture. Passive partnerships may not add much value to ongoing activities; nor are they likely to generate the learning and reflection that may often arise from joint discussion and action. Such partnerships are also likely to be unsustainable. Many partnerships may begin this way, but the challenge is then to transform them into something more worthwhile. The study argued that partnership is best understood as a process based on both structural factors and negotiation between actors.

Table 10.1 presents a set of criteria for identifying and building active partnerships based on the findings. While respective roles between agencies and individuals needed to be clearly agreed in advance in the design of the project, there was value in the idea that project actors can renegotiate and reassess their roles over time. Linkages should not be premised on an over-rigid notion of 'comparative advantage', such as one that requires NGOs to deliver inputs to farmers while government the carries out research on new technologies. While this had been the idea informing the project design, it was not one that survived for long, since NGOs themselves were found to be innovating and researching new technologies themselves, and that government research capacities had been overstated. Synergies may

TABLE 10.1 Contrasting characteristics of 'active' and 'dependent' partnerships

Active partnerships	Dependent partnerships
Process	Blueprint, fixed term
Negotiated, changing roles	Rigid roles based on static assumptions about 'comparative advantage'
Clear purposes, roles and linkages but an openness to change as appropriate	Unclear purposes, roles and linkages
Shared risks	Individual interests
Debate and dissent	Consensus
Learning and information exchange	Poor communication flows
'Activity-based' origins – emerging from practice	'Resource-based origins' – primarily to gain access to funds

Source: adapted from Lewis (1998b)

result in unintended outcomes, some of which may be useful, others not. For example, some forms of dependent partnership also run the risk of 'agency creation' by powerful international NGOs who seek to use partnerships as a vehicle for their own interests, a fact rarely considered in the partnership literature (Box 6.3).

Partnership also needs to embody a sharing of risks across collaborating agencies and individuals, otherwise there is little chance of generating efficiency, innovation or creativity. Discussion concerning progress needs to be open and honest, with mistakes acknowledged and failures faced up to. The free exchange of information between agencies and individuals in partnership is a prerequisite for learning within the project or programme. Dependent partnership, on the other hand, is characterized by blueprint thinking and a superficial clarity about the purposes of the partnership which may obscure the need to face up to creativity, risk taking and learning. Partnerships are also diverse, varying from sector to sector and country to country, and it may be difficult to 'replicate' successful ones. Partnerships are also highly sensitive to external factors, including economic conditions, political climate, culture and ecology, and may be strongly influenced by support or obstruction from key individuals in positions of power and authority. For example, sudden changes in key government personnel (such as the director of the government's NGO unit moving to another post) can alter the balance of NGO/government relationships at a stroke in a particular country context.

In a recent study of international and local NGO partnerships in India and Ghana, Elbers (2012) discusses what he calls 'the partnership paradox'. He concludes that partnership practices are structured by a set of rules, but that there is always ambiguity around the meaning and application of these rules. While international NGO funders have more power and resources in the relationship, their partners can make use of the flexibility this ambiguity offers to build room for manoeuvre in the relationship (through personal relationships and negotiation skills), even though setting the formal rules remain out of their reach. However, as these rules have become increasingly shaped by new managerialist logic, they have become less reflective of the values and principles of partnership in three main ways: they reflect the notion of measured, quantified value rather than that of social solidarity; the instrumentalization of the relationship in which the main purpose is now for the local partner to contribute to the policy objectives of the international organization rather than being autonomous; and the assumption that local partners will be motivated to 'maximize personal advantage' in the relationship leading to the increased use of monitoring instruments and surveillance that ultimately erode trust.

The idea of partnership is a complex one, embodying ideas about instrumentality, process, informal personal relationships and the context of growing managerialism. Arguing against the rise of complex bureaucratic forms of inter-agency relationship, Mawdsley *et al.* (2005) suggest that a greater level of personal interaction in the form of face-to-face visits and relationships is an essential ingredient for the formation of effective North–South partnerships. Each specific partnership will require new definition and adaptation and continuous review. Partnerships cannot be replicated in any straightforward way from one setting to another. The first step is to identify the goals of partnership, the second is to design mechanisms for achieving the necessary linkages and communication channels, while the third is to review purposes and progress regularly. Active partnership is only likely to emerge as a result of shared risk, joint commitment and negotiated roles that are linked to a clear set of purposes.

Conclusion

This chapter has discussed the management of the relationships that NGOs need to maintain with government, business and other development actors, along with NGO interactions at community level. The work of development NGOs depends on the successful management of these interactions, although the environment in which NGOs operate is both diverse, and an increasingly turbulent and uncertain one. The strategic management framework provides a useful way through which to analyse these relationships. The framework also illustrates the need for NGOs to balance internal management with the management of relationships in the NGO's wider environment. The growing importance of global and local networks in the maintenance of their relationships, and the increasing role and sophistication of information technology, are likely to become more important for the management of activities beyond the formal boundaries of the organization.

11

NGOs AND THE DYNAMICS OF INTERNAL MANAGEMENT

> ... some professional management, with its emphasis on management by objectives rather than mission, on job descriptions rather than roles, on financial sophistication rather than political will, could lead to the development of static and uncreative organizations ...
>
> *Dartington (1992: 31)*

Introduction

The aim of this chapter is to take us further inside the world of the non-governmental organization to examine the main internal management issues faced by development NGOs. We begin with the question of how third sector organizations as a whole have approached internal management, where a specialized field has emerged that has focused on issues of particular concern to the sector such as leadership, governance and working with volunteers. We consider the sometimes problematic relationship between mainstream management thinkers and ideas and those in the third sector. The remainder of the chapter then moves to a discussion of some of the specific issues faced by development NGOs, including debates around organizational development and capacity, leaderships and governance, organizational change and the management of information.

Inside third sector organizations

Common internal management problems faced by third sector organizations include: a tendency for vague organizational objectives; challenges of monitoring performance effectively; the need to balance multiple accountabilities of a range of stakeholders inside and outside the organization; the intricate management structures that evolve in order to try do this; the centrality of the difficult concept of 'voluntarism', and the need to maintain organizational values over time in addition to demonstrating effective actions (Hudson 1995). Given our earlier discussion of the need for a composite model of NGO management, the most useful starting point for what is still a relatively under-researched topic is with the study of third sector management.

As with the world of development NGOs, the third sector management field has long been characterized by tensions and ambiguities: between those who remain suspicious of management on principle and those for whom management is important, as well as between those who favour the importation of wider principles from outside, and those who see the need to evolve distinctive styles and tools within the sector.

Such tensions continue to be played out. For example, in a recent discussion with a senior manager in a leading UK development NGO, the central internal management challenge of the past decade was identified as the need to professionalize an organization that senior managers had come to see as excessively participatory and consultative, while 'keeping the passion'. This meant making the effort to reform the internal management systems and culture of the organization in ways that 'make it clear that leaders do have a right to lead, and managers have a right to manage ... and that everybody can't be involved in everything'. The reforms embodied the idea that 'it is not a democracy, but an organization', and the need to create a new culture in which it is recognized that managers sometimes need to direct, 'sometimes need to consult, sometimes need to co-create, or sometimes just need to take decisions'.[89]

Writing in the early days of the field, McGill and Wooton's (1975) initial ideas have largely stood the test of time. They noticed that despite a growing interest in the third sector's importance, roles and relevance, studies at the time 'reveal[ed] little about the internal workings of third sector organizations' (p.447). Drawing on an earlier conceptual framework developed by economist A.G. Frank (1959) that aimed to challenge the assumption that organizations can realistically plan according to clear and unambiguous goals, they identified two central management problems at the heart of third sector management: 'goal ambiguity' and 'conflicting performance standards'.

Unlike those in the private and public sectors, third sector managers were seen to define future objectives in terms of general directions or thrusts and not by formally stated, definable goals. The process of setting goals becomes highly politicized by a range of external stakeholder pressures, leading to confusion between means and ends. It becomes difficult, therefore, to make use of formal rational management planning tools based on the Weberian model of a bureaucracy with stable roles and hierarchies.[90] Third sector organizations also tend to exhibit a relatively wide gap between the formal public statements made by the organization about what it is doing, and the unofficial goals which are being pursued on a day-to-day level by people within the organization, a difference between what organizational theorist Charles Perrow (1967) termed 'official' and 'operative' goals.

In this view, the people working in third sector organizations tended to have distinctive characteristics, such as a strong or different value motivations. They tended to prefer informal management procedures rather than stable roles and hierarchies. The attempt is often to build 'a highly flexible management system built around temporary project groups, collegial management, etc' (p.451). Organizations tended to plan their work on the basis of contingency and incremental learning based on a general sense of 'organizational direction', rather than on a set of clearly defined, achievable goals. This meant also that performance evaluation was far more complex in third sector organizations.

Third sector organizations were best seen as open systems, where there was always a need to respond to contingencies, in contrast to the goal-oriented, task-specific procedures that lend themselves to techniques such as 'management by objectives' in the private sector. The legitimacy of a third sector organization was always under threat, because its goals may be constantly under challenge both from within, and from outside in the organization's environment. Its very existence is also regularly called into question through unstable funding conditions, and by the possibility that the need that an organization is trying to meet may itself be subject to change.

In contrast to the more familiar idea of the functional executive who works on hierarchically devolved, goal-specific tasks, McGill and Wooton (1975: 452) saw the third sector manager essentially as

> a facilitator, an information gatherer, a person who thrives on giving and receiving feedback. This type of executive operates effectively in unstructured environments where policy making and implementation are constantly linked in a decentralised organization. A key theme for the existential executive is enabling others throughout the organization to exercise a high degree of choice and responsiveness.

The authors suggested too that this idea of the 'existential executive' was also gradually becoming influential in other sectors as well, as changing global conditions began to demand more flexible approaches.

Others within the third sector research community pointed out that there was also a downside to all this flexibility and informality. Tim Dartington (1992: 30–1) was concerned that third sector organizations tend to build management skills on a rather *ad hoc* basis, as and when they were needed. They shunned the formal management training and techniques found elsewhere, and instead developed their management skills through 'the experience of doing and through peer support'. This generated a set of strongly expressive (rather than instrumental) management priorities that focused on mission rather than objectives, and on roles rather than job descriptions. Charles Landry *et al.* (1992: 23) were similarly concerned that this lack of attention to management contributed to the danger that organizations were 'concentrating on swabbing the decks of the Titanic while failing to look out for icebergs'.

Much of the third sector was by now moving in the other direction, with many organizations seeking to professionalize in response to criticisms that they needed a more managerial approach. Management trends from the business world began to impact upon the third sector at regular intervals, including management by objectives (MBO) in the 1970s, total quality management (TQM) in the 1980s and results-based management in the 1990s (Smillie and Hailey 2001). In the case of development NGOs, donors were often driving these changes, themselves influenced by the private sector.

There was perhaps some irony that just as many NGOs were beginning to look to management ideas to professionalize (and perhaps formalize the complex spirit of voluntary action), the private sector was also discovering the value of participatory management and leadership, the importance of 'flatter' organizational structures and the need for improved organizational learning. For example, writing about global management trends, Parker (1998: 146) documents the decline of the top-down management style and the supremacy of top-level managers:

> In a rapidly changing global world where flexibility is a critical variable, resources are less than abundant, and learning and thinking at all levels have become important, lower level employees also have become involved in all aspects of organizational change and development.

From the vantage point of the present, the prediction made by McGill and Wooton (1975) that third sector management issues and concerns could point the way to new directions for mainstream management can now be seen to be coming true. Most up-to-date management thinking now stresses many of the characteristics associated with the ideal type of third sector management – open systems thinking, flexibility, reduced hierarchy and decentralized structures. The interesting question, perhaps, is the fact that while many businesses now practise aspects of a participatory management approach, there are still many NGOs which remain stuck in outmoded or inappropriate models, half-borrowed from the business sector of old, or haphazardly evolved 'on the hoof' within a rapidly changing environment.

For example, the case of strategic planning in the third sector is a good example of this phenomenon. Strategic planning is 'a disciplined effort to produce fundamental decisions and actions that shape and guide what an organization (or other entity) is, what it does, and why it does it' (Bryson 1994: 155). As we discuss later in this chapter, strategic planning has been a popular management tool used since the 1960s for deciding what an organization wants to do, and how it will therefore proceed. Reflecting a technical-rational view of organizational life, it aimed to provide a clear framework of directions and priorities within which an organization's members can make long-term decisions and plans, and on a day-to-day basis help guide an organization's work towards a set of common goals and shared vision (Eade and Williams 1995).

Yet many development NGOs became interested in strategic planning during the 1990s (as part of efforts to professionalize their management) at precisely the time it was being questioned and re-evaluated within the mainstream management field. Henry Mintzberg (1994), one of the best-known originators of the strategic planning concept, had begun arguing that its usefulness had been exaggerated. The key weakness, as he saw it, was that strategic planning carried the assumption that organizational events could be predicted and controlled. It therefore separated strategies from operational activities, when in practice the two are very closely linked, with planning associated with analysis, and strategy linked to synthesis. In the third sector, and among many development NGOs, debates were way behind. Strategic planning was becoming regarded as an example of 'best practice', despite the 'waning confidence' of business theorists in the approach (Mulhare 1999).[91]

Attention from mainstream management writers

By the 1990s some mainstream business management writers were now discovering third sector management. Charles Handy (1988) for example argued that the important difference is that third sector organizations were 'value-driven' organizations, and that this posed distinctive management challenges. This was because people work in these voluntary organizations from a variety of public and private motives – such as altruism, an escape from dominant ideologies, increasing public status from being on an NGO board, or simply for experience, friendship and to add something new to their CVs. How does one manage such complex multiple interests and objectives?

Bestselling business guru Peter Drucker (1990) also set out a view of third sector management. He argued that third sector organizations lacked a clear bottom line and therefore faced distinctively complex management challenges. Mike Hudson (1995) built further on this view by suggesting third sector organizations differed from organizations in the public and private sectors because there was no clear link between the providers of funds and the users of the services. In the private sector, customers pay for goods and services at a market price, and if the organization fails to provide these at the 'right' quality and price, either the organization improves its performance or goes out of business. In the public sector, if people within a democratic political system are not receiving an acceptable level or quality of services then they can, at least in theory, vote officials out of office. For third sector organizations, this lack of clear accountability through markets or political process creates an unusually complex set of management challenges and problems.

Voices within third sector research did not always agree with these new management ideas. For example, Helmut Anheier (2000) argued that Peter Drucker was not correct in suggesting that there is no bottom line for third sector organizations, arguing instead that the problem was actually one of *too many* bottom lines. This reflects the complex pattern of stakeholders in each organization, and, coupled with the high level of diversity of structure and purpose, gives rise to the distinctive complexity of third sector management. Nor was the primacy of values argument left unchallenged. Rob Paton (1999) feared that there was a new third sector variant of 'managerialism' evolving based on the idea of the centrality of third sector values. This can lead to management 'solutions' that are merely based on static or rigid notions of values instead of the evolving, often conflictive processes of value-based action within the third sector. The emphasis on values, Paton pointed out, was sometimes used to mask organizational confusion and rhetoric.[92]

Such views move us closer to a view of third sector management as a process of choice and balance that takes place around a particularly complex set of themes. While wider management thinkers have offered some useful insights into third sector management, its main concerns cannot of course be addressed adequately by simply relying on the importation of 'one size fits all' business models – but also requires approaching on its own terms.

Third sector management research

Today a rich field of research on third sector management exists, particularly in the United States and Britain. Rather than trying to import standard management ideas, many third sector management researchers have gone about trying to develop new concepts and models based on new theorizing and empirical research. The growth of third sector management, despite its focus on Northern contexts, has useful implications for understanding how NGOs are organized. It represents a starting body of knowledge that can be approached, adapted or rejected when considering organizations working in different cultures and contexts. There is comparatively little, for example, that has been written on governance or staffing within development NGOs, particularly in the South, yet these are subjects explored in comparative detail in relation to the Northern third sectors.

As we saw earlier, Billis (1993a) developed an influential general theory that sought to explain common organizational problems arising from rapid growth and change in the British voluntary sector. A third sector organization normally tends to start with a loose, informal 'associational' structure and a single purpose, but if successful it grows and experiences the emergence of hierarchical 'bureaucratic' structures, along with more complex multiple purposes, often driven by pressures from the wider policy environment. He identified the roots of these problems in an organization's journey from one organizational 'world' to another, and the ambiguity that arises from this. Billis' 'worlds theory' suggests a common source of management problems lies in an organization's ambiguous positioning on this boundary between these 'associational' and the 'bureaucratic' worlds. For example, having begun as a small-scale organization providing a service to its members, organized around face-to-face relationships and relying mainly on volunteers, an organization faces pressures to formalize. Its informal systems are no longer sufficient and it requires more formal bureaucratic structures, such as the introduction of paid staff.

As it formalizes, an organization tends to lose touch with its earlier values and goals, and some basic and often predictable problems result. These include tensions between volunteers and paid staff, between personnel with formal job descriptions and those without, and between the head of the organization and other stakeholders such as the governing body. The key issue is that these changes tend to occur incrementally and are not sufficiently appreciated by managers. Unless growth and change take place with a proper sense of awareness and accountability, David Billis argues, the tensions that emerge cannot be managed effectively. Change is neither inevitable nor necessarily bad but the organizational consequences of 'sliding into change' will cause serious management problems that will affect the organization's accountability and effectiveness.

A second important area, for which it is also largely impossible to import useful ideas from the other sectors, is the management of the third sector governing body. Margaret Harris (1996) considers the ways in which formal structures are supposed to function in theory, and then to compare these 'assumed' roles with those encountered in the messy world of real organizations. In the UK 'charity' world there are, she argues, five main functions which are usually claimed for the board, in the organization's own public statements or which are required by British charity law: (i) serving as the point of final accountability for the organization, such that it is answerable for the organization's conduct to government, clients and regulatory bodies, and responsible for the action of the agency's staff and its use of resources; (ii) acting as the employer of the third sector organization's staff, whether paid or voluntary, taking final decision on such issues as appointments, promotion and disciplinary action (even though these may be handled by paid staff on a day-to-day basis within the organization); (iii) formulating and developing the organization's policy in terms of its overall mission and purposes, and setting priorities and planning monitoring activities; (iv) taking responsibility for ensuring the availability of resources, from finance to staff and office space, and in this sense responsible for the organization's continuation and survival; and finally (v) mediating between organization and environment, representing the organization to outside actors and bringing information and ideas back in from outside. Studies of this kind highlight the fact that there is normally a significant gap between the 'assumed' and the 'manifest' functions of the governing body.

One reason for this disjuncture is sometimes ignorance among governing body members that they have been allocated certain duties. They see the executive director of the agency as being in charge, in the way that the chief executive officer of a commercial business organization operates. Another may be that unless there is a crisis of some kind, the day-to-day management of a reasonably stable and successful organization will be taken care of by its professional paid staff without much involvement by the governing body. The relationship between governing body and paid staff may also help explain the gap between theory and practice, since it is a relationship vulnerable to tensions and communication difficulties unless both sides are committed to making it work. Finally, the structure of service-providing organizations may offer another area of explanation. Harris (1996) outlines an 'entrepreneurial model', common among newer agencies in Britain, in which the power of the governing body is curtailed by the existence of energetic staff and guardians (the people who have set up the organization, and care about its future) who then take care of many of the prescribed functions of the governing body and leave it without a clear role or purpose. These issues continue to animate third sector researchers. For example, recent research from Canada highlights the importance of focusing more strongly on the competencies of board chairs in particular as a way of enhancing effectiveness (Harrison and Murray 2012).

Leadership in the third sector is another key area. This is a concept that has fallen from fashion in the wider management literature, and often simply used interchangeably with that of 'management'. Kay (1996: 131) suggests that interpretative approaches have begun again to favour a definition of leadership

> as a multi-dimensional process of social interaction, creating and sustaining acceptable meanings of issues, events and actions. Leaders are conceptualised as those who have involvement and influence in this leadership process.

In this way, leadership is seen as a process of sense-making rather than as a measurable aspect of individual human behaviour, and one which is characterized by the creation and sustaining of acceptable meanings of issues and actions rather than simply as the responsibility of a particular individual in a formal leadership position. In Kay's (1996: 145) research it was found that in the UK third sector the role of chief executive was an important one in shaping such processes, but that there was activity throughout the organization that also played a part. The pattern of leadership that was identified was therefore seen in terms of an essentially participatory ideal rather than the heroic leader model:

> It is therefore seen as important that all staff and volunteer members at all levels of voluntary organizations, *and* service users, need to be enabled to exercise leadership and to develop the skills to participate in this process.

However, it is not always clear in the study how frequently this form of leadership is actually found among third sector organizations. The problem of over-dominant 'charismatic' leaders remains common in the third sector. Furthermore, Henry Mintzberg has recently written about the need for what he sees as the US model of heroic model of leadership to take a back seat in the relation to development management in the context of the global South in favour of 'engaging management' models in which leaders earn trust by helping other staff to be important and by bringing out their energies and creativity (Mintzberg 2010).

Finally, involving volunteers is another distinctive area of third sector research with relevance for NGOs. The people who make up the governing body of a third sector organization are usually volunteers, and even if the organization does not make use of volunteer staff, these people may constitute the 'voluntary' element of a third sector organization which gives it its distinctive character (Salamon and Anheier 1992).

Many third sector organizations also involve volunteers more widely, making volunteering another distinctive area of management that increasingly receives attention in the research literature. For example, Davis Smith (1996) analyzed the trend towards formalizing the activities of volunteers within agencies, and the overtones of managerialism that may threaten the complex bundle of motivations that make up the volunteer 'ethos' in the UK. Recent work by Hager and Brudney (2011) considers the ways both organizational factors and issues in the wider environment help to condition the opportunities that are available to managers to recruit volunteers. In the context of international development, volunteering has grown into a large-scale field, underpinned by ideas that range from the rationale of providing technical assistance at one end of the scale to those of building social solidarity and contributing to the humanization of the impersonal forces of globalization at the other (Lewis 2006b).

Since the 1960s there has been a questioning of the idea that volunteers can be left to themselves in third sector organizations as well-meaning amateurs if their

---

BOX 11.1 VOLUNTEERING AND SOCIAL MEDIA IN INDIA

Organizing volunteers is an important concern for NGO management. Traditionally, Indian NGOs have reached out to volunteers mainly through word of mouth. The internet has changed this, making it possible to reach larger numbers through websites and social media. NGOs can now share their work with a far larger audience and across boundaries. Many NGOs have dedicated volunteer managers, or outsource this to other service provider NGOs. The past decade or so has seen a rise in NGOs such as Volunteer Match, iVolunteer, and the Hands-on network. These partner with other NGOs and recruit volunteers based on partner requirements, managing a volunteer's progress and ensuring their retention.

With the advent of social media, the environment around volunteering has become very much more dynamic. Social media sites such as Facebook, Twitter and LinkedIn make it possible to share and promote volunteering stories, thus attracting more people. Volunteers share their stories with their friends, creating more awareness and knowledge and stimulating more people to volunteer. However, recruiting more volunteers this way is not always straightforward. Unlike websites, social media thrive on live content. Managing social media requires a dedicated resource both in terms of manpower and finances, both of which tend to be in short supply in many organizations. Furthermore the competition to get people's attention is fierce. In the entire social media space, NGOs are not only competing with other NGOs. The potential volunteer for an NGO is also a potential business customer. Some NGOs find they are competing with bigger brands. Despite these hurdles, an NGO may be able to develop a large follower base. But the main challenge that NGOs face is then converting these potential volunteers into actual volunteers. In the virtual world it is easy for someone to show support by 'liking' something or 're-tweeting' a thought. But in the real world, an organization probably cannot count on more than 1% of their registered volunteers to *actually* volunteer. Social media provides some new opportunities, but also some challenges. Organizations, at least in India, are still trying to get it right with social media.

Source: Ashima Goyal Siraj, personal communication

work has important social consequences, and a gradual move towards professionalization can be detected – a combination of pressure from government and from
inside many third sector organizations, where both paid staff and volunteers themselves have urged greater levels of professional support. This has led to a somewhat
managerialist view that volunteers should be treated as 'unpaid professionals' with
parity with paid staff in every other respect, a trend which has met with considerable resistance in some quarters of the third sector.

Returning to the ambiguous position of the third sector organization where
both personal informality and bureaucratic systems may coexist within a single
agency, there may be a clash with the essentially heterogeneous motivations and
needs of volunteers. Formal training and job descriptions may only appeal to one
section of the volunteer community. Davis Smith (1996: 198) makes the case that
many third sector organizations will therefore require a management style that is
closer to the enabling model than the controlling one:

> For some this will mean the workplace model of individual job descriptions
> and the like; for others it will mean a much more informal and flexible
> approach.

New technology is leading NGOs to develop interesting new ways of mobilizing
and managing volunteers, as Box 11.1 from India describes.

At the same time, the third sector literature does of course have certain weaknesses. The main one is the problem of context-specific assumptions that inform
research undertaken in the UK or the US.[93] For example, some development NGOs
prefer to see themselves in professionalized terms and do not identify with the ethos
of 'voluntarism'. Also, the governing body model, though common in many countries, is far from universal, and many development NGOs do not operate in this way
(Fowler 1997, for example, outlines a non-governing body structure common in
Latin America). Smillie and Hailey (2001: 108) argue from their study of South
Asian NGOs that the much-observed tensions between staff and board in the third
sector literature is actually quite rare in Southern NGOs, simply because 'many
NGO boards act more as rubber-stamp cheering sections than as the policy formulation bodies so beloved of non-profit management literature'. Third sector management research is also strongly focused on service delivery organizations, and
engages somewhat less with organizations concerned with advocacy and social
change.

Internal management issues in development NGOs

In Chapter 3, we explored an 'NGO management debate' that surfaced for a while
in the latter half of the 1980s, driven in part by contributors to the NGO management
newsletter produced in Geneva by the ICVA. After the ICVA activity, less was written
on the subject of NGO management for a time until the late 1990s, when two major
books on this theme emerged, one by Alan Fowler (1997), who pulled together

many of his previous writings into a vast, detailed text, and Naoki Suzuki (1997), whose work with a Japanese NGO in Africa prompted a detailed research study.

Suzuki's (1997) book takes as its focus the world of international development NGOs. It concentrates mainly on the internal management questions rather than on programmatic issues for NGOs. Suzuki argues that these NGOs are characterized by a series of organizational tensions that generate a set of specific management dilemmas. He locates the key dimension of NGO management in terms of a struggle between headquarters and field offices (another popular topic in the third sector literature). The different roles and activities of the two parts of an organization create a basic tension: the headquarters office tends to be physically distant and concerned with fundraising efforts, while the local office is concerned with relationships with the local community and the implementation of poverty reduction programmes. This study is based on detailed interviews with NGO staff, and one of its strengths is the ability to examine NGO management through the stories told by staff themselves.

Three sets of tensions are revealed within NGOs. The first is between 'organizational maintenance and project implementation', in the sense that NGOs which are funded by donors must always prioritize the provision of reports and information to these donors, but at the same time the organization must maintain a focus on the implementation of projects and the maintenance of effective relationships with the beneficiaries. The second is the tension between 'diversity and similarity', in which staff within the same organization must undertake potentially contradictory tasks while still seeking to work together to achieve common goals. The third tension that is highlighted is that 'between flexibility and consistency', such that on the one hand donors may impose a set of systematic rules and regulations about performance and accountability, but for the field office the local realities of development work are inevitably 'messy' and difficult to build systems around.

Alan Fowler's (1997) *Striking a Balance* is a key text that needs discussing in depth. The author is concerned with outlining what he terms the 'capacities approach' to understanding NGO management issues, which has five dimensions: the organization's set up, its leadership, its stakeholders, its fund mobilization, and its achievements.

The organizational 'set up' needs to link vision, mission and role clearly and use strategic planning to turn strategy into programmes. He suggests that an emphasis on reflection and learning is necessary for effectiveness, and discusses the importance of linking micro- and macro-level activity for maximum impact. Within the organization Fowler (1997: 61) argues that effective management requires a combination of both the 'participatory' and the 'instrumental' dimensions of management, pointing out that 'decision-making must be consultative enough for shared ownership of the outcomes and directive enough to be timely'. To improve leadership and human resources, the organization's culture needs to properly reflect its values and approach, including challenging wider issues of gender and power. The challenges of leadership and succession, and of the use of expatriate staff both need careful planning. Moving on to the third set of issues, Fowler emphasizes the importance to an NGO of managing external relationships with 'primary stakeholders' (i.e. beneficiaries or clients) and with other NGOs. He outlines a concept of 'authentic partnerships' and the struggle to build more equal donor–recipient relation-ships, and broader working coalitions. He also stresses the task of influencing govern-ment, and the need for NGOs to provide distinctive development inputs that avoid duplicating government efforts. In terms of the mobilization of funds, Fowler insists these should be of sufficient 'quality' to allow an NGO to pursue its work properly. He distinguishes 'hot' from 'cold' money (in terms of its conditionality levels) and reviews three sources of funding in the form of gifts, taxes and market-based transac-tions, and crucially points out that sustainable development is 'neither cheap nor quick'. Fowler's final set of capacities involves 'managing through achievement'. This section discusses the problems of the complexity of the development task, the blunt tools available for the measurement of success, and the dominant NGO culture of action over reflection that may often inhibit organizational learning (Box 11.2).

Fowler (1997) favoured moving from an emphasis on measurement of develop-ment impact towards one of 'interpretation', mainly through working with different 'stakeholders' and incorporating their feedback and perspectives on progress, rather than seeking to develop quantitative evaluation tools. This allows an NGO to build its

---

BOX 11.2 CONTRASTING ORGANIZATIONAL CHARACTERISTICS OF TWO NGOs IN SOUTH ASIA

Edwards (1999a) contrasts the organizational characteristics of two NGOs in South Asia. The first organization, which was the more successful, had 'inspira-tional but not overbearing' leadership, which was respected both by staff within the organization and by members of the disadvantaged communities within which the NGO was active. However, a shared organizational culture had been built up through long-term education and dialogue about the causes of poverty and the appropriate response to it, which created a high level of commitment, selflessness and 'a determination to hand over power at every opportunity' during the course of the NGO's development work. This had the result that local community groups, rather than the NGO itself, were gradually strength-ened through the NGO's work. By contrast, another NGO which was judged less successful in the study, was characterized by a strong director whose per-sonal influence shaped the work undertaken to the detriment of middle-level and junior staff further down the hierarchy, who found themselves with very little opportunity to influence decisions or events. For example, a new credit scheme was introduced from the top without consultation, despite the fact that local staff had learned from their own informal efforts that such a design could not work properly. Consultation at the country office level took place not with country staff, but with the headquarters in London, which led not only to missed opportunities for learning, but also to extremely high overheads. Important preconditions for success such as risk-taking, communication and initiative were all discouraged by this excessive centralization and bureaucracy.

Source: Edwards (1999a)

legitimacy through achievement and accountability. The final parts of the book are concerned with improving NGO effectiveness by developing the five capacities through both 'organizational development' as well as strengthening wider 'civil society', a process which Fowler distinguished as 'institutional development' (ID). He is careful to characterize this as a process, not a means or an end. Ending the book with a set of future choices for NGOs, Fowler mixes a strong identification with and support for development NGOs with a sense of realism about the future. He sees the priority as creating NGO distinctiveness (building people's capacities rather than providing global welfare, linking with wider social movements) as well as learning from practice in order to gain leverage on aid, states and markets. The author suggests that NGO leaders need to think carefully about the future, because they need to improve their effectiveness and reduce their dependence upon foreign aid, which is in decline:

> It seems to me that this is a moment in NGDO history when leaders have to [be] ... motivators charting future directions for development and then mobilising followers ... the ball is in the court of NGDO leaders and followers to generate a vision of the future they want *beyond aid*.
>
> (p.234)

The idea of 'non-governmental development organizations' is slanted firmly towards organizations promoting social change, and Fowler is somewhat dismissive of NGOs that deliver services or provide 'welfare' (p.223), which as we saw in Chapter 9, is a key NGO activity.[94] The book also focuses mainly on NGOs that are part of the 'aid industry' as opposed to other kinds of organizations – such as small-scale campaigning groups or self-help community organizations – which play a developmental role and which form part of the broader NGO sector or civil society. In later work, Alan Fowler has subsequently shifted his focus away from NGOs and the development industry to argue for a more political concept of 'civic driven change' driven by civil society groups positioned outside the aid system (Fowler and Biekart, 2011):

> an NGO choosing an alternative concept of civil society and other roles tends to self-exclude from direct support from official aid agencies. But, it also means that it is better able to mitigate against overly growth-driven organizational strategies which – in the name of the poor – would make them supplicants to donors that typically demand compliance with officially 'approved' technocratic development practices.

There have been few studies of NGO management issues in development NGOs beyond the West. Ian Smillie and John Hailey's (2001) book on management and leadership in South Asian development NGOs was an exception, and contributed many important insights into the internal workings of NGOs. Based on detailed interviews with NGO leaders in India, Pakistan and Bangladesh and case studies produced by local researchers, a key strength of the book is the way that each organization described is located firmly within its organizational history. Among the more surprising conclusions from the study is the relatively heavy investment in training and research observed in these NGOs as compared to what the authors see as the relative neglect of such investment by many international NGOs:

> This failure to invest in their own learning and self-reflection stands in marked and odd contrast with their willingness to build the same capacities in their Southern counterparts.
>
> (p.79)

At the same time, individual founder-leaders' perspectives on organizations may sometimes be seen in retrospect to have presented a somewhat rosy view of the organization as a whole. At least one of the organizations described in this study has subsequently run into serious difficulties, reflecting a higher degree of fragility in internal management and leadership than expected.[95]

Books dealing specifically with internal NGO management issues were then fairly few and far between until Paul Ronalds' (2010) *The Change Imperative*. In this book Ronalds, a practitioner with a longstanding background in the international NGO sector, sounds the alarm for international NGOs to pay more attention to organizational issues if they wish to survive and prosper. In particular, he argues that the large international NGOs need to better embrace change if they were to become effective within the changing global context in which NGO work takes place. He sets out a set of issues around management that will be familiar to those who have followed the debate in recent decades, but with the additional urgent twist that today the environment is far tougher and more competitive for development NGOs.[96] Ronalds' (2010: 152) book was a reminder that many of the old issues from the NGO management debate of the 1980s were far from resolved:

> INGOs must begin to take management seriously and invest in developing highly effective and context appropriate leaders and managers ...

The large international development NGOs, he argued, have tended to lack flexibility in their internal operational structures and need to find ways to promote better information flow, networking capacities and responsiveness to change. He also drew attention to the shortcomings of the strategic planning approach for NGOs forced to operate in increasingly complex and unpredictable contexts:

> Large INGOs need to ensure they sufficiently emphasise creativity, immediacy, experimentation and initiative. Otherwise, they risk their growing size and bureaucracy leading to them prioritizing predictability over improvisation, constraints rather than opportunities and accounting over goal flexibility.
>
> (p.152)

The book continues and extends the view that there is a need to maintain a high level of diversity among INGO organizational structures to maximize effectiveness and impact, and once again warns against 'one size fits all' recommendations.

Two other key themes are important in relation to internal management: leadership and boards. There has been much less research into issues of NGO leadership than in the wider third sector literature. The leadership model most strongly associated with development NGOs is the charismatic founder-leader model. Tom Carroll (1992: 92) found that NGOs with strong capacities in participatory service delivery were often headed by a strong, charismatic single leader possessing 'extraordinary vision and personal commitment'. This has sometimes been viewed, particularly by donors, in negative terms as a 'Lawrence of Arabia syndrome', implying the idea of a heroic but unaccountable leader. Yet as Carroll (1992: 140) suggests, this form of leadership offers both strengths and weaknesses:

> strong central leadership has been essential to the survival and strength of these organizations and has generally not spawned the autocratic, paternalistic relationships often attributed to it.

Carroll's view is that strong centralized leadership is very important, especially in the early years of an NGO's existence. By contrast, Zadek and Szabo's (1994: 30) analysis of charismatic leadership highlighted the more negative side. The influential Sri Lankan NGO Sarvodaya had been established by a leader who sought to combine participatory decision-making with his personal abilities to inspire, but over time this created a decision-making structure that showed signs of paternalism and ultimately led to an organization that was left weakened by a subsequent difficult process of leadership transition.

A second common (and related) area of internal NGO weakness is that of governance structure and process, which is rarely discussed in the NGO literature. One exception is a useful study by Rajesh Tandon (1995) on NGO board relationships in India. Many South Asian NGOs legally registered as societies and trusts, which dictates that there should be an executive council and committee or governing board, a chief executive officer (CEO) such as a secretary, president, director or coordinator. Tandon identifies a range of strategies pursued in South Asia, which he calls 'board games'.

For example, in the case of 'family boards', NGO boards may operate like a small family business based on kinship, informality and trust, which provides a supportive structure in the early stages of an NGO but which over time may lead to patriarchal governance structures and few entrances for new staff. In the case of 'invisible boards', there is a small group of family and friends brought together by the founder from time to time simply as a 'rubber stamp' in order to meet the legal requirements of NGO registration, with the result that governance and management are clearly separated. Also common is the 'staff board', in which the NGO staff also acts as the board. While this can be effective in the short term, the lack of separation of the governance function from the demands of day-to-day management can prove an inadequate system for dealing rationally with senior staff conflicts, and rarely allows for fresh perspectives to enter the organization. Finally, for 'professional boards', in which competent people are brought together formally (and sometimes remunerated), it may be difficult to generate a shared vision and a sustained commitment. Each of these NGO board types, while displaying certain strengths, nevertheless contains important weaknesses that limit the organizational capacity of the NGO in important ways.

In addition to basic management and governance of an organization, another reason for taking boards seriously is in relation to 'social capital' ideas. By contributing to internal democracy within the associations of civil society – as well as to 'bridging' roles across organizations – effective boards may also contribute to the creation of social capital and therefore to more democratic politics and prosperous communities in the wider sense. Tandon (1995) argues that, at its best, board membership is a means of civil engagement. It can strengthen the networks of trust and collaboration that can contribute to healthy communities and democratic process. Well-organized boards have the potential to cut across class, race and gender lines, with members bringing their own skills as well as the perspectives of the communities that they serve.

If the NGO has a charismatic founder-leader, research suggests that this tends to limit the autonomy of the board. The leader builds up 'sweat equity' by continually providing the bulk of the ideas and energy. As the NGO moves through its life cycle from the early days of defining its vision and mission and building its programmes (during which time the dominant leader model can prove effective) towards a second period of growth and expansion, the board is needed more and more but performs less and less well. For NGOs that are engaged in 'internationalizing', there is a further set of distinctive organizational issues that emerges (Box 8.1).

Just as Harris showed in relation to third sector boards and governance in the UK, boards remain a relatively weak (and under-researched) area in the management of development NGOs. Ronalds' (2010) analysis of INGO boards bears out many of these continuing problems, along with some additional ones specific to the INGO context. He finds that many organizations experience difficulties recruiting sufficiently knowledgeable, experienced and independent people, especially given the increasing complexity of the work these organizations undertake. A second problem he identified is the challenge of finding suitable ways for such individuals to have a genuine voice in the organization's governance. A third is the issue of making sure that there is developing country representation on the board as a means for improving representation and local accountability.

Finally, the growth of NGOs also raises the issue of increased bureaucratization, sometimes seen as being at odds with the idea that NGOs can operate more flexibly than governments and are closer to people on the ground. On the one hand, popular views of bureaucracy have negative connotations of red tape, slowness and corruption, but on the other as Weber showed, bureaucracy is the foundation stone of administrative practice, offering the potential for an optimization of precision, speed and impartiality. Narayana (1992: 135) writes about the bureaucratization of NGOs in India and finds that though many NGOs have not taken on 'bureaucratic' characteristics, some are becoming increasingly bureaucratic in terms of 'structure, process and behaviour'. For example, many older 'Gandhian' NGO leaders are being replaced by new professionals who may be more interested in maximizing resources and economic incentive systems. This process of bureaucratization is also being conditioned by external factors such as sources of funding and government control bodies. These demands each produce pressures that can lead NGOs to formulate and adhere to bureaucratic procedures such that there was a general observed tendency for 'NGOs to adjust to their complex environment by becoming increasingly bureaucratic'. This finding is also born out by Wallace *et al*.'s (2006: 165) study of NGOs in Uganda and South Africa, where

> Many staff in both north and south complained that they felt more like bureaucratic aid administrators than development workers and that more time was spent on paperwork than development ...

Internal management and capacity building

Despite the lack of profile of management issues within the literature on NGOs, there has been a considerable amount of writing devoted to the issue of 'capacity building' (or 'capacity development' as it is often now known). Like many of the terms employed in relation to NGOs (such as participation and empowerment), capacity building is somewhat imprecise, but usually refers to strengthening the organizational dimensions of NGOs. Rick James (1994: 5) defines capacity building as: 'an explicit outside intervention to improve an organization's effectiveness and sustainability in relation to its mission and context'.

The idea of capacity building was originally used in relation to efforts to strengthen the public sector in developing countries (Polidano and Hulme 1999). It referred to external efforts to strengthen government's capacity to carry out various tasks, from service delivery to policy analysis. The idea arose as a reaction against the tendency for development projects to generate dependency and an inability to sustain performance beyond the end of the project, as Umeh (1992: 58) explains:

> the process of identifying and developing the management skills necessary to address policy problems; attracting, absorbing and managing financial, human and information resources; and operating programmes effectively.

In the NGO field, the discourse of capacity building began emerging when increased aid began to flow more freely into the NGO sector at the time of the 'new policy agenda' during the 1990s.

International NGOs were encouraged by donors to 'strengthen' local partner NGOs to increase roles in service delivery and advocacy.[97] If NGOs were to be more central to development efforts, donors felt that they should strengthen their organizational capacities. Early organizational assessments of development NGOs had not been particularly positive. For example, Stark Biddle's (1984) analysis of data from more than one hundred senior staff of US NGOs (commissioned by USAID) had identified a lack of leadership capacity, poor communications between headquarters and field offices, weak financial planning, poor fund-raising management, problems in the governance relations and the functioning of boards, and inadequate attention to human resources.

Capacity building also spoke to the changing relationship between international and 'Southern NGOs' (Lewis 1998c). For reasons of sustainability, many international NGOs had become interested in making a transition from simply implementing projects and providing services directly towards helping to build local organizations and structures. This involved working with and, if necessary, strengthening the local 'partner' organizations. International NGOs began to judge their own effectiveness in terms of how far they were managing to strengthen their

---

BOX 11.3 CHALLENGING THE NORTH/SOUTH CONVENTIONS OF 'CAPACITY BUILDING'

There are currently some interesting examples of NGOs that move beyond the rhetoric of capacity building towards radical organizational support and change.

The NGO Resource Centre in Karachi is an example of capacity building that moves beyond the conventional North/South model. Established with the support of the Aga Khan Foundation in 1991, the Centre has provided capacity building support in the form of training, information provision and linkage support to local NGOs in Pakistan. It is now the Civil Society Resource Centre (CSRC) (www.csrc.org.pk).

The Transform Programme began in the UK as a capacity building programme for the Southern partners of a group of UK NGOs including Christian Aid, CAFOD, World University Service and Oxfam. Over time, it has evolved into a network of NGOs and consultants in Southern and East Africa which aims to strengthen the capacity of organizations and businesses to build organizational support locally and reduce dependence on Northern organizations and resource channels. It has now become Transform Africa, an independent organization (www.transformafrica.org).

At the same time, NGOs in the South are also increasingly making use of the growing sophistication of web sites that offer wider advice on third sector management, such as Blue Avocado in the United States which focuses on board management issues and offers 'practical, provocative and fun food-for-thought for non-profits'. One director of a Mexican NGO recently reported the usefulness of sites such as this one for planning leadership succession in a small NGO. Although ideas may originate from one context, there is increasing willingness for organizations to learn from and adapt ideas as many varied sources as possible in putting together viable management strategies (www.blueavocado.org).

Source: author interview notes

partners not just with funding but also in terms of skills and capacities (Egeland and Kerbs 1987). At the same time, capacity building helped bolster the organizational identity of international NGOs. As they moved away from direct operational work, they could present themselves as more developmental and less welfare service oriented. At the same time, if they were now helping to build the capacity of local NGOs – and civil society more widely – then this could be seen as contributing to the new wider agenda of 'good governance'.

Fowler's (1997) approach briefly discussed above sets out five categories of NGO capacities and discusses agendas and organizational approaches for enhancing them.[98] Capacity building can therefore be understood as a form of 'organization development' (OD) that will be familiar to many from the management literature.[99] Fowler *et al.* (1992: 18) define OD in terms of 'an ongoing process that optimises an organization's performance in relation to its goals, resources and environments'. Cooke (1996) distinguishes two different main ideological variants of OD. One he terms 'development organization development' (DOD), which tends to be flexible and experiential, and the other 'managerialist organization development' (MOD) that is planned and systematic in nature.

Many different forms of support are provided to and by NGOs under the general heading of 'capacity building' (Sahley 1995). The first is technical assistance, which is usually concerned with basic operation issues of the NGO and can include technical resources such as a monitoring system or computer software, specialized advice, or exchange or secondment of staff in order to strengthen certain skills. The second is provision of organizational assistance as a response to overall organizational needs, and may take the form of management training or short-term consultancy inputs designed to build capacity in an area such as strategic planning in a problem-solving approach. The third is 'organizational development intervention', in which a longer-term view is formed of organizational capacity overall, leading to a facilitative programme over a number of years of interventions designed to help the organization diagnose and solve present and future challenges itself.

Drawing partly on Oxfam GB's long experience in this field, Deborah Eade (1997: 35) identifies three views of capacity building within an NGO – which she distinguishes from other forms of capacity building such as institutional development – and points out that while these are clearly interrelated they are often muddled and can usefully be separated out. First, capacity building can be understood as a 'means' through which an organization is strengthened to perform specific activities. Second, it can be viewed as a 'process' of searching for greater coherence within an organization based on reflection and leadership in relation to mission, structure and activities. Third, it can be understood as an end, that is, to provide an organization with the means to survive and fulfil its mission and objectives.

Critics of the capacity building agenda have sometimes argued that the overall discourse carries a 'subtle paternalism', associated with an instrumentalist view of NGOs as delivery systems for donor funds and with an assumption that international NGOs have all the answers (Fisher 1994). For Kaplan (1999) there is also a problem that standardized views of how NGO capacities should be strengthened can lead to a disjuncture between proposed solutions and local problems, between what is offered and what is required. He argues that we need to move away from a 'simplistic delivery' view of capacity building, which instead needs to be rooted in the specifics of an individual organization's history and distinctive processes, rather than 'one size fits all' solutions. The idea that each organization is unique and needs to be in overall control of its own organizational evolution is also explored in Biggs and Lewis (2009) in the context of a fair trade organization in Nepal.

Despite the criticisms, Fowler (1997) argues that capacity building can provide a useful opportunity to reflect on organization issues and development approaches, and for a possible renegotiation of international NGO roles *vis-a-vis* local societies, perhaps leading to a move beyond the bland rhetoric of 'partnership'. Shifts away from more traditional models of 'North-South' capacity building are illustrated in Box 11.3.

There has been a resurgence of the idea of capacity building – or 'capacity enhancement' as it is often now termed – in the context of the changed environment in which NGOs increasingly operate. International NGOs increasingly see themselves as agencies with decades of experience on the ground, tackling poverty and providing basic services to people. This is leading NGOs such as CARE and Oxfam to provide capacity building to a range of institutions in the Middle East, Africa and Asia to develop their expertise in training staff, advocacy work and fundraising competencies (Cooper 2012):

> That's become the main selling point of international NGOs: their experience in scaling up community projects and achieving real results for thousands more than a local grassroots organization could. Few small NGOs, for example, would dare to aim at saving the lives of 50 million minors – Save the Children's goal over the next five years.

For the discussion of NGO management, the importance of 'capacity building' is the recognition that factors both inside *and* outside the NGO are important for an organization's effectiveness. Any comparative advantage that NGOs may have over other sectors is only 'potential' and not innate, and therefore needs to be realized.

The management of information

Another key issue for internal management is the management of information. NGOs can be seen as being increasingly concerned in their work with 'linkages and information flows', both with national and international development agencies, and with the people that they work with (Madon 1999: 253). However, while most NGOs are conscious of the need to collect and manage information, not all information is actually useful. The challenge for NGOs is to distinguish between gathering and utilizing different kinds of information for different purposes – including *data* (which are quantitative or qualitative facts), *information* (data and other objective facts which have been given meaning) and *knowledge* (the product of people giving some kind of significance or value to this information). This can be seen as building 'a chain of increasing value, whereby data can become information, which can then be transformed into knowledge' (Powell 1999: 11).

It is almost self-evident that good information management can improve an organization's efficiency, effectiveness and creativity. But as Powell (1999: 21) argues, it is the current high speed of technological change and the growing complexity of task that causes many NGOs problems:

> Everyone is agreed that information and knowledge are of vital importance. However, no one knows which knowledge, applied to which information, in which way, will prove to be the most effective way in shaping the new realities.

This produces and reinforces conceptual uncertainty among NGO managers and managing information is clearly getting more difficult. Turning the mass of information into 'useable knowledge' is difficult for NGOs, because it requires well-developed analytical skills, including an understanding of the linkages between micro and macro levels.

This is particularly apparent for NGOs engaging with markets, where there is rapid change and a high economic cost to out of date or inadequate information. For example, in the course of an initiative by NGOs working in Mozambique to support emerging entrepreneurship among small producers in the recently privatized cashew nut industry, it was found that learning to manage information effectively was a key constraint in building and supporting successful businesses in conditions in which global markets can change rapidly (Artur and Kanji 2005). Unequal access to information remains a key dilemma. Information is ultimately linked to power, since participation in the 'informational economy' remains highly uneven, as the work of influential work of Manuel Castells (1996) shows.

As resource dependency theory tells us, organizations need to be able to manage all resources, and not only material forms. Michael Edwards (1994) has highlighted some of the barriers that tend to restrict information management within NGOs. There may be an overall organizational culture that restricts information exchange. For some activists, information gathering may simply be seen as a luxury that the organization cannot afford. At the level of structure, NGO staff may be geographically scattered and compartmentalized and this too may restrict the generation of useful knowledge. Most important of all is the need to acknowledge the role of power within organizations and between stakeholders. In practice, many NGOs view themselves as vulnerable (and they often are, subject either to government interference, or donor changes of funding policy) and therefore behave defensively. They may have incentives to reject information that does not fit with their existing practices, or which they feel some stakeholders will not wish to hear. They may also be reluctant to face up to information that suggests a level of failure, since admitting failure may be perceived as likely to increase vulnerability (see Chapter 7).

Managers deploy power consciously or unconsciously to control information. For example, it is common in any work place for informal networks to emerge that exclude certain people and create knowledge cliques. This links us back to earlier discussions about power, knowledge and information that were raised in Chapter 7 in the work of Ebrahim (2003), set out in Box 7.2. NGO managers need to understand and in some cases challenge the assumptions that are made at different levels about what kinds of knowledge and information are most valued (such as 'formal' – normally quantitative – data as opposed to informal, qualitative or local forms of information). At the same time, as Smyth (2002) suggests, NGOs are interested in the opportunities presented by the new technologies, but at the same time are pressured by donors to demonstrate that what they do has impact, raising the concern that 'the current emphasis is too heavily on management, of both information and people, which could lead to the neglect of social relations embedded in knowledge' (p.103).

Issues of representation are also an important component of NGO information management. Bebbington (2005) shows how dominant NGO representations of

---

BOX 11.4 CLOSING THE CIRCLE: A SPANISH NGO USES BLOGGING TO LINK SPONSORS WITH COMMUNITY RECIPIENTS

The NGO Ayuda en Accion – Spain's Action Aid – has been experimenting with social media to strengthen connections between its supporters and the communities where it works in Latin America. Individual sponsors typically contribute around 20 euros a month to local education and health projects, but numbers have been falling in recent years, and the NGO needs to reinvigorate its business model. The public's willingness to donate was negatively affected by a scandal in Spain in 2007 when two charities were accused of fraud, and by the 2008 financial crisis. Typically, sponsors receive updates from communities a couple of times a year, including a Christmas message, as a way of attempting to create a relationship between sponsor and beneficiary.

In a new pilot scheme, the Vidas en Directo (Lives Live) initiative has tried to make the connection a more immediate one. Members of these communities are being trained by the NGO to communicate with those who support them via a weekly blog. Esther Alonso, head of organization and projects, explains: 'We want people to communicate directly without intermediaries. That improves accountability, brings more transparency, works on their technical capacities and empowers them...We want to say to sponsors: "Here is your window into these projects, you can look through it in real time"'. The next stage of the experiment is to give sponsors who are interested special usernames so they can 'write back' and talk about their own lives, in an effort to create a less unequal and a more equal type of international aid relationship.

Source: The Guardian Poverty Matters, 'Spanish NGO uses blogging to link donors with Latin American recipients', Mark Tran, (accessed 6 November 2012)

Andean people by Dutch and Peruvian NGOs have often served to perpetuate a largely out-of-date picture of these people as primarily depending upon agrarian livelihoods, which the very poorest households no longer did. This misrepresentation resulted in development interventions that were biased towards the less poor groups and that ignored the needs of those most marginalized. At the same time, David Mosse's (2005: 8) work on the ethnography of project processes underlines the point that power is exercised through 'control over the interpretation of events' and in 'the narratives that maintain an organizations definition of the problem'. The narratives and problem definitions are important because they play a large part in the judgments and decisions surrounding discussions of what constitutes the 'success' of an organization or an intervention.

Generating knowledge from information, argues Powell (1999), while increasingly reliant on technology, is essentially a human process. Reaction to information necessarily draws upon peoples' experience, judgement, values, insights, and is not therefore necessarily objective. This point is made forcefully by Wallace and Kaplan (2003: 61) in a study of organizational change experienced by Action Aid in Uganda, where the local country office is caught between the demands of head office and those of funders, each requiring different forms of information for different purposes:

> ... the entire system in which Action Aid Uganda is embedded relies on the kind of thinking which revels in lists, which insists upon logical frameworks, quantitative analysis and reporting, boxes, compartments, tables. The tendency is towards reduction of complexity and nuance and contradiction to lowest common denominators of facts and numbers which can be perused and assessed in the quickest possible time, with the least amount of effort. This remains the Action Aid centre's main expectation, as it does the expectations of the aid world generally. Uncertainty, ambiguity, nuance, complexity – all these are to be avoided. They demand high levels of emotional and thinking ability, and they don't easily bring in the money.

The recent emphasis on results and quantification across large parts of the development industry that was discussed in Chapter 5 may be closing down the scope for NGOs to manage and use information effectively in diverse ways. It may also be damaging their capacity to produce knowledge that can speak effectively to a people-centred development perspective (see Wallace *et al.* 2013). For example, NGOs will also need to improve their capacity to access and analyse information and evidence if the new much-vaunted 'theories of change' approaches to planning are to be used effectively.

The rapid growth in communications technology is transforming the ways in which organizations approach their work (Scott Morton 1996). These technologies may make it possible for NGOs to react more quickly to events, and make it easier for information to be deployed for advocacy purposes. New technology also makes an impact on the ways in which NGOs relate with actors in their external environment, making coordination efforts potentially more effective, and bringing new dimensions to the tasks of internal management (Box 11.4). The increase in quantity and quality of information available generates complex challenges for NGO managers, but it could also allow better 'sensing' by organizations of events within their external environment. An abuse of human rights in a country can be signalled around the world in seconds so that NGOs can immediately take action.

Clark and Themudo (2006: 70) point out that new technology increasingly allows smaller flexible network structures to react more quickly to rapidly changing events and issues than the traditional NGOs with their unwieldy systems and structures:

> Most established NGOs are hobbled by elaborate management and board processes that must approve major policy statements; dotcauses do not have such constraints. Hence, we find that, today, there are strong advantages to being small, flexible, and dependent primarily on web-based communications.

NGOs have responded to improved communication opportunities through the forging of alliances, the construction of networks, and what Brown has termed the 'bridging' role – between local community organizations and government, between consumers and producers, between constituents in rich countries and those in poor countries. The result has been increasing levels of inter-organizational and inter-sectoral partnership (Lindenberg and Bryant 2001). Information technology also potentially brings increases in the controlling dimension of management work, such as in terms of performance measurement (Scott Morton 1996), and these may be an unwelcome trend for NGOs if it adds to pressures for technocratic forms of evaluation at the expense of more participatory learning-based approaches.

Organizational change within NGOs

If we consider prevailing ideas about organizational change in the business world, we find that it is likely to be influenced by two main types of factors: the wider environment that both drives and constrains change, and specific efforts by managers to secure change within the organization. Change may also be both planned and unplanned.

As we saw in Chapter 7, the neo-institutionalist perspective suggests that organizations that share the same overall environment will engage in similar practices and take on similar characteristics. They will come under pressure to legitimize themselves by adopting institutionalized ideas and practices, assisting them to understand and operate in the wider context of the social world, and generating an institutional logic that signals to different stakeholders, referents and constituents that the organization is legitimate. Leading neo-institutionalists DiMaggio and Powell (1991) famously argued that organizations therefore tend to change primarily to be more like each other. They may be pressured, for example, by government (or donors) to conform to accepted norms and practices, creating a process of convergence that they term 'isomorphism'.

Planned change, as we have seen, is central to rational, top-down thinking about organizations where ordered restructuring is seen as both desirable and possible. Such ideas reflected the dominant post-1960s Western model of organizational change, which uses military language of 'planning', 'scenarios' and 'objectives' and identifies definable problems that need to be overcome in organizations. As we have seen, an example of this can be found in Henry Mintzberg's model of strategic planning. There have been many other variations and adaptations of this basic idea. For example, an 'incremental' variant acknowledges the role of politics, power, incremental change and feedback (Quinn 1980). This type of approach follows Charles Lindblom's (1959) idea of 'the science of muddling through'. He demonstrates the importance of emergent, incremental change based on a series of small but significant changes – negotiations of multiple demands and competing values – along with a process of mutual adjustments. In this way, formal techniques such as strategic planning are beyond the capacities of real people because both technique and organization are so complex, and that only a longer process of 'successive limited comparison' can produce change through small, incremental steps.

A wider exploration of the management and organization literature reveals a great many different theoretical perspectives on change. Andrew Pettigrew (1987) argued that securing strategic change is extremely complex and requires understanding of context, content and process by managers often over a long period. In Peter Senge's (1990) work there is an emphasis on the need for organizations to have a systems approach to change, in which they seek to build a 'learning organization' that can change effectively. This requires the acquisition of important new disciplines in thinking by managers. Tom Peters (1994) argues that the most important thing for managers to do is not to think consciously about change processes but to instead seek out unusual new challenges and make their organization an exciting place to work in – by building the 'curious corporation' – and success will automatically follow. Finally, Gareth Morgan (1994) stressed the symbolic dimension of change within organizations. Managers need to apply appropriate 'images' to conceive of possible changes, e.g. the spider plant, which grows and changes simultaneously through multiple centres and strands in more complex ways than linear models of change may allow.

Although the potential for achieving change may be circumscribed by pressures in the environment, individual organizations nevertheless still have choices about how to try to manage change and how to determine its trajectory. Two basic groups of ideas or models exist about managing organizational change (Tassie *et al.* 1996).

First, we have what might be termed programmatic or 'rational change' models. These tend to draw upon linear ideas of transition and change followed by periods of calm. A three-step change process for organizations is commonly conceptualized, involving *unfreezing, moving* and *refreezing* (Robbins 1990). This model recognizes that change does not take place within an organization simply because a decision has been taken for it to occur, and it conceptualizes change management as a process rather than an event. Such an approach allows useful recognition of the fact that change is likely to be resisted, for various reasons: by people with power fear losing what they have; by bureaucratic structures that favour the status quo; by organizational cultures that resist change (see Chapter 8); and by organizational efforts to 'manage' the environment in order to protect the organization from the need for change. Recognition of pressures to postpone or delay necessary change lay, for example, at the heart of a learning exercise that was undertaken by IIED on participation (Box 11.5).

A second group of perspectives are broadly non-linear. In chaos and complexity theory, for example, causes and effects are seen as unclear and multidirectional, and change process patterns emerge from apparent disorder through a process of self-organization. For example, if an organization takes a decision to acquire a computerized system to improve its record keeping, this may generate unanticipated discussions about precisely which records are to be kept, and the ripples from this change may eventually feed into wider negotiations about changing the mission of the organization.

This approach acknowledges the rapidity of change and turbulence in the environment, and the likelihood that this creates more complexity and ambiguity for managers. It suggests that planned change often fails to yield the desired results, leading to more 'new recipes for success' that repeatedly disappoint. It also challenges

---

BOX 11.5 INTERNAL PROCESSES AND PARTICIPATION: LEARNING WITHIN IIED

The International Institute for Environment and Development (IIED) is a non-governmental research organization that works extensively with a range of partners in the South on research and advocacy. In 2001 IIED undertook a review of its internal systems and structures and external project relationships in order to stimulate learning and increase IIED's transparency to its partners. While the review found plenty of evidence to indicate that IIED remained at the forefront of using and promoting participatory approaches and methods, it was also agreed that – like many NGOs – IIED also needed 'to draw out, disseminate and incorporate lessons from our work much more systematically than we do' (p.33). Issues raised by the study included the need to: (a) recognize the demands on the time of staff and partners and ensure that there are adequate incentives in place to encourage learning and exchange; (b) understand that there can be trade-offs between interesting processes and useful high quality products, so that judgements sometimes need to be made in cases where time and/or resources are tight; (c) ensure that dissemination and influencing strategies are better planned and budgeted for with partners; and (d) understand that there are several different understandings of participation that exist and that it is necessary to negotiate these clearly with staff and partners. The authors concluded that the experience of doing the review 'illustrates the complexities involved in "practising what we preach" and reminds us how difficult it is to keep to the values that underpin "participation" in a demanding and competitive environment' (p.v).

Source: Kanji and Greenwood (2001)

the idea of open systems thinking in which organizations are viewed as being in equilibrium with their environments. If there is no linear cause and effect operating, and with each individual managers' realities often quite different within any organization, then simple 'means–ends' thinking becomes unable to deal with complexity and change effectively.

Complexity theory is therefore leading researchers to refine earlier models such as 'organizational learning' in order to emphasize features of organizations as the existence of informal spontaneous networks among staff which 'shadow' formal structures (e.g. resistance, favouritism, etc.), and the need to encourage 'spontaneous self control' during periods of organizational change which does not tip over into an 'unstable zone' in which change becomes impossible to guide. For example, in one study of an organizational change programme within an international NGO and its field offices it was found that staff perceived change very differently in different parts of the organization. There was a particular discrepancy between the headquarters and the overseas field offices. Organizational change was being promoted ostensibly to promote regionalization, with devolution of many powers to the local offices (with overall control retained by the centre), but was perceived by the field offices simply as a concentration of power by the centre. The process of organizational change in the NGO was closer to one of 'organized anarchy' than planned change. In this case, there was no shared vision across the NGO because goals were ambiguous, technologies were unclear and structures were loosely coupled (DiBella 1992).

Tassie *et al.* (1996: 144) argue that both of the main views of organizational change can be reconciled, because each has validity in certain circumstances. Managing a realistic model of change (in line with De Graaf's [1987] conceptual framework) calls for a good fit between the level of unpredictability in the environment, the links between means and ends in terms of assessing whether a given process will produce a given outcome, and the level of 'programmability' possible in the change process:

> the failure of most change initiatives in … [third sector organizations] … can be attributed to an inability to match the adopted approach to change (programmatic or self-organized) with the situation (external environment or means/ends relationships orientated).

From the third sector literature we can take away the idea that change management is probably best seen as an art rather than a precise science. Managers can try to create a context for change that allows for both planned and unplanned patterns to emerge, rather than trying simply to impose a top-down master plan. Once a leader realizes that they cannot easily predict or control change, then a context may be built by articulating a commitment to the process and to the core vision and values of the organization, but then by leaving the precise trajectory of different parts of the change process to managers. These are then free to pursue diverse initiatives as long as they fall within the overall context domain.

Third sector management trends

While discussions about NGO management have generally been relatively slow to take shape, there have by contrast been lively debates taking place about wider third sector management issues, particularly in the United States. Paul Light (2000) examines the overall trends in non-profit management reform in the United States based on large-scale surveys of non-profit organizations in 19 states, and identifies a set of pressures on organizations to reform their management practices. These include pressure from funders and clients, higher levels of public scrutiny arising from legitimacy problems generated by recent public scandals, the growth of specialized consultants and advisers to the sector, and the growth of increasingly similar, professionalized non-profit organizations seeking uniqueness in a competitive marketplace.

Light goes on to identify four 'tides of reform', each of which is based on different assumptions about non-profit organizations and their roles, and each of which has distinctive strengths and weaknesses. The 'scientific management' model (a) seeks to establish a set of core best practices that all organizations should follow, based on developing standards and codes of conduct. Taking its cue from the 'patron saint' of scientific management F.W. Taylor, the approach requires organizations to work towards improving their internal systems and structures over time, but it can be costly to implement and runs the risk of placing emphasis on relatively unimportant elements of organizational performance. By contrast the 'liberation management' model (b) takes a different tack. Rather than focusing on the rules, systems and structures of organizations, this approach argues that an assessment of outcomes (in relation to an organization's mission statement) should be the ultimate indicator of non-profit effectiveness. The model stresses employee empowerment, deregulation and entrepreneurialism, but runs the risk that an organization might lose internal discipline or lose sight of its original target group.

The third management approach of 'war on waste' is influenced mainly by private sector thinking. This model (c) draws on ideas from the corporate sector to improve efficiency through mergers, strategic alliances and shared administrative costs. Placing an emphasis on re-engineering and downsizing, the main assumption is that by reorganizing the non-profit organization, gains in efficiency can be achieved. The strengths of the approach lie in its ability to reduce duplication and allocate funds more efficiently, but the danger is that an emphasis on uniformity will lead to a reduction in the diversity of the non-profit sector, and that it may impact negatively on staff morale within organizations. Finally, the 'watchful eye' approach (d) stresses the need for more public scrutiny of non-profit organizations in order to promote a higher level of overall management discipline. Focusing on the concept of transparency, it assumes that the availability of financial and performance information will create competition and reduce inefficiency, and while its openness is a key strength, there are fears that the model is also open to manipulation and the use of inaccurate information to maintain a good public image.

All four 'tides of reform' were found to be active in the sector. Some trends are apparent, with 'scientific management' seen as suitable for small emergent non-profits seeking to improve their capacity, while larger established organizations have been drawn into the 'watchful eye' model as the government increases financial reporting regulations. While the 'liberation management' idea has been found attractive to many organizations, it has generated debates about the practice of effective evaluation and the definitions of 'success' among different stakeholders. While (a) and (b) are based on the assumption that the organization can undertake reforms from within and regulate itself, (c) and (d) instead place an emphasis on the need for outside pressure. Given the diversity of organizations, the study concludes by suggesting that what is needed is for organizations to set their own priorities and avoid being drawn either by management reform fashions, or by simply importing practices from the government or business sectors, and instead to build capacity to improve their performance.

Moving to the world of development, it is the 'war on waste' approach that has become most relevant to NGOs. It has found traction because of the donors' increased emphasis on 'value for money' issues, as Cooper (2012) suggests:

> To increase value for money, aid groups are slashing overhead costs, red tape and transaction costs. They are enhancing coordination between headquarters and field offices. They are harmonizing global operations, rooting out fraud and waste, and optimizing the use of their resources

Donors such as DFID are themselves facing pressures to increase cost effectiveness, partly as a result of the new public management agendas and partly as a consequence of the financial crisis that has affected public sectors in many Western countries.

While broader contexts may change, debates around the internal management of NGOs have stayed fairly constant. For example, Grant and Crutchfield (2007) recently attempted to identify the characteristics of 'high impact non-profits' based on a study of a combination of domestic non-profit organizations and international NGOs. They considered a mix of well-known and little-known organizations, across a range of sectors. The findings led to them offering a robust critique of conventional non-profit management wisdom with its usual emphasis on leadership, governance, strategies, programmes, marketing, and fundraising, along with the strategy of securing small-scale success and then trying to scale it up site by site.

By contrast, the researchers found that strong impact depended on a range of other factors that they distilled into six key activities that they term: (i) serve and advocate; (ii) make markets work; (iii) inspire evangelists; (iv) nurture non-profit networks; (v) master the art of adaptation; and (vi) share leadership. This led them to go on to challenge and dismantle some of what they saw as a set of 'non-profit myths' about preconditions for creating successful organizations. The first is that of 'perfect management', finding that some successful organizations are far from exemplary models of generally accepted management principles, and that while 'adequate management is necessary, it is not sufficient for creating significant social impact'. The second is 'brand name awareness', since they find that most of the organizations are not household names, and few focus much on marketing themselves or their work. Nor is there a 'breakthrough new idea' involved in this success, with most mostly old ideas being 'tweaked' and made to work. Organizations do not tend to spend time creating 'textbook mission statements', and organizations find it better to 'live' their values and ideas rather than fine-tuning them on paper. The fifth myth is the need to rely on conventional metrics such as 'overhead ratios', which are often misleading in the way they present information. And sixth and finally, there was no correlation apparent in their sample between success and 'large budgets'.

Grant and Crutchfield (2007: 34) conclude by questioning the idea that internal management is a key ingredient of success, suggesting that what probably matters more is that organizations should simply focus on what goes on 'outside their own walls' and enlist help from others:

> We had assumed that there was something inherent in these organizations that helped them have great impact – and that their success was directly tied to their growth or management approach. Instead, we learned that becoming a high-impact nonprofit is not just about building a great organization and then expanding it to reach more people. Rather, high-impact nonprofits work with and through organizations and individuals *outside themselves* to create more impact than they ever could have achieved alone. They build social movements and fields; they transform business, government, other nonprofits, and individuals; and they change the world around them.

Studies such as this one suggest that what we think we know about managing in the third sector, and what has relatively quickly – in the short period of time that research has been ongoing – become seen as conventional wisdom, may still not amount to very much. It shows once again just how complex, diverse and difficult it is to understand and manage organizations in the third sector.

Conclusion

This chapter has examined some of the issues that emerge in the internal management of NGOs, focusing on aspects of both the third sector and the wider management literature. On the whole there is surprisingly little written on the internal management of NGOs. Starting with the wider third sector literature, it is possible to identify a set of distinctive management issues which apply to most third sector organizations, such as leadership, governance and volunteerism. However, there are important differences among development NGOs in terms of context and approaches. Finally, not everyone agrees that getting internal management right is necessarily *the* critical factor for NGOs to be successful in their work. What *is* more certain is that additional research is needed by both practitioners and researchers to more fully understand the internal organizational landscape of NGO management, which is unlikely to be understood simply as an extension of mainstream management, nor, in the practical realm, as responding to 'one size fits all' management prescriptions.

12

CONCLUSION

NGO management and the future

> Twenty years ago most NGOs concentrated on what they thought they did best, whether relief, self-help, conservation, micro-credit or advocacy. Now leading NGOs are seeing the need to do all these things and take a holistic view of development.
>
> *Clark (2003a: 147)*

Introduction

In this book, we have traced the history of ideas around NGO management and developed a conceptual framework that allows us to understand it as a complex field of research and practice. We conclude with a discussion of the conceptual framework for NGO management that has been assembled during the course of this book, and with some ideas about where the field is going. While the NGO management debate can never be fully resolved, individual organizations will need to build approaches that help to maximize their potential in line with their own values and priorities and the opportunities and constraints offered by the environments in which they work.

The emergence of NGO management

When the donor-led expansion of development NGOs took place during the late 1980s, the new resources being made available to them soon became the subject of much debate. For many NGOs, a reliance on commitment, goodwill and sound values was seen as the key to doing effective work, and there was distrust of the idea of management itself. Others saw this as not enough. They began arguing that NGOs needed to take management more seriously than they did if they were to improve their performance, build more solid reputations and justify the increasing resources they received. In response to the suspicion of management expressed by some development NGOs, Piers Campbell (1987) suggested that there was nothing inherently 'good' or 'bad' about the concept of management *per se*, arguing that management was simply 'the process of mobilizing resources towards a given purpose'.

Different perspectives on the subject of NGO management began to emerge. The first was the *generic management* view. This assumed that 'management is management' and places a strong emphasis on a 'one size fits all' approach. According to this view, there is no particular reason why NGOs should not seek to strengthen and improve their management by drawing strongly on mainstream business thinking. One practical implication of this perspective was that NGOs should consider sending their staff to the established management training courses alongside colleagues from the worlds of business and government. It was a view that was often reinforced by the observed failures of many development NGOs to engage with the 'nuts and bolts' of basic management due to a preoccupation with what he terms 'fancy' alternative, value-driven management ideas (Dichter 1989a).

The second was the idea that a *distinctive* view of NGO management was needed. This perspective was particularly found in some quarters of the new community of wider 'third sector' management researchers who, frustrated at the neglect that their subject had received, argued that new management models and concepts needed to be developed based on the distinctive, specific experiences of third sector managers (Billis 1993a; Harris 1996). Following from this, Billis and MacKeith (1992: 44) went on to argue that NGO management is 'a massive uncharted territory awaiting exploration' and hypothesize that NGO management may embody a unique 'combination of challenges' for managers, which will need to be explored through further investigative research.

A third *adaptive* view of NGO management is the most realistic and the most useful. Within this perspective, it was argued that while generic or mainstream management ideas may be useful and relevant to development NGOs (as well as those from the wider third sector), these cannot be applied in any simple, straightforward way. Instead, they need to be adapted in the light of NGO distinctiveness in relation to organizational structure and culture, and in terms of the complex and distinctive work which development NGOs seek to undertake (Campbell 1987). A synthesis of different types of management is required. At the same time, NGOs needed to be viewed not only in terms of their organizational characteristics, but also the wider contexts in which they operate. This emphasis on context was essential if the overly technical and depoliticizing tendencies encountered within some strands of the 'NGO management science' (critiqued by Stewart 1997) were to be countered effectively.

Similar views emerged from the work of David Korten (1990) and Alan Fowler (1997), both of which emphasize the need for development NGOs to learn from other sectors, and to build innovative management approaches of their own which can both get the work done more effectively, *and* which remain appropriate to core NGO principles and values. In this perspective, NGO management becomes associated with improvisation, hybridity and synthesis – key themes that we have been exploring in the course of this book.

The nature of NGO management

From this adaptive view, we therefore arrive at what we have termed a 'composite' model, which is set out in Table 12.1 below. It recognizes the diversity of NGOs, and the fact that an organization's operating context is crucial to the opportunities and constraints it faces in relation to management, and the uncertainty that this implies. This environment includes the institutional context, the level of political stability, the resource availability, and the cultural norms that exist both within and beyond an organization's boundaries. NGO management is represented as a hybrid, based on an organization-, task- and context- specific improvisation and synthesis that draws on ideas and practices from four different areas of management.

The composite model of NGO management draws on four areas of management: business, public, development and third sector. First, *generic management* (drawn mainly from the business sector) is important because development NGOs like any other organization need to give priority to well established 'nuts and bolts' management principles. The private sector has also come to be seen as far more central to international development than it once was, making it necessary for NGOs to engage with it and sometimes to adopt some of its ideas and approaches. Second, relevant principles need to be drawn from *public sector management*. These might include the need to empower the users of services, improving levels of public participation in local level decision making, or ensuring that equal opportunities policies are in place within an organization to challenge discrimination. Public management may also be particularly relevant to NGOs that become engaged in contracting and the delivery of public services. Third, *development management* seeks to achieve a good fit between both the outcomes of activities undertaken and the manner in which such work is carried out. This becomes a vital area for development NGOs seeking to build distinctive values into their work and reduce the gap

TABLE 12.1 A composite framework for understanding NGO management

	Contextual features	*Organizational features*
All organizations	Environment (culture, context, institutions)	Generic management (mainly from the 'for-profit' business world)
Development NGOs	Development management (from 'Southern' projects and programmes)	Third sector management (mainly from 'Northern' voluntary/ non-profit sectors)
		Public sector management (from government in 'North' and 'South')

Source: adapted from Campbell 1987.

between the values they espouse and the way they go about doing their work ('walking the talk'). Finally, *third sector management* ideas are potentially useful to development NGOs because third sector organizations (of which NGOs form a subset) face distinctive challenges of structure and context that go beyond, or are inappropriate to, generic management. For example, there is little in mainstream management theory which would properly equip an NGO for the difficult tasks of managing the demands of different funding agencies, or balancing its accountabilities simultaneously to both a formal governing body and to its large numbers of geographically remote, impoverished users. These are the kinds of questions that third sector management seeks to address.

NGOs management as synthesis and improvisation

As we have seen, NGO management is best viewed as a distinctive synthesis from other fields. The sector origins of concepts, ideas and approaches central to NGO management lie outside the immediate experience of development NGOs – in the worlds of business or government organizations, or among the non-profit or voluntary sectors of the industrialized countries of Europe and North America. Table 12.2 shows how many of the key issues faced by NGO managers in fact have origins in the other sectors.

For example, the concept of public accountability, an important issue for NGOs, goes back to debates within public administration. For example, Selznick's (1966) study of the TVA examined constraints to public participation in a large public sector development project. Moving to the private sector, we have discussed how NGOs have frequently drawn upon forms of 'strategic planning' tools, drawn from the private sector, as a means to address perceived weaknesses in planning their work. At the same time, the 'social audit' as a method for improving performance and accountability draws upon earlier private sector debates about business practices and social responsibility (Goyder 1961). NGO managers and researchers need to be aware of the sector origins of these ideas, for they are far from unique and NGOs are not the first face organizations to face such challenges. Uncovering more of this hidden history may help NGO managers avoid the risks and waste of resources associated with 'reinventing the wheel'.

Of course, NGO management is not only concerned with the recycling and adaptation of old ideas. Many NGOs are also generating their own management

TABLE 12.2 The sector origins of selected concepts relevant to NGO management

Public sector	Private sector	Third sector
Accountability	Strategic planning	Volunteer management
Empowerment	Management by objectives	Fund-raising management
Capacity building	Social audit	Governance and governing bodies
Participation	Stakeholder analysis	Participatory evaluation
Equal opportunities	Organizational learning	Advocacy

innovations. For example, some NGOs have evolved novel approaches to managing relationships, such as the concept of 'accompaniment' in Latin America as a reaction against discredited earlier forms of top-down 'partnership' in which local NGOs often found themselves subordinate players (Hoyer 1994). More recently, Oxfam International has been seeking to harmonize the work undertaken by its alliance of international NGOs based on a 'one-affiliate, one-vote' system' under a new 'single management structure'. Up to four affiliates can work together in a country under a single managing affiliate in ways that still allow for affiliate diversity to flourish but where multiple complementary approaches are selected based on context, combined with a streamlining of areas where diversity is less useful, such as in finance systems and 'business processes' (Hobbs 2013). Such innovations frequently go undocumented, and more systematic research will be needed in order to understand them, particularly those emerging in non-Western contexts.

At the same time, both organizations, and the contexts in which they operate, are becoming more complex. Activism is a diverse and constantly changing terrain of experience and activity (Gellner 2010). Managers are constantly required to move into new territory, often relying on experimentation and experiential learning. For example, in his description of global action networks (GANs) Waddell (2011: xiv) writes of the ways that activists move beyond the confines of traditional NGO work into more open-ended, cross boundary activity:

> They are figuring things out as they go along, since there are no role models. This means that they are often borrowing approaches and ideas from traditions with strategies and goals quite different from their own ... Sometimes these can be adapted ... but often other traditions are problematic and actually hinder GANs' ability to realize their goals.

As they carry out their day-to-day work, NGO managers are both synthesizing and adapting ideas from these various sources to fit their needs, and improvising and innovating new approaches to NGO management practice.

Complexity, hybridity and ambiguity

The continuing growth of *complexity* is a key challenge for development NGOs. Some mainstream management theory sees the growth of complexity as linked to the increasingly dispersed spatial dimension of business activities and the multicultural character of business practices (Harzing 1995). For example, the use of some familiar management techniques may not work in unfamiliar contexts, and it becomes more difficult for organizations to implement uniform personnel practices and performance standards. Kelleher and McLaren (1996) emphasize the turbulent context in which many development NGOs tend to work, and use the phrase 'grabbing the tiger by the tail' to encapsulate the challenge of taking control of organizational change under difficult and volatile circumstances. The rise of rights-based development is another factor that has increased the complexity of the work that

NGOs do. As Hobbs (2013: 3) argues, this has increasingly made development 'about political alliances and action, rather than service delivery, technical projects and large grants'. It is also focusing attention more and more on issues in developed countries, where the roots causes of problems of 'stalled trade talks, gridlocked climate negotiations, unequal access to natural resources' often lie – creating the need for new forms of political agility and action.

Nevertheless, the work of many development NGOs remains located in particularly difficult areas, such as places where there is continuous conflict and instability or in remote, isolated communities. Many NGOs operate under conditions of extreme danger and instability, while others may simply face long-term environmental factors that make it slow and difficult to achieve progress with difficult challenges. Development NGOs have perhaps not done enough to convey a clear narrative that encapsulates the difficulty, riskiness and complexity of the work that they do – preferring instead to present fundraising images that suggest that they can provide straightforward solutions to problems while maintaining unrealistically low administrative overheads within their organizations.[100]

Mainstream management theory has increasingly paid attention to the idea of *hybridity* as a post-bureaucratic organizational form, and Parker (1998: 236) sees 'expanding choices for organizations' which 'involve more complex, hybrid structures and processes capable of surviving and thriving in the global marketplace'. Hybridity is now also a dominant theme within writing on the third sector around the world. In recent work on the theme of hybridity in the UK third sector, David Billis (2010: 12) writes

> One thing is sure. We are not going to return – at least in the near future – to an (apparently) benign era of more straightforward organizational boundaries… What we are now facing are fundamental changes in the nature of the organizations that are financing, planning and delivering welfare. It is not just the economy, but also the organizations themselves that have become 'mixed' …

In the world of development NGOs, we are also seeing new combinations of organizational structures and objectives emerge, from the rise of the ethical business organization to the commercializing world of micro-credit provision. While conventional organizational choices, such as self-management systems, decentralized structures and classic bureaucracies, can all be found amongst the NGO sector, mixed organizational forms are also becoming increasingly common. For example, NGOs that operate micro-credit programmes may draw upon private sector financial management techniques and practices to calculate administrative and loan recovery costs, while remaining within the overall framework of the not-for-profit form. As Brett (2009) has argued, at the centre of successful development is the search for 'viable hybrid solutions'.

Hybridity is also relevant at the level of sector, where boundaries have for some time been blurring. While it may be useful to conceive of an NGO as being part of the third sector, it is just as important to understand its position in relation to the other two sectors. For example, an NGO that moves into not-for-profit trading activity in order to reduce its dependence on donors may find itself increasingly drawing upon private sector business management thinking. An NGO that undertakes contract work within a government-run service provision system may need to engage with and take on many of the public sector management traditions. Organizational success increasingly depends not just on boundary spanning between the NGO and the wider environment, but also on managing effectively across sector boundaries.

In earlier chapters, we saw that *ambiguity* has also been a central theme throughout our discussion of NGO management, whether in the tensions between charitable and business management styles in the context of NGO work with 'fair trade' (Lewis 1998), or in the organization tensions that emerge when an organization contains elements of both the associational and the bureaucratic 'worlds' (Billis 1993a). In particular, NGO managers may find themselves struggling to reconcile managerialist pressures and people-focused work. This was particularly apparent from Wallace *et al.*'s (2006: 165) study of organizations in Uganda and South Africa in which it was found that

> The disjuncture between the paper-based plans, objectives, activities and indicators and the day-to-day realities that poor people and NGO staff try to grapple with in a wide range of contexts and cultures is too great to be bridged. The paper-based plans and timetables are left in the office, while NGO staff try to find ways – many innovative, others very inappropriate – to work with poor communities, marginalized groups and the neglected. They then revert to the written tools again when it comes to reporting and accounting for donor aid money …

Critics of the new aid environment argue that it is now one that 'rewards crude declarations of success, and discourages subtle and critical reflection' (Scott-Smith 2013: 101).

Ambiguity is also found in relation to the identities and self-representations of development NGOs. For example, many development NGOs have long combined mainstream economic income generation work alongside more politically sensitive empowerment activities aimed at political transformation. Such organizations present complex justifications for combining such approaches, including the need to balance meeting peoples' immediate needs with the longer-term aims of contributing to structural change. This makes it possible for local NGOs to present a non-threatening face to donors and government in order to widen membership and activities, while offering ideological attractions to supporters from radical backgrounds. It may also allow NGOs to adapt to working within a repressive political environment while working towards longer-term change. David Hulme (1994: 260) calls this the 'double-headed strategy', which allows NGOs to present different sides to different stakeholders, a useful strategy under conditions of uncertainty and change, but often difficult to maintain and manage. There may be contradictions when NGOs attempt to be all things to all people:

> the income generation activities operated by SNGOs commonly integrate members more deeply into the processes that their consciousness-raising and dialogical activities identify as causes of poverty-profit maximisation, competition among the poor reducing group solidarity and the acquisition of the assets of the poor by entrepreneurs.

Many development NGOs may also seek to present a non-political image for state approval, but then project the language of small-scale political action locally. This can confuse its membership and may also bring conflicts with charity laws or with suspicious governments. Yet as Mitlin *et al.* (2005) argue in support of the idea of NGOs producing development 'alternatives', the need to build linkages more broadly with social movements and political parties in order to support political change processes will require NGOs to build skills that will allow them to negotiate as effectively as possible in this difficult area.

Changing aid agendas around civil society bring contradictions about NGO roles and orientation into sharper focus. NGO identities may be confused by two divergent trends: 'some NGOs are moving further into the global service-providing marketplace, while others see themselves as part of international social movements' (Edwards 1999b: 198). These reflect the long-running dichotomy, which has often been observed in the wider third sector between service provision and advocacy, and there is every reason to suppose that both types of agencies will remain important within development work. Organizations that remain caught between these trends may face tensions. While it may sometimes be possible to combine both trends effectively within a single, flexible organization, there are increasing numbers, particularly of international NGOs, which lack a clear strategy and structure and whose disorientation is apparent from the continuing crises of reorganization involving efforts at decentralization, regionalization, harmonization and indigenization. There may come a point at which ambiguity, like hybridity, becomes more clearly a source of weakness than a source of strength.

NGO management in the world

Turbulence continues to characterize the wider global context, and the first decade of the twenty-first century has been increasingly unstable. The primacy of Western style neoliberalism that has followed the Cold War is increasingly under challenge, and the US-dominated 'uni-polar' world that was has begun to fade. The limits to the project of European integration have become strikingly apparent and its increasing level of economic prosperity has come to a sudden and dramatic halt with rising unemployment and the crisis of the Euro currency. What explains these dramatic changes? According to Michael Cox (2012), Western policy makers in particular have shown themselves to be increasingly incautious, having financed economic growth on the back of unsustainable debt, allowed the creation of impenetrable banking instruments through weak regulation of the banking sector, and over-reached themselves militarily in the ill-advised attempt to transform Iraq.

Another factor has been the faster than predicted rise of the BRIC economies and the pace of China's economic growth in particular, especially around the time of the 2008 banking crisis, and the Euro crisis and its associated political challenges that followed soon afterwards. There will of course be positive trends in the return to a multi-polar world including the diversification of development approaches and funding. But there remains considerable uncertainty as to how these changes in the world economy will eventually play out, with important implications for the world of international development, whose assumptions about the way change happens – and the approaches and resources required to bring these about – are likely to undergo a wholesale re-evaluation.

All this brings new complexity and unpredictability. At the same time, aid policy – particularly in the West – continues to be dominated by technocratic approaches and neoliberal policy ideas. For a time, the mainstream aid system opened up to multiple NGO identities and roles – as deliverers of humanitarian relief goods, as social service providers contracted by governments and donors, and as advocates of human rights, democracy and social justice. But space has gradually contracted. The world of aid, as Hulme (1994: 257) points out, increasingly limits the room for manoeuvre available for pursuing diverse strategies:

> The third sector is being encouraged to restructure itself from a source of innovation, organizational pluralism, alternative knowledge creation and 'new' political force into a contractor for national governments and international aid agencies.

At the level of wider politics and policy, there are continuing changes in the regulatory frameworks operated by governments, with a continuing shift towards enablement and competition, alongside contracting and a greater role for the private sector as both an aid manager and a deliverer of services. In the context of the UK third sector, a recent report from the Barings Foundation (2013) restated long run-ning concerns about the loss of the third sector's independence in the face of the growth of service delivery and statutory funding, mostly in the form of 'contracting' (which demands measureable outcomes) rather than grants. This undermines the independence of the sector's 'purpose, action and voice'. There is a risk that specialist expertise on the needs of different groups, better delivered services because of high levels of user engagement, and stronger sector diversity because of the capacity of the sector to give expression to different voices, may be lost. The report also cites two additional trends in the form of increased competition from for-profit tendering, and the financial crisis that has led to new financial challenges for NGOs. As sector bounda-ries become further blurred within the 'big society' agenda the report concludes that a key danger is that those parts of the sector that deliver public services 'could in effect become not for profit businesses, virtually interchangeable with the private sector' (p.27), echoing David Korten's output vendor versus development catalyst concerns of the early 1990s.

Despite a more flexible language of development, funding processes are becoming more complex and bureaucratic. In some cases, they have involved governments imposing unwieldy management and reporting tools that ironically have long been left behind by public and private sectors (Wallace *et al.* 2005: 168):

> It some ways it was hard for the researchers to understand why a set of tools based on approaches to planning, development and change that have been so questioned and discredited over decades, has come to dominate aid funding processes.

The MDGs signalled a commitment at the international level to poverty reduction, but they also symbolized a new form of far-reaching managerialist targeting within international development. The arrangements being put in place to supersede the MDGs look unlikely to challenge these principles to any significant degree, although civil society efforts to include the reduction of inequality as a component of whatever follows may still bear fruit.

The increased private sector influence in development has added to the complexity. Business, as we have seen, has come to be seen by donors (and many NGOs) as a key player in the fight against poverty, through its creation of employment and its growing (and increasingly publicized) range of social and ethical activities. The growth of interest in the social accountability of the business community may bring new opportunities for NGOs to influence business practice (Zadek 2000; Forstater *et al.* 2002). Business has increasingly been brought into the management of development work by donors such as DFID in the form of private consultancy groups. The private sector is also increasingly influencing the way NGOs are managed. As Cooper (2012) asserts

> Many NGOs are sharpening their business ethos when it comes to hiring and project implementation; performance based pay and cost-benefit analyses, once considered a corporate mainstay, have now entered the non–profit realm … NGOs aren't just partnering with the private sector. In many ways they are adopting corporate principles and strategies, hiring staff with business backgrounds and contemplating long term social impact investment …

At the same time, development work requires NGOs to make more and more connections in terms of levels and ideas. NGOs that were previously content to try to make a difference at the local project level, perhaps combined with some national level advocacy work, are finding themselves participating in more wide-ranging debates and forms of action. Issues that were previously debated nationally are now 'up for grabs internationally' such as pharmaceutical testing, accounting standards, multilateral trade negotiations and financial regulation (Keohane and Nye 2003). At the same time, there are concerns that closer ties with donors have led many development NGOs too far into 'non-political arenas' where it is difficult for them to address the structural causes of poverty and exclusion (Banks and Hulme 2012).

Implications for NGO management

How will the management of NGOs evolve over the coming decade? The days of the reluctant NGO manager seem to be over for many NGOs, replaced by a new NGO professionalism, a dominance of mainstream development delivery approaches, and a rapprochement both with working with the private sector and adopting more of its management assumptions and tools. For Dichter (1999: 54), there has been a general shift among development NGOs towards a sort of commercialization:

> To survive, today's NGO has been forced to become more corporation-like and less church-like. Its primary concern, though rhetorically still to actualise social visions, is also to cater to a marketplace (of ideas, funders, backers, supporters).

As more and more professionalized NGOs operate in which Dichter calls a 'global marketplace of altruism', we are faced with more and more calls for development NGOs to rethink the implications of their recent growth and to return to their roots, working for change 'quietly, locally, and modestly'. As part of this trend, writers such as Alan Fowler (2008) continue to argue for growth and recognition of the importance of the 'non-aided' NGO sector as a key foundation of civil society. There are also calls for NGOs to go back to what originally made NGOs important – the ideas of innovation and grassroots people-centred approaches – alongside concern that the continuing split between those organizations focused mainly on service provision and those others focused on advocacy is unhelpful and still needs to be overcome. Following from this, Banks and Hulme (2012) suggest that a key new direction for development NGOs is to 'step back' and find ways to let citizens do more.

The recent rise of the 'my NGO' phenomenon in which concerned citizens set up their own small organization to assist or show solidarity in direct ways with others in need perhaps reflects a dissatisfaction with the more corporate aspects of the international NGO industry and the desire for smaller scale, people-to-people development work. But there may also be a danger in idealizing small, informal NGOs, which may also reproduce paternalistic approaches and reinvent the wheel. The NGO universe will be a poorer place without diversity and pluralism. The more corporate NGO model embodied for example by BRAC in Bangladesh challenges many prevailing wisdoms. It has evolved into a key player in that country's struggle against poverty, while at the same time it coexists with the thousands of smaller, less bureaucratised third sector organizations that remain active locally.

At the broader level, a key danger has always been that the NGO management agenda brings with it a narrowing and a depoliticization of the approaches to development work undertaken by NGOs. As NGO management becomes a formalized

part of wider management training within universities and institutes, a predominantly technical approach that draws mainly on assumptions from the corporate
world may squeeze out those staff who come from an activist tradition and create a
'local managerialism that emphasises organizational governance over radical politics'
(Choudry and Kapoor 2013: 11).

In Fowler and Malunga's (2010) overview, three important internal issues for
NGOs are highlighted. First is the importance of achieving accountable and effective
approaches that can take into account both careful planning and evaluation, and the
capacity to learn and address complexity and uncertainty. Achieving this balance, or
what they call 'an organizational blend' (p.6), is the key challenge for which there are
'no rules', meaning that improvisation remains key. Budget cuts are, they suggest,
placing even more pressure on managers to manage this challenge. Second is the
search for revitalized NGO identities within civil society that are viable and credible
beyond the world of aid, including in different ways the renewal of the various values
of charity, social justice, activism and welfare to which the sector in all its diversity has
its roots. Third is the need to 'optimize the political economy' of NGOs as organizations, in which there is increasing money available for certain activities and very little
for others, leaving some organizations in expansion and others in a continual struggle
to survive. Organizations will need to experiment with further alliances, localization
and voluntarism if the NGO sector is to remain diverse and credible.

The vast diversity of NGOs and issues means that the activities 'mix' will be different for each NGO, and that this may also change as the organization evolves, takes
new decisions and develops new strategies. Over time, some NGOs may move
closer towards the market sector and sell services in order to become sustainable,
while others may choose to rely on a more value-based, voluntarist motivation to
their work and remain true to founding principles. Some NGOs may decide that
entering into contracting arrangements with government for service delivery is
appropriate to their objectives, and these organizations may then grow to take on
more of the characteristics of government agencies.

These trajectories will each have a set of advantages and disadvantages in terms
of the work NGOs undertake and the management implications of these activities.
A dynamic model of NGO management therefore needs to encapsulate organizational diversity, learning and change. The model reflects a 'process' view of management that recognizes that NGOs are adaptive, constantly changing organizations
that operate within increasingly uncertain and unpredictable contexts, and that there
is therefore no single 'blueprint' for managing NGOs. It also acknowledges that
there are increasingly many management issues – such as the new information technology – with which all three kinds of organization may be simultaneously grap-
pling. At the organizational level, development NGOs need to be able to manage
change either by being clear enough about their goals and purposes to resist pressures to grow or change, or else by building change strategies that allow structures
and practices to evolve that are in keeping with the organization's own values and
ethics.

The main risks to NGOs may be linked more to ideology than to organizational scale. The extension of managerialism into almost every aspect of international development NGO work by donors is deeply problematic for the capacities of NGOs to remain diverse and creative organizations. For example, the relentless emphasis on innovation – as opposed to genuine creativity – may actually reduce the organizational space for new thinking. Seelos and Mair (2012: 46) suggest that 'innovation is not the Holy Grail', writing that:

> First, we found that both longterm evidence from studies of social sector organizations and recent empirical evidence challenge the mantra that *more innovation is better*. Second, we found that many of the assumptions about innovations in the social sector may be misleading. And third, we discovered that pushing innovation can stifle progress just as much as it can enable it.

Will there be a trend towards strength through a diversity of structures and approaches, or will there be a process of standardization – what Foreman (1999), writing about the influence of Northern or international over Southern organizations, has termed the 'McDonaldization of NGOs' – in which NGOs tend towards a unidirectional isomorphism? What is clear from our discussion is that there are just as many pitfalls for NGOs if they simply rely upon 'high moral purpose, good will, hard work, and common sense' (Korten 1987: 155) as there are if they respond unthinkingly to pressures from the environment to professionalize. Ultimately these are political rather than technical choices which development NGOs will need to make.

NOTES

1 By 'grey' literature, I refer to documents produced by agencies such as donors and NGOs, including evaluations, country overviews or training manuals. While these may not have the rigour of systematically produced formal research studies, they may still be valuable sources of information for researchers because they contain up to date, difficult to find data with a practical focus.

2 The complex issue of NGO terminologies is discussed in more detail in Chapter 4.

3 Not everyone uses the term 'third sector' in in the same way. For example, Norman Uphoff (1995) argues that only membership-based, self-help organizations should be seen as part of the third sector. He reasons – incorrectly in my view – that public benefit NGOs that provide services to third parties should more properly be considered part of the not-for-profit *private* sector.

4 However, as we will see in Chapter 3, it is also recognized that development can be defined broadly to include elements of these fields. For example, the rise of 'right-based approach' within development – as practised by many of the NGOs that make up the Save the Children alliance of organizations – makes an explicit link between human rights and development.

5 As we will see in Chapter 3, development can be defined broadly to include elements of these other fields. For example, the rise of right-based development makes an explicit link.

6 Context also refers to sector as well, where we must beware of 'one size fits all' approaches. As Staudt (1991: 3) has put it: 'development management ... involves more than adopting some bag of tricks from, say, western corporations, assuming techniques work the same way everywhere'.

7 'The charitable-industrial complex', *The New York Times*, July 26, 2013, http://www.nytimes.com (accessed 27 August 2013).

8 What constitutes a progressive position is of course highly subjective, and is here left up to the reader.

9 'Russia raids human rights groups in crackdown on "foreign agents"', The *Guardian*, Wednesday 27 March 2013, www.guardian.co.uk (accessed 7 June 2013).

10 BRAC once stood for the Bangladesh Rural Advancement Committee, but since it now works beyond rural areas and beyond Bangladesh, it briefly changed to Bridging Resources Across Communities, before settling on the idea that its name should no longer be regarded as an abbreviation at all. BRAC's website, which contains a wealth of information, is at www.brac.net

11 BRAC has substantially reduced its earlier dependency on foreign aid by establishing a range of social enterprises, including a bank and a university, and by charging for some of its services. Its 2004 Annual Report stated that of its annual budget of US$245 million, around 77 per cent was now self-financed.

12 Vetwork's website can be found at www.vetwork.org.uk

13 The MSc in Management of NGOs began in 1995 at the London School of Economics' Centre for Civil Society in the Department of Social Policy. A wide variety of students from all over the world (but mostly from the global South) have graduated from this and successor programmes. Some current and former students have contributed to this book in the form of case study material illustrating some of the NGO challenges that they have faced since graduating. The programme has continued to evolve and in 2011 became a distinctive stream within a newly configured MSc in Social Policy and Development.

14 The BBC website reported that 30 staff at 14 leading UK international NGOs were paid more than £100,000 per year, and that the UK Charity Commission was urging pay restraint. The site quoted a Save the Children spokesperson saying: 'To run an organisation that reaches 10 million children in more than 50 countries, with thousands of staff, in some of the toughest places in the world, takes real leadership, experience, knowledge and skill... Without this talent we would not, in the past five years, have almost doubled our income from £161m to £284m, enabling us to reach more of the neediest children on earth than at any point in our 90-year history'. ('Charity Commission chairman issues charity pay warning', www.bbc.co.uk, 6 August 2013, accessed 6 August 2013).

15 However, as third sector organizations engage in closer relationships with states and donors in contractual service delivery roles, they may take on more and more of the characteristics of private sector or public sector organizations and lose this distinctive, value-driven character (Edwards 1996; Fowler 1997).

16 Since the 2008 financial crisis, the reduction of resources available to many development NGOs creates a new challenge for managers now having to think not about unplanned growth and expansion, but about the new landscape of contraction and shrinkage for which NGOs may be particularly unprepared in organizational terms (Brian Pratt, INTRAC, personal communication).

17 The preoccupation with NGO 'capacity building' which arose in the 1990s was a reflection of many things, such as the search for new useful roles by Northern NGOs. No longer wishing to implement their own projects directly in low-income countries, and bypassed in some cases by bilateral donors eager to work directly with third sectors in these countries, many turned instead to the challenge of 'building the capacity' of their local 'partner' third sector organizations (Smillie 1994; Lewis 1998c).

18 It is not clear whether this was because it had already served its purpose of putting the subject on the agenda or whether its members ran out of funding or enthusiasm.

19 Information about INTRAC's work and publications can be found at www.intrac.org

20 The 'management guru' phenomenon is one in which charismatic individuals claim to have all-purpose, novel answers to important management questions. A lively and provocative overview of the world of the management gurus can be found in Micklethwait and Wooldridge (1996). The authors conclude that while management theory is a commercially successful industry that acts as a 'magnet to charlatans', it does offer some general lessons and is 'not entirely devoid of intellectual context'. Some private sector management gurus went on to 'discover' the third sector and went about propagating and adapting their ideas, with sometimes interesting results (e.g. Peter Drucker 1990; Charles Handy 1988).

21 Brown (2011) writes that ANT is 'an approach to the study of mediated relationships between people and things. Its central proposition is that there is nothing outside of what it terms "heterogeneous" or "hybrid" networks of human and non-human materials'.

22 The influential bundle of approaches and ideas previously known by different names such as participatory rural appraisal' (PRA) or rapid rural appraisal (RRA) and associated with the work of Robert Chambers and others.

23 Hybridity is a term from biology that refers to the case in which two species that do not normally interbreed are found to do so under artificial or unnatural conditions. This gives potentially useful new characteristics to the union that neither species might have possessed singly.

24 Kiggundu (1989: 30), however, suggests that too much emphasis tends to be placed on 'cultural variables' within organization and management studies of non-Western cultures, and not enough on the process of managing task, performance and technology.

25 The full document can be downloaded from the Centre for Civil Society Studies at the Johns Hopkins University (http://ccss.jhu.edu).

26 Vakil (1997) suggests that the 'voluntary' element of the structural-operational definition be dropped to reflect the growing professionalization of NGOs. Although this may be appropriate in some cases, it would arguably close off a key element of most third sector organizations. Even BRAC, perhaps the largest NGO in the world, and one which now sports a strong private, even corporate image, still has a voluntary board of directors and still relies on village-level volunteers for aspects of its work. However, Fowler (1997) noted the existence of NGOs in Latin America that do not follow the governing body structure but are managed and governed by an executive director. In a recent interview with the director of a Mexican NGO, the same issue was raised.

27 See for example Horton Smith's (1997) passionate case for arguing that informal grassroots groups are perhaps best seen as the 'true' third sector, a position closer to that of Norman Uphoff (see Chapter 2).

28 The world of policy tends to be characterized by an ahistorical, short-term perspective that tends to ignore the past in favour of promised successful action in the future (Lewis 2009). As Alan Fowler (2012: 3) also points out in relation to his biography of the NGO ACORD, 'the past influences the future'.

29 Blair (1997: 24–5) argues that only those NGOs engaged in working towards public goals (such as those third sector organizations concerned with influencing state policy) can be seen as true civil society actors. Self-help groups or service delivery NGOs primarily concerned with meeting members' needs are not CSOs. This means that while all "CSOs" are NGOs, by no means are all NGOs "CSOs"'.

30 It could be argued that an organization such as NK is representative of the original radical impulse of the development NGO sector in 1980s Bangladesh from which market-oriented NGOs have subsequently deviated. This raises a problem with the pejorative concept of 'NGO-ization' as used by Choudry and Kapoor (2013), which could instead actually be seen as a form of 'de-NGOization' in this context.

31 Kaldor (2003) sees the emergence of the 'anti-globalization movement' in the late 1990s as a sign that other less progressive streams within civil society, such as certain NGOs which represent 'tamed social movements' and those which embody nationalist or fundamentalist interests, are under an increased challenge.

32 There are different views about where the third sector term came from, with Etzioni (1972) usually credited as the originator. Levitt however, writing around the same time in the 1970s, does not refer to Etzioni's work. Another possible contender for the originator of the term is Daniel Bell who refers to it in his 1976 book *The Coming of Post-Industrial Society* (Martin Albrow, personal communication). Fisher (1998) seems to attribute the origins of the term to Nielsen's 1979 book *The Endangered Sector*, but this would appear to be a later derivative usage.

33 An interesting parallel can be found in the participatory development movement embodied in the work of Robert Chambers (1994, 1995, 2005) whose ideas also centre on a critique of 'normal professionalism'.

34 There are increasing numbers of 'hybrid' organizations existing around the alliances and networks which spring up within changing institutional environments (Kramer 1995). This increasing hybridization of the third sector is discussed further in Chapter 8.

35 While Nerfin (1986) asserts the moral superiority of the citizen, Najam makes no judgements at all about the relative values of these three different sectors, merely that they are different.

36 Adalbert Evers (2013) suggests that today's policy debates in Europe make an unhelpful conflation between the distinctive concepts of 'civil society' and 'third sector'. He argues that the first is best viewed as a political concept (about the intermediation of conflict in the public domain) and the second an economic one (increasingly linked to the restructuring of welfare policies, such as the 'big society' idea in the UK). Despite the origins of the term third sector, it seems that its popular usage has become narrowed to the economic emphasis on state and market failure and the role of NGOs as gap fillers.

37 This term 'faith-based organization' has become commonly used around the world and accepted by policy makers. It may be less appropriate when applied to religious NGOs from traditions such as Hinduism and Buddhism in which the concept of 'faith' is less central than in Christianity, Islam or Judaism.

38 By the mid-2000s, there were concerns that development theory had run out of stream and that development studies had become overly concerned with policy and practice – too focused on the needs of donors in particular (Thomas 2006). This was ironic given the earlier and widely debated concerns raised by Michael Edwards during the 1980s in a powerful critique in which he wrote the 'irrelevance of development studies' (due to its heavy emphasis on theoretical debates).

39 The UNDP *Human Development Reports* can be found at www.hdr.undp.org/reports/

40 Many critics advocate rejection of development as an idea. This is not the place to engage in depth with concepts such as 'post-development'. But it is worth noting that such critiques, despite many useful ideas, at times can appear perverse and surprising. For example, one radical post-development writer opposes the idea of development because it destroys 'noble forms of poverty' and 'arts of suffering' (Rahnema 1997: x).

41 Chhotray (2008) correctly warns us against the use of simple binary distinctions such as 'mainstream' and 'alternative' development paradigms, and suggests that effective NGO work depends instead on both challenging and moving between realms and categories.

42 There has long been a set of changing geographical terminologies around development. A global demarcation of 'First World' (Western capitalist), 'Second World' (Soviet, Eastern Bloc and other socialist areas) and 'Third World' (the rest) became common during the Cold War. The still commonly used distinction between a wealthy developed 'North' and a poor, less developed 'South' originated in the UN-sponsored Brandt Commission report of 1980.

43 In many developing countries, the donor fashion for NGOs that emerged at this time greatly enlarged the size and numbers of the NGO community. In some areas, this led to the creation of NGOs that had not evolved organically but were instead vehicles to receiving the funds that were being made available. This fed into the highly uncomplimentary view of NGOs simply as vehicles for unscrupulous entrepreneurial individuals to 'get rich quick' (Lofredo 1995).

44 The official donor scruples about core costs rarely seem to apply to consulting firms, which receive overheads from donors, often multiplying by three- or four-fold the salary component (Brown and Korten 1989).

45 Some organizations such as Oxfam GB have responded to this problem by starting a poverty programme in the UK (Lewis 1999a).

46 Interview with UK NGO manager, 27 November 2012.

47 Despite this changing landscape, OECD countries continue to deliver $120 billion in aid each year.

48 See UN (2013).

49 Empowerment is used widely within business and management as well as in development (Wright 1994). The operating staff is seen as the starting point for action, as a source of skills and capacities. Empowerment implies encouraging them to take the initiative in solving problems (e.g. Holcombe [1995] on the Grameen Bank model).

50 See http://www.actionvillageindia.org.uk/index.php?/our-partners/assefa/ for more up-to-date information about ASSEFA's work.

51 Despite the high profile achieved by the Make Poverty History campaign, there were critics who remained disappointed by the lack of coordination among organizations and the tangible changes on the trade reform agenda (Hertz 2005).

52 Organization theory has not traditionally identified third sector organizations as being distinctive, and NGO researchers themselves have been slow to consider whether organizational theory might offer insights into how NGOs are managed. We do not therefore pretend to offer a comprehensive review of organization theory, which is a vast field, but instead review potential links with NGO issues.

53 Many of these ideas have strongly influenced work in the third sector management literature (e.g. Billis 1993a), which is discussed in Chapter 7.

54 Avina (1993) set out a framework to provide NGO managers with a 'map' to help plan and adapt an organization's structure and strategies, and perhaps resist external pressures for change. Drawing on his own observations rather than the formal life-cycle literature, he sketched a four-stage model: start up, expansion, consolidation and finally close-out. He suggested that both external and internal factors help determine an organization's transition from one stage to another.

55 There is a wide literature on social movements (e.g. McAdam *et al.* 1996). Approaches to social movements vary. The 'resource mobilization' approach in the US argues that the civil rights and women's movements rely on the availability of resources as the critical factor that makes it possible to turn 'grievance' into action and protest (McCarthy and Zald 1977). By contrast, the 'new social movement' tradition from Latin America examines the ways in which social movements constitute local responses and resistance to processes of globalization and cultural imposition (Escobar and Alvarez 1992, Canel 1997). Such literature still needs closer linking with the literature on NGOs (Norrell 1999).

56 The idea that sector boundary crossing is itself an important source of creativity and innovation is explored in recent work by Lewis (2008, 2011) who studied the life histories of NGO leaders and activists who had carried ideas from one sector into another at different points in their careers.

57 For example, Tom Peters and Robert Waterman's *In Search of Excellence* (1982) was a million-selling popular management book that listed eight themes – such as 'sticking to the knitting' that were identified as common to successful companies.

58 This is not to imply that the discipline of anthropology has any more relevance to the study of NGOs than say political economy or geography, but simply that certain kinds of anthropological work interact in potentially useful ways with some current themes in organization theory relevant to NGO management. This approach also reflects my own personal interest and training in social anthropology.

59 Like anthropology, the field of third sector research began in Western settings and has over time diversified and internationalized. The study of Western third sector organizations, whether US non-profit organizations, UK voluntary agencies or international development NGOs, brings with it a set of assumptions and biases rooted in the history, values and cultures of the West. Within the study of the third sector, researchers have only comparatively recently begun to widen and internationalize their focus. Discussions about which types of third sector organizations 'belong' and those which do not became a lively debate in the efforts of the Johns Hopkins comparative non-profit research project, as it moved beyond its initial origins in the contexts of North America and Europe (Salamon and Anheier 1997).

60 He uses Slovenian philosopher Slavoj Žižek's concept of ideology to suggest that development workers remain embedded in the idea of development as an unquestionable good that gives meaning and validity to their work, and leads them to disregard the obvious limitations of what they do and the oversimplifications inherent in many NGO project assumptions.

61 Such an approach warns us to move beyond static ideas in which cultural characteristics are seen to exist in the psyches of people within certain communities or societies. For example, Jaeger and Kanungo (1990) are rightly critical of the notions of 'traditionalism' propounded by authors such as McClelland (1961), which insisted that cultures which emphasized familism and fatalism were antithetical to development because they

could not espouse 'modern' values, a line of thinking which informed much of the 'modernization' theory of the 1960s and 1970s.

62 One of the problems of such an approach is that it assumes that differences between large national groups are stronger than those within populations, which of course runs the risk of stereotyping cultural characteristics.

63 Management by Objectives (MBO) is another logic model informed by the same means-ends thinking as the log frame.

64 An important postmodern critique of cross-cultural training work within multinational corporations – which partly draws on Hofstede's ideas – is made by Leggett (1999: 2), who argues that despite its admirable integrative goals, such training rests on the misguided modernist universalizing assumption that trainees from other cultures are seeking to participate in emerging global systems 'without quite understanding the rules' and need therefore to be 'helped up the ladder'.

65 Here Claeyé draws upon Homi Bhabha's (1984) work on mimicry – as a way of engaging with wider structural power relations and local values by translating ideas and transgressing boundaries.

66 In 2001, PDI changed its name to People's Development Institute.

67 Such a view is implicit in Brett's (1993) study, which argues that we are finally starting to develop methods of accounting for the relative efficiency of different kinds of institutional actors, and therefore envisages a plurality of institutional actors, based on their relative strengths and weaknesses, as the ideal.

68 BBC News Africa, www.bbc.co.uk/news/ (accessed 15 August 2013).

69 Freire's (1972) ideas were politically radical, envisaging class empowerment as the outcome. Within Freire's framework, the idea of groups is important, supported by facilitative, non-directive external professional help. He later became critical of the use of the term 'empowerment' in the US as a form of individual self-improvement. Empowerment also became part of 'management speak' in the business world, in the sense of managers who want to empower their workers and unleash their creativity for greater profit.

70 Participation also has a political meaning, such that liberal theory sees participation as a crucial element of democratic responsive government by providing a voice for ordinary people in decision making, and the UNDP *Human Development Report* (1993) saw participation as the key to innovation and the creation of more democratic and just societies.

71 See Kabeer *et al.* (2009) for a discussion of the case of this homogenization taking place in the Bangladesh NGO sector.

72 For example, in a study of NGO advocacy work around land rights in Kenya and Mozambique, advocacy strategies by NGOs were found to be significantly influenced by contextual factors such as the continuing periodic hostility to NGOs from the Kenyan government, and the struggle by a new NGO sector in Mozambique to absorb relatively large amounts of donor funds very quickly (Kanji *et al.* 2002).

73 There are of course many different ways of conceptualizing the policy process. Some emphasize technical and instrumental dimensions, while others highlight the role of politics and power. NGO managers will find a useful and concise overview of these different perspectives in Sutton (1999).

74 Annis (1992) reflects on the idea of 'informational empowerment' as a tool for evolving greater connectedness among environmental networks in Central America.

75 Such problems are also very real ones for NGOs elsewhere too. For example, in Armenia the PRSP process has been a reasonably inclusive one at the formal level, but since most participating NGOs remain heavily dependent on the major international bilateral and multilateral donors it is not surprising that they do not choose to voice critical views (Ishkanian 2006).

76 In the agricultural development sector, a series of case studies can be found drawn from Asia (Farrington and Lewis 1993), Latin America (Bebbington and Thiele 1993) and Africa (Wellard and Copestake 1993).

77 These authors suggest two new and memorable metaphors for thinking about NGOs: 'as jelly': the NGO focuses on the process of building relationships, becomes pushed and pulled in different directions, but manages to hold a coherent policy agenda together; and as 'microchip': the NGO is more proactive and seeks to convene relationships based around an intellectual contribution which gives them a 'convening legitimacy' among other actors. This is achieved by NGOs that can add value by bring a broader perspective to discussions and creating a specific space for discussion (Mitlin *et al.* 2005).

78 Private sector techniques include the 'social audit', first outlined in Goyder (1961) and outlined in the NGO context in Zadek and Gatwood (1995); and the idea of 'developmental market research', which adapts conventional market research for development work, and has been pioneered in this context by S. Epstein (Marsden *et al.* 1995).

79 This may in part be due to the difficulty for outside researchers of gaining access to data relating to a subject that is understandably sensitive.

80 The *Guardian* newspaper, 28 January, 2006.

81 In some rare cases, people may be able to 'exit' and simply use the services of another NGO.

82 http://guidestar.org/news/features/sarbanes_oxley.jsp (accessed 27 May 2005).

83 There are now signs that rural elites may be losing some of this power as rural communities become more connected through better infrastructure and economic opportunities, leading to a loosening of 'the net' (Lewis and Hossain 2005).

84 For a short and clearly written introductory overview of the main issues and complex debates around the concept of social capital, see Bebbington (2004).

85 The concept of 'governmentality' was coined by Michel Foucault to encapsulate the multiple ways in which the conduct of a population is governed, through organizations and institutions of the state, through norms and identities and through individual self-regulation.

86 More details of the ETI, an alliance of companies, trade unions and voluntary organizations, can be found at www.eti.org.uk

87 BRAC's efforts to develop its social business has at times been resisted by established interests claiming unfair trading practices. BRAC was challenged in the courts in 1999 when it sought to expand into commercial banking, which some saw as inappropriate for a charitable non-profit organization. The Supreme Court upheld BRAC's right to establish a bank as long as its profits were ploughed back into development activities, but it required that tax be paid on commercial revenues arising from banking (Sidel 2004).

88 This type of arrangement has led to the preference in some quarters for the term 'not-for-profit' to be used rather than 'non-profit', which embodies the issue of primary purpose more clearly.

89 Interview with UK NGO manager, 29 November 2012.

90 Most discussions of bureaucracy start with the work of German sociologist Max Weber, whose work connected the idea of bureaucracy with developments in wider politics and society.

91 Mintzberg's later view was that only by linking strategic planning to a wider, processual approach to organizational learning could it be useful. As Bryson (1988) says, 'strategic thinking and acting are what count, not strategic plans in and of themselves'.

92 There is now considerable emphasis on the building of shared values within corporations as a precondition for successful business enterprise (Parker 1998: 206). Perhaps the key point is not the importance of values in third sector management, but the nature of those values. Clashes over different values are common in the NGO sector, for example, between charitable and more political approaches to tackling problems of poverty.

93 There are of course important differences between the UK and the US that have to be negotiated within the third sector management field as well.

94 As we saw in Chapter 9, in practice the boundaries between service delivery and advocacy can be blurred.

95 In Bangladesh, Proshika's problems have been strongly linked to political issues in the organizational environment, but may also have reflected a lack of attention to management and leadership issues within the organization (see Lewis 2010).

96 The older NGO management debate took place during a period of NGO expansion and wide access to resources. Today's climate is much tougher, with fewer available resources and a set of higher, more rigidly defined expectations from many donors.

97 As we saw in Box 6.6, this capacity building effort can sometimes result in the creation of new organizations in the South rather than changes to an existing organization.

98 In contrast to Alan Fowler, Sahley (1995) identified three main NGO 'capacities': (i) identity, culture and purpose, such as the capacity for a clear overall ideology of development, good staff/management relations and effective conflict resolution mechanisms; (ii) management systems and structure such as clear procedures, roles and responsibilities, effective decision making and financial management; and (iii) effective programme and technical capacity, which refers to the ability of an NGO to deliver services effectively and develop strategies based on an informed understanding of social, political and economic contexts.

99 OD can be distinguished from the wider concept of institutional development (ID). Institutions are stable sets of widely recognized rules such as laws, markets or civil society, while organizations are structures bringing together people to work towards a common purpose. ID in relation to NGOs is concerned with efforts to improve the performance of the wider context in which NGOs operate, such as network building between organizations, the reform of the legal environment in which NGOs operate, and efforts to influence the policy environment (Fowler *et al.* 1992).

100 I am grateful to John Hailey for this useful observation.

APPENDIX

A selection of useful NGO management websites

AccountAbility

This is an organization dedicated to strategies for promoting improved accountability and stakeholder involvement in relation to civil society, business and public sector organizations.
www.accountability.org.uk

Board Café/Blue Avocado

Used by development NGOs beyond its domestic US constituency, this site justifiably claims to be 'Short enough to read over a cup of coffee, Board Café has everything you need and want to know to help you give and get the most out of board service'.
www.blueavocado.org/category/topic/board-cafe

Capacity.org

Capacity.org describes itself as a 'gateway on capacity development' and offers a quarterly newsletter as well as a platform for access and exchange for materials and ideas on capacity development. Its materials are available in French and English.
www.capacity.org

Feinstein International Center, Tufts University

Highly relevant particularly to the world of humanitarian NGOs, The Feinstein International Center's research is on the politics and policy of aiding the vulnerable, on protection and rights in crisis situations. It has long-term partnerships with a range of humanitarian and human rights agencies.
http://sites.tufts.edu/feinstein/

INTRAC

The International NGO Training and Research Centre (INTRAC) has undertaken research, consultancy and training on NGO management for more than 15 years. Its newsletter Ontrac provides a wealth of useful information for the NGO manager.

www.intrac.org

Management Accounting for Non-Governmental Organizations (Mango)

Founded in 1999, Mango is a UK-registered charity that aims to strengthen the financial management of NGOs.

www.mango.org.uk

Management Assistance Group

Another US site, the focus is exclusively on social justice organizations and the site covers a wide range of third sector management issues that will be of interest to many NGOs, including strategic planning, innovation and managing people.

www.managementassistance.org/

Management Help

A good general site that carries access to basic information on key management ideas and tools. It has a very useful section that covers non-profit organizations.

www.managementhelp.org

Most Significant Change (MSC) monitoring and evaluation

MSC is a technique aimed at organizations and individuals who wish to monitor and evaluate their social change programmes and projects. By 2004, the MSC technique had been used both by NGOs and governments in Africa, Asia, Latin America, Europe and Australasia.

www.mande.co.uk/docs/MSCGuide.htm

NGO Management Association

Formed by former participants of the LSE's NGO Management MSc course as a site run by NGO managers for NGO managers, this initiative has now grown to include a wide range of resources relating to all aspects of NGO management, including management tools, training and education and upcoming jobs.

www.ngomanager.org

RAPID Programme

The Research and Policy in Development (RAPID) programme is an initiative at the Overseas Development Institute (ODI) that aims to improve the use of research and evidence within development policy and practice through research and debate. The site has useful materials on the link between research and policy that NGOs will find useful.

www.odi.org.uk/rapid

GLOSSARY

Accountability	a process in which an organization builds and maintains a relationship with stakeholders based on transparency and influence
Advocacy	an activity in which an NGO seeks changes in policy, and ultimately in the allocation of power, through political influence based on representing members' and supporters' interests to policy makers
Ambiguity	the coexistence of two or more meanings within a single subject or entity
Association	an organizational form based around membership, usually but not necessarily, informal in structure
Capacity building	originally a public sector term, it became widely used in relation to NNGO/SNGO relationships during the 1990s, usually referring to processes of organization development (OD), but sometimes used more generally
Civil society	a complex term with many different definitions, but which usually refers to the set of organizations and institutions situated between the state, the business world and the household, and to the 'space' in which various kinds of organized entities (religious groups, NGOs, social movements, the media, professional associations, etc.) negotiate and pursue diverse (and sometimes contradictory) social interests
Community-based organization	local, 'grassroots' membership organizations, which often form part of the 'coping strategies' of low-income households (also sometimes known as 'people's organizations')
Complexity	a condition in which there are numerous elements within a system, and many relationships among the elements
Corporate social responsibility	an approach to citizenship and ethics by businesses in which mere compliance is transcended and forms of social good are attempted
Dotcause	a flexible civil society network that draws on new information technology to organize campaigning and protest

Empowerment	an imprecise term which refers to a transformative process in which individuals and groups move from insight to action in pursuit of changes in the exercise of power
Global civil Society	a diverse collection of non-state actors (including associations, organizations and networks) operating transnationally within civil society spaces
Global South	a term used in place of 'third world'
Governance	the ongoing process within organizations by which guidelines for decision-making, mission and action are developed and compliance with them is monitored
Hybridity	a combination of two different elements, such as organizational characteristics
Legitimacy	a term that refers to the credibility of an organization, based on perceived moral justifications for its social and political actions
NGO	non-governmental organization, a highly imprecise term which usually refers to the subset of 'third sector' organization involved in poverty reduction, human rights and environmental concerns
'The North'	the group of rich countries that used to be generally referred to as 'developed'
Non-profit organization	the term commonly used in the United States for 'third sector organization', so labelled because it is distinguished from the culturally dominant model of profit-making organization
Not-for-profit	a term which has tended to replace 'non-profit', meaning that an organization may engage in profit-making activities (such as selling goods or services) but that the proceeds are ploughed back into the organization's activities rather than distributed to shareholders as in the case of a for-profit company
Participation	a somewhat imprecise term which refers to the complex political process of increasing people's involvement in decision-making which can sometimes result in greater 'voice', but on the other may simply legitimize existing decision-making
People's organization	a term often used to refer to local, membership organizations. These can be contrasted with non-membership forms of NGO sometimes called 'intermediary organizations' or 'grassroots support organizations' which provide support and services to POs
Philanthropy	the ethical notion of giving and serving to people beyond one's own family, a term which is common particularly in the United States
PVO	a term commonly used in the United States to describe its development NGOs working in the 'third world'
Scaling up	the process in which NGOs seek to move beyond transitory or localized activities to achieve greater impact through a variety of possible strategies
Service delivery	provision by government agencies, private sector organizations or NGOs of services such as education, healthcare, agricultural extension, etc.
Social economy	economic activities which serve social rather than primarily economic aims such as profit maximization; a term commonly used in continental Europe

Social entrepreneur	creative individuals in the civil society, public or business sector who seek to put underutilized resources to use to satisfy unmet social needs
Social movements	loosely organized groups of organizations and individuals around pressing problems of a local, national or global nature, such as environment, identity, poverty or human rights
Stakeholder	any person or group that is able to make a claim on an organization's attention, resources or output, or who may be affected by the organization
'The South'	a term which has been used in preference to earlier terms for poorer countries such as 'third world' or 'developing countries' (but which excludes Australia and New Zealand)
Third sector	a term referring to the collection of institutions and organizations which, particularly in the West, are seen as separate from state and market (which are said to form the other two sectors) and which has emerged to challenge this 'two sector' view of the world. Also refers to the institutional 'space' between state and market
Transition country	an area of the former Soviet bloc in transition from a planned socialist economy towards free market capitalism
TSO	an organization, such as a trade union, religious group, NGO or community organization which is neither formally part of government nor a for-profit organization
Voluntarism	the tradition of organized voluntary action, but also the philosophical idea that the will dominates the intellect
VO	a term used commonly in Britain to refer to third sector organization; effectively a synonym for non-profit organization or non-governmental organization. Sometimes it is misleadingly used to refer to organizations composed of volunteers (as opposed to more professionalized third sector organizations)
Volunteer	a person who enters into a service or a transaction of their own freewill without an expectation of remuneration

BIBLIOGRAPHY

Abdel Ati, H.A. (1993) 'The development impact of NGO activities in the Red Sea province of Sudan: a critique'. *Development and Change*, 24: 103–30.

Abramson, D.M. (1999) 'A critical look at NGOs and civil society as means to an end in Uzbekistan'. *Human Organization*, 58, 3: 240–50.

Abzug, R. and Forbes, D. (1997) 'Is civil society unique to nonprofit organizations?', paper presented at Association for Research on Nonprofit Organizations and Voluntary Action (ARNOVA) conference, Indianapolis.

Action Aid Bangladesh (2009) *Climate Change Adaptation in an Uncertain Environment: Lessons from a Targeted Community Based Adaption Approach in Bangladesh*. Dhaka: Action Aid.

Africa, S. (2013) 'Philippine NGOs: defusing dissent, spurring change'. Chapter 5 in A. Choudry and D. Kapoor (eds) *NGOization: Complicity, Contradictions and Prospects*. London: Zed Books.

Alvesson, M. (1993) *Cultural Perspectives on Organizations*. Cambridge: Cambridge University Press.

Amendola, M. and Bruno, S. (1990) 'The behaviour of the innovative firm: relations to the environment'. *Research Policy*, 19: 419–33.

Anderson, K. and Rieff, D. (2005) 'Global civil society: a sceptical view'. Chapter 1 in H. Anheier, M. Glasius and M. Kaldor (eds) *Global Civil Society 2004/5*. London: Sage.

Anheier, H.K. (1987) 'Indigenous voluntary associations, non–profits and development in Africa', in W.W. Powell (ed.) *The Nonprofit Sector: A Research Handbook*. New Haven, CT: Yale University Press.

—— (1990) 'Private voluntary organizations and the Third World: the case of Africa', in H.K. Anheier and W. Seibel (eds) *The Third Sector: Comparative Studies of Non-profit Organizations*. Berlin and New York: Walter de Gruyter.

—— (2000) 'Managing nonprofit organizations: towards a new approach'. Civil Society Working Paper 1, Centre for Civil Society, London School of Economics.

—— (2005) *Nonprofit Organizations: Theory, Management, Policy*. London: Routledge.

Anheier, H. (2011) 'Of ties, holes and folds: the power of transnational civil society networks', in M. Albrow and H. Seckinelgin (eds) *Global Civil Society 2011: Globality and the Essence of Justice*. Basingstoke: Palgrave Macmillan, pp. 62–3.

Anheier, H., Glasius, M. and Kaldor, M. (2001) *Global Civil Society 2001*. Oxford: Oxford University Press.

Annis, S. (1987) 'Can small-scale development be a large-scale policy? The case of Latin America'. *World Development*, 15 (supplement): 129–34.

—— (1992) 'Evolving connectedness among environmental groups and grassroots organizations in protected areas of Central America'. *World Development*, 20, 4: 587–95.

Archer, R. (1994) 'Markets and good government', in A. Clayton (ed.) *Governance, Democracy and Conditionality: What Role for NGOs?*. Oxford: INTRAC.

Arellano-Lopez, S. and Petras, J.F. (1994) 'Non-governmental organizations and poverty alleviation in Bolivia'. *Development and Change*, 25: 555–68.

Argyris, C. and Schön, D. (1978) *Organizational Learning: A Theory of Action Perspective*. New York: Addison-Wesley.

Artur, L. and Kanji, N. (2005) *Satellites and Subsidies: Learning from Experience in Cashew Processing in Northern Mozambique*. London: International Institute for Environment and Development (IIED).

Ashby, J. (1997) *Towards Voluntary Sector Codes of Practice: A Starting Point for Voluntary Organizations, Funders and Intermediaries*. York: Joseph Rowntree Foundation.

Ashworth, G. (1996) 'Gender, culture and NGOs', in A. Clayton (ed.) *NGOs, Civil Society and the State*. Oxford: International NGO Research and Training Centre (INTRAC).

Atack, I. (1999) 'Four criteria of development NGO legitimacy'. *World Development*, 27, 5: 855–64.

Avina, J. (1993) 'The evolutionary life-cycles of non-governmental development organizations'. *Public Administration and Development*, 13: 453–74.

Avritzer, L. (2004) Civil society in Latin America: uncivil, liberal and participatory models. Chapter 6 in M. Glasius, D. Lewis and H. Seckinelgin (eds) *Exploring Civil Society: Political and Cultural Contexts*. London: Routledge, pp. 53–60.

Badalt, C. (1997) 'Entrepreneurship theories of the non-profit sector'. *Voluntas*, 8, 2: 162–78.

Baig, Q. (1999) 'NGO governing bodies and beyond: a Southern perspective on third sector governance issues', in D. Lewis (ed.) *International Perspectives on Voluntary Action: Reshaping the Third Sector*. London: Earthscan.

Baillie Smith, M. and Jenkins, K. (2012) 'Existing at the interface: Indian NGO activists as strategic cosmopolitans'. *Antipode*, 44, 3: 640–62.

Banerjee, A. and Duflo, E. (2011) *Poor Economics: A Radical Rethinking of the Way to Fight Global Poverty*. Philadelphia, PA: Perseus Books.

Banfield, E. (1958) *The Moral Basis of a Backward Society*. Chicago: The Free Press.

Banks, N. and Hulme, D. (2012) 'The role of NGOs and civil society in development and poverty reduction'. Working Paper 171, Brooks World Poverty Institute, University of Manchester.

Baring Foundation (2013) *Protecting Independence: The Voluntary Sector in 2012*. Report by the Panel on the Independence of the Voluntary Sector.

Barlett, C.A. and Ghoshal, S. (1990) 'Matrix management: not a structure, a frame of mind'. *Harvard Business Review*, 68, 4: 138–45.

Bate, S.P. (1997) 'Whatever happened to organizational ethnography?'. *Human Relations*, 50, 9: 1147–75.

Batsleer, J., Cornforth, C. and Paton, R. (eds) (1992) *Issues in Voluntary and Non-Profit Management*. Milton Keynes: Open University Press/Wokingham: Addison-Wesley.

Beall, J. (2005) *Funding Local Governance: Small Grants for Democracy and Development*. Rugby: ITDG Publishing.

Bebbington, A. (1991) 'Sharecropping agricultural development: the potential for GSO-government collaboration'. *Grassroots Development*, 15, 2: 20–30.

—— (2004) 'Social capital and development studies 1: critique, debate, progress?'. *Progress in Development Studies*, 4, 4: 343–9.

—— (2005) 'Donor-NGO relations and representations of livelihood in nongovernmental aid chains'. *World Development*, 33, 6: 937–50.

Bebbington, A., Guggenheim, S., Olson, E. and Woolcock, M. (2004) 'Exploring social capital debates at the World Bank'. *Journal of Development Studies*, 40, 5, 33–64.

Bebbington, A., Guggenheim, S., and Woolcock, M. (2006) 'The ideas-practice nexus in international development organizations: social capital at the World Bank'. Chapter 1 in A. Bebbington, S. Guggenheim, M. Woolcock and E. Olson (eds) *The Search for Empowerment: Social Capital as Idea and Practice at the World Bank*. Bloomfield, CT: Kumarian.

Bebbington, A., Hickey, S. and Mitlin, D.C. (2008) (eds) 'Introduction: can NGOs make a difference: the challenge of development alternatives'. Chapter 1 in *Can NGOs Make a Difference?: The Challenge of Development Alternatives*. London: Zed Books, pp. 3–37.

Bebbington, A., Lewis, D. and Batterbury, S. (2007) 'Beyond the development text: the World Bank and empowerment in practice'. *Journal of Development Studies*, 43, 4: 597–621.

Bebbington, A. and Thiele, G. (eds) (1993) *Non-Governmental Organizations and the State in Latin America: Rethinking Roles in Sustainable Agricultural Development*. London: Routledge.

Bell, D. (1976) *The Coming of Post-Industrial Society: A Venture in Social Forecasting*. London: Harper.

Bennett, J. (ed.) (1995) *Meeting Needs: NGO Coordination in Practice*. London: Earthscan.

Benthall, J. (2003) 'Humanitarianism, Islam and 11 September'. *HPG Briefing No 11*, July. London: Overseas Development Institute.

Bhabha, H.K. (1984) 'Of mimicry and man: the ambivalence of colonial discourse'. *October*, 28, 125–33.

Bhalla, A. and Lapeyre, F. (1997) 'Social exclusion: towards an analytical and operational framework'. *Development and Change*, 28, 3: 413–34.

Bielefeld, W. (1994) 'What affects nonprofit survival?', *Nonprofit Management and Leadership*. 5, 1: 19–36.

Biggs, S. (1997) 'Livelihood, coping and influencing strategies of rural development person-nel'. *Project Appraisal*, 12, 2: 101–6.

Biggs, S. and Lewis, D. (2009) 'Fair Trade and organizational innovation in Nepal: lessons from 25 years of growth of the Association of Craft Producers (ACP)'. *European Journal of Development Research*, 21, 3: 377–96.

Biggs, S. and Neame, A. (1995) 'Negotiating room for manoeuvre: reflection concerning NGO autonomy and accountability within the new policy agenda', in M. Edwards and D. Hulme (eds) *Beyond the Magic Bullet: NGO Performance and Accountability in the Post-Cold War World*. London: Earthscan.

Biggs, S. and Smith, G. (1998) 'Beyond methodologies: coalition building for participatory technology development'. *World Development*, 26, 2: 239–48.

Billis, D. (1993a) *Organising Public and Voluntary Agencies*. London: Routledge.

—— (1993b) 'What can nonprofits and businesses learn from each other?', in D.C. Hammack and D.R. Young (eds) *Nonprofit Organizations in a Market Economy*, San Francisco: Jossey-Bass.

—— (2010a) 'From welfare bureaucracies to welfare hybrids'. Chapter 1 in D. Billis (ed.) *Hybrid Organizations in the Third Sector: Challenges for Practice, Theory and Policy*. Basingstoke: Palgrave Macmillan, pp. 3–24.

—— (2010b) 'Towards a theory of hybrid organizations', in D. Billis (ed.) *Hybrid Organizations in the Third Sector: Challenges for Practice, Theory and Policy*. Basingstoke: Palgrave Macmillan, pp. 46–69.

Billis, D. and Harris, M. (eds) (1996) *Voluntary Agencies: Challenges of Organization and Management*. London: Macmillan.

Billis, D. and MacKeith, J. (1992) 'Growth and change in NGOs: concepts and comparative experience', in M. Edwards and D. Hulme (eds) *Making a Difference: NGOs and Development in a Changing World*. London: Earthscan.

—— (1993) *Organising NGOs: Challenges and Trends in the Management of Overseas Aid*. London: LSE Centre for Voluntary Organization.

Black, J.K. (1991) *Development in Theory and Practice: Bridging the Gap*. Boulder, CO: Westview.

Blackburn, J. (2000) 'Understanding Paulo Freire: reflections on the origins, concepts and possible pitfalls of his educational approach'. *Community Development Journal*, 35, 1: 3–15.

Blair, H. (1997) 'Donors, democratisation and civil society: relating theory to practice', in D. Hulme and M. Edwards (eds) *Too Close for Comfort? NGOs, States and Donors*. London: Macmillan.

Blond, Philip (2010) *Red Tory: How Left and Right Have Broken Britain and How We Can Fix It*. London: Faber.

Booth, D. (1994) 'Rethinking social development: an overview', in D. Booth (ed.) *Rethinking Social Development: Theory, Research and Practice*. London: Longman.

Bordt, R.L. (1997) *The Structure of Women's Nonprofit Organizations*. Bloomington, IN: Indiana University Press.

Bornstein, E. (2005) *The Spirit of Development: Protestant NGOs, Morality, and Economics in Zimbabwe*. Stanford, CA: Stanford University Press.

Borg, M. and Harzing, A.-W. (1995) 'Internationalisation and the international division of labour', in A.-W. Harzing and J. van Ruysseveldt (eds) *International Human Resource Management*. London: Sage.

Borras, Saturnino M. Jr. (2001) 'State–society relations in land reform implementation in the Philippines'. *Development and Change* 32, 3: 545–75.

BRAC (1983) *The Net: Power Structure in Ten Villages*, Rural Study Series. Dhaka: Bangladesh Rural Advancement Committee.

BRAC (2004) *Annual Report 2004*. Dhaka: Bangladesh Rural Advancement Committee.

Bratton, M. (1989) 'The politics of NGO-government relations in Africa'. *World Development*, 17, 4: 569–87.

—— (1990) 'Non-governmental organizations in Africa: can they influence public policy?'. *Development and Change*, 21: 87–118.

—— (1994) 'Civil society and political transitions in Africa', in J. W. Harbeson, D. Rothchild and N. Chazan (eds) *Civil Society and the State in Africa*. Boulder, CO: Lynne Reinner.

Brett, E.A. (1993) 'Voluntary agencies as development organizations: theorising the problem of efficiency and accountability'. *Development and Change*, 24: 269–303.

—— (2009) *Reconstructing Development Theory: International Inequality, Institutional Reform and Social Emancipation*. Basingstoke: Macmillan.

Brinkerhoff, D. and Brinkerhoff, J. (2013) 'Development management and policy implementation'. Chapter 28 in E. Araral Jr, S. Fritzen, M. Howlett, M. Rajesh and X. Wu (eds) *Routledge Handbook of Public Policy*. London: Routledge, pp. 374–83.

Britton, B. (1998) 'The learning NGO'. INTRAC Occasional Papers Series no. 17, Oxford: The International NGO Training and Research Centre.

Brodhead, T. (1987) 'NGOs: in one year, out the other?'. *World Development* (supplement), 15: 1–6.

Brown, L.D. (1987) 'Development organizations and organization development: towards an expanded paradigm'. *Research in Organizational Change and Development*, 1: 59–87.

—— (1991) 'Bridging organizations and sustainable development'. *Human Relations*, 44, 8: 807–31.

—— (1994) 'Creating social capital: nongovernmental development organizations and intersectoral problem solving'. *IDR Reports*, 11, 3, Boston: Institute for Development Research.

Brown, L.D. and Ashman, D. (1996) 'Participation, social capital and intersectoral problem-solving: African and Asian cases'. *World Development*, 24, 9: 1467–79.

Brown, L.D. and Covey, J. (1983) 'Organizational microcosms and ideological negotiation', in M.H. Bazerman and R.J. Lewicki (eds) *Negotiating in Organizations*. Newbury Park, CA: Sage Publications.

—— (1987) 'Organizing and managing private development agencies: a comparative analysis'. Boston: Institute for Development Research/Newhaven: Yale Program on Non-profit Organization (PONPO) Working Paper no. 129.

Brown, L.D. and Fox, J. (2001) 'Transnational civil society coalitions and the World Bank', in M. Edwards and J. Gaventa (eds) *Global Citizen Action*. Boulder, CO: Lynne Rienner.

Brown, L.D. and Korten, D.C. (1989) 'Understanding voluntary organizations: guidelines for donors'. Working Paper 258, Country Economics Department, Washington DC: World Bank.

—— (1991) 'Working more effectively with nongovernmental organizations'. Chapter 3 in S. Paul and A. Israel (eds) *Nongovernmental Organizations and the World Bank*. Washington DC: World Bank.

Brown, L.D. and Tandon, R. (1994) 'Institutional development for strengthening civil society'. *Institutional Development (Innovations in Civil Society)*, 1, 1: 3–17.

Brown, S. (2011) 'Actor–network theory', in M. Tadajewski, P. Maclaran, E. Parsons, and M. Parker (eds) *Key Concepts in Critical Management Studies*. London: Sage.

Bryman, A. (1992) *Charisma and Leadership in Organizations*. London: Sage.

Bryson, J. (1988) *Strategic Planning for Public and Non-Profit Organizations*. San Francisco, CA: Jossey-Bass.

—— (1994) 'Strategic planning and action planning in nonprofit organizations', in R.D. Herman and Associates (eds) *The Jossey-Bass Handbook of Nonprofit Leadership and Management*. San Francisco, CA: Jossey-Bass.

Buchanan-Smith, M. and Maxwell, S. (1994) 'Linking relief and development: an introduction and overview'. *IDS Bulletin*, 25, 4: 2–16.

Bunch, R. (1985) *Two Ears of Corn: A Guide to People-Centred Agricultural Improvement*. Oklahoma: World Neighbors.

Bunting, M., The *Guardian*, 17 January 2011.

Buxton, A. and Wilson, E. (2013) *FPIC and the Extractive Industries: A Guide to Applying the Spirit of Free, Prior and Informed Consent in Industrial Projects*. Sustainable Markets Group, IIED.

Buxton, C. (2011) *The Struggle for Civil Society in Central Asia*. Sterling, VA: Kumarian.

Campbell, P. (1987) 'Management development and development management for voluntary organizations'. ICVA Occasional Paper no. 3. Geneva: International Council of Voluntary Agencies.

—— (1994) 'Alternative financing strategies for Southern NGOs'. Mimeo, Geneva: International Council of Voluntary Agencies.

Canel, E. (1997) 'New social movement theory and resource mobilisation theory: the need for integration', in M. Kaufman and H.D. Alfonso (eds) *Community Power and Grassroots Democracy*. London: Zed Books.

Carroll, T.F. (1992) *Intermediary NGOs: The Supporting Link in Grassroots Development*. Hartford, CT: Kumarian Press.

Castells, M. (1996) *The Rise of the Network Society*. Oxford: Blackwell.

Cernea, M.M. (1988) 'Non-governmental organizations and local development'. World Bank Discussion Papers, Washington DC: World Bank.

Chambers, R. (1983) *Rural Development: Putting the Last First*. Harlow: Longman.

—— (1987) 'Sustainable livelihoods, environment and development: putting poor rural people first'. Discussion paper no. 240, Brighton: Institute of Development Studies.

—— (1992) 'Spreading and self-improving: a strategy for scaling up', in M. Edwards and D. Hulme (eds) *Making a Difference: NGOs and Development in a Changing World*. London: Earthscan.

—— (1994) *Challenging the Professions*. London: Intermediate Technology Publications.

—— (1995) 'Participatory rural appraisal (PRA): challenges, potentials and paradigm'. *World Development*, 22: nos. 7, 9, 10 (in three parts).

—— (2005) *Ideas for Development*. London: Earthscan.

Charnovitz, S. (1997) 'Two centuries of participation: NGOs and international governance'. *Michigan Journal of International Law*, 18, 2: 183–286.

Chhetri, R. (1995) 'Rotating credit associations in Nepal: dhikuri as capital, credit, saving and investment'. *Human Organization*, 54, 4: 449–54.

Chhotray, V. (2008) 'Political entrepreneurs or development agents: an NGO's tale of resistance and acquiescence in Madhya Pradesh, India'. Chapter 13 in *Can NGOs Make A Difference?: The Challenge of Development Alternatives*. London: Zed Books.

Choudry, A. and Kapoor, D. (2013) 'NGOization: complicity, contradictions and prospects', in A. Choudry and D. Kapoor (eds) *Introduction to NGOization*. London: Zed Books.

Claeyé, F. (2012) 'Culture, power and resistance: hybridization of management systems in South African NPOs'. Unpublished PhD thesis, Middlesex University Business School, UK.

—— (2014) *Managing Nongovernmental Organizations: Culture, Power and Resistance*. London: Routledge.

Clark, J. (1991) *Democratising Development: the Role of Voluntary Organizations*. London: Earthscan.

—— (1992) 'Policy influence, lobbying and advocacy', in M. Edwards and D. Hulme (eds) *Making a Difference: NGOs and Development in a Changing World*. London: Earthscan.

—— (1997) 'The state, popular participation and the voluntary sector', in D. Hulme and M. Edwards (eds) *Too Close for Comfort? NGOs, States and Donors*. London: Macmillan.

Clark, J. (2003a) (ed.) *Globalizing Civic Engagement: Civil Society and Transnational Action*. London: Earthscan.

—— (2003b) *Worlds Apart: Civil Society and the Battle for Ethical Globalization*. Hartford, CT: Kumarian.

Clark, J. and Themudo, N. (2005) 'Linking the web and the street: internet-based "dotcauses" and the "anti-globalization" movement'. *World Development*, 34, 1: 50–74.

Clark, N., Hall, A., Sulaiman, R. and Naik, G. (2003) 'Research as capacity building: the case of an NGO facilitated post-harvest innovation system for the Himalayan Hills'. *World Development*, 31, 11: 1845–63.

Clarke, G. (1998) 'Nongovernmental organizations and politics in the developing world'. *Political Studies*, XLVI: 36–52.

Cohen, D., de la Vega, R. and Watson, G. (2001) *Advocacy for Social Justice: A Global Action and Reflection Guide*. Bloomfield, CT: Kumarian.

Coleman, J. (1988) 'Social capital in the creation of human capital', reprinted in P. Dasgupta and I. Seargeldin (eds) (1999) *Social Capital: A Multifaceted Perspective*. Washington DC: World Bank.

Coleman, J. (1990) *Foundations of Social Theory*. Cambridge, MA: Harvard University Press.

Comaroff, J.L. and Comaroff, J. (2000) *Civil Society and the Critical Imagination in Africa: Critical Perspectives*. Chicago, IL: University of Chicago Press.

Constantino-David, K. (1992) 'The Philippine experience in scaling-up', in M. Edwards and D. Hulme (eds) *Making a Difference: NGOs and Development in a Changing World.*, London: Earthscan.

Cooke, B. (1996) 'Organization development and institutional development'. Mimeo, Institute for Development Policy and Management, Manchester.

—— (1997) 'Participation, "process" and management: lessons for development in the history of organization development'. *Journal of international Development*, 10, 1: 35–54.

Cooke, B. and Kothari, U. (2001) (eds) *Participation: The New Tyranny?* London: Zed Books.

Cooper, G. (2012) 'Reinventing the international NGO', Devex, 8 October, www.devex. com (accessed 14 October 2012).

Cooprider, D.L. and Srivastva, S. (1987) 'Appreciative enquiry in organizational life'. *Research in Organizational Change and Development*, 1: 129–69.

Cornwall, A. and Brock, K. (2005) 'What do buzzwords do for development policy? A critical look at "participation", "empowerment" and "poverty reduction"'. *Third World Quarterly*, 26, 7: 1043–60;

Court, J., Menidizbal, E., Osbourne, D. and Young, J. (2006) *Policy Engagement: How Civil Society Can Be More Effective*. Research and Policy in Development (RAPID), London: Overseas Development Institute.

Covey, J. (1995) 'Accountability and effectiveness in NGO policy alliances'. *Journal of International Development*, 7, 6: 857–67.

Cowen, M.P. and Shenton, R.W. (1996) *Doctrines of Development*. London: Routledge.

Cox, M. (2012) 'A hell of a decade'. *LSE Connect*, 24, 1, Summer, pp. 15–16.

Cox, T. (1994) *Cultural Diversity in Organizations: Theory, Research and Practice*. San Francisco, CA: Berret-Koehier.

Craig, D. and Porter, D. (2003) 'Poverty reduction strategy papers: a new convergence'. *World Development*, 31, 1: 53–69.

Crutchfield, L.R. and Grant, H.M. (2007) *Forces for Good: The Six Practices of High-Impact Nonprofits*. New York: Wiley.

Curtis, D. (1994) 'Owning without owners, managing with few managers: lessons from Third World irrigators', in S. Wright (ed.) *Anthropology of Organizations*. London: Routledge.

Cushing, C. (1995) 'Humanitarian assistance and the role of NGOs'. *Institutional Development (Innovations in Civil Society)*, 2, 2: 3–17.

Dale, R. (2004) *Development Planning: Concepts and Tools for Planners, Managers and Facilitators*. London: Zed Books.

Dartington, T. (1992) 'Professional management in voluntary organizations: some cautionary notes', in J. Batsleer, C. Cornforth and R. Paton (eds) *Issues in Voluntary and Non-Profit Management*. Milton Keynes: Open University/Wokingham: Addison-Wesley.

Davies, R. (1997) 'Donor information demands and NGO institutional development'. *Journal of International Development*, 9, 4: 613–20.

Davis Smith, J. (1996) 'Should volunteers be managed?', in D. Billis and M. Harris (eds) *Voluntary Agencies: Challenges of Organization and Management*. London: Macmillan.

Davis Smith, J., Rochester, C. and Hedley, R. (eds) (1995) *An Introduction to the Voluntary Sector*. London: Routledge.

de Graaf, M. (1987) 'Context, constraint or control? Zimbabwean NGOs and their environment'. *Development Policy Review*, 5: 277–301.

de Haan, A. (2009) *How the Aid Industry Works: An Introduction to International Development*. Bloomfield, CT: Kumarian Press.

de Haan, A. and Maxwell, S. (1998) 'Poverty and social exclusion in North and South', *IDS Bulletin*, 29, 1: 1–9.

de Waal, A. and Omaar, R. (1993) 'Doing harm by doing good? The international relief effort in Somalia'. *Current History*, 92, 574: 198–202.

Deacon, B. (2012) 'The post-MDG 2015 UN Development Policy: from the global politics of poverty alleviation to the global politics of solidarity'. Global Cooperation Newsletter, December 2012. International Council on Social Welfare (ICSW). Entebbe: Uganda.

Deacon, B., Hulse, M. and Stubbs, P. (1997) *Global Social Policy: International Organizations and the Future of Welfare*. London: Sage.

Dechalert, P. (1999) 'NGOs, advocacy and popular protest: a case study of Thailand'. Centre for Civil Society International Working Paper 6. London: London School of Economics.

—— (2002) 'Non-governmental organizations and resources: case studies of four NGOs in Thailand'. Unpublished PhD thesis, London School of Economics.

DeMars, W.E. (2005) *NGOs and Transnational Networks: Wild Cards in World Politics*. London: Pluto Press.

Denning, S. (2000) *The Springboard: How Storytelling Ignites Action in Knowledge-Era Organizations*. Boston, Butterworth-Heinemann.

Desai, U. and Snavely, K. (1998) 'Emergence and development of Bulgaria's environmental movement'. *Nonprofit Management and Leadership*, 27, 1: 32–48.

DFID (Department for International Development) (1997) *Eliminating World Poverty: A Challenge for the 21st Century*. London: The Stationery Office.

—— (2009) *Eliminating World Poverty: Building Our Common Future*. London: The Stationery Office.

Diaz-Albertini, J. (1991) 'Non-government development organizations and the grassroots in Peru'. *Voluntas*, 2, 1: 26–57.

—— (1993) 'Nonprofit advocacy in weakly institutionalised political systems: the case of NGDOs in Lima, Peru'. *Nonprofit and Voluntary Sector Quarterly*, 27, 4: 317–37.

DiBella, A. (1992) 'Planned change in an organized anarchy: support for a postmodernist perspective'. *Journal of Organizational Change Management*, 5, 3: 55–65.

Dichter, T.W. (1989a) 'Development management: plain or fancy? Sorting out some muddles'. *Public Administration and Development*, 9: 381–93.

—— (1989b) 'NGOs and the replication trap'. *Technoserve Findings 89*, Norwalk, CT: Technoserve Inc.

—— (1996) 'Questioning the future of NGOs in micro-finance'. *Journal of International Development*, 8, 2: 259–70.

—— (1997) 'Appeasing the gods of sustainability: the future of international NGOs in microfinance', in D. Hulme and M. Edwards (eds) *Too Close for Comfort? NGOs, States and Donors*. London: Macmillan.

—— (1999) 'Globalisation and its effects on NGOs: efflorescence or a blurring of roles and relevance?'. *Nonprofit and Voluntary Sector Quarterly* (supplement), 28, 4: 38–86.

Dickmann, M., Parry, E., Emmens, B. and Williamson, C. (2010) *Engaging Tomorrow's Global Humanitarian Leaders Today*. Enhancing Learning and Research for Humanitarian Assistance, People in Aid Cranfield University, School of Management, UK.

Dignard, L. and Havet, J. (1995) *Women in Micro- and Small-Scale Enterprise Development*. London: Intermediate Technology Publications.

DiMaggio, P. and Powell, W.W. (1991) 'The iron cage revisited: institutional isomorphism and collective rationality in organizational fields', in P. DiMaggio and W. W. Powell (eds) *The New Institutionalism in Organizational Analysis*. Chicago, IL: University of Chicago Press.

Downing, J. (1991) 'Gender and the growth of micro-enterprises'. *Small Enterprise Development*, 2, 1: 4–12.

Drabek, A. G. (1987) 'Development alternatives: the challenge for NGOs'. *World Development*, 15 (supplement): ix–xv.

Drucker, P. (1990) *Managing the Nonprofit Organization*. New York: Collins.

Duffield, M. (1993) 'NGOs, disaster relief and asset transfer in the Horn: political survival in a permanent emergency'. *Development and Change*, 24, 1: 131–57.

—— (2002) 'Social reconstruction and the radicalization of development: aid as a relation of global liberal governance'. *Development and Change* 33, 5: 1049–71.

Dunleavy, P., Margetts, H., Bastow, S. and Tinkler, J. (2005) 'New public management is dead – long live digital-era governance'. *Journal of Public Administration and Theory*, 16, 3: 1–28.

Eade, D. (1997) *Capacity Building: An Approach to People-Centred Development*. Oxford: Oxfam Publications.

Eade, D. and Williams, S. (1995) *The Oxfam Handbook of Development and Relief*. Oxford: Oxfam Publications.

Ebrahim, A. (2003) *NGOs and Organizational Change: Discourse, Reporting and Learning*. Cambridge: Cambridge University Press.

Ebrahim, A. (2010) *The Many Faces of Nonprofit Accountability*. Harvard Business School, Working Paper 10-069, Harvard University.

Ebrahim, A. and Kasturi Rangan, V. (2010) *The Limits of Nonprofit Impact: A Contingency Framework for Measuring Social Performance*. Harvard Business School, Working Paper 10–099, Harvard University.

Economist (2000) 'NGOs: sins of the secular missionaries', 29 January, pp. 25–8.

Edoho, F. (1998) 'Management capacity building: a strategic imperative for African development in the twenty-first century', in V. Udoh James (ed.) *Capacity Building in Developing Countries: Human and Environmental Dimensions*. New York: Praeger.

Edwards, M. (1993) 'Does the doormat influence the boot? Critical thoughts on UK NGOs and international advocacy'. *Development in Practice*, 3, 3: 163–75.

—— (1994) 'NGOs in the age of information'. IDS Bulletin, Spring 1994.

—— (1996) 'International development NGOs: legitimacy, accountability, regulation and roles', Discussion paper prepared for the Commission of the Future of the Voluntary Sector and the British Overseas Aid Group (BOAG), London.

—— (1998) 'Nailing the jelly to the wall: NGOs, civil society and international development', unpublished draft mimeo.

—— (1999a) 'NGO performance: what breeds success?'. *World Development*, 27, 2: 361–74.

—— (1999b) *Future Positive: International Co-Operation in the 21st Century*. London: Earthscan.

—— (2008) 'Have NGOs made a difference? From Manchester to Birmingham with an elephant in the room'. Chapter 2 in A. Bebbington, S. Hickey and D.C. Mitlin (eds) *Can NGOs Make A Difference?: The Challenge of Development Alternatives*. London: Zed Books, 38–54.

Edwards, M. and Gaventa, J. (eds) (2001) *Global Citizen Action*. Boulder, CO: Lynne Rienner.

Edwards, M. and Hulme, D. (eds) (1992) *Making a Difference: NGOs and Development in a Changing World*. London: Earthscan.

—— (1995) *Beyond the Magic Bullet: NGO Performance and Accountability in the Post-Cold War World*. London: Earthscan.

Edwards, M, Hulme, D. and Wallace, T. (2000) 'Increasing leverage for development: challenges for NGOs in a global future'. Chapter 2 in D. Lewis and T. Wallace (eds) *New Roles and Relevance: Development NGOs and the Challenge of Change*. Hartford, CT: Kumarian.

Egeland, J. and Kerbs, T. (eds) (1987) *Third World Organizational Development: A Comparison of NGO Strategies*. Geneva: Henry Dunant Institute.

Elbers, W. (2012) 'The partnership paradox: principles and practice in North-South NGO relations'. Unpublished PhD thesis, University of Nijmegen, The Netherlands.

Ellis, G. (1984) 'Making PVOs count more: a proposal', in R.F. Gorman (ed.) *Private Voluntary Organizations as Agents of Development*. Boulder, CO: Westview Press.

Empson, W. (1930/1966) *Seven Types of Ambiguity*. New York: New Directions.

Escobar, A. (1995) *Encountering Development: The Making and Unmaking of the Third World*. Princeton, NJ: Princeton University Press.

Escobar, A. and Alvarez, S.E. (eds) (1992) *The Making of Social Movements in Latin America: Identity, Strategy and Democracy*. Boulder, CO: Westview Press.

Escobar, J.S. (1997) 'Religion and social change at the grassroots in Latin America'. *Annals of the American Academy of Political and Social Science*, 554: 81–103.

Etzioni, A. (1961) *A Comparative Analysis of Complex Organizations: On Power, Involvement and their Correlates*. New York: The Free Press of Glencoe.

—— (1972) 'The untapped potential of the third sector'. *Business and Society Review*, 1, Spring: 39–44.

—— (1973) 'The third sector and domestic missions'. *Public Administration Review*, July/August: 314–27.

—— (1993) *The Spirit of Community*. London: Harper Collins.

Evans, P. (1996) 'Government action, social capital and development: reviewing the evidence for synergy'. *World Development*, 24, 6: 1119–32.

Evers, A. (1995) 'Part of the welfare mix: the third sector as an intermediate area'. *Voluntas*, 6, 2: 159–82.

—— (2013) 'The concept of "civil society": different understandings and their implications for third sector policies'. *Voluntary Sector Review*, 4, 2: 149–64.

Eyben, R. (2013) 'Uncovering the politics of "evidence" and "results": a framing paper for development practitioners'. Unpublished paper, IDS Sussex. www.bigpushforward.net

Farrington, J. and Bebbington, A., with Wellard, K. and Lewis, D. (1993) *Reluctant Partners?: NGOs, the State and Sustainable Agricultural Development*. London: Routledge.

Farrington, J. and Lewis, D. with Satish, S. and Miclat-Teves, A. (eds) (1993) *NGOs and the State in Asia: Rethinking Roles in Sustainable Agricultural Development*. London: Routledge.

Fechter, A-M. and Hindman, H. (2011) 'Introduction', *Inside the Everyday Lives of Development Workers: The Challenges and Futures of Aidland*. Sterling, VA: Kumarian Press.

Ferguson, J. and Gupta, A. (2002) 'Spatializing states: towards an ethnography of neoliberal governmentality'. *American Ethnologist*, 29, 4: 981–1002.

Ferlie, E., Ashburner, L., Fitzgerald, L. and Pettigrew, A. (1996) *The New Public Sector Management in Action*. Oxford: Oxford University Press.

Fernando, J.L. (2011) *The Political Economy of NGOs and State in Sri Lanka and Bangladesh*. London: Pluto Press.

Fernando, J.L. and Heston, A. (eds) (1997) 'The role of NGOs: charity and empowerment', introduction to *Annals of the American Academy of Political and Social Science*, 554, November: 8–20.

Financial Times (2002) 'Alliances between companies and non-governmental organizations attracts varying degrees of enthusiasm', 29 November 2002.

Fisher, J. (1993) *The Road from Rio: Sustainable Development and Nongovernmental Movement in the Third World*. New York: Praeger.

—— (1994) 'Is the iron law of oligarchy rusting away in the third world?'. *World Development*, 22, 4: 129–44.

—— (1998) *Nongovernments: NGOs and the Political Development of the Third World*. Hartford, CT: Kumarian.

Fisher, W.F. (1997) 'Doing good? The politics and anti-politics of NGO practices'. *Annual Review of Anthropology*, 26: 439–64.

—— (2010) 'Civil society and its fragments'. Chapter 10 in David N. Gellner (ed.) *Varieties of Activist Experience: Civil Society in South Asia*. London: Sage, pp. 250–68.

Foreman, K. (1999) 'Evolving global structures and the challenges facing international relief and development organizations'. *Nonprofit and Voluntary Sector Quarterly*, 28, 4 (supplement): 178–97.

Forstater, M., MacDonald, J. and Raynard, P. (2002) *Business and Poverty: Bridging the Gap*. Resource Centre for the Social Dimensions of Business Practice, Prince of Wales International Business Leaders Forum, London.

Fowler, A. (1995) 'Capacity building and NGOs: a case of strengthening ladles for the global soup kitchen?'. *Institutional Development (Innovations in Civil Society)*, 1, 1: 18–24.

—— (1997) *Striking a Balance: A Guide to Enhancing the Effectiveness of NGOs in International Development*. London: Earthscan.

—— (1999) 'Advocacy and third sector organizations', in D. Lewis (ed.) *International Perspectives on Voluntary Action: Reshaping the Third Sector*. London: Earthscan.

—— (2000) *The Virtuous Spiral: A Guide to Sustainability for NGOs in International Development*. London: Earthscan.

—— (2008) 'Development and the new security agenda: w(h)ither(ing) NGO alternatives? Chapter 6 in A. Bebbington, S. Hickey and D.C. Mitlin (eds) *Can NGOs Make a Difference?: The Challenge of Development Alternatives*. London: Zed Books, 111–32.

—— (2012) *ACORD's Transformation: Overcoming Uncertainty 1976–2010*. London: Agency for Cooperation and Research in Development.

Fowler, A. and Biekart, K. (1996) 'Do private agencies really make a difference?', in D. Sogge, K. Biekart and J. Saxby (eds) *Compassion and Calculation: the Business of Private Foreign Aid*. London: Pluto Press.

Fowler, A. and Biekart, K. (2011) 'Civic driven change: a narrative to bring politics back into civil society discourse'. Working Paper 159, ISS, The Hague, Netherlands.

Fowler, A., Campbell, P. and Pratt, B. (1992) *Institutional Development and NGOs in Africa: Policy Perspectives for European Development Agencies*. NGO Management Series no. 1, Oxford: INTRAC.

Fowler, A. and Edwards, M. (2002) (eds) *The NGO Management Reader*. London: Earthscan.

Fowler, A. and Malunga, C. (2010) (eds) *NGO Management: The Earthscan Companion*. London: Earthscan.

Fowler, A. and Malunga, C. (2010) 'Introduction: NGOs in a world of uncertainties', in A. Fowler and C. Malunga (eds) *NGO Management: The Earthscan Companion*. London: Earthscan, 1–12.

Fox, J. (1992) 'Democratic rural development: leadership accountability in regional peasant organizations'. *Development and Change*, 23, 2: 1–36.

Frank, A.G. (1959) 'Goal ambiguity and conflicting standards: an approach to the study of organization'. *Human Organization* (Winter 1958–9): 8–13.

Freeman, J. (1973) 'The tyranny of structurelessness'. *Berkeley Journal of Sociology*, 17: 151–64.

Freire, P. (1972) *Pedagogy of the Oppressed*. Harmondsworth: Penguin.

Friedmann, J. (1992) *Empowerment: the Politics of Alternative Development*. Oxford: Blackwell.

Fry, R. (1995) 'Accountability in organizational life: problem or opportunity for nonprofits?'. *Nonprofit Management and Leadership*, 6, 2: 181–96.

Fyvie, C. and Ager, A. (1999) 'NGOs and innovation: organizational characteristics and constraints in development assistance work in the Gambia'. *World Development*, 27, 8: 1383–96.

Gardner, K. (2012) *Discordant Development: Global Capitalism and the Struggle for Connection in Bangladesh*. London: Pluto Press.

Gardner, K. and Lewis, D. (1996) *Anthropology, Development and the Postmodern Challenge*. London: Pluto Press.

—— (2000) 'Dominant paradigms overturned or business as usual? Development discourse and the White Paper on international development'. *Critique of Anthropology*, 20, 1: 15–29.

Gaventa, J. (1999) 'Building links and learning between NGOs and community-based organizations in North and South', in D. Lewis (ed.) *International Perspectives on Voluntary Action: Reshaping the Third Sector*. London: Earthscan.

Geertz, C. (1973) *The Interpretation of Cultures*. New York: Basic Books.

Gellner, D.N. and Hirsch, E. (eds) (2001) *Inside Organizations: Anthropologists at Work*. Oxford: Berg.

Gellner, D.N. (2010) 'Introduction: making civil society in South Asia'. Chapter 1 in D.N. Gellner (ed) *Varieties of Activist Experience: Civil Society in South Asia*. London: Sage, pp. 1–16.

Ghani, A. and Lockhart, C. (2008) *Fixing Failed States: A Framework for Rebuilding a Fractured World*. Oxford: Oxford University Press.

Gioia, D.A. and Thomas, J.B. (1996) 'Identity, image and issue interpretation: sensemaking during strategic change in academia'. *Administrative Science Quarterly*, 41: 370–403.

Glasius, M., Lewis, D. and Seckinelgin, H. (eds) (2004) *Exploring Civil Society: Political and Cultural Contexts*. London: Routledge.

Glasius, M. Kaldor, M. and Anheier, H. (2006) *Global Civil Society 2005/6*. London: Sage.

Gledhill, J. (1994) *Power and Its Disguises: Anthropological Perspectives on Politics*. London: Zed Books.

Glennie, J. (2012) 'Does aid from Africa from Brics differ from traditional aid'. *The Guardian* Poverty Matters website, posted Thursday 26 April (accessed 12 November 2012).

Goetz, A.M. (ed.) (1997) *Getting Institutions Right for Women in Development*. London: Zed Books.

Goetz, A.M. and Sen Gupta, R. (1996) 'Who takes the credit? Gender, power and control over loan use in rural credit programmes in Bangladesh'. *World Development*, 24: 1.

Gomez, G.M. and Helmsing, A.H.J. (2010) 'Social entrepreneurship: a convergence of NGOs and the market economy?'. Chapter 30 in A. Fowler and C. Malunga (eds) *NGO Management: The Earthscan Companion*. London: Earthscan, 391–402.

Gosling, L. and Edwards, M. (1995) *Toolkits: A Practical Guide to Assessment, Monitoring, Review and Evaluation*. London: Save the Children Fund Development Manual no. 5.

Goyder, G. (1961) *The Responsible Company*. Oxford: Blackwell.

Grant, H.M. and Crutchfield, L.R. (2007) 'Creating high-impact nonprofits'. Stanford Social Innovation Review, 10, Fall, pp. 32–41.

Greiner, Larry (1972) 'Evolution and revolution as organizations grow'. *Harvard Business Review*, 50, July/August, pp. 37–46.

Grey, C. and Willmott, H. (2005) *Critical Management Studies: A Reader*. Oxford: Oxford University Press.

Grint, K. (1995) *Management: A Sociological Introduction*. Cambridge: Polity Press.

Guardian (2004) 'Hearts and minds at any cost', 13 July 2004.

Guareschi, P. and Jovchelovitch, S. (2004) 'Participation, health and the development of community resources in Southern Brazil'. *Journal of Health Psychology*, 9, 1: 303–14.

Guha, R. (1989) *The Unquiet Woods: Ecological Change and Peasant Resistance in the Himalaya*. Oxford: Oxford University Press.

Guijt, I. (2008) 'Civil society participation as the focus of Northern NGO support: the case of Dutch co-financing agencies'. Chapter 8 in A. Bebbington, S. Hickey and D.C. Mitlin (eds) *Can NGOs Make a Difference?: The Challenge of Development Alternatives*. London: Zed Books.

Guijt, I. and Gaventa, J. (1998) 'Participatory monitoring and evaluation: learning from change'. IDS Policy Briefing no. 12, Brighton: Institute of Development Studies.

Guijt, I. and Shah, M.K. (1998) 'General introduction: waking up to power, process and conflict', in I. Guijt and M.K. Shah (eds) *The Myth of Community*. London: Intermediate Technology Publications.

Gulrajani, N. (2010) 'New vistas for development management: examining radical reformist possibilities and potential'. *Public Administration and Development*, 30(2): 136–48.

Gupta, A. and Ferguson, J. (2002) Spatializing states: towards an ethnography of neoliberal governmentality. *American Ethnologist*, 29, 4: 981–1002.

Hadenius, A. and Uggla, F. (1996) 'Making civil society work, promoting democratic development: what can states and donors do?'. *World Development*, 24, 10: 1621–39.

Hadjipateras, A. (1997) 'Implementing a gender policy in ACORD: strategies, constraints, and challenges'. *Gender and Development*, 5, 1: 28–34.

Hager, M.A. and Brudney, J.L. (2011) 'Problems recruiting volunteers: nature versus nurture'. *Nonprofit Management and Leadership*, 22, 2: 137–51.

Hailey, J. (1999) 'Charismatic autocrats or development leaders? Characteristics of first generation NGO leadership'. Draft presented to the UK Development Studies Association Conference, University of Bath, September.

—— (2000) 'Learning for growth: organizational learning in South Asian NGOs', in D. Lewis and T. Wallace (eds) *New Roles and Relevance: Development NGOs and the Challenge of Change*. Hartford, CT: Kumarian Press.

—— (2006) 'NGO leadership and development: a review of the literature'. Praxis Paper, Oxford: International NGO Training and Research Centre (INTRAC).

Hailey, J. and James, R. (2010) '"Trees die from the top": international perspectives on NGO leadership development'. Chapter 31 in A. Fowler and C. Malunga (eds) *NGO Management: The Earthscan Companion*. London: Earthscan, 405–13.

Hall, M. (2012) 'Evaluation logics in the third sector'. *Voluntas*, November.

Hamada, T. (1992) 'Anthropology and organizational culture', in T. Hamada and W.E. Sibley (eds) *Anthropological Perspectives on Organizational Culture*. Lanham, MD: University Press of America.

Handy, C. (1988) *Managing Voluntary Organizations*. Harmondsworth: Penguin.

—— (1995) 'Trust and the virtual organization'. *Harvard Business Review* (May–June): 40–50.

Hanlon, J. (1991) *Mozambique: Who Calls the Shots?*. London: James Currey.

Hann, C. and Dunn, E. (eds) (1996) *Civil Society: Challenging Western Models*. London: Routledge.

Harding, P. (1991) 'Qualitative indicators and the project framework'. *Community Development Journal*, 26: 4.

Harmer, A. and Cotterrell, L. (2005) 'Diversity in donorship: the changing landscape of official humanitarian aid'. Humanitarian Policy Group Report 20, September, London: Overseas Development Institute (ODI).

Harmer, A. and Macrae, J. (2003) 'Humanitarian action and the global war on terror: a review of trends and issues'. HPG Briefing No 9, July. London: Overseas Development Institute.

Harris, M. (1996) 'Do we need governing bodies?', in D. Billis and M. Harris (eds) *Voluntary Agencies: Challenges of Organization and Management*. London: Macmillan.

—— (1999) 'Voluntary sector governance: problems in practice and theory in the United Kingdom and North America', in D. Lewis (ed.) *International Perspectives on Voluntary Action: Reshaping the Third Sector*. London: Earthscan.

—— (2010) 'Third sector organizations in a contradictory policy environment'. Chapter 2 in D. Billis (ed.) *Hybrid Organizations in the Third Sector*. Basingstoke: Palgrave Macmillan.

Harrison, Y.D. and Murray, V. (2012) 'Perspectives on the leadership of chairs of nonprofit organization boards of directors: a grounded theory mixed-method study'. *Nonprofit Management and Leadership*, 22, 4: 411–37.

Harriss, J. (1997) 'Social capital: missing link or analytically missing?', *Journal of International Development*, 9: 7.

Harsh, M., Mbatia, P. and Shrum, W. (2010) 'Accountability and inaction: NGOs and resource lodging in development'. *Development and Change* 41, 2: 253–78.

Harzing, A.-W. (1995) 'Internationalization and the international division of labour', in A.-W. Harzing and J. van Ruysseveldt (eds) *International Human Resource Management*. London: Sage.

Hashemi, S.M. (1989) 'NGOs in Bangladesh: development alternative or alternative rhetoric?'. Mimeo, Jahangirnagar University, Bangladesh.

—— (1995) 'NGO accountability in Bangladesh: beneficiaries, donors and the state', in M. Edwards and D. Hulme (eds) *Beyond the Magic Bullet: NGO Performance and Accountability in the Post-Cold War World*. London: Earthscan.

Hashemi, S.M. and Hassan, M. (1999) 'Building NGO legitimacy in Bangladesh: the contested domain', in D. Lewis (ed.) *International Perspectives on Voluntary Action: Reshaping the Third Sector*. London: Earthscan.

Hatch, M.J. (1997) *Organization Theory: Modern, Symbolic and Postmodern Perspectives*. Oxford: Oxford University Press.

Hayman, R. (2012) 'The Busan Partnership: implications for civil society'. Briefing Paper 29, Oxford: INTRAC.

Hertz, N. (2005) 'We achieved next to nothing'. *New Statesman*, 12 December.

Hickey, S. and Mohan, G. (2004) (eds) *Participation: From Tyranny to Transformation*. London: Zed Books.

—— (2005) 'Relocating participation within a radical politics of development'. *Development and Change*, 36, 2: 237–62.

Hilhorst, D. (2003) *The Real World of NGOs: Discourses, Diversity and Development*. London: Zed Books.

Hinton, R. and Groves, L. (2004) 'The complexity of inclusive aid'. Chapter 1 in L. Groves and R. Hinton (eds) *Inclusive Aid: Changing Power Relationships in International Development*. London: Earthscan.

Hirschmann, A. (1970) *Exit, Voice and Loyalty*. Cambridge, MA: Harvard University Press.

Hobbs, J. (2013) 'Responding to complexity and change: Oxfam International's approach'. *ONTRAC*, 54, May, pp. 3–4.

Hofstede, G. (1991) *Cultures and Organizations: Software of the Mind – Intercultural Cooperation and its Importance for Survival*. London: HarperCollins.

Hoksbergen, R. (2005) 'Building civil society through partnership: lessons from a case study of the Christian Reformed World Relief Committee'. *Development In Practice*, 15, 1: 16–27.

Holcombe, S. (1995) *Managing to Empower: the Grameen Bank's Experience of Poverty Alleviation*. London: Zed Books.

Holmén, Hans (2010) *Snakes in Paradise: NGOs and the Aid Industry in Africa*. Sterling, VA: Kumarian Press.

Honey, R. and Okafor, S. (1998) *Hometown Associations: Indigenous Knowledge and Development in Nigeria*. London: Intermediate Technology.

Hood, C. (1998) *The Art of the State: Culture, Rhetoric and Public Management*. Oxford: Clarendon Press.

Hopgood, S. (2006) *The Keepers of the Flame: Understanding Amnesty International*. Ithaca, NY: Cornell.

Horton Smith, D. (1997) 'Grassroots associations are important: some theory and a review of the impact literature'. *Non-Profit and Voluntary Sector Quarterly*, 26, 3: 269–306.

Howell, J. (2006a) 'Gender and civil society', in M. Glasius, M. Kaldor, H. Anheier (eds) *Global Civil Society Yearbook 2005/6*. London: Sage.

—— (2006b) 'The global war on terror, development and civil society'. *Journal of International Development*, 18, 1: 121–35.

Howell, J. and Pearce, J. (2000) 'Civil society: technical instrument or force for change?, in D. Lewis and T. Wallace (eds) *New Roles and Relevance: Development NGOs and the Challenge of Change*. Hartford: Kumarian Press.

—— (2001) *Civil Society and Development: A Critical Exploration*. London: Lynne Rienner.

Howes, M. (1997) 'NGOs and the institutional development of membership organizations: the evidence from six cases'. *Journal of International Development*, 9, 4: 597–604.

Howes, M. and Sattar, M.G. (1992) 'Bigger and better? Scaling-up strategies pursued by BRAC 1972-1991', in M. Edwards and D. Hulme (eds) *Making a Difference: NGOs and Development in a Changing World*. London: Earthscan.

Howlett, M. and Giest, S. (2013) 'The policy-making process'. Chapter 2 in E. Araral Jr, S. Fritzen, M. Howlett, M. Rajesh and X. Wu (eds) *Routledge Handbook of Public Policy*. London: Routledge, 17–28.

Hoyer, H.J. (1994) 'Reflections on partnership and accompaniment'. *Institutional Development*, 1, 1.

Hudock, A. (1995) 'Sustaining Southern NGOs in resource-dependent environments'. *Journal of International Development*, 7, 4: 653–67.

—— (1997) 'Institutional interdependence: capacity-enhancing assistance for intermediary NGOs in Sierra Leone and the Gambia'. *Journal of International Development*, 9, 4: 589–96.

—— (1999) *NGOs and Civil Society: Democracy By Proxy?* Cambridge: Polity Press.

Hudson, M. (1995) *Managing Without Profit: The Art of Managing Non-Profit Organizations*. Harmondsworth: Penguin.

Hulme, D. (1990) 'Can the Grameen Bank be replicated? Recent experiments in Malaysia, Malawi and Sri Lanka'. *Development Policy Review*, 8: 287–300.

—— (1994) 'NGOs and social development research', in D. Booth (ed.) *Rethinking Social Development: Theory, Research and Practice*. London: Longman.

Hulme, D. and Edwards, M. (eds) (1997) *Too Close for Comfort? NGOs, States and Donors*. London: Macmillan.

Hulme, D. and Shepherd, A. (2003) 'Chronic poverty and development policy: an introduction'. *World Development*, 31, 3: 399–403.

IDS (Institute of Development Studies) (2003) 'The rise of rights: rights-based approaches to international development'. IDS Policy Briefing, Issue 17, May. www.ids.ac.uk

IFRC (1997) *Code of Conduct for International Red Cross and Red Crescent Movement and NGOs in Disaster Relief*. Geneva: International Federation of the Red Cross.

Igoe, J. and Kelsall, T. (eds) (2005) *Between a Rock and a Hard Place: African NGOs, Donors and the State*. Durham, NC: Carolina Academic Press.

Ilchman, W.F., Katz, S.N. and Queen, E.L. (eds) (1998) *Philanthropy in the World's Traditions*. Indianapolis: Indiana University Press.

INTRAC (2012) 'Theory of change: what's it all about?' *ONTRAC*, the newsletter of INTRAC, 51, May. Oxford: International NGO Training and Research Centre.

—— (2013) 'The rise of INGO families: perspectives, iuses, and experiences' *ONTRAC*, the newsletter of INTRAC, 54, May. Oxford: International NGO Training and Research Centre.

Ishkanian, A. (2006) 'From inclusion to exclusion: Armenian NGOs' participation in the PRSP'. *Journal of International Development*, 18, 5: 729–40.

Ishkanian, A. and Szreter, S. (2012) *The Big Society Debate: A New Agenda for Social Welfare?* Cheltenham: Edward Elgar.

Jaeger, A.M. and Kanungo, R.N. (eds) (1990) *Management in Developing Countries*. London: Routledge.

Jain, P.S. (1996) 'Managing credit for the rural poor: lessons from the Grameen Bank'. *World Development*, 24, 1: 79–90.

Jalali, R. (2002) 'Civil society and the state: Turkey after the earthquake'. *Disasters*, 120–39.

James, R. (1994) 'Strengthening the capacity of Southern NGO partners: a survey of current NNGO approaches'. *INTRAC* Occasional Papers Series no. 5. Oxford: The International NGO Training and Research Centre.

—— (2003) 'Exploring OD in Africa'. *Nonprofit Management and Leadership*, 14, 313–24.

—— (2010) 'Managing with spirit'. Chapter 20 in A. Fowler and C. Malunga (eds) *NGO Management: The Earthscan Companion*. London: Earthscan, 255–68.

Jenkins, J.C. (1987) 'Nonprofit organizations and policy advocacy', in W.W. Powell (ed.) *The Nonprofit Sector: A Research Handbook*. New Haven, CT: Yale University Press.

Jenkins, R. and Goetz, A.M. (1998) 'Accounts and accountability: theoretical implications of the right-to-information movement in India'. Unpublished mimeo, Brighton: Institute of Development Studies.

Jennings, M. (2012) 'International NGOs must address their accountability deficit'. *Guardian* Poverty Matters Blog, 9 February (accessed 19 August 2013).

Jones, B.D. (1995) '"Intervention without borders": humanitarian intervention in Rwanda 1990-94'. *Millennium: Journal of International Studies*, 24, 2: 225–49.

Jones, F.E. (1996) *Understanding Organizations: A Sociological Perspective*. Toronto: Copp Clark.

Kabeer, N. and Huq, L. (2010) 'The power of relationships: love and solidarity in a landless women's organisation in rural Bangladesh'. *IDS Bulletin*, 41, 2: 79–87.

Kabeer, N. with Haq Kabir, A. and Huq, T.Y. (2009) 'Quantifying the impact of social mobilisation in rural Bangladesh: donors, civil society and "the road not taken"'. IDS Sussex Working Paper.

Kabeer, N., Mahmud, S. and Castro, J.G. Isaza (2012) 'NGOs and the political empowerment of poor people in rural Bangladesh: cultivating the habits of democracy?'. *World Development*, 40, 10: 2044–62.

Kaijage, F.J. (1993) (ed.) *Management Consulting in Africa: Utilizing Local Expertise*. West Hartford, CT: Kumarian Press.

Kaimowitz, D. (1993) 'The role of NGOs in agricultural research and technology transfer in Latin America'. *World Development*, 21, 7: 1139–50.

Kaldor, M. (2003) *Global Civil Society: An Answer to War*. Cambridge: Polity Press.

Kanji, N. and Greenwood, L. (2001) *Participatory Approaches to Research and Development in IIED: Learning from experience*. International Institute for Environment and Development (IIED). Available at www.iied.org

Kanji, N., Braga, C. and Mitullah, W.V. (2002) *Promoting Land Rights in Africa: How do NGOs Make a Difference?* International Institute for Environment and Development (IIED). Available at www.iied.org

Kanji, N., Kapiriri, M., Hearn, J. and Manyire, H. (2000) 'An assessment of DFID's engagement with civil society in Uganda: past work and current shifts'. Department for International Development office, Uganda.

Kanji, N., Sherbut, G., Fararoon, R. and Hatcher, J. (2012) 'Improving quality of life in remote mountain communities'. *Mountain Research and Development*, 32, 3: 353–63.

Kanter, R.M. and Summers, D. (1987) 'Doing well while doing good: dilemmas of performance measurement in nonprofit organizations and the need for a multiple constituency approach', in W.W. Powell (ed.) *The Nonprofit Sector: A Research Handbook*. New Haven, CT: Yale University Press.

Kaplan, A. (1999) 'The development of capacity'. Non-Governmental Liaison Service (NGLS) Development Dossier, Geneva: United Nations Organization.

Kardam, N. (1993) 'Development approaches and the role of advocacy'. *World Development*, 21, 11: 1773–86.

Karim, M. (2000) 'NGOs, democratisation and good governance: the case of Bangladesh', in D. Lewis and T. Wallace (eds) *New Roles and Relevance: Development NGOs and the Challenge of Change*. Hartford, CT: Kumarian Press.

Karnani, A. (2007) 'Microfinance misses its mark'. *Stanford Social Innovation Review*, Summer.

Karsten, M. F. (1994) *Management and Gender: Issues and Attitudes*. London: Praeger.

Kaufman, G. (1997) 'Watching the developers: a partial ethnography', in R.D. Grub and R.L. Stirrat (eds) *Discourses of Development: Anthropological Perspectives*.

Kawashima, N. (1999) 'The emerging non-profit sector in Japan'. Centre for Civil Society International Working Paper 9, London School of Economics.

Kay, R. (1996) 'What kind of leadership do voluntary organizations need?', in D. Billis and M. Harris (eds) *Voluntary Agencies: Challenges of Organization and Management*. London: Macmillan.

Keane, J. (1998) *Civil Society: Old Images, New Visions*. Cambridge: Polity Press.

Keck, M. and Sikkink, K. (1998) *Activists Beyond Borders: Advocacy Networks in International Politics*. Ithaca, NY: Cornell University Press.

Kelleher, D. and McLaren, K. (1996) *Grabbing the Tiger by the Tail: NGOs Learning for Organizational Change*. Ottawa: Canadian Council for International Cooperation.

Kendall, J. and Knapp, M. (1999) 'Evaluation and the voluntary (non-profit) sector: emerging issues', in D. Lewis (ed.) *International Perspectives on Voluntary Action: Reshaping the Third Sector*. London: Earthscan.

Keohane, R.O. and Nye, J.S. (2003) 'What's new? What's not? (And so what?)'. Chapter 4 in D.Held and A.McGrew (eds) *The Global Transformations Reader* (2nd edition). Cambridge: Polity Press, pp. 75–83.

Khan, T.A. (1999) 'The Muslim Buddhist: Akhtar Hameed Khan (1914–1999)'. *Himal*, 12, 11: 49–50.

Kickul, J. and Lyons, T.S. (2012) *Understanding Social Entrepreneurship: The Relentless Pursuit of Mission in an Ever Changing World*. London: Routledge.

Kiggundu, M.N. (1989) *Managing Organizations in Developing Countries: An Operational and Strategic Approach*. Hartford, CT: Kumarian Press.

Kilby, P. (2011) *NGOs in India: the Challenges of Women's Empowerment and Accountability*. London: Routledge.

Kinsbergen, S. and Schulpen, L. (2011) 'Taking stock of PIs: the what, why and how of private initiatives in development', in Paul Hoebink (ed.) *The Netherlands Yearbook on International Cooperation*. Assen, The Netherlands: Van Gorcum, pp. 161–86

Koch, D-J. Dreher, A. NunnenKamp, P. and Rainer, T. (2008) 'Keeping a low profile: what determines the allocation of aid by non-governmental organizations?', *World Development*, 37(5): 902–18.

Koenig, B. (1996) 'The management of international non-governmental organizations in the 1990s'. *Transnational Associations*, 2: 66–72.

Korten, D.C. (1980) 'Community organization and rural development: a learning process approach'. *The Public Administration Review*, 40: 480–511.

—— (1987) 'Third generation NGO strategies: a key to people-centred development'. *World Development*, 15 (supplement): 145–59.

—— (1990) *Getting to the 21st Century: Voluntary Action and the Global Agenda*. West Hartford, CT: Kumarian Press.

Korten, F.F. and Siy, R.Y. (1989) *Transforming a Bureaucracy: the Experience of the Philippines National Irrigation Administration*. West Hartford, CT: Kumarian Press.

Kothari, U. and Cooke, B. (2001) (eds) *Participation: The New Tyranny?* London: Zed Books.

Kramer, R. (1994) 'Voluntary agencies and the contract culture: dream or nightmare?'. *Social Service Review*, 63, 1: 33–60.

—— (1995) 'Is the third sector concept obsolete?'. *Inside ISTR*, 4, 4: 6–7, International Society for Third Sector Research.

Kramsjo, B. and Wood, G. (1992) *Breaking the Chains: Collective Action for Social Justice Among the Rural Poor in Bangladesh*. London: Intermediate Technology Publications.

Kubicek, P. (2002) 'The earthquake, civil society, and political change in Turkey: Assessment and comparison with Eastern Europe'. *Political Studies*, 50: 761–78.

Landry, C., Morley, D., Southwood, R. and Wright, P. (1985) 'What a way to run a railroad', in J. Batsleer, C. Cornforth and R. Paton (eds) *Issues in Voluntary and Non-profit Sector Management*. Milton Keynes: Open University Press/Wokingham: Addison-Wesley.

—— (1992) 'An analysis of radical failure', in J. Batsleer, C. Cornforth and R. Paton (eds) *Issues in Voluntary and Non-Profit Sector Management*. Wokingham: Addison-Wesley.

Leadbeater, C. (1997) *The Rise of the Social Entrepreneur*. London: Demos.

Leat, D. (1988) *Voluntary Organizations and Accountability*. London: National Council for Voluntary Organizations.

—— (1993) *Managing Across Sectors: Similarities Between For-Profit and Voluntary Non-Profit Organizations*, London: City University Business School.

—— (1995) 'Challenging management: an exploratory study of perceptions of managers who have moved from for-profit to voluntary organizations'. London: City University Business School.

Leggett, W.H. (1999) 'Tensions of business: processes of identification in a transnational corporate office'. Unpublished draft conference paper, American Anthropological Association Conference, Chicago.

Levitt, T. (1975) *The Third Sector: New Tactics for a Responsive Society*. New York: AMACOM, American Management Association.

Lewis, D. (1997) 'NGOs and the state in Bangladesh: donors, development and the discourse of partnership'. *Annals of the American Academy of Political and Social Science*, 554: 33–45.

—— (1998a) 'Nonprofit organizations, business and the management of ambiguity: case studies of "fair trade" from Nepal and Bangladesh'. *Nonprofit Management and Leadership*, 9, 2: 135–52.

—— (1998b) 'Inter-agency partnerships in aid-recipient countries: lessons from an aquaculture project in Bangladesh'. *Nonprofit and Voluntary Sector Quarterly*, 27, 3: 323–38.

—— (1998c) 'Development NGOs and the challenge of partnership: changing relations between North and South'. *Social Policy and Administration*, 32, 5: 501–12.

—— (ed.) (1999a) *International Perspectives on Voluntary Action: Reshaping the Third Sector*. London: Earthscan.

—— (1999b) 'Revealing, widening, deepening? A review of the existing and potential contribution of anthropological approaches to "third sector" research'. *Human Organization*, 58, 1: 73–81.

—— (2002a) 'Civil society in African contexts: reflections on the "usefulness" of a concept'. *Development and Change*, 33, 4: 569–86.

—— (2002b) 'Organization and management in the third sector: towards a cross-cultural research agenda'. *Nonprofit Management and Leadership*, 13, 67–83.

—— (2003) 'Theorising the organisation and management of non-governmental development organisations: towards a composite approach'. *Public Management Review*, 5, 3: 325–44.

—— (2004) 'On the difficulty of studying "civil society": Reflections on NGOs, state and democracy in Bangladesh'. *Contributions to Indian Sociology*, 38, 3: 299–322.

—— (2005) 'Actors, ideas and networks: trajectories of the non-governmental in development studies', in U. Kothari (ed.) *A Radical History of Development Studies*. London: Zed Books.

—— (2006a) 'Non-governmental organizations and international politics', in N. Tate (ed.) *Governments of the World*. Farmington Hills, MI: Macmillan Reference USA.

—— (2006b) 'Globalization and international service: a development perspective'. *Voluntary Action*, 7, 2: 13–26.

—— (2009) 'International development and the "perpetual present": anthropological approaches to the re-historicisation of policy'. *European Journal of Development Research*, 21, 1.

—— (2010) 'Disciplined activists, unruly brokers? Exploring the boundaries between non-governmental organisations, donors and state in Bangladesh', in D.N. Gellner (ed.) *Varieties of Activist Experience: Civil Society in South Asia*. New Delhi: Sage Publications.

—— (2011) *Bangladesh: Politics, Economy and Civil Society*. Cambridge: Cambridge University Press.

—— (2012) 'Is innovation essential for development work?' Poverty Matters Blog, The *Guardian*, 25 July, www.guardian.co.uk/global-development/poverty-matters (accessed 2 January 2013).

—— (2013) 'Sideways strategies: civil-society-state reformist crossover activities in the Philippines 1986-2010'. *Contemporary Southeast Asia*, 35, 1, April, pp. 27–55.

—— (2014 forthcoming) 'Contesting "parallel wolds": time to abandon the distinction between the international and domestic contexts of third sector scholarship?', *Voluntas*.

Lewis, D., Bebbington, A., Batterbury, S., Shah, A., Olson, E., Siddiqi, M.S. and Duvall, S. (2003) 'Practice, power and meaning: frameworks for studying organizational culture in multi-agency rural development projects'. *Journal of International Development*, 15, 1–17.

Lewis, D. and Hossain, A. (2004)) 'Beyond the net?: The changing rural power structure in Bangladesh'. Report to Swedish International Development Agency. Stockholm: Sida.

Lewis, D. and Kanji, N. (2009) *Non-Governmental Organisations and Development*. London: Routledge.

Lewis, D. and Madon, S. (2003) 'Information systems and non-governmental development organizations (NGOs): Advocacy, organizational learning and accountability in a Southern NGO'. *The Information Society*, 20, 2: 117–26.

Lewis, D. and Mosse, D. (2006) (eds) *Development Brokers and Translators: The Ethnography of Aid and Agencies*. Bloomfield, CT: Kumarian Press.

Lewis, D. and Opoku-Mensah, P. (2006) 'Moving forward research agendas on international NGOs: theory, agency and context'. *Journal of International Development*, 18: 1–11.

Lewis, D. and Siddiqi, M.S. (2006) 'Social capital from sericulture?', in A. Bebbington, M. Woolcock and S. Guggenheim (eds) *Social Capital and the World Bank*. Bloomfield, CT: Kumarian Books.

Lewis, D. and Sobhan, B. (1999) 'Routes of funding, roots of trust? Northern NGOs, Southern NGOs and the rise of direct funding'. *Development in Practice*, 9, 1 and 2: 117–29.

Lewis, D. and Wallace, T. (eds) (2000) *New Roles and Relevance: Development NGOs and the Challenge of Change*. Hartford, CT: Kumarian Press.

Light, P.C. (2000) *Making Nonprofits Work: A Report on the Tides of Nonprofit Management Reform*. Aspen, CO: The Aspen Institute/Brookings Institution Press.

Lindblom, C. (1959) 'The science of muddling through'. *Public Administration Review*, 19: 79–88.

Lindenberg, M. and Bryant, C. (2001) *Going Global: Transforming Relief and Development NGOs*. Bloomfield, CT: Kumarian.

Lister, S. (2000) 'Power in partnership? An analysis of an NGO's relationships with its partners'. *Journal of International Development*, 12: 227–39

Little, D. (2003) *The Paradox of Wealth and Poverty: Mapping the Ethical Dilemmas of Global Development*. Boulder, CO: Westview.

Lofredo, G. (1995) 'Help yourself by helping the poor'. *Development in Practice*, 5: 4.

Long, N. (2001) *Development Sociology: Actor Perspectives*. London: Routledge.

Long, N. and Long, A. (eds) (1992) *Battlefields of Knowledge: The Interlocking of Theory and Practice in Social Research and Development*. London: Routledge.

Lovegrove, N. and Thomas, M. (2013) 'Triple-strength leadership'. *Harvard Business Review*, September: 46–57.

Lovell, C. (1992) *Breaking the Cycle of Poverty: The BRAC Strategy*. Hartford, CT: Kumarian Press.

Luetchford, P. (2006) 'Brokering Fair Trade: relations between coffee cooperatives and alternative trade organizations – a view from Costa Rica'. Chapter 5 in *Development Brokers and Translators: the Ethnography of Aid and Agencies*. Hartford, CT: Kumarian Press, 127–148.

Lyman, S.M. (1995) *Social Movements: Critiques, Concepts and Case-Studies*. London: Macmillan.

MacDonald, L. (1994) 'Globalizing civil society: interpreting international NGOs in Central America'. *Millennium: Journal of International Studies*, 23, 2: 267–85.

MacDonald, N. (2004) 'Success is extinction: scenario planning in INGOs'. *Development*, 47, 4: 115–20.

MacKeith, J. (1992) 'Raising money or raising awareness? Issues and tensions in the relationship between fundraisers and service providers'. Centre for Voluntary Organization Working Paper 12, London School of Economics.

—— (1993) *NGO Management: A Guide Through the Literature*. London: Centre for Voluntary Organization, London School of Economics.

Mackintosh, M. (1992) 'Questioning the state', in M. Wuyts, M. Mackintosh and T. Hewitt (eds) *Development Policy and Public Action*. Milton Keynes: Open University Press/Oxford: Oxford University Press.

Macrae, J. and Zwi, A. (eds) (1994) *War and Hunger: Rethinking International Responses to Complex Emergencies*. London: Zed Books/Save the Children Fund.

Madon, S. (1999) 'International NGOs: networking, information flows and learning'. *Journal of Strategic Information Systems*, 8 (1999) 251–61.

Mallaby, S. (2004) 'NGOs: "Fighting poverty, hurting the poor"'. *Foreign Policy*, September/October.

Mansour, K. and Ezzat, H.R. (2009) 'Faith-based action in development and humanitarian work'. Chapter 6 in F. Holland (ed.) *Global Civil Society 2009: Poverty and Activism*. London: Sage, 118–46.

Marsden, D. (1994) 'Part I: Indigenous management (Introduction)', and 'Indigenous management and the management of indigenous knowledge', in S. Wright (ed.) *Anthropology of Organizations*. London: Routledge.

Marsden, D. and Oakley, P. (1990) *Evaluating Social Development Projects*. Oxford: Oxfam Publications.

Marsden, D., Oakley, P. and Pratt, B. (1995) *Measuring the Process: Guidelines for Evaluating Social Development*. Oxford: INTRAC.

Martens, K. (2006) 'NGOs in the United Nations system: evaluating theoretical approaches'. *Journal of International Development*, 18, 5: 691–700.

Martin, J. and Meyerson, D. (1988) 'Organizational cultures and the denial, channeling and acknowledgement of ambiguity', in L.R. Pondy, R.J. Boland and H. Thomas (eds) *Managing Ambiguity and Change*. New York: Wiley.

Maskovsky, J. (2013) 'Protest anthropology in a moment of global unrest'. *American Anthropologist*, 115, 1: 126–9.

Mawdsley, E. (2012) *From Recipients To Donors: Emerging Powers and the Changing Development Landscape*. London: Zed Books.

Mawdsley, E., Townsend, J. and Porter, G. (2005) 'Trust, accountability, and face-to-face interaction in North-South NGO relations'. *Development In Practice*, 15, 1: 77–82.

Maxwell, S. (1997) 'Implementing the World Food Summit Plan of Action'. *Food Policy*, 22: 6.

McAdam, D., McCarthy, J.D. and Zald, M.N. (1996) *Comparative Perspectives on Social Movements*. Cambridge: Cambridge University Press.

McAdam, D. and Scott, W.R. (2005) 'Organizations and Movements', Chapter 1 in G.F. Davis, D. McAdam, W.R. Scott and M.N. Zald (eds) *Social movements and Organization Theory*. Cambridge: Cambridge University Press, 4–40.

McCarthy, J.D. and Zald, M.N. (1977) 'Resource mobilisation in social movements: a partial theory'. *American Journal of Sociology*, 82: 1212–34.

McClelland, D.C. (1961) *The Achieving Society*. New Jersey: Van Nostrand.

McGee, R. (2004) 'Unpacking policy: actors, knowledge and spaces', in K. Brock, R. McGee and J. Gaventa (eds) *Unpacking Policy*. Kampala: Fountain Publishers.

McGill, M.E. and Wooton, L.M. (1975) 'Management in the third sector'. *Public Administration Review*, 35, 5: 444–56.

McGregor, J.A. (1989) 'Towards a better understanding of credit in rural Bangladesh'. *Journal of International Development*, 1: 467–86.

McSweeney, B. (2001) 'The fallacy of "national culture" identification'. *Human Relations*, 55, 1: 89–118.

Messer, J. (1998) 'Agency, communion and the formation of social capital', *Nonprofit and Voluntary Sector Quarterly*, 27, 1: 5–12.

Meyer, C. (1997) 'The political economy of NGOs and information sharing', *World Development*, 25, 7: 1127–40.

Michels, R. (1962) *Political Parties*, New York: The Free Press.

Micklethwait, I. and Wooldridge, A. (1996) *The Witch Doctors: What the Management Gurus are Saying – Why it Matters and How to Make Sense of it*. London: Heinemann.

Midgley, J. (1995) *Social Development: The Development Perspective in Social Welfare*. London: Sage.

Millard, E. (1996) 'Appropriate strategies to support small community enterprises in export markets'. *Small Enterprise Development*, 7, 1: 4–16.

Minogue, M., Polidano, C. and Hulme, D. (eds) (1998) *Beyond the New Public Management: Changing Ideas and Practices in Governance*. Cheltenham: Edward Elgar.

Mintzberg, H. (1994) 'The fall and rise of strategic planning'. *Harvard Business Review* (January–February): 107–14.

—— (2010) Developing leaders? Developing countries? Chapter 32 in A. Fowler and C. Malunga (eds) *NGO Management: The Earthscan Companion*. London: Earthscan, 414–25.

Mitlin, D., Hickey, S. and Bebbington, A. (2005) 'Reclaiming development: NGOs and the challenge of alternatives'. Background paper presented at conference on Reclaiming Development: Assessing the Contribution of NGOs to Development Alternatives, University of Manchester, UK, 27–29 June.

Molyneux, M. and Lazar, S. (2003) *Doing the Rights Thing: Rights-Based Development and Latin American NGOs*. London: Intermediate Technology Development Group (ITDG) Publishing.

Moore, H. (1988) *Feminism and Anthropology*. Cambridge: Polity Press.

Moore, M. and Stewart, S. (1998) 'Corporate governance for NGOs?'. *Development in Practice*, 8, 3: 335–42.

Morgan, G. (1994) *Imaginization*. London: Sage.

—— (1997) *Images of Organization*, (2nd edition). London: Sage.

Morgan, T. (ed.) (1994) *Women in Management: A Developing Presence*. London: Routledge.

Morris, S. (1999) 'Defining the nonprofit sector: some lessons from history'. Centre for Civil Society International Working Paper 3, London School of Economics.

Morris-Suzuki, T. (2000) 'For and against NGOs'. *New Left Review*, March/April, 63–84.

Moser, C.O. (1989) *Gender Planning and Development: Theory, Practice and Training*. London: Routledge.

Mosse, D. (2005) *Cultivating Development*. London: Pluto Press.

Mosse, D. and Lewis, D. (2006) 'Theoretical approaches to brokerage and translation in development'. Chapter 1 in D. Lewis and D. Mosse (eds) *Development Brokers and Translators: The Ethnography of Aid and Agencies*. Bloomfield CT: Kumarian Press.

Mukasa, S. (1999) 'Are expatriate staff necessary in international development NGOs? A case study of an NGO in Uganda'. Centre for Civil Society International Working Paper 4, London School of Economics.

Mulhare, E.M. (1999) 'Mindful of the future: strategic planning ideology and the culture of nonprofit organizations'. *Human Organization*, 58, 3: 323–30.

Murray Li, T. (2007) *The Will to Improve: Governmentality, Development and the Practice of Politics*. Durham, N.C: Duke University Press.

Najam, A. (1996a) 'NGO accountability: a conceptual framework'. *Development Policy Review*, 14: 339–53.

—— (1996b) 'Understanding the third sector: revisiting the prince, the merchant and the citizen'. *Nonprofit Management and Leadership*, 7, 2: 203–19.

—— (1999) 'Citizen organizations as policy entrepreneurs', in D. Lewis (ed.) *International Perspectives on Voluntary Action: Reshaping the Third Sector*. London: Earthscan.

Narayana, E.A. (1992) 'Bureaucratisation of non-governmental organizations: an analysis of employees' perceptions and attitudes'. *Public Administration and Development*, 12: 123–37.

Naschold, F. (2002) 'Aid and the millennium development goals'. Overseas Development Institute. ODI Opinions Number 4.

Nauta, W. (2006) 'Ethnographic research in a non-governmental organization: revealing strategic translations through an embedded tale'. Chapter 7 in D. Lewis and D. Mosse (eds) *Development Brokers and Translators*. Hartford, CT: Kumarian Books, 149–72.

Nerfin, M. (1986) 'Neither prince nor merchant: citizen – an introduction to the Third System', in K. Ahooja-Patel, A.G. Drabek and M. Nerfin (eds) *World Economy in Transition*. Oxford: Oxford University Press.

Nelson, P. (2006) 'The varied and conditional integration of NGOs into the aid system: NGOs and the World Bank'. *Journal of International Development*, 18.

Newsweek (2005) 'The $1.6 trillion non-profit sector behaves (or misbehaves) more and more like big business', 5 September 2005.

Nielsen, W. (1979) *The Endangered Sector*. New York: Columbia University Press.

Norrell, A. (1999) 'Bridging gaps or "a bridge too far"? The management of advocacy within service providing NGOs in the UK'. Centre for Civil Society International Working Paper 3, London School of Economics.

North, L. (2003) Rural progress or rural decay?: an overview of the issues and case studies. Chapter 1 in L. North and J.D. Cameron (eds) *Rural Progress, Rural Decay: Neoliberal Adjustment Poilcies and Local Initiatives*. Bloomfield, CT: Kumarian.

Obadare, E. (2003) 'White collar fundamentalism: youth, religiosity and uncivil society in Nigeria'. Unpublished ongoing PhD research paper.

ODI (Overseas Development Institute) (1995) 'NGOs and official donors'. Briefing Paper 1995 (4) August, London: Overseas Development Institute. www.odi.org.uk

—— (1997) *The People in Aid Code of Best Practice in the Management and Support of Aid Personnel*. Relief and Rehabilitation Network, February. London: Overseas Development Institute. www.odi.org.uk

—— (1999) 'What can we do with a rights-based approach to development?'. Briefing Paper 1999 (3) September. London: Overseas Development Institute. www.odi.org.uk

OECD (2009) *Better Aid: Civil Society and Aid Effectiveness: Findings, Recommendations and Good Practice*. Paris: Organization for Economic Cooperation and Development.

—— *How DAC Members Work with Civil Society Organizations: An Overview*. Paris: Organization for Economic Cooperation and Development.

Olie, R. (1996) 'The culture factor in personnel and organization policies', in A.-W. Harzing, and J. van Ruysseveldt (eds) *International Human Resource Management*. London: Sage.

Onis, Z. and Senses, F. (2005) 'Rethinking the emerging post-Washington consensus'. *Development and Change*, 36, 2: 263–90.

Osborne, M. and Homer, L. (1996) 'Managing equal opportunities and anti-oppressive practice', in S.P. Osborne (ed.) *Managing in the Voluntary Sector*. London: International Thomson Business Press.

Owusu, C. (2004) 'An international NGO's staff reflections on power, procedures and relationships'. Chapter 8 in L. Groves and R. Hinton (eds) *Inclusive Aid: Changing Power Relationships in International Development*. London: Earthscan.

Parker, B. (1998) *Globalization and Business Practice: Managing Across Boundaries*. London: Sage.

Parry-Williams, J. (1992) 'Scaling up via legal reform in Uganda', in M. Edwards and D. Hulme (eds) *Making a Difference: NGOs and Development in a Changing World*. London: Earthscan.

Paton, R. (1991) 'The social economy: value-based organizations in the wider society', in J. Batsleer, C. Cornforth and R. Paton (eds) *Issues in Voluntary and Non-profit Management*. Milton Keynes: Open University Press/Wokingham: Addison-Wesley.

—— (1999) 'The trouble with values', in D. Lewis (ed.) *International Perspectives on Voluntary Action: Reshaping the Third Sector*, London: Earthscan.

Pearce, J. (1997) 'Between co-option and irrelevance? Latin American NGOs in the 1990s', in D. Hulme and M. Edwards (eds) *Too Close for Comfort? NGOs, States and Donors*. London: Macmillan.

People in Aid (2012) *The 2012 INGO Management Agenda: A Benchmarking Report for the INGO Sector*. People in Aid & The Roffey Park Institute, Horsham, UK.

Perera, J. (1997) 'In unequal dialogue with donors: the experience of the Sarvodya Shramadana Movement', in D. Hulme and M. Edwards (eds) *Too Close for Comfort? NGOs, States and Donors*. London: Macmillan.

Perri 6 (1993) 'Innovation by non-profit organizations: policy and research issues'. *Nonprofit Management and Leadership*, 3, 4: 397–414.

Perrow, C. (1967) 'The analysis of goals in complex organizations'. *American Sociological Review*, April: 194–208.

Peters, T.J. (1994) *The Tom Peters Seminar*. New York: Vintage Books.

Peters, T.J. and Waterman, R.H. (1982) *In Search of Excellence*. New York: Harper and Row.

Pettigrew, A.M. (1987) 'Context and action in the transformation of the firm'. *Journal of Management Studies*, 24, 6: 649–70.

Pfeffer, J. and Salancik, G. (1978) *The External Control of Organizations: A Resource Dependence Perspective*. New York: Harper and Row.

Phillips, S.D. and Rathgeb Smith, S. (2011) *Governance and Regulation in the Third Sector: International Perspectives*. London: Routledge.

Polanyi, K. (1957) *The Great Transformation: The Political and Economic Origins of Our Time*. Boston, MA: Beacon Press.

Polidano, C. and Hulme, O. (1999) 'Public management reform in developing countries'. *Public Management*, 11, 1: 121–32.

Pollard, A. and Court, J. (2008) 'How civil society organizations use evidence to influence policy processes'. Chapter 7 in A. Bebbington, S. Hickey and D.C. Mitlin (eds) *Can NGOs Make a Difference?: The Challenge of Development Alternatives*. London: Zed Books, 133–52.

Pollitt, C. (1993) *Managerialism and Public Services*, Oxford: Blackwell.

Pondy, L.R., Boland Jr, R.J. and Thomas, H. (eds) (1988) *Managing Ambiguity and Change*. London: Wiley.

Poole, N. (1994) 'The NGO sector as an alternative delivery system for agricultural public services'. *Development in Practice*, 4, 2: 100–11.

Postma, W. (1998) 'Capacity building: the making of a curry'. *Development in Practice*, 8, 1: 54–63.

Powell, M. (1999) *Information Management for Development Organizations*. Oxford: Oxfam Publications.

Powell, W.W. (ed.) (1987) *The Nonprofit Sector: A Research Handbook*. New Haven, CT: Yale University Press.

Power, M. (1997) *The Audit Society: Rituals of Verification*. Oxford: Oxford University Press.

Pratt, B. (2009) 'Civil society and development: challenges from European governments? A review of official aid policies in Europe and their implications for civil society'. *INTRAC Policy Briefing Paper No. 24*. Oxford: International NGO Training and Research Centre.

Pratt, B. (2010) 'Strategic issues facing NGO into the foreseeable future', Chapter 11 in A. Fowler and C. Malunga (eds) *NGO Management: The Earthscan Companion*. London: Earthscan, 165–74.

Putnam, R.D. (1993) *Making Democracy Work: Civic Traditions in Modern Italy*. Princeton, NJ: Princeton University Press.

Putzel, J. (1997) 'Accounting for the "dark side" of social capital: reading Robert Putnam on democracy'. *Journal of International Development*, 9, 7: 939–50.

Quinn, J.B. (1980) *Strategies for Change: Logical Incrementalism*. Homewood, IL: Irwin.

Rahman, M. (1995) 'Development of people organization through NGOs: a study of RDRS support to its federations'. *Grassroots*, XVI, April–June.

Rahnema, M. (1992) 'Participation', in W. Sachs (ed.) *The Development Dictionary: A Guide to Knowledge as Power*. London: Zed Books.

—— (1997) *The Post-Development Reader*. London: Zed Books.

Rajak, D. (2011) *In Good Company: An Anatomy of Corporate Social Responsibility*. Stanford, CA: Stanford University Press.

Rao, A. and Kelleher, D. (1995) 'Engendering organizational change: the BRAC case'. *IDS Bulletin*, 26: 3.

—— (1998) 'Gender lost and gender found: BRAC's gender quality action-learning programme'. *Development Practice*, 8, 2: 173–85.

Raymond, P. (2013) 'There is hope for Haiti, despite what the critics say'. *The Guardian* Poverty Matters Blog, 10 January 2013 (accessed 16 August 2013).

Reifner, U. and Ford, J. (eds) (1992) *Banking for People*. Berlin and New York: Walter de Gruyter.

Ridde, V. (2006) 'Performance-based partnership agreements for the reconstruction of the health system in Afghanistan'. *Development In Practice*, 15, 1: 4–15.

Riddell, R. (1999) 'Evaluation and effectiveness in NGOs', in D. Lewis (ed.) *International Perspectives on Voluntary Action: Reshaping the Third Sector*. London: Earthscan.

Riddell, R.C. and Robinson, M. (1995) *NGOs and Rural Poverty Alleviation*. Oxford: Clarendon Press.

Robbins, S.P. (1990) *Organization Theory: Structure, Design and Applications*. New York: Prentice-Hall.

Robinson, M. (1993) 'Governance, democracy and conditionality: NGOs and the new policy agenda', in A. Clayton (ed.) *Governance, Democracy and Conditionality: What Role for NGOs?*. Oxford: International NGO Research and Training Centre.

—— (1995) 'Strengthening civil society in Africa: the role of foreign political aid', in M. Robinson (ed.) *Towards Democratic Governance*. IDS Bulletin 26: 2, April.

—— (1997) 'Privatising the voluntary sector: NGOs as public service contractors', in D. Hulme and M. Edwards (eds) *Too Close for Comfort? NGOs, States and Donors*. London: Macmillan.

Robinson, M. and White, G. (1997) 'The role of civic organizations in the provision of social services'. Research for Action Papers no. 37, Helsinki: United Nations University/World Institute for Development Economics Research.

Rochester, C. (1995) 'Voluntary agencies and accountability', in J.D. Smith, C. Rochester and R. Hedley (eds) *An Introduction to the Voluntary Sector*. London: Routledge.

Rodrik, D. (2012) 'After the Millennium Development Goals', www.project-syndicate.org/commentary (accessed 13 November 2012).

Ronalds, P.D. (2010) *The Change Imperative: Creating the Next Generation NGO*. Sterling, VA: Kumarian Press.

Rondinelli, D. (1993) *Development Projects as Policy Experiments*. London: Routledge.

Rostow, W.W. (1960) *The Stages of Economic Growth: A Non-Communist Manifesto*. Cambridge: Cambridge University Press.

Rotberg, R.I. (ed.) (1996) *Vigilance and Vengeance: NGOs Preventing Ethnic Conflict in Divided Societies*. Washington DC: Brookings Institution Press.

Rowlands, J. (1995) 'Empowerment examined'. *Development in Practice*, 15, 2: 101–7.

Sachs, J. (2005) *The End of Poverty: How We Can Make it Happen in Our Lifetime*. London: Penguin.

Sahley, C. (1995) 'Strengthening the capacity of NGOs: cases of small enterprise development agencies in Africa'. INTRAC Management and Policy Series no. 4, Oxford: International NGO Training and Research Centre.

Salamon, L. (1994) *Partners in Public Service: Government-Nonprofit Relations in the Modern Welfare State*. Baltimore, MD: Johns Hopkins University Press.

Salamon, L. and Anheier, H. (1992) 'In search of the non-profit sector: in search of definitions', *Voluntas*, 13, 2: 125–52.

—— (1994) *The Emerging Sector: The Nonprofit Sector in Comparative Perspective – an Overview*. Baltimore, MD: Johns Hopkins University Press.

—— (1996) *The Emerging Nonprofit Sector*. Manchester: Manchester University Press.

—— (1997) *Defining the Nonprofit Sector: A Cross-National Analysis*. Manchester: Manchester University Press.

—— (1999) 'The third sector in the third world', in D. Lewis (ed.) *International Perspectives on Voluntary Action: Reshaping the Third Sector*. London: Earthscan.

Salamon, L.E., Wojciech Sokolowski, S. and List, R. (2003) *Global Civil Society: An Overview*. Baltimore, MD: Centre for Civil Society Studies, The Johns Hopkins University.

Sanyal, B. (1991) 'Antagonistic cooperation: a case study of NGOs, government and donors' relationships in IG projects in Bangladesh'. *World Development*, 19, 10: 1367–79.

Satish, S. and Prem Kumar, N. (1993) 'Are NGOs more cost-effective than government in livestock service delivery? A study of artificial insemination in India', in J. Farrington and D.J. Lewis (eds) *NGOs and the State in Asia: Rethinking Roles in Sustainable Agricultural Development*. London: Routledge.

Satterthwaite, D. (2005) 'Introduction: Why local organizations are central to meeting the MDGs'. Chapter 1 in T. Bigg and D. Satterthwaite (eds) *How to Make Poverty History*. London: International Institute for Environment and Development (IIED).

Saxby, J. (1996) 'Who owns the private aid agencies?', in D. Sogge, K. Biekart and J. Saxby (eds) *Compassion and Calculation: The Business of Private Foreign Aid*. London: Pluto Press.

Schaffer, B. (1969) 'The deadlock in development administration', in C. Leys (ed.) *Politics and Change in Developing Countries*, Cambridge: Cambridge University Press.

Schmidt, R.H. and Zeitinger, C.P. (1996) 'Prospects, problems and potential of credit granting NGOs'. *Journal of International Development*, 8, 2: 241–58.

Schuller, M. (2012) *Killing with Kindness: Haiti, International Aid, and NGOs*. Foreword by P. Farmer. New Brunswick, NJ: Rutgers University Press.

Schulpen, L. and Habraken, R. (2013) 'Southern civil society in perspective: a literature review'. Working Paper, Centre for Internatinoal Development Issues (CIDIN), University of Nijmegen, The Netherlands.

Schumacher, E.F. (1973) *Small is Beautiful: A Study of Economics as if People Mattered*. London: Abacus.

Schuurman, F. J. (1993) 'Modernity, post-modernity and the new social movements', in F. J. Schuurman (ed.) *Beyond the Impasse: New Directions in Development Theory*. London: Zed Books.

Scott, M.J.O. (2001) 'Danger – landmines! NGO-government collaboration in the Ottawa process', in M. Edwards and J. Gaventa (eds) *Global Citizen Action*. Boulder, CO: Lynne Rienner, pp. 121–34.

Scott Morton, M. S. (1996) 'Information and communication technologies', in R. Paton, G. Clark, G. Jones, J. Lewis and P. Quintas (eds) *The New Management Reader*, London: International Thomson Business Press and the Open University.

Scott-Smith, T. (2013) 'Insulating the developing classes'. Chapter 7 in T. Wallace, F. Porter and M. Ralph-Bowman (eds) *Aid, NGOs and the Realities of Women's Lives: A Perfect Storm*. Rugby: Practical Action.

Seckinelgin, H. (2006) 'The multiple worlds of NGOs and HIV/AIDS: rethinking NGOs and their agency'. *Journal of International Development*, 18: 715–27.

Seelos, C. and Mair, J. (2012) 'Innovation is not the holy grail'. *Stanford Social Innovation Review*, Fall, pp. 45–9.

Seibel, W. (1999) 'Successful failure: an alternative view of organizational coping'. Chapter 6 in H.K. Anheier (eds) *When Things Go Wrong: Organizational Failures and Breakdowns*. London: Sage, 91–104.

Selznick, P. (1966) *TVA and the Grassroots*. New York: Harper and Row.

Semboja, J. and Therkildsen, O. (1995) *Service Provision Under Stress in East Africa: State, NGOs and People's Organizations in Kenya, Tanzania and Uganda*. London: James Currey.

Sen, A. (1981) *Poverty and Famines: An Essay on Entitlement and Deprivation*. Oxford: Oxford University Press.

—— (1983) 'Poor, relatively speaking'. *Oxford Economic Papers*, 35: 153–69.

Sen, B. (1987) 'NGO self-evaluation: issues of concern'. *World Development*, 15 (supplement): 161–7.

Sen, S. (1992) 'Non-profit organizations in India: historical development and common patterns'. *Voluntas*, 3, 2: 175–93.

Senge, P.M. (1990) *The Fifth Discipline: The Art and Practice of the Learning Organization*. New York: Doubleday.

Senillosa, I. (1998) 'A new age of social movements: a fifth generation of non-governmental organization in the making?'. *Development in Practice*, 8, 1: 40–53.

Shaw, M. (1994) 'Civil society and global politics: beyond a social movements approach'. *Millennium: Journal of International Studies*, 23, 3: 647–67.

Sidel, M. (2004) 'States, markets and the nonprofit sector in South Asia: judiciaries and the struggle for capital in comparative perspective'. *Tulane Law Review* 78, 5: 1611–69.

—— (2005) 'The guardians guarding themselves: a comparative perspective on non-profit self-regulation'. *Chicago-Kent Law Review*, 80: 803–35.

Simbi, M. and Thom, G. (2000) '"Implementation by proxy"?: the next step in power relationships between Northern and Southern NGOs', in D. Lewis and T. Wallace (eds) *New Roles and Relevance: Development NGOs and the Challenge of Change*. Hartford, CT: Kumarian Press.

Simukonda, H.P.M. (1992) 'Creating a national NGO council for strengthening social welfare services in Africa: some organizational and technical problems experienced in Malawi'. *Public Administration and Development*, 12: 417–31.

Skloot, E. (1987) 'Enterprise and commerce in non-profit organizations', in W.W. Powell (ed.) *The Nonprofit Sector: A Research Handbook*. New Haven, CT: Yale University Press.

Smillie, I. (1988) 'Northern "donors" and Southern "partners": arguments for an NGO consortium approach'. Mimeo, Development Assistance Committee (DAC) Paris NGO meeting.

—— (1994) 'Changing partners: Northern NGOs, Northern governments'. *Voluntas*, 5, 2: 155–92.

—— (1995) *The Alms Bazaar: Altruism Under Fire – Non-Profit Organizations and International Development*. London: Intermediate Technology Publications.

—— (1998) 'NGOs in their dotage', *Appropriate Technology*, 25, 1: 21–2.

—— (2009) *Freedom From Want: The Remarkable Success of BRAC, the Global Grassroots Organization That's Winning the Fight Against Poverty*. Sterling, VA: Kumarian Press.

Smillie, I. and Hailey, J. (2001) *Management for Change: Leadership, Strategy and Management in Asian NGOs*. London: Earthscan.

Smith, B. (1987) 'An agenda of future tasks for international and indigenous NGOs: views from the North'. *World Development*, 15 (supplement): 87–93.

Smith, C. and Friedmann, A. (1972) *Voluntary Associations: Perspectives on the Literature*. Cambridge, MA: Harvard University Press.

Smith, G. (2002) 'Faith in the voluntary sector: a common or distinctive experience of religious organizations?'. Centre for Institutional Studies, University of East London.

Smith, S.R. and Lipsky, M. (1993) *Nonprofits for Hire: The Welfare State in the Age of Contracting*. Cambridge, MA: Harvard University Press.

Smith, W.E., Lethem, F. and Thoolen, B.A. (1980) 'The design of organizations for rural development projects: a progressive report'. Washington DC: World Bank Staff Working Paper no. 375.

Smyth, I. (2002) 'Slaying the serpent: knowledge management in development NGOs'. Chapter 6 in P. Newell, S.M. Rai and A. Scott (eds) *Development and the Challenge of Globalization*. Rugby: Practical Action.

Sogge, D. (1996) 'Settings and choices', in D. Sogge (ed.) with K. Biekart and J. Saxby, *Compassion and Calculation: The Business of Private Foreign Aid*. London: Pluto Press, 1–23.

Solomon, B.B. (1976) *Black Empowerment: Social Work in Oppressed Communities*. New York: Columbia University Press.

Stacey, R., Griffin, D. and Shaw, P. (2000) *Complexity and Management: Fad or Radical Challenge to Systems Thinking?* London: Routledge.

Stark Biddle, C. (1984) *The Management Needs of Private Voluntary Organizations*. Washington DC: USAID.

Staudt, K. (1991) *Managing Development: State, Society and International Contexts*. London: Sage.

Stern, E. (1992) 'Evaluating innovatory programmes: an external evaluator's view', in J. Batsleer, C. Cornforth and R. Paton (eds) *Issues in Voluntary and Non-Profit Management*. Milton Keynes: Open University Press/Wokingham: Addison-Wesley.

Stewart, S. (1997) 'Happy ever after in the marketplace: non–government organizations and uncivil society'. *Review of African Political Economy*, 71: 11–34.

Stirrat, R.L. and Henkel, H. (1997) 'The development gift: the problem of reciprocity in the NGO world'. *Annals of the American Academy of Political and Social Science*, special issue on 'The Role of NGOs: Charity and Empowerment', November, 554: 66–80.

Stoddard, A. (2003) 'Humanitarian NGOs: challenges and trends'. HPG Briefing No 12, July. London: Overseas Development Institute.

Stoddard, A., Harmer, A. and DiDomenico, V. (2009) 'Providing aid in insecure environments: trends in violence against aid workers and the operational response (2009 update)'. HPG Policy Brief 34, Humanitarian Policy Group, London: Overseas Development Institute.

Sumner, A. and Mallett, R. (2012) *The Future of Foreign Aid: Development Cooperation and the New Geography of Global Poverty*. London: Palgrave.

Sutton, R. (1999) 'The policy process: an overview'. Working Paper No. 118. London: Overseas Development Institute (ODI).

Suzuki, N. (1997) *Inside NGOs: Learning to Manage Conflicts Between Headquarters and Field Offices*. London: Intermediate Technology Publications.

Tandon, R. (1995) 'Board games: governance and accountability in NGOs', in M. Edwards and D. Hulme (eds) *Beyond the Magic Bullet: NGO Performance and Accountability in the Post-Cold War World*. London: Earthscan.

—— (1997) 'Organizational development and NGOs: an overview'. *Institutional Development*, IV, 1: 3–19.

Tandon, Y. (1996) 'An African perspective', in D. Sogge, K. Biekart and J. Saxby (eds) *Compassion and Calculation: the Business of Private Foreign Aid*. London: Pluto Press.

Tassie, B., Zohar, A. and Murray, V. (1996) 'The management of change', in S.P Osborne (ed.) *Managing in the Voluntary Sector*. London: Thomson Business Press.

Tayeb, M.H. (1988) *Organizations and National Culture: A Comparative Analysis*. London: Sage.

Taylor, J. (2010) 'The phases of organization development'. Chapter 13 in A. Fowler and C. Malunga (eds) *NGO Management: The Earthscan Companion*. London: Earthscan, 191–201.

Tembo, F. (2004) 'NGDOs' role in building poor people's capacity to benefit from globalization'. *Journal of International Development*, 16, 1023–37.

Tendler, J. (1982) 'Turning private voluntary organizations into development agencies: questions for evaluation'. Program Evaluation Discussion Paper 12, Washington DC: United States Agency for International Development.

—— (1997) *Good Governance in the Tropics*. Baltimore, MD: Johns Hopkins University Press.

Themudo, N. (2003) 'Managing the Paradox: NGOs, resource dependence, and independence in environmental NGOs – case studies from Portugal and Mexico'. Unpublished PhD dissertation, University of London.

Therkildsen, O. and Semboja, J. (1995) 'A new look at service provision in East Africa'. Chapter 1 in J. Semboja and O. Therkildsen (eds) *Service Provision Under Stress in East Africa: The State, NGOs and People's Organizations*. London: James Currey.

Thomas, A. (1992) 'NGOs and the limits to empowerment', in M. Wuyts, M. Mackintosh and T. Hewitt (eds) *Development Action and Public Policy*. Oxford: Oxford University Press.

—— (1996) 'What is development management?'. *Journal of International Development*, 8, 1: 95–110.

—— (1999) 'What makes good development management?', *Development in Practice*, 9, 1 and 2, February: 9–17.

—— (2000) 'Development as practice in a liberal capitalist world'. *Journal of International Development*, 12: 773–87.

TIB (2006) *Problems of Governance in the NGO Sector: The Way Out*. Dhaka: Transparency International Bangladesh.

Tran, M. (2012) 'Spanish NGO uses blogging to link donors with Latin American recipients', The *Guardian*, 6 November 2012.

Turner, M. and Hulme, D. (1997) *Governance, Administration and Development: Making the State Work*. London: Macmillan.

Tvedt, T. (1998) *Angels of Mercy or Development Diplomats? NGOs and Foreign Aid*. Oxford: James Currey.

—— (2006) 'The international aid system and the non-governmental organizations: a new research agenda'. *Journal of International Development*, 18, 5: 677–90.

Udoh James, V. (ed.) (1998) *Capacity Building in Developing Countries: Human and Environmental Dimensions*. New York: Praeger.

Umeh, O.J. (1992) 'Capacity building and development administration in Southern African countries'. *International Review of Administrative Sciences*, 58, 1: 57–70.

UN (2013) *A New Global Partnership: Eradicate Poverty and Transform Economies through Sustainable Development*. Report of the High-Level Panel of Eminent Persons on the Post-2015 Development Agenda, United Nations 2013.

UNDP (United Nations Development Programme) (1993) *Human Development Report*. New York: United Nations Development Programme.

—— (2013) *Human Development Report 2013: The Rise of the South: Human Progress in a Diverse World*. New York: United Nations Development Programme.

Uphoff, N. (1995) 'Why NGOs are not a third sector: a sectoral analysis with some thoughts on accountability, sustainability and evaluation', in M. Edwards and D. Hulme (eds) *Beyond the Magic Bullet: NGO Performance and Accountability in the Post-Cold War World*. London: Earthscan.

USAID (2013) *Theories and Indicators of Change Briefing Paper. Concepts and Primers for Conflict Management and Mitigation*. Washington DC: United States Agency for Intrnational Development.

Uvin, P. (1995) 'Fighting hunger at the grassroots: paths to scaling up'. *World Development*, 23, 6: 927–39.

Vakil, A. (1997) 'Confronting the classification problem: toward a taxonomy of NGOs'. *World Development*, 25, 12: 2057–71.

Van Maanen, J. (2001). 'Natives "R" us: Some notes on the ethnography of organizations', in D. Gellner and E. Hirsch (Eds) *Inside Organizations: Anthropologists at Work*. Oxford: Berg.

Van Rooy, A. (1997) *Civil Society and the Aid Industry*. London: Earthscan.

—— (1998) 'The frontiers of influence: NGO lobbying at the 1974 World Food Conference, the 1992 Earth Summit and beyond'. *World Development*, 25, 1: 93–114 (offprint P5031).

Vivian, J. (1994) 'NGOs and sustainable development in Zimbabwe'. *Development and Change*, 25: 181–209.

Vivian, J. and Maseko, G. (1994) *NGOs, Participation and Rural Development: Testing the Assumptions with Evidence from Zimbabwe*. Geneva: UN Research Institute for Social Development.

Waddell, S. (2011) *Global Action Networks: Creating Our Common Future Together*. London: Palgrave.

Wallace, T. (1998) 'Institutionalizing gender in UK NGOs'. *Development in Practice*, 8, 2: 159–72.

Wallace, T. and Kaplan, A. (2003) 'The taking of the horizon: Lessons from ActionAid Uganda's experience of changes in development practice'. Working Paper Series, Number 4, Kampala: ActionAid Uganda.

Wallace, T., Bornstein, L. and Chapman, J. (2006) *Coercion and Commitment: Development NGOs and the Aid Chain*. Rugby: Practical Action/Intermediate Technology Development Group (ITDG).

Wallace, T., Porter, F. and Ralph-Bowman, M. (2013) *A Perfect Storm: Aid, NGOs and the Realities of Women's Lives*. Rugby: Practical Action Publishing.

Watson, H. and Laquihon, W. (1993) 'The MBRLC's Sloping Agricultural Land Technology (SALT) research and extension in the Philippines', in J. Farrington and D. Lewis (eds) *NGOs and the State in Asia: Rethinking Roles in Sustainable Agricultural Development*. London: Routledge.

Wedel, J., Shore, C., Feldman, G. and Lathrop, S. (2005) 'Towards an anthropology of public policy'. *Annals of the American Academy of Political and Social Science*, 600, July, pp. 30–51.

Wellard, K, and Copestake, J. (eds) (1993) *Non-Governmental Organizations and the State in Africa: Rethinking Roles in Sustainable Agricultural Development*. London: Routledge.

White, G. (1994) 'Civil society, democratisation and development'. *Democratisation*, 1, 3: 375–90.

White, J. and Morton, J. (2005) 'Mitigating impacts of HIV/AIDS on rural livelihoods: NGO experiences in sub-Saharan Africa'. *Development In Practice*, 15, 2: 186–99.

White, S. (1995) 'Depoliticising development: the uses and abuses of participation'. *Development in Practice*, 6, 1: 6–15.

Wilson, E. and Blackmore, E. (2013) *Dispute or Dialogue: Community Perspectives on Company-Led Grievance Mechanisms*. Sustainable Markets Group, IIED.

Wood, G.D. (1997) 'States without citizens: the problem of the franchise state'. Chapter 5 in D. Hulme and M. Edwards (eds) *Too Close for Comfort? NGOs, States and Donors*. London: Macmillan.

World Bank (1999) 'Turkey Marmara Earthquake Assessment'. Turkey Country Office, Ankara, September.

World Bank (2002) *Empowerment and Poverty Reduction: A Sourcebook*. Washington DC: The World Bank.

Wright, D. (1996) 'The perils and pleasures of donor consortia'. *Small Enterprise Development*, 7, 4: 32–8.

Wright, S. (ed.) (1994) *Anthropology of Organizations*. London: Routledge.

Wuthnow, R. (1991) *Between States and Markets: the Voluntary Sector in Comparative Perspective*. Princeton, NJ: Princeton University Press.

Yaziji, M. and Doh, J. (2009) *NGOs and Corporations: Conflict and Collaboration*. Cambridge: Cambridge University Press.

Young, D. (1992) 'Organizing principles for international advocacy associations'. *Voluntas*, 3, 1: 1–28.

Zadek, S. (2000) 'The future of non-government organizations in a world of civil corporations', in D. Lewis and T. Wallace (eds) *New Roles and Relevance: Development NGOs and the Challenge of Change*. Hartford, CT: Kumarian Press.

Zadek, S. and Gatwood, M. (1995) 'Social auditing or bust?', in M. Edwards and D. Hulme (eds) *Beyond the Magic Bullet: NGO Performance and Accountability in the Post-Cold War World*. London: Earthscan.

Zadek, S. and Szabo, S. (1994) *Valuing Organization: The Case of Sarvodaya*. London: The New Economics Foundation.

INDEX

Made in the USA
Middletown, DE
30 August 2018